LIBRARY OF HEBREW BIBLE/ OLD TESTAMENT STUDIES

523

Formerly Journal for the Study of the Old Testament Supplement Series

Editors
Claudia V. Camp, Texas Christian University
Andrew Mein, Westcott House, Cambridge

Founding Editors
David J. A. Clines, Philip R. Davies and David M. Gunn

Editorial Board
Richard J. Coggins, Alan Cooper, John Goldingay, Robert P. Gordon,
Norman K. Gottwald, Gina Hens-Piazza, John Jarick, Andrew D. H. Mayes,
Carol Meyers, Patrick D. Miller, Yvonne Sherwood

THE SIN OF THE CALF

The Rise of the Bible's Negative Attitude Toward the Golden Calf

Youn Ho Chung

t &t clark

NEW YORK • LONDON

Published by T & T Clark International
A Continuum imprint
80 Maiden Lane, New York, NY 10038
The Tower Building, 11 York Road, London SE1 7NX

www.continuumbooks.com

Visit the T & T Clark blog at www.tandtclarkblog.com

Library of Congress Cataloging-in-Publication Data
A catalog record for this book is available from the Library of Congress.

ISBN: 978-0-567-42590-4

Typeset and copy-edited by Forthcoming Publications Ltd. (www.forthpub.com)
Printed in the United States of America

CONTENTS

ACKNOWLEDGMENTS

Since I began my study in the Bible, one of my interests has been to know (לָדַעַת) how *knowledge* (דַּעַת) activities of the characters in the Bible and of its authors had been channels for the revelation of God's will. The study of the calf image helped me expand my horizon of understanding of such an interest. This monograph is a revised version of my Ph.D. dissertation, originally written in Hebrew and submitted to the Hebrew University of Jerusalem in January 2007. I am deeply indebted to my dissertation advisor, Professor Baruch J. Schwartz, whose unselfish guidance, thorough comments, insightful advice, and kind encouragement, made the work possible. My special thanks go to Professor Alexander Rofé, who guided me to complete the Hashulama course and advised me to go more deeply into the world of Judaism, and to Professor Israel Knohl, who not only inspired me with critical advice, as a member of my examination committee, but also encouraged me pursue the publication of my work. I am also very thankful to my professors, who expanded my biblical *Erkenntnis* (דַּעַת) horizon: the late Moshe Weinfeld, Menaham Haran, Shalom Paul, Immanuel Tov, and other committee members, Professor Mordechai Cogan and Dr. Ilan Sharon.

Yossi Garfinkel, Professor of Biblical Archaeology at the Hebrew University of Jerusalem, has always been a kind friend. Not only did Professor Garfinkel offer valuable guidance on archaeological issues relating to my research, but he (and his lovely family) extended warm invitations to join them in their Jewish festival celebrations. Professor Garfinkel's wife, Tal Ilan, Professor at Freie Universität, read a draft of the Hebrew manuscript and corrected my Hebrew.

In addition, I would like to thank Professors Menahem Kister, Daniel Schwartz, and Joshua Levenson for their helping me to enter into the world of the Second Temple studies and the study of Rabbinic literature.

Glad thanks are due to Professor Claudia V. Camp, co-editor of the LHBOTS series, and to the staff at T&T Clark/Continuum for accepting my work into this series. With regard to the publication of the present work, I must admit that I owe gratitude to the enthusiastic suggestion of

Professor Alan Cooper at Jewish Theological Seminary of New York, as one of my dissertation's examiners, who is looking forward to the publication of the work and debates he foresees it will generate among scholars.

I would like to thank Aaron Anish for preparing the first translation of my Hebrew manuscript into English. Thanks go also to my colleague, Rev. Jay Kronish, who corrected my English further, and to Janice Karnice for her proof-reading of the manuscript.

I am very thankful for the encouragement and financial support given to me by my Professors at PCTS (Presbyterian College & Theological Seminary of Seoul), Sa-Moon Kang, Joong-Eun Kim, and Young-Ihl Chang, and the associate directors of Jerusalem Branch of PCTS, Rev. Kwang-Sun Rhee, Sei-Yun Chang, and Elder Chul Kwon. Thanks are due to my colleagues at the University of the Holy Land. I am grateful to Professors Claire and Steve Pfann, as well as the faculty and students for mutual teaching and learning.

Finally, my heartfelt thanks go to my mother, who prays incessantly for me, and to my wife, You-Soon, without whose devotional support, this work would not see the light of day. This book is dedicated to them. I am thankful for Ye-Joong, Ye-One, and Ye-Hyung, who are the Lord's children entrusted to me. My children are always joy and encouragement to me, and it is because of them I understand (יוֹדֵעַ) the Lord's words: 'He will rejoice over you with gladness' (Zeph 3:17).

ABBREVIATIONS

AB	Anchor Bible
ABD	*Anchor Bible Dictionary*. Edited by D. N. Freedman. 6 vols. New York, 1992
AbrN	*Abr-Nahrain*
AJBI	*Annual of the Japanese Biblical Institute*
AJSL	*American Journal of Semitic Languages and Literatures*
AJSR	*Association for Jewish Studies Review*
ANEP	*The Ancient Near East in Pictures Relating to the Old Testament*. Edited by J. B. Pritchard. Princeton, 1954
ANET	*Ancient Near Eastern Texts Relating to the Old Testament*. Edited by J. B. Pritchard. 3d ed. Princeton, 1969
AOAT	Alter Orient and Altes Testament
ASV	American Standard Version
ATD	Das Alte Testament Deutsch
AuOr	*Aula orientalis*
BA	*Biblical Archaeologist*
BAR	*Biblical Archaeology Review*
BASOR	*Bulletin of the American Schools of Oriental Research*
BDB	Brown, F., S. R. Driver, and C. A. Briggs. *A Hebrew and English Lexicon of the Old Testament*. Oxford, 1907
BHS	*Biblia Hebraica Stutgartensia*
Bib	*Biblica*
BN	*Biblische Notizen*
BR	*Biblical Review*
BTB	*Biblical Theology Bulletin*
BWANT	Beiträge zur Wissenschaft vom Alten und Neuen Testament
BZAW	Beihefte zur Zeitschrift für die alttestamentlische Wissenschaft
CBC	Cambridge Bible Commentary
CBQ	*Catholic Biblical Quarterly*
CC	Continental Commentary
CurBS	*Currents in Research: Biblical Studies*
DBAT	*Dielheimer Blätter zum Alten Testament und seiner Rezeption in der Alten Kirche*
DDD	*Dictionary of Deities and Demons in the Bible*. Edited by K. van der Toorn, B. Becking, and P. W. van der Horst. Leiden, 1995
EAEHL	*Encyclopedia of Archaeological Excavations in the Holy Land*. Edited by M. Avi-Yonah. 4 vols. Jerusalem, 1975
EncJud	*Encyclopaedia Judaica*. 16 vols. Jerusalem, 1972

EvQ	*Evangelical Quarterly*
ETL	*Ephemerides theologicae lovanienses*
ESV	English Standard Version
EV	English Bible verse numbering
EvQ	*Evangelical Quarterly*
GKC	*Gesenius' Hebrew Grammar*. Edited by E. Kautzsch. Translated by A. E. Cowley. 2d. ed. Oxford, 1910
HeyJ	*Heythrop Journal*
HS	*Hebrew Studies*
HTR	*Harvard Theological Review*
HUCA	*Hebrew Union College Annual*
ICC	International Critical Commentary
IEJ	*Israel Exploration Journal*
Int	*Interpretation*
JAOS	*Journal of the American Oriental Society*
JARCE	*Journal of the American Research Center in Egypt*
JBL	*Journal of Biblical Literature*
JNES	*Journal of Near Eastern Studies*
JPS	Jewish Publication Society of America, Translations to the Holy Scriptures
JQR	*Jewish Quarterly Review*
JSOT	*Journal for the Study of the Old Testament*
JSOTSup	Journal for the Study of the Old Testament: Supplement Series
JSS	*Journal of Semitic Studies*
JTS	*Journal of Theological Studies*
KAR	*Keilschrifttexte aus Assur religiösen Inhalts*. Edited by E. Ebeling. Leipzig, 1919–23
KJV	King James Version
KTU	*Die keilalphabetischen Texte aus Ugarit*. Edited by M. Dietrich, O. Loretz, and J. Sanmartín. AOAT 24/1. Neukirchen–Vluyn, 1976. 2d enlarged ed. of *KTU: The Cuneiform Alphabetic Texts from Ugarit, Ras Ibn Hani, and Other Places*. Edited by M. Dietrich, O. Loretz, and J. Sanmartín. Münster, 1995
LXX	Septuagint
MDB	*Mercer Dictionary of the Bible*. Edited by W. E. Mills. Macon, 1990
MT	Masoretic text
NAS	New American Standard Bible with Codes (1977)
NAU	New American Standard Bible with Codes (1995)
NIB	New International Version (BR)
NIV	New International Version (1984) (US)
NEB	The New English Bible
NCBC	The New Century Bible Commentary
OLP	*Oriental lovaniensia periodica*
OTL	Old Testament Library
OTWSA	*Oudtestamentiese Werkgemeenskap van Suid-Africa*
RevExp	*Review and Expositor*

RSV	Revised Standard Version
RV	Revised Version
SEÅ	*Svensk exegetisk årsbok*
SEL	*Studi epigrafici e linguistici*
SBLSP	*Society of Biblical Literature: Seminar Papers*
SJOT	*Scandinavian Journal of the Old Testament Studia Theologica*
StudBib	*Studia Biblica*
TDOT	*Theological Dictionary of the Old Testament.* Edited by G. J. Botterweck and H. Ringgren. Translated by J. T. Willis, G. W. Bromiley, and D. E. Green. 8 vols. Grand Rapids, 1974–
TLOT	*Theological Lexicon of the Old Testament.* Edited by E. Jenni, with assistance from C. Westermann. Translated by M. E. Biddle. 3 vols. Peabody, Mass., 1997
TRev	*Theologische Revue*
UF	*Ugaritic-Forschungen*
VAS	*Vorderasiatische Schriftdenkmäler der königlichen Museen zu Berlin*
VT	*Vetus Testamentum*
VTSup	Vetus Testamentum Supplements
WBC	Word Biblical Commentary
ZAW	*Zeitschrift für die alttestamentliche Wissenschaft*
ZTK	*Zeitschrift für wissenschaftliche Theologie*

Chapter 1

INTRODUCTION

1. *The Aim of the Study*

The relationship of the biblical tradition to golden calf worship seems to be entirely negative. In the Torah and the books of Kings, harsh criticism is wielded against the golden calf the Israelites made in the wilderness (Exod 32; Deut 9:7–10:11) and the calves erected by Jeroboam ben Nebat (1 Kgs 12:26–33) at Dan and Bethel during his reign over the northern kingdom of Israel. The book of Hosea contains a polemic against the calf at Samaria, which is perceived as the object of idolatrous worship (and is rejected by YHWH) (8:5; 10:5; 13:2). The calf is also referred to derogatorily in the book of Psalms (Ps 106:19) and in the sermonizing historical survey in the book of Nehemiah (Neh 9:18).

The antiquity of calf worship in Israel is confirmed by a bronze icon found in the region of the tribe of Manasseh, and dated to the Judges period (Iron Age I).[1] This discovery may support the hypothesis that calf worship was practiced in Jeroboam's northern kingdom of Israel, as related in the story in 1 Kgs 12:26–33. And even if this narrative, in its current version, is certainly a Deuteronomistic work, it apparently relies on an ancient, pre-Deuteronomistic version of the story, based on a reliable historical tradition.

The attribution of the establishment of calf worship to Jeroboam is credible therefore, but given the evidence of the antiquity of the practice in Israel, it becomes clear that Jeroboam did not invent it, but rather merely breathed new life into it. Hence, the question arises as to whether Jeroboam in truth set up the golden calves in order to buck the postulates of the Israelite religion of his time; that is: Was Jeroboam's golden calf really meant to lure Israel into worship of other gods or idolatry? This question is also raised from another direction: the scathing criticism of Jeroboam in the books of Kings for committing the "sin" of the golden

---

1. A. Mazar, "The 'Bull Site'—An Iron Age I Open Cult Place," *BASOR* 247 (1982): 27–42.

calf belongs entirely to its Deuteronomistic editing layer. This layer includes, as aforementioned, the narrative attributing the establishment of calf worship to Jeroboam (1 Kgs 12:26–32), and the same applies to the story of the prophet from Judah who comes to Bethel (1 Kgs 13), in the characterization of Jehu's sins (2 Kgs 10:29), and in the typical Deuteronomistic concluding remarks (1 Kgs 14:16; 16:2; 2 Kgs 10:28; 17:16). Yet this layer is merely reflective of the position of the Deuteronomistic editor of the books of Kings in the middle of the sixth century B.C.E., while in the pre-Deuteronomistic layer of 1 Kgs 12 there is no indication that this act on the part of Jeroboam was considered deserving of repudiation from the perspective of Israelite religion in his day.

Similarly, the polemic against calf worship in the Torah merely reflects the attitude of the composers of the documents, which postdate Jeroboam's time: the Elohist narrative dates at the earliest to the second half of the eighth century B.C.E., while Deuteronomy was composed no earlier than the seventh century B.C.E.

Hence, the most ancient source in which the calf cult in the northern kingdom meets with condemnation is a collection of prophecies preserved in the book of Hosea (8:4–5; 10:5–6; 13:2), which have been dated to the middle of the eighth century B.C.E. Before that, at least as far as we know, even the greatest zealots in the kingdom of Israel—Elijah, Elisha, and King Jehu—neither spoke out nor acted against it. Moreover, it appears, based on a close examination of 1 Kgs 12, that the motives of Jeroboam himself were purely Yahwistic in nature. Jeroboam's aim was to win the loyalty of those who supported belief in YHWH but opposed the religious policies of Solomon. It can be deduced from such that Jeroboam's golden calves were not designed to entice Israel into the worship of other gods but rather to serve the God of Israel himself.

Seeing that calf worship was an age-old practice, and that Hosea was probably the first to criticize it, it becomes clear that up until his time calf worship was considered a legitimate practice. The golden calf, therefore, met with negative treatment only at a later stage in the history of the Israelite faith.

If this is the case, what were the factors involved in calf worship being rendered taboo in Israelite religion? The aim of the present study is to explore these factors. To this purpose, I will begin with a review of the existing research on the subject.

2. *Survey of the Research*

The opinions of researchers as to the motive behind the polemic against the golden calf are normally divided into two categories. On the one hand, there are those who contend that the golden calf was, *a priori*, an idol, that is, a molten image of a pagan god, and that criticism of it arose naturally (§2.1). On the other hand, there are those who suggest that opposition to calf worship actually resulted from external circumstances (§2.2).

2.1. *The Calf as Idol*

Most of the traditional commentators and some modern researchers are of the opinion that the golden calf was an idol, namely, the iconic representation of a pagan god. As to just which god, the views are divided. Three possibilities have been suggested: (1) Egyptian gods (§2.1.1), (2) Mesopotamian gods (§2.1.2), and (3) Canaanite gods (§2.1.3).

2.1.1. *Egyptian Gods*. In Egypt, rites associated with bulls (the god Apis in Memphis, and later Mnevis in Heliopolis) and cows (Hathor) were widespread. Accordingly, up until the middle of the nineteenth century, most researchers held the view that the golden calf comprised an imitation of the bull god Apis, or was related to Mnevis, the sacred bull deity whose worship was centered in Heliopolis.[2] Even today, there are scholars who adhere to this stance.[3] They attempt to back this position by citing evidence of bull worship as far as the Nile Delta region, where the Israelites dwelled, and where Shishaq provided refuge to Jeroboam I until Solomon's death, as recounted in 1 Kgs 11:40.

In particular, Oswalt claims that the Hebrews in Egypt identified YHWH with the sun god Amon-Re, the king of Egyptian gods, and represented YHWH with the image of a bull, a symbol also associated with Amon-Re.[4] Danelius[5] argues that the golden calf refers to the cow-goddess Hathor (who gave birth to the sun every morning as a calf), based on the fact that the Septuagint and Josephus Flavius use the term

2. H. Ewald, *Geschichte des Volkes Israel*. Bd. 2, *Geschichte Moses und der Gotterrschaft in Israel* (Göttingen: Dieterichschen Buchhandlung, 1865), 275ff.; H. Graetz, *Geschichte der Israeliten*. Bd. 1, *von ihren Uranfängen (um 1500) bis zum Tode des Königs Salomo (um 977)* (Leipzig: Leiner, 1874), 11ff. (esp. 18). According to Graetz, "Abir" refers to "Apis" in Egypt. See also J. Robertson, *The Early Religion of Israel* (Edinburgh: Blackwood, 1892), 151.

3. R. Pfeiffer, "Images of Yahweh," *JBL* 45 (1926): 217ff.; M. Murray, *The Splendour that was Egypt* (London: Sidgwick & Jackson, 1964), 98–99; S. Morenz, *Egyptian Religion* (trans. A. E. Keep; Ithaca, N.Y.: Cornell University Press, 1973), 20, 103, 143–44, 148, 157, 259, 265, 268.

4. J. N. Oswalt, "The Golden Calves and the Egyptian Concept of Deity," *EvQ* (1973): 13ff.

5. E. Danelius, "The Sins of Jeroboam ben-Nabat," *JQR* 58 (1967): 95–114.

δαμάλεις ("cow") in reference to the calf in 1 Kgs 12, and the assumption that Nebat, Jeroboam's father's name, is derived from the Egyptian root NBT, which means "mistress," a name used in connection with Hathor.

2.1.2. *Mesopotamian Gods.* Regarding the origin and nature of the golden calf as an object of idolatrous worship, there is another argument that claims that its worship in Israel was the product of Mesopotamian influence, Mesopotamia being the place of origin of the Hebrew Patriarchs.[6] According to this view, the golden calf is associated with the bull, symbol of the moon god Sin, the worship of whom was adopted by the Patriarchs in the Mesopotamian cultural center of Harran, and passed down to their descendants, who perpetuated it in Egypt and later still, after their passage into Canaan.

2.1.3. *Canaanite Gods.* Since the beginning of the twentieth century, important archaeological excavations have been conducted whose findings support a Canaanite origin of the golden calf. As a result, many scholars tend to hold the view that the bull icon in Israel can be traced to the Canaan region,[7] where the primary deities linked with the bull image are Hadad (or Hadad-Rimmon), El, and Baal.

2.2. *External Circumstances*

Views holding that censure of the golden calf derived from external circumstances are also divided into three categories: those who see it as resulting from a conflict between priesthoods, namely, between the Aaronic (Levitical) priesthood and a competing one (§2.2.1); a second group who believe that it primarily comprised an indictment of Jeroboam's religious policies (§2.2.2); and a third group, which is of the opinion that it actually constituted a critical assault on Jeroboam's system of government (§2.2.3).

---

6.   J. Lewy, "The Late Assyro-Babylonian Cult of the Moon and Its Culmination at the Time of Nabonidus," *HUCA* 19 (1945): 405–89; A. F. Key, "Traces of the Worship of the Moon God Sîn among the Early Israelites," *JBL* 84 (1965): 20–26; L. Bailey, "The Golden Calf," *HUCA* 42 (1971): 97–115.

7.   J. Hehn, *Die biblische und die babylonische Gottesidee* (Leipzig: Hinrichs, 1913), 296ff.; W. F. Albright, *Archaeology and the Religion of Israel* (Baltimore: The Johns Hopkins University Press, 1946), 71ff., 84–87, 149, 156; E. L. Ehrlich, *Geschichte Israels von den Anfängen bis zur Zerstörung des Tempels (70 n. Chr)* (Berlin: de Gruyter, 1958), 44; H. Ringgren, *Israelite Religion* (trans. D. Green; Philadelphia: Fortress, 1966), 42ff.; R. E. Clements, *Exodus* (CBC; Cambridge: Cambridge University Press, 1972), 206.

2.2.1. *Power Struggle Between Priesthoods*. Numerous scholars hold the view that the Elohist's narrative in the Torah, which wholly repudiates the golden calf, reflects an attack on the Aaronic (Levitical) priesthood in Bethel. This approach was first suggested by Kennett,[8] who hypothesized that Aaron established calf worship at Bethel, and was further advanced by Meek,[9] Eissfeldt,[10] and North.[11] However, these scholars failed to identify which competing priesthood initiated such an attack on the Aaronic priesthood. In the opinion of Aberbach and Smolar,[12] it is a Jerusalemite Zadokite priesthood of the First Temple period. Cross[13] agrees that the narrative in Exod 32 was constructed as a polemic against the Aaronic priesthood at Bethel, but denies the suggestion that it was contrived by the Jerusalemite priesthood. He contends that the negative attitude toward the golden calf originated among one of the northern priesthoods. In his estimation, the Elohist's narrative reflects an attack launched by the Mushite priests—who considered the cherubs the only legitimate symbol of YHWH's presence—against the Aaronite priests, who backed the calf. Noth,[14] Lehming,[15] Beyerlin,[16] Losa,[17] and Childs,[18] even while they may be divided on the matter of attributing the calf narrative in the Torah to an Elohistic source, share the view that the Exod 32 narrative was produced as an assault on the Aaronite priesthood at Bethel.

2.2.2. *Jeroboam's Religious Policies*. A number of researchers, in pointing out the kinship between Exod 32 and 2 Kgs 12:26–33, hypothesize that the Exod 32 narrative was written after 2 Kgs 12 and that it was

8. R. H. Kennett, "The Origin of the Aaronite Priesthood," *JTS* 6 (1905): 161–68.

9. T. J. Meek, "Aaronites and Zadokites," *AJSLL* 45 (1929): 149–66.

10. O. Eissfeldt, "Lade und Stierbild," *ZAW* 58 (1940–41): 190–215.

11. F. S. North, "Aaron's Rise in Prestige," *ZAW* 66 (1954): 191–99.

12. M. Aberbach and L. Smolar, "Aaron, Jeroboam, and the Golden Calves," *JBL* 86 (1967): 129–40.

13. F. M. Cross, *Canaanite Myth and Hebrew Epic: Essays in the History of the Religion of Israel* (Cambridge, Mass.: Harvard University Press, 1973), 198–206.

14. M. Noth, *Überlieferungsgeschichte des Pentateuch* (Stuttgart: Kohlhammer, 1948), 195–97; *A History of Pentateuchal Traditions* (trans. B. W. Anderson; Englewood Cliffs, N.J.: Prentice-Hall, 1972), 178–80; *Exodus* (OTL; trans. J. S. Bowden; Philadelphia: Westminster, 1962), 244–46.

15. S. Lehming, "Versuch zu Ex. xxxii," *VT* 19 (1960): 16–50.

16. W. Beyerlin, *Origins and History of the Oldest Sinaitic Traditions* (Oxford: Blackwell, 1965), 128–32.

17. J. Losa, "Exode xxxii et la Redaction JE," *VT* 23 (1973): 31–55.

18. B. S. Childs, *The Book of Exodus* (OTL; Louisville, Ky.: Westminster John Knox, 1976), 560–61.

meant to besmirch Jeroboam's name. In their judgment, the polemic
nature of the golden calf narrative in the Torah emanates from a critique
of Jeroboam's religious policies.[19] Yet even those who assert that the
Exod 32 narrative was composed prior to 2 Kgs 12 agree that the golden
calf narrative in the Torah comprises a critical assault on the religious
policies of Jeroboam.[20]

2.2.3. Jeroboam's Government System. According to Jenks,[21] the reason
for the polemic against the golden calf was opposition to Jeroboam's
system of government. Jeroboam, going against the prophetic group,
which preferred a system of tribal confederacy, adopted a Jerusalemite
(and Canaanite) model for his government. The ensuing struggle between
Jeroboam and the prophets led, therefore, to the polemic against the
golden calves erected by the king at Dan and Bethel.

2.3. The Need for Reassessment
The research to date on this matter, then, is insufficient, and there
remains, in my view, a vital need to re-examine the factors behind the
shift from an attitude that saw the golden calf as a legitimate appurtenance used in the worship of YHWH, the God of Israel, to an attitude that
wholly rejected it.

The conception that the golden calf comprised an idol, a molten image
of a pagan god, is not convincing. On the one hand, the assertion that the
Israelite people adopted calf worship and identified the God who brought
them out of Egypt with an Egyptian god appears unlikely, since it is hard
to believe that the Israelites, who were enslaved and repressed by the
Egyptians, would associate the God who liberated them precisely with an
Egyptian god. This is reasonable to assume even in the absence of a
discussion of the historical validity of the Exodus story. Furthermore, the

---

19. Noth, *Exodus*, 243–47, and *Pentateuchal Traditions*, 142–45; Lehming,
"Versuch," 16–50; J. Gray, *I and II Kings* (Philadelphia: Westminster, 1970), 289;
G. W. Coats, *Rebellion in the Wilderness: The Murmuring Motif in the Wilderness
Tradition of the Old Testament* (Nashville: Abingdon, 1968), 184–86; B. S. Childs,
"The Etiological Tale Re-Examined," *VT* 24 (1974): 386–97, and *The Book of
Exodus*, 566; H. D. Hoffmann, *Reform und Reformen* (Zurich: Theologischer Verlag,
1980), 62–70; J. P. Hyatt, *Exodus* (NCBC; Grand Rapids: Eerdmans, 1983), 305;
J. Van Seters, "The Golden Calf: Exodus 32," in *The Life of Moses: The Yahwist
as Historian in Exodus–Numbers* (Kampen: Kok, 1994), 290–318.

20. Aberbach and Smolar, "Aaron, Jeroboam," 129–40; Beyerlin, *Origins*,
128–29.

21. A. W. Jenks, *The Elohistic and North Israelite Traditions* (Missoula, Mont.:
Scholars Press, 1977), 101–4.

Egyptians only worshipped the living bull, and not a sculpture or icon of it. Hence, the view that traces the origin of the golden calf to an Egyptian god is unconvincing. On the other hand, the hypothesis that links the golden calf with the bull, symbol of the moon god Sin, in Mesopotamia, birthplace of the Hebrew Patriarchs, and suggests that bull worship persisted among the Israelites even in the monarchic times, also appears to lack foundation. If the golden calf were related to some Mesopotamian god, why is it that not a single polemic against calf idols can be found among the zealous Yahwists, such as Elijah, Elisha, Jehu, and the like, in the time of kingdom.

It appears that the range of views cited above (§2.2) regarding the polemic against the golden calf stem, to a certain extent, from the tendency to examine the biblical story through sociological lenses, and to assume that it was the product of power struggles between priesthoods or between Jeroboam and the prophets. However, scholars who attempt to locate the motive for the polemic in such circumstances are unable to explain why it only appears during a later period,[22] when according to these same researchers, the struggles began even before Jeroboam's reign[23] or immediately after his enthronement.[24] If this is the case, we would expect to find a polemic against the calf from this period. However, as aforementioned, none exists.

3. *Aniconism in the Israelite Religion and the Nature of the Calf Image*

As indicated above, the proposition that the golden calf was originally associated with a pagan god is implausible. This is because the aforementioned view does not provide a clear answer to the question why a polemic against the calf does not emerge prior to Hosea in the middle of the eighth century B.C.E., even though there were zealots for YHWH, who vocally opposed idolatry before that time. Hence, one can deduce that from the very beginning the golden calf was associated with the worship of YHWH. From this deduction a question arises: What, then, was the nature of the golden calf? Was it a symbol or an image of YHWH? If the answer is affirmative, another question arises: Was it permissible within the Israelite religion to use an image of YHWH in worship prior to the

---

22. The polemic cannot be found in Elijah, Elisha, or even Jehu, but only in Hosea during the eighth century B.C.E.
23. See Cross, *Canaanite Myth*, 197–99.
24. See Jenks, *Traditions*, 104–5.

iconoclastic events of the second half of the eighth century B.C.E.?[25] And if the golden calf was not originally considered an image of YHWH, what was its essential character? In order to provide answers to these questions, one should, first of all, take into account the aniconism of Israelite religion. If in Israelite religion an "aniconic practice" predominated, that is, anthropomorphic images of YHWH were not produced, even prior to the active opposition to religious symbols or images in the eighth century B.C.E., then there is a greater probability that the golden calf originally was not considered an image or symbol of YHWH.

There is no clear reference in the Bible to the existence of anthropomorphic images of YHWH in the temples of the kingdom of Judah[26] or the northern kingdom of Israel (if we ignore momentarily the image of the calf and the question of whether it comprised a theriomorphic representation of YHWH). The majority of biblical scholars agree that during the First Temple period in the kingdom of Judah, and specifically the Jerusalem Temple, YHWH was represented in worship by the empty throne flanked by two cherubs, and not by an anthropomorphic or theriomorphic form.[27] This type of worship, in which an icon of YHWH is

---

25.   The iconoclastic reforms of Hezekiah and Josiah follow Hosea's polemic in the eighth century B.C.E. This can be inferred on the basis of the associations between Hosea and Deuteronomy, which are also linked to the reforms of Josiah. These connections lead us to assume a flow of northern traditions into Judah after the fall of Israel in 722/21 B.C.E. (see M. Weinfeld, *Deuteronomy and the Deuteronomic School* [Oxford: Clarendon, 1972], 366ff.); one connection is the polemic around the figures mentioned in the books of Hosea and Deuteronomy.

26.   To the best of my knowledge, there are virtually no scholars who claim that "Nehushtan," the copper serpent mentioned in Num 21:8–9; 2 Kgs 18:4, was a theriomorphic image of God. Olyan's interpretation of "Nehushtan" as a ritual symbol of the goddess Asherah is based on inadequate evidence, as suggested by S. Wiggins ("The Myth of Asherah: Lion Lady and Serpent Goddess," *UF* 23 [1991]: 386). It seems that "Nehushtan" is related to a traditional symbol indicating the healing power of God (see R. Hendel, "Nehushtan," *DDD*, 1159).

27.   R. Albertz, *A History of Israelite Religion in the Old Testament Period*, vol. 1 (trans. J. Bowden; London: SCM, 1994), 131; T. N. D. Mettinger, *No Graven Image? Israelite Aniconism in Its Ancient Near Eastern Context* (Stockholm: Almqvist & Wiksell, 1995), 16ff., 139, 167ff.; Th. Podella, *Das Lichtkleid JHWHs* (Tübingen: Mohr Siebeck, 1996), 2, 37, 88, 160, 164, 186, 267. Attempts have been made by a few researchers (B. B. Schmidt, "The Aniconic Tradition: On Reading Images and Viewing Texts," in *The Triumph of Elohim: From Yahwisms to Judaism* [ed. D. V. Edelman; Grand Rapids: Eerdmans, 1996], 75–105; H. Niehr, "In Search of YHWH's Cult Statue in the First Temple," in *The Image and the Book: Iconic Cults, Aniconism, and the Rise of Book Religion in Israel and the Ancient Near East* [ed. K. van der Toorn; Leuven: Peeters, 1997], 73–95, and, in the same volume, C. Uehlinger, "Anthropomorphic Cult Statuary in Iron Age Palestine and the Search

absent, seems to be compatible with ancient Israelite aniconic practice, and is supported by archaeological findings from the Iron Age I.

Archaeological excavations point to discontinuity in the presence of anthropological images between the Late Bronze Age and the Iron Age I in the ancient settlements throughout Israel prior to the division of the kingdom. Male and female statuettes dating to the late Bronze Age are common,[28] while no male representations of deities from the Iron Age I were found at Israelite sites. There are two exceptions to the rule: a bronze figurine from the twelfth century B.C.E. found at Hazor, and an engraving on a miniature altar from the tenth century B.C.E., found at Gezer. And yet neither of these is necessarily Israelite.[29] There is no example of a bronze male icon from an Israelite site that can be dated with absolute certainty to the Bronze Age.[30] Even the primary female

for Yahweh's Cult Images," 97–155) to prove that there were ritual anthropomorphic images of YHWH, based on the assumption that worship in the time of the First Temple was not unlike that in the rest of the ancient Near East. However, these attempts were refuted by Na'aman, who showed, through a comparison of ritual objects, which were suggested as representations of YHWH, with examples from Mesopotamia, that there is no clear evidence of the existence of an anthropomorphic image of YHWH in the Second Temple period (N. Na'aman, "No Anthropomorphic Graven Image: Nots on the Assumed Anthropomorphic Cult Statues in the Temples of YHWH in the Pre-Exilic Period," *UF* 31 [1999]: 391–415).

28. See O. Negbi, *Canaanite Gods in Metal* (Tel Aviv: Tel Aviv University, 1976), 112ff.

29. See W. G. Dever, "Material Remains and the Cult in Ancient Israel: An Essay in Archeological Systematics," in *The Word of the Lord Shall Go Forth* (ed. C. L. Meyers and M. C. O'Connor; Winona Lake, Ind.: Eisenbrauns, 1983), 573–74; R. Hendel, "The Social Origins of the Aniconic Tradition in Early Israel," *CBQ* 50 (1988): 367. Regarding the bronze figurine from Hazor, Ahlström offers a different interpretation, suggesting that it represents an Israelite god (G. W. Ahlström, "An Israelite God Figurine from Hazor," *Orientalia Suecana* 19–20 [1970–71]: 54–62, and "An Israelite God Figurine, Once More," *VT* 25 [1975]: 106–9). However, as O. Keel ("Das Vergraben der 'fremden Götter' in Genesis XXXV 4b," *VT* 23 [1973]: 305–36 [esp. 325f.]) and W. W. Hallo ("Cult Statue and Divine Image: A Preliminary Study," in *Scripture in Context II: More Essays on the Comparative Method* [ed. L. G. Perdue; Winona Lake, Ind.: Eisenbrauns, 1983], 1–16 [esp. 1–4]) have pointed out, a close reading of the findings of the archaeological excavation shows that Ahlström was incorrect. According to Dever ("Material Remains," 583), Layer XI (in which the figurine was discovered) can be properly dated to the twelfth century B.C.E., but what Ahlström terms "foundation level" is actually a collection of utensils from the Late Bronze Age (thirteenth century B.C.E.) and, of course, is representative of the material culture that preceded Israelite settlement.

30. T. J. Lewis, "Divine Images and Aniconism in Ancient Israel," *JAOS* 118 (1998): 43. A few bronze objects were mistakenly dated to Iron Age I–II by Negbi

cultic icon form of the Bronze Age, namely, a tablet depicting a standing goddess, seems to be entirely absent.[31] Furthermore, Israelite aniconism can possibly be linked to aniconism among the nomads of the Sinai and Arabian deserts.[32] Excavations at Timna, north of the Bay of Eilat, show that Midianites, who built the "Tent Shrine" on the ruins of the Egyptian temple on the site, deliberately broke the images of the goddess Hathor and effaced the stone pillars bearing her face.[33]

It appears, therefore, that the lack of an anthropomorphic representation of YHWH, at least during the First Temple period, can be explained by the general lack of anthropomorphic images of deities in the Israelite settlements of Iron Age I. This can be viewed as confirmation of the argument that Israelite religion had a tradition of aniconism since at least Iron Age I. Yet this does not mean that due to this tradition or aniconic custom, no images were used in the worship of YHWH. Actually, "legitimate" ritual images, which were neither anthropomorphic nor theriomorphic, were employed.[34] At this point, in order to understand the relationship between aniconism and "legitimate" representations, the concept of aniconism should be defined.

The term aniconism is simply defined as the absence of representations; more specifically, those of living or divine beings, and more generally, any type of human representation. Aniconism also sometimes refers, as it does here, to the religious prohibition of the ritual use of idols and images depicting a deity. However, this does not mean that

(*Gods*, 49, 57). Among them were icons from Beit Shemesh, Megiddo, Beit Shean, and perhaps also Shechem. All should be properly dated to the Late Bronze Age (see T. J. Lewis, "The Identity and Function of El/Baal Berith," *JBL* 115 [1996]: 418–22).

31. See M. Tadmor, "Female Cult Figurines in Late Canaan and Early Israel: Archaeological Evidence," in *Studies in the Period of David and Solomon and Other Essays* (ed. T. Ishida; Winona Lake, Ind.: Eisenbrauns, 1982), 139–40, 157, 161, 171ff.

32. See Mettinger, *No Graven Image*, 57–79. Regarding the nomadic character of the Israelite people prior to the Iron Age, see A. Rainey, "Israel in Merneptah's Inscription and Reliefs," *IEJ* 51 (2001): 57–75; T. E. Levy et al., "Archaeology and the Shasu Nomads: Recent Excavations in the Jabal Hamrat Fidan, Jordan," in *"Le-David Maskil": A Birthday Tribute for David Noel Friedman* (ed. R. E. Friedman and W. H. C. Propp; Winona Lake, Ind.: Eisenbrauns, 2004), 63–89.

33. See B. Rothenberg, "Timna," *NEAEHL* 4:1475–85 (esp. 1482ff.).

34. For example, images of cherubs were woven into "curtains" (יְרִיעוֹת, Exod 26:1; 36:8) and a partition (פָּרֹכֶת) placed in front of the Ark (Exod 26:31; 32:35) in the Tabernacle (2 Chr 3:14). They were also engraved on the walls (1 Kgs 6:29; 2 Chr 3:7), doors (1 Kgs 6:32, 35), and bronze stands (1 Kgs 7:29, 36) in Solomon's Temple. There were two golden cherubs in the Tabernacle (Exod 26:18–22; 37:7–9) and in Solomon's Temple (1 Kgs 6:21–28; 8:5–9; 2 Chr 3:10–13).

objects symbolic of a deity are necessarily forbidden. According to Gladigow, aniconic cults are defined as those in which "no 'images' are known or accepted as objects of worship, especially not in the form of anthropomorphic images."[35] Mettinger expands Gladigow's definition, describing it as referring to "cults where there is no iconic representation of the deity (anthropomorphic or theriomorphic) serving as the dominant or central cultic symbol."[36] In sum, aniconism refers to a form of worship in which anthropomorphic or theriomorphic representations of the deity are absent. This definition clarifies why some ritual objects were regarded as legitimate even within aniconic practice: they were not seen as representing God or his image. Israelite aniconism can be divided into two types: aniconic symbols and "sacred emptiness."[37] The first type includes some ritual symbols, such as unprocessed stones[38] and steles,[39] which were considered legitimate prior to the Deuteronomic admonitions (see Deut 16:21). The second type includes the seat/pedestal of the deity or empty throne as exemplified by the Ark/cherubs.[40]

I will turn now to a discussion of the calf, an example frequently used by those opposing the claim that iconic representations of YHWH were not "made"[41] in Israelite religion within the framework of aniconic practice. As previously mentioned, I have reached the conclusion that in Israelite religion the calf image was not originally conceived of as a ritual object of "other god."[42] If that is the case, what was the calf's function in the worship of YHWH? Given Israelite aniconism, it is reasonable to assume that the calf image did not serve as an iconic representation of YHWH, but rather as an expression of sacred emptiness, like the Ark/cherubs. The function of Jeroboam's calves, it appears, was similar to that of the Ark/cherubs in the Jerusalem Temple.

35. B. Gladigow, *Handbuch religionswissenschaflicher Grundbegriffe*, vol. 1 (Stuttgart: Kohlhammer, 1988), 472.

36. Mettinger, *No Graven Image*, 19.

37. Mettinger (ibid.) calls this "empty-space aniconism."

38. The crude form of many of the steles (מַצֵּבוֹת) can be understood given the biblical imperative of using "uncut stones" for religious purposes (Exod 20:25; Deut 27:6; Josh 8:31; 1 Kgs 6:7).

39. The standing stone stele found in the inner sanctum of the Arad temple is an outstanding example of an aniconic object symbolizing YHWH's presence. For a detailed examination of these objects, see Mettinger, *No Graven Image*, 135ff.

40. Gladigow, *Handbuch*.

41. This statement regarding the existence of an iconic representation of YHWH demands clarification. It is possible that there was an object that was not originally made as a representation of YHWH, but over time became considered as such.

42. The term "other god" will be used throughout the present work to refer to refer to the object of "foreign," that is, non-YHWH worship.

Already in Shiloh, we encountered a tradition associating the Ark with cherubs: the Ark/cherubs are linked here to a divine epithet that appears in 1 Sam 4:4.[43] In the Jerusalem Temple, the Ark is similarly associated with the cherubs. When the Ark is brought to Solomon's Temple, it is placed "under the wings of the cherubs" (2 Kgs 8:6). The cherubs in the priestly Tent of Meeting faced one another (Exod 25:20), while those in Solomon's Temple stood parallel to one another. Each cherub touched with its outer wing one of the walls of the structure, while their inner wings touched in the center of the structure. Apparently, M. Haran is correct in his hypothesis that this coupling of inner wings composed the throne of YHWH.[44] This interpretation is also supported by Ezek 10:1, which shows that the cherubs were part of the form of the throne (compare also Ezek 1:22–26). The Ark, which was only one-and-a-half cubits in height (compare Exod 25:10), served as YHWH's footstool (Pss 99:5; 132:7; 1 Chr 28:2). The explanation is that YHWH sits invisible, in his majesty, above the cherubs and the Ark.[45] The divine epithet "sits between the cherubs" must be understood in this context.

Assuming that Jeroboam was a conservative and that his religious policy was one of restoration rather than invention or innovation,[46] and that his calves were not idolatrous in nature,[47] Jeroboam's use of the representation of the calf can reasonably be viewed as a counterpart of the cherubs, that is, as a pedestal of the invisible YHWH. The comparative material provided by iconic art of the ancient Near East further

---

43. 1 Sam 4:4 reads: "…and from there they carried the Ark of the Covenant of YHWH of hosts, who sits upon the Cherubim." Compare to 2 Sam 6:2: "…to bring up from there the ark of YHWH, which bears the name of YHWH of hosts, who sits upon the cherubim." The same mention of YHWH as "sitting upon the cherubim" also appears in 1 Kgs 19:15; Isa 37:16; Pss 80:2; 99:1; 1 Chr 13. Cf. 2 Sam 22:11; Ps 18:11.

44. M. Haran, "The Ark and the Cherubim: Their Symbolic Significance in Biblical Ritual," *IEJ* 9 (1959): 30ff. (35ff.).

45. T. Mettinger, "The Veto on Images and the Aniconic God in Ancient Israel," in *Religious Symbols and Their Functions* (ed. H. Biezais; Stockholm: Almqvist & Wiksell, 1979), 21ff.

46. See S. Talmon, "Divergences in Calendar-Reckoning in Ephraim and Judah," *VT* 8 (1958): 58–74. A further examination will be made in the following section (§4).

47. Had the calves been idolatrous in nature, they would have already drawn criticism from zealots such as Elijah, Elisha, and Jehu, prior to Hosea's polemic surrounding them, as mentioned above. The divine nature of the cultic formula outlined in 1 Kgs 12:28 will be discussed in detail in the following section (§4 of the present chapter).

corroborates this insight. In the glyptic art of the Canaan region there is a clear pictorial progression from a young bull ridden by a lightning bolt-wielding storm-god, to a bull bearing only lightning bolts, to a young bull with nothing on its back. A complete bronze figurine of a god riding a bull, made in a single casting, was found at Carchemish and dated to the seventh century B.C.E.[48] Earlier evidence of bull images associated with Baal-Hadad or other weather gods was also found: a roll-stamp from Tel Mardich, dated to approximately 1725 B.C.E., depicts a seated bull on a background in which Baal-Hadad is discernable.[49] Three reliefs, one from north-east Halab, dated to the eighth or seventh century B.C.E., the second from Arslan Tash, dated to the period of Tiglath-pileser III, and the third from Til Barsib, from the twelfth or eleventh century B.C.E., depict bearded weather gods, carrying three-pronged lightning bolts, who stand on the backs of bulls.[50] This evidence and more from Near Eastern art, in which deities stand on the backs of animals, and mainly bulls and lions,[51] leads me to conclude that in the Bible, the calf (or bull) comprised the tangible pedestal upon which the invisible YHWH was presumed to stand. Accordingly, since the late 1920s, biblical researchers have argued, following Obbink[52] and gaining further reinforcement from Albright,[53] that the golden calf did in fact represent the footstool of the invisible YHWH. Despite Eissfeldt's attempts to offer an alternative interpretation,[54] this view has justifiably met with general agreement among scholars.[55]

Toews is one of the scholars who have questioned this interpretation of the calf. It is his contention that the bull carrying an upright god on his back is associated mainly with the storm god Baal-Hadad, who appears in finds from the Middle to Late Iron Age I. Yet YHWH is not a storm

48. C. L. Woolley, *Carchemish*, vol. 3 (Oxford: Oxford University Press, 1914), Table 71b.

49. O. Keel, *Die Welt der altorientalischen Bildsymbolik und das Alte Testament: Am Beispiel der Psalmem* (Zurich: Benziger, 1977), 192, fig. 290.

50. *ANEP*, 500, 501, 532.

51. *ANEP*, 74, 470, 479, 522, 525, 526, 531, 534, 537, 830, 835.

52. H. Th. Obbink, "Jahwebilder," *ZAW* 47 (1929): 264–74.

53. W. F. Albright, *From the Stone Age to Christianity: Monotheism and the Historical Process* (Baltimore: The Johns Hopkins University Press, 1957), 299ff.; idem, *Yahweh and the Gods of Canaan* (Garden City, N.Y.: Doubleday, 1968), 172.

54. Eissfeldt, "Lade und Stierbild," 190ff. Eissfeldt is of the opinion that we are talking here about a ritual standard with the image of a bullhead, in Exod 32 and 1 Kgs 12.

55. See M. Weippert, "Heiliger Krieg in Israel und Assyrian," *ZAW* 84 (1972): 103 n. 55; S. E. Loewenstamm, *The Evolution of the Exodus Tradition* (trans. B. J. Schwartz; Jerusalem: Magnes, 1992), 53.

god like Baal-Hadad, so it is unlikely that the Israelite people perceived the calf image as the footstool upon which YHWH stood.[56] Toews goes on to suggest that the calf image symbolized YHWH, but not necessarily his footstool.[57] However, in my opinion, Toews misses the point, which is that YHWH unifies within himself all of the characteristics of a storm god. As several scholars have already pointed out,[58] the original characterization of YHWH is that of a storm god. One should note the etymological meaning of the name YHWH (יְהוָה) itself, that is, "exhale/breathe out" (related also secondarily to the verb הָיָה, "to be"), and the descriptions of his physical manifestation in Deut 33:2–3; Judg 3:4–5; Hab 3:3; and Ps 68:8–9.[59] Therefore, Toews' position, that YHWH does not belong to the category of gods who stand upon the backs of calves simply because he is not a storm god, is unconvincing.

4. *Relevant Questions*

Although calf worship existed in Israel before the time of Jeroboam ben Nebat,[60] it can safely be said that the calf cult under Jeroboam was the first instance in which it gained official religious and national status in the northern kingdom of Israel. Therefore, we will begin by examining the two calves of Jeroboam, which appear in the books of Kings. The calf descriptions in the books of Kings seem to reflect the Deuteronomistic

---

56. W. I. Toews, *Monarchy and Religious Institution in Israel under Jeroboam I* (Atlanta: Scholars Press, 1993), 52.

57. Ibid., 53.

58. It should be mentioned that 1 Kgs 17–19 emphasizes YHWH's power over thunder and lightning, which is linked to different phenomena related to Baal in Ugarit rituals. See Cross, *Canaanite Myth*, 190–94; F. C. Fensham, "A Few Observations on the Polarisation between Yahweh and Baal in 1 Kings 17–19," *ZAW* 92 (1980): 227–36; S. M. Olyan, *Asherah and the Cult of Yahweh in Israel* (Atlanta: Scholars Press, 1988), 8, 88.

59. See T. N. D. Mettinger, "The Elusive Essence: YHWH, El and Baal and the Distinctiveness of Israelite Faith," in *Die hebräische Bibel und ihre zweifache Nachgeschichte* (ed. E. Blum et al.; Neukirchen–Vluyn: Neukirchener Verlag, 1990), 393–417 (410–12). It should be noted that the descriptions of YHWH's corporeal manifestation are found mainly in northern sources; see L. E. Axelsson, *The Lord Rose Up from Seir: Studies in the History and Traditions of the Negev and Southern Judah* (trans. F. H. Cryer; Lund: Almqvist & Wiksell, 1987), 48–65.

60. The existence of calf worship in Israel before the time of Jeroboam ben Nebat was substantiated with the archaeological discovery of a bronze bull figurine from a ritual site in the area of the tribe of Manasseh dated to the period of the Judges, that is, Iron Age I (see Mazar, "The 'Bull Site,'" 27–42).

position. A number of questions arise regarding the Deuteronomistic aspects of the depiction of Jeroboam's calves.

First, what is the substance of "Jeroboam's sins"[61] that "caused Israel to sin" and led to the destruction of the state?[62] And what is the relation between "Jeroboam's sins" and the calf?

Secondly, some argue that the narrative in Exod 32 was created with reference to the cult of Jeroboam's golden calves, because the cultic formula in plural form in 1 Kgs 12:28 and Exod 32:4, 8 does not accord with Aaron's single calf. In other words, the reference to the cultic formula in plural form[63] shows that the Exod 32 narrative was invented or composed in order to denigrate the cult of Jeroboam, who made two golden calves,[64] rather than Aaron who made only one calf. Here the following questions are evoked: Was there not a cult that included the image of the calf in Israel prior to Jeroboam's reign? And was the cultic formula also presented for the first time by Jeroboam?

Thirdly, what is the nature of Jeroboam's calves as reflected in the books of Kings? In the opinion of Mullen,[65] who cites Halpern's interpretation,[66] the term "molten image" (מַסֵּכָה) in 1 Kgs 14:9 and 2 Kgs 17:16 is the "Deuteronomistic euphemism" for Jeroboam's "golden calf," and in the plural form in 1 Kgs 14:9 ("molten images," מַסֵּכֹות) it clearly reflects the interpretation of the author regarding Jeroboam's calves as representations of "other gods." The view that the Deuteronomist interpreted Jeroboam's calves as idols is justified in light of 2 Kgs 17:7–18, according to which the cause of the demise of the northern kingdom of Israel was the worship of other gods (v. 7). However, it is hard to link the cultic formula in 1 Kgs 12:28, "behold your gods, O Israel, who brought you up out of the land of Egypt," to an idol.[67] The formula refers

---

61. 1 Kgs 14:16; 15:31; 16:31; 2 Kgs 3:3; 10:31; 13:2, 6; 15:9, 18, 24, 28; 17:22.

62. On the reason for the fall of Israel, see 2 Kgs 17:6–16, 20–23; cf. 1 Kgs 14:14–16.

63. "These are your gods, O Israel, who brought thee out of the land of Egypt" (Exod 32:4).

64. Noth, *Exodus*, 247ff., and *Pentateuch*, 157ff.; Lehming, "Versuch," 49; Ringgren, *Israelite Religion*, 37; G. Fohrer, *History of Israelite Religion* (trans. D. E. Green; London: SPCK, 1973), 82.

65. E. T. Mullen, "The Sins of Jeroboam: A Redactional Assessment," *CBQ* 49 (1987): 214 n. 5.

66. B. Halpern, "Levitic Participation in the Reform Cult of Jeroboam I," *JBL* 95 (1976): 36.

67. See J. Pakkala, "Jeroboam's Sin and Bethel in 1 Kgs 12:25–33," *BN* 112 (2002): 88.

to "liberation from Egypt" in the book of Exodus and in the Deuteronomistic History, and always revolves around YHWH.[68] The formula
"God brought you up out of the land of Egypt" is stressed in E[69] and D,
as opposed to J, where it does not appear.[70] Apparently, the tradition of
Israel's exodus from Egypt was marginalized in the kingdom of Judah
from the time of the reign of David and Solomon as part of an emphasis
on royal theology, which sought to ensure the stability of the Davidic
dynasty.[71] By contrast, in the northern kingdom of Israel a royal theology
aimed at solidifying the kingdom did not develop. Therefore, an atmosphere prevailed there of restraint as far as the kingship was concerned.
Given the repressiveness of Solomon, as absolute ruler,[72] it seems that
at the dawn of the northern kingdom "all the congregation of Israel"
anticipated a leadership similar to that of the tribal confederacy.[73] In the
system of the tribal confederacy, YHWH ruled and redeemed his people
through his charismatic earthly representatives (the "judges"). His representatives were merely agents performing his will. Hence, the authority of YHWH's representatives was limited, non-absolute, indeterminate,
and even non-inheritable, in contrast to that of the absolute king.[74] As
in Samuel's case, some of the early prophets[75] in the northern kingdom backed the leadership according to this system, and opposed the

68. For example, Exod 5:6; 6:12, 21; 7:8; 8:14; 13:6, 11; 16:1; 20:1; 26:8; 1 Sam
12:6; 1 Kgs 8:16, 21, 51, 53; 9:9; 2 Kgs 17:7, 36.
69. Exod 18:1; 20:2; 32:1, 4, 7, 8, 11, 23; and also Num 23:22.
70. The contention is not that there is no reference to Israel's exodus from Egypt
in J, but rather that there is no formula according to which YHWH liberated Israel
from Egypt.
71. See Albertz, *Israelite Religion*, 227. The Yahwist of the ninth century B.C.E.
supported the continuity and stability of the Davidic dynasty through the everlasting
covenant between God and Abraham (see G. Fohrer, *Introduction to the Old
Testament* [London: SPCK, 1976], 152).
72. See 1 Kgs 12:3–16.
73. Since Noth published his book *Das System der Zwölf Stämme Israels* (Darmstadt: Wissenschaftliche Buchgesellschaft, 1930), the theory that the early political
system of the tribes of Israel was a confederacy has been accepted. However, few
accept all of his suggestions in detail, and his original proposition demands a certain
degree of revision. Regarding modifications to Noth's theory, see M. Weinfeld, "The
Pattern of the Israelite Settlement in Canaan," *SVT* 40 (1986): 270. Overall, there is
little controversy surrounding the fact that the Israelite political system prior to the
kingdom was that of a tribal confederacy.
74. J. Bright, *A History of Israel* (Philadelphia: Westminster, 1981), 167.
75. For example, Ahiah (1 Kgs 11:29–39; 14:1–16; 15:29); Shemaiah (1 Kgs
12:21–24); Jehu (1 Kgs 16:1–7, 12).

absolutist system.[76] The negative attitude of these prophets toward the authority of the king apparently influenced the later prophets.[77] It also characterizes the Elohist, who was influenced by the northern prophetic tradition.[78] More than the Yahwist, the Elohist repeatedly emphasizes the importance of Moses.[79] Thus, in E, YHWH's covenant with Moses on Mt. Sinai is stressed.[80] From here, several passages in 1 Samuel,[81] which are attributed to an Elohistic source,[82] show that YHWH was king of the tribal

76. The insistence of the prophets—including Ahiah (1 Kgs 11:29–39; 14:1–16; 15:29), Shemeiah (1 Kgs 12:21–24), and Jehu (1 Kgs 15:1–7, 12)—on establishing a confederative leadership led to the instability of the throne in Israel. In other words, while in Judah the Davidic dynasty endured throughout its history, the crown changed hands at least three times, and each time violently, in the first fifty years of the kingdom of Israel (922–876 B.C.E.): Jeroboam's son Nadab was slain by Basha (1 Kgs 15:28); Ela, Basha's son, was killed by Zimri (1 Kgs 16:9–10); Zimri committed suicide when the Israelites enthroned Omri (1 Kgs 16:15–18) (see Bright, *History of Israel*, 238–39). In other words, the desire for a charismatic leadership for the tribal confederacy remained.

77. For example, see Hos 3:4; 7:3–7; 8:7, 15; 13:10–11. Hosea even stated that the kingship was not from YHWH (8:4). By contrast, Isaiah, a Jerusalemite and a contemporary of Hosea, says nothing against the kings.

78. The Elohist's opposition to the king's authority is apparent in the words of Balaam, who serves as spokesman of the God of Israel: "Lo, I am come to you; have I now any power at all to speak any thing? The word that God puts in my mouth, that shall I speak" (Num 22:38). Balaam's statement not only expresses resistance to Balak's order to curse Israel, but also reflects the Elohistic view that the true king of Israel is not Balak but God himself. On the link between E and the prophets of northern Israel, see Fohrer, *Introduction*, 156; Jenks, *Traditions*, 83ff., and "Elohist," *ABD* 2:482.

79. The Elohist depicts Moses as the man to whom God revealed his name (YHWH) for the first time (Exod 3:13–15), as the representative of God before Israel and Pharaoh (Exod 3:15; 7:14ff.), as the leader of the people upon their exodus from Egypt (Exod 3:9–12; 13:17–19), as the judge of the people (Exod 18:13ff.), as a leader of the people in war (Exod 17:8–16), as the mediator in the establishment of the covenant between the people and God (19:2–9, 16–17, 19; 27:3–8, 11–15), and as the mediator and intercessor in cases of apostasy (Exod 32:11–14, 30–34). In addition, God speaks to Moses "face to face" and "mouth to mouth," unlike the other prophets (Num 11:6–8); see Jenks, *Elohistic*, 90–91.

80. Fohrer, *Introduction*, 156.

81. 1 Sam 8; 10:17–27; 12:12, 19.

82. The attribution of these passages to E is based on the close relationship between E and the prophetic traditions of 1 Samuel: the story of the election of Samuel (1 Sam 3:1–4:1a) demonstrates the link to similar traditions in E, especially the story of Moses' election (Exod 3:1, 4, 9–13, 15); the role of Samuel's endeavors as prophet (7:5; 8:6; 19:19, 23) is similar to that of the "prophets" in E (Abraham—

confederacy before the establishment of the kingdom.[83] Therefore, if the traditions of Samuel show that the political system in the time of the tribal confederacy was theocratic, then it can be said that in the Sinai covenant of E, which can be seen as the source for the traditions of Samuel, YHWH is regarded as king of the people. Yet, in contrast to E, the Yahwist, who supports the continuity and stability of the Davidic dynasty, emphasizes the covenant of Abraham (Gen 15 and 16), which was devised as an ideological model for the Davidic dynasty and the covenant of David (1 Sam 7:14–16). The tradition of the Sinai covenant, which emphasizes the God who liberates Israel from Egypt,[84] was marginalized in the southern kingdom of Judah. If this is the case, the tradition (or the formula) according to which "God brought Israel up out of Egypt" appears in the book of Deuteronomy and the Deuteronomistic editing as it does due to the fact that the Deuteronomic and the Deuteronomistic writers to a great extent minimized royal theology, and in their

Gen 20:7; Moses—Num 11:2; Exod 32:7–14, 31–33). Furthermore, Samuel is described in the same way that Moses is described in E, as mentioned above, as God's messenger to Israel (8:4–22), as judge (7:15–17), as leader (12:2ff.), and as leader of the people in war (7:5ff.); see Jenks, *Traditions*, 89ff.

83. When the people request a king from Samuel, YHWH says to Samuel: "Listen to the voice of the people in regard to all that they say to you, for they have not rejected you, but they have rejected me from being king over them" (1 Sam 8:7); and in his farewell speech, Samuel ponders the people's request: "When you saw that Nahash the king of the sons of Ammon came against you, you said to me, 'No, but a king shall reign over us,' although the LORD your God *was* your king" (1 Sam 12:12).

84. If it can properly be held that a parallel exists between the structure of the Sinai covenant and the form of the suzerainty treaty in the ancient Near East, then the Sinai covenant demands a "prologue" establishing the compassion of the suzerain (sovereign God) toward the vassal (the people), and this is God's liberation of Israel from Egypt. For an examination of the similitude between the Sinai covenant and the suzerainty treaty, see G. Mendenhall, "Covenant Forms in Israelite Tradition," *BA* 17 (1954): 50–76; recently, Polak attempted to confirm this analogy: "The Covenant at Mount Sinai in the Light of Texts from Mari," in *Sefer Moshe: The Moshe Weinfeld Jubilee Volume* [ed. C. Cohen, A. Hurvitz, and S. M. Paul; Winona Lake, Ind.: Eisenbrauns, 2004], 119–34). Although D. J. McCarthy (*Treaty and Covenant* [Rome: Pontifical Biblical Institute, 1978], 245–56) has refuted this comparison, apparently the tradition of the Sinai covenant could not have been established in the absence of the tradition of God's release of Israel from Egypt, in light of Exod 20:2, whose basic premise is the laws of the Sinai covenant (the Ten Commandments). (On the close link between the Exodus tradition and the Sinai covenant, see E. W. Nicholson, *Exodus and Sinai in History and Tradition* [Atlanta: John Knox, 1973], 27.)

work adopted sources originating in the northern kingdom.[85] Hence, in the light of the formula according to which God is the one who freed Israel from bondage in Egypt, and the annotation of the Deuteronomist construing Jeroboam's calves as images of "other gods," it must be concluded that the source of the cultic formula in 1 Kgs 12:28, "behold your gods, O Israel, who brought thee up out of the land of Egypt,"[86] is not of the Deuteronomist. One can say, then, that he embedded in his composition the cultic formula regarding calf worship, which existed before his time and was known to him. Why did the editor, who viewed Jeroboam's calves as images of other gods, use this formula, even though the term "Elohim" in it refers to YHWH? A reply to this question will be provided in an analysis of Deut 9:7–10:11, along with an observation on the historical and theological background that led to the formation of the law forbidding images.

Fourthly, if the Deuteronomist states regarding Ahab, "…and Ahab did yet more to provoke YHWH, the God of Israel, than all the kings of Israel that were before him" (1 Kgs 16:33), why does he not blame Ahab for the downfall of Israel, but rather Jeroboam, who made the two calves? Or while the Deuteronomist casts the blame on Jeroboam's calves, why does the prophet Jeremiah declare in Jer 23:13 that the cult of Baal led to the demise of Israel and Samaria?[87]

The four questions indicated above will help to uncover the factors contributing to the negative approach to the calf image. The first question will be examined in Chapter 2, the second one in Chapter 3, the third one

---

85. See Albertz, *Israelite Religion*, 227. In Deut 17:14–20, a positive estimation of the role of the king in Israelite life is absent: these verses echo the prophetic traditions of Samuel, who sees the kingdom opposing the confederative ideology as an example of the pagan cultures (1 Sam 8). Therefore, the Deuteronomic school, which inherited the negative attitude toward the kingship from the prophetic tradition in the northern kingdom, bound the king to the laws of the Torah (Deut 17:18–19); see Jenks, *Traditions*, 129; Albertz, *Israelite Religion*, 225–26.

86. Opinions are divided on the question of whether the source of the cultic formula in 2 Kgs 12:28 is from Exod 32:4, 8, or vice versa. This issue will be discussed further in Chapter 3.

87. See M. S. Smith, *The Early History of God: Yahweh and the Other Deities in Ancient Israel* (Grand Rapids: Eerdmans, 2002), 75; in Jer 23:13–23, Jeremiah declares to his contemporaries that the fall of the northern kingdom of Israel resulted from the worship of Baal, and thus cautions Judah that God's judgment would be harsher upon it than upon Israel, and that it would be unavoidable and like that imposed on Sodom and Gomorrah in 23:14 (see also Jer 1:3). For a detailed interpretation of Jer 23:13, see J. M. Bracke, *Jeremiah 1–29* (Louisville, Ky.: Westminster John Knox, 2000), 187; M. Bole, *The Book of Jeremiah* (Jerusalem: Mosad Harav Kook, 1984 [Hebrew]), 296.

in Chapters 3 and 5, and the fourth one in Chapter 4. Below, I will
provide a general outline of the issues to be examined in the following
chapters.

In Chapter 2, I will seek out the hidden motive behind the Deuteronomist's negative stance regarding Jeroboam's calves through an explora-
tion of the nature of the calves, an examination of the ideological system
implicit in the Deuteronomist's historical account, and a close reading of
1 Kgs 12:26–13:10 (and also 2 Kgs 23:15–20).

In Chapter 3, through an analysis of the relevant texts on calf worship
and a comparison between them, I will clarify the points of contention
with calf worship in all of them, and which polemical criteria were used.

In Chapter 4, I will inquire into the religious background that led the
Elohist to the polemic against the calf image. I will examine particularly
the religious situation at the end of the eighth century B.C.E., bearing in
mind that this state of affairs is reflected in the book of Hosea, who was a
contemporary of the Elohist.

In Chapter 5, I will reveal the historical background and the theological factors that led to the composition of Deut 9:1–10:11. In this context,
I will ask when the aniconic custom assumed a statutory form, that is,
when was the law prohibiting images formed.

5. *The Motives Behind the Negative Attitude*
Toward the Calf Image—Methodological Considerations

In order to understand the motives behind the negative attitudes of the
critics of the calves in the Bible, one must take into account the negative
components of calf worship, as well as the background of the theological
(or ideological) critics who denounce the calf. In dealing with this point,
I will examine the motives for the aforementioned negative stance in
three directions:

The first direction is an examination of the negative position in relation
to the image of the calf itself. Although in the beginning the calf image
served as the pedestal of an invisible YHWH, it can be assumed that over
time it came to be considered as a sculptural representation of YHWH or
as an image of other god. In such a case, one must inquire into the causes
for this shift in the public's understanding of the calf.

The second direction is an examination of the negative attitude toward
calf worship. One must check here whether the cultic acts involved in the
calf cult deviated from the normative worship of YHWH.

The third direction is an examination of the question of whether there
is an ulterior motive for the negative stance regarding the calf. In other

words, the critics of the calf could have stressed the "sin of the calf" in order to denounce something else. In such an instance, the polemic against this other thing could be the underlying motive for the polemic against the calf.

My objective in the present study is to try to uncover the motive for the negative position on golden calf worship, and for the development of a literary tradition expressing this position, by tracing golden calf traditions in Israelite religious history. I will attempt to examine the possibility that a change in religious outlook generated the polemic against the golden calf. In tracing this shift in religious view, I will ask, first of all, what are the polemic viewpoints implicit in the negative attitude toward calf worship, and afterwards, following which I will explore the reasons or historical background that led to these viewpoints.

I intend to approach the research issues using exegetical methods, especially the tradition-historical method, with respect to the texts under discussion, and thus avoid sociological postulations that view the golden calf narrative in the framework of power struggles.

Chapter 2

THE SINS OF JEROBOAM AND THE CALVES

1. *The Sins of Jeroboam and the Calves*

1.1. *The Sin of the Calf as Jeroboam's Primary Sin*

The phrase "the sins of Jeroboam which he sinned, and which he made Israel to sin" is a standard expression used by the Deuteronomist to criticize the kings of Israel.[1] The author uses the sins of Jeroboam in order to explain the fall of the northern kingdom of Israel (2 Kgs 17:20–23; see also 1 Kgs 14:14–16). Jeroboam's sins, which are discussed in detail by the Deuteronomist in 1 Kgs 12:26–32, are the making of the two golden calves, one at Bethel and the other at Dan, the appointing of non-Levite priests, and the changing of the dates of religious festivals. In the framework of the discussion of these sins, harsh criticism is reserved especially for the sin of the golden calf, of which it is said "and this thing became a sin" (1 Kgs 12:30). In the books of Kings, the sin of the golden calf is the only one of Jeroboam's sins that is referred to several times, while the other two are not mentioned further. Through the prophecy of Ahiah the Shilonite, which tells of the divine plan to annihilate King Jeroboam's dynasty (1 Kgs 14:6–16), the Deuteronomist explicitly points out in v. 9 that the golden calves of Jeroboam were what aroused God's fury. In 1 Kgs 10:29, "Jeroboam's sins" are clearly identified with "the golden calves." We can infer from such, therefore, that the Deuteronomist considered the sin of the golden calf to be the primary sin committed by the Israelites, and the cause of the downfall of the northern kingdom.

---

1. This expression, or a number of variations upon it, were used to attack the kings of northern Israel: Nadab, 1 Kgs 15:15–30; Basha, 1 Kgs 15:34; Zimri, 1 Kgs 16:16; Ahab, 1 Kgs 16:31; Ahaziah, 1 Kgs 22:53; Jeroboam, 2 Kgs 3:3; Jehu, 2 Kgs 10:29; Jehoahaz, 2 Kgs 13:6; Jehoash, 2 Kgs 13:11; Jeroboam ben Jehoash, 2 Kgs 14:23; Zachariah, 2 Kgs 15:9; Menahem, 2 Kgs 15:18; Pekahiah, 2 Kgs 15:24; Pekah, 2 Kgs 15:28.

1.2. *Motives for the Condemnation of Jeroboam's Calves*

If the erection of the golden calves was the most grievous of Jeroboam's sins in the Deuteronomist's eyes, what was the background to the Deuteronomist's indictment of the calves? As mentioned above, a motive for the negative attitude toward the calf can be suggested in three directions: (1) the negative attitude toward the calf image itself; (2) the cultic acts involved in the worship of Jeroboam's calves; and (3) the Deuteronomist's ulterior motive behind the "sin of the calf." As was observed above, Jeroboam's calves are considered "other gods" in 1 Kgs 14:9 and 2 Kgs 17:16. However, disclosing the background to the censure of the calf image in the books of Kings is possible only after an analysis of the relevant texts pertaining to the calves, as well as an examination of the prohibition of the image. The reason is that the text in Deuteronomy dealing with the calf (Deut 9:1–10:11) was apparently formed by the Deuteronomist in the process of editing the Elohist's writings, and one must examine the sin of the calf in light of the prohibition of the image. Accordingly, the background to the Deuteronomist polemic against Jeroboam's calves will be discussed by way of an analysis of texts related to the calves (Chapter 3) and an examination of the texts dealing with the prohibition of the image (Chapter 5). Incidentally, the books of Kings contain no reference to the cultic activities involved in calf worship, and so there is no need to explore the second direction mentioned above. In this context, therefore, the present study will be confined exclusively to an examination of the third direction.

The suspicion that there is an ulterior motive behind the Deuteronomist's indictment of the calf as a cardinal sin stems from the following question: Why does the Deuteronomist not attribute responsibility for Israel's demise to the sins of Ahab, but rather only to the sins of Jeroboam,[2] despite his admission that "Ahab did more to provoke YHWH God of Israel than all the kings of Israel who were before him" (1 Kgs 16:33)? It seems that the Deuteronomist has a particular reason for detesting Jeroboam more than Ahab when it comes to the downfall of Israel, even while admitting that Ahab's sin was more deplorable than any committed by the kings of Israel, certainly including Jeroboam. It is possible, therefore, that the Deuteronomist is concealing the true reason for his loathing of Jeroboam.

---

2. See 2 Kgs 17:20–23; also 1 Kgs 14:14–16.

2. *The Deuteronomist and the Ulterior Motive*
Behind the Polemic on the Calf Image

It is hard to deny that the Deuteronomist's work, that is, what is termed "Deuteronomistic History," was composed according to a certain schema,[3] especially in all that concerns the criteria used by the Deuteronomist in compiling the books of Kings. It turns out that the Deuteronomist uses David and Jeroboam ben Nebat as criteria for the appraisal of kings in the northern and southern kingdoms. In other words, his historiographic schema assumes that because of David's righteousness, Judah will stand (1 Kgs 15:3–5), and because of Jeroboam's sins, Israel will fall (1 Kgs 14:16). What, then, was the Deuteronomist's motivation for proposing such a historiographic model? We can deduce that it was related to the religious policies adopted by David and Jeroboam respectively as founders of the southern kingdom[4] and northern kingdom. The books of Kings in their entirety support such a conclusion. We find no flaw in David's cultic activity, as lauded in 1 Kgs 15:5, "For David had done what was right in the eyes of YHWH and had not failed to keep any of YHWH's commands all the days of his life—except in the case of Uriah the Hittite," while Jeroboam is condemned for his religious policy as depicted in 1 Kgs 12:26–32.[5] However, as Jones well points out,[6] the Deuteronomist's condemnation of Jeroboam's religious policies is characterized by unjustness and bias, since his point of view is essentially Judean, that is, it originates in the southern kingdom.[7] Where, then, can

---

3. Since Noth's hypothesis that "First Prophets" should be attributed to a single Deuteronomistic editor or author in exile (*Überlieferungsgeschichte des Pentateuch*), there still is little agreement regarding the number of editing layers. In the present study, for the sake of convenience, I refer to a Deuteronomistic Historian in the singular, that is, "the Deuteronomist" rather than "the Deuteronomists," despite evidence of later additions in Deuteronomistic History.

4. Although David was king of the United Kingdom of Israel, at the time of the divided kingdom, he was the founder of the southern kingdom, considering the fact that he was crowned at Hebron with the support of the tribe of Judah, while Jeroboam was the founder of the northern kingdom.

5. See also 1 Kgs 14:9, 16.

6. G. H. Jones, *1 and 2 Kings* (The New Century Commentary 1; Grand Rapids: Eerdmans, 1984), 256. The point of view of Judah in this passage is clearly revealed through the reference to Rehoboam as "their master."

7. Scholars usually agree that 1 Kgs 12:26–32 was written entirely from the perspective of Judah. Some scholars have attempted, therefore, to uncover the reality behind Jeroboam's religious policies. This reality is described below in relation to the identity of the golden calf, as I understand it. Halpern ("Levitic Participation," 32) argues that the exclusivity of the Levite priesthood did not take hold before the

we find a clue suggesting this point of view? We need to look at ch. 13 of 1 Kings,[8] in which the Deuteronomist speaks through the mouth of "a man of God" from Judah in order to say that Jeroboam's religious policies were denounced as intolerable and sinful from the very beginning. Verse 33 of ch. 12 links 12:26–32 to ch. 13 (especially vv. 1–10). First of all, in order to clarify this link, one must pay particular attention to the expression "and went up to the altar..." in v. 33bβ, since it appears also in 12:32aβ and 12:33aα. The phrase "and went up to the altar," which occurs three times, precedes the phrase "so did he in Bethel, to sacrifice to the calves..." in 12:32aβ and the phrase "which he had made in Bethel..." in 12:33aα. It turns out that "Bethel" and "calves" are correlated with "altar."[9] Apart from 12:33bβ, the word "altar" appears another ten times in 13:1–10, and thus serves as a link between "Bethel" and "calves," between ch. 12 and ch. 13. One can understand from this literary schema that the condemnation of the altar in vv. 1–10 of ch. 13 is aimed at Bethel and the calves referred to in 12:26–32. Moreover, the fact that the Deuteronomist places the expression "and went up to the altar, to make sacrifice smoke (לְהַקְטִיר)"[10] precisely before ch. 13, in which YHWH's judgment of Bethel is declared, demonstrates that the beginning of Jeroboam's new rite and YHWH's judgment of it occurred on the very same day. It should be noted that the expression "and went up to the altar, to make sacrifice smoke" in v. 33 of ch. 12 is aimed directly at the expression "and Jeroboam was standing by the altar to make sacrifice smoke," in v. 1b of ch. 13. This is indicative of the

---

end of the seventh century B.C.E. J. Morgenstern ("The Festival of Jeroboam I," *JBL* 83 [1964]: 109–18) also claims that Jeroboam's calendar was not an innovation, but rather a reconstruction of an ancient system, which well fit the agrarian society that was deeply ingrained in the tribal confederacy. Compare Talmon, "Divergences," 48–74. Talmon rightly contends that Jeroboam's actions were meant to restore the political, social, and religious conditions that prevailed in Israel before it became the United Kingdom under David's rule (ibid., 49). Z. Zevit ("Deuteronomistic Historiography in 1 Kings 12–2 Kings 17 and the Reinvestiture of the Israelian Cult," *JSOT* 32 [1985]: 57–73) supports Talmon's view.

8. For a discussion of 1 Kgs 13 and a survey of the relevant scholarly literature, see G. N. Knoppers, *Two Nations Under God: The Deuteronomistic History of Solomon and the Dual Monarchies 2: Reign of Jeroboam, the Fall of Israel, and the Reign of Josiah* (Atlanta: Scholars Press, 1994), Chapter 3.

9. Note: "to the altar...in Bethel" (v. 32aβ, v. 33aα); "to the altar...to sacrifice to the calves" (v. 32aβ).

10. On the understanding of the verb לְהַקְטִיר, see D. V. Edelman, "The Meaning of QIṬṬĒR," *VT* 35 (1985): 395–404, and R. E. Clements, "קטר," *TDOT* 13: 9–16.

Deuteronomist's intention to emphasize that Jeroboam's cult at Bethel was deemed intolerable and sinful from the outset. In other words, 1 Kgs 12:32–13:10[11] is skillfully edited so as to argue through the "personification"[12] of the word "altar" that both "Bethel" and "calves" were censured from day one. Yet, when we read 1 Kgs 13:1–10 (and particularly v. 2[13]) in the context of 2 Kgs 23:15–20 (especially vv. 16 and 20), in which it is said that the prophecy of the anonymous man of God from Judah was realized through the desecration of the altar at the cultic site at Bethel by Josiah, it is understood that the Deuteronomist wishes to condemn Bethel itself.[14]

Why, then, does the Deuteronomist deny the legitimacy of Bethel and condemn it? We can identify a hint of his loathing for and criticism of Bethel in 1 Kgs 12:26–27: "And Jeroboam said in his heart: 'Now will the kingdom return to the house of David. If this people go up to offer sacrifices in the house of YHWH at Jerusalem, then will the heart of this people turn back to their lord, even to Rehoboam king of Judah; and they will kill me, and return to Rehoboam king of Judah." According to this

11. The prophetic episode relating to Jeroboam ben Nebat (13:1–10) is not essentially related to the parabolic episode of the aged prophet from Bethel (13:11–32). See W. B. Barrick, "Burning Bones at Bethel: A Closer Look at 2 Kgs 23:16a," *SJOT* 14 (2000): 3–16 (4).

12. When the man of God declares "the word of God" before Jeroboam in v. 2 of ch. 13, he does not address Jeroboam, but rather the altar ("And he cried against the altar by the word of YHWH, and said: 'O altar, altar'"). Here, the Deuteronomist personifies the altar and turns it into a living being capable of hearing. The personification of the altar can be interpreted as referring either to a messenger of God capable of transmitting the message of YHWH, or to Jeroboam himself. The latter possibility is more appropriate since Jeroboam, who is standing next to the altar, hears YHWH's message from the man of God. Therefore, the personified altar is none other than Jeroboam himself.

13. 1 Kgs 13:2 reads: "… Behold, a son shall be born to the house of David, Josiah by name; and on you he shall sacrifice the priests of the high places who burn incense on you, and human bones shall be burned on you."

14. It seems that the prophecy of the man of God in 1 Kgs 13:2, that Josiah will slaughter the priests of the high places and burn their bones, is incompatible with Josiah's reforms further on in the books of Kings since, according to the latter, Josiah burned human bones on the altar at Bethel (v. 16), but slew priests of high places in other areas of Samaria, but not Bethel itself (v. 20). Yet, it should be noted that the Deuteronomist's most significant message is the rejection of Bethel through the desecration of the altar and the destruction of its high places. The report according to which Josiah burned all the vessels for "other gods" in the Jerusalem Temple and carried their ashes to Bethel (2 Kgs 23:4) is suggestive of the Deuteronomist's strong disgust for Bethel. For commentary on the burning of bones on the altar, see Barrick, "Burning Bones."

Deuteronomistic account, Jeroboam established his cultic centers at Bethel and Dan in order to prevent his people from going up to worship at the Temple in Jerusalem. Why, then, does the Deuteronomist only disparage Bethel in the books of Kings? Apparently Dan ceased to be active after its destruction at the hands of Tiglath-pileser during the second half of the eighth century B.C.E., as evidenced by archaeological excavations,[15] while worship at Bethel continued well after the fall and exile of the northern kingdom of Israel.[16] In order to elucidate the Deuteronomist's polemic against Bethel, we must pay heed to the term "high place" (בָּמָה) or "high places" (בָּמוֹת), which refers to the ritual site at Bethel, and serves for the Deuteronomist as a sort of criterion by which he judges the kings of Judah. The question of whether the kings of Judah were considered by the Deuteronomist to be flawless like David pivots around whether they conducted worship at the "high place" or removed it. According to this condition, even if the kings conformed to YHWH's will, they still did not do all that was expected of them.[17] Generally speaking, the decisive reason for the Deuteronomist's negative estimation of the kings of Judah is related to the high places.[18]

Nevertheless, in an earlier period in Israelite history, the high places were undoubtedly considered legitimate sites for the worship of YHWH.[19]

---

15. A. Biran, "Tel Dan: Biblical Texts and Archaeological Data," in *Scripture and Other Artifacts* (ed. M. D. Coogan et al.; Louisville, Ky.: Westminster John Knox, 1994), 15.

16. 2 Kgs 17:28 tells us of the importance of the city as a cultic center even after the exile of the kingdom of Israel, and this argument is supported by the description of Josiah's reforms.

17. For an evaluation of these kings, see the following sources: Asa, 1 Kgs 15:11–15; Jehoshaphat, 1 Kgs 22:43–44; Joash, 2 Kgs 12:3–4; Amaziah, 2 Kgs 14:3–4; Azariah, 2 Kgs 15:1–7; Jotham, 1 Kgs 15:34–35. Hezekiah was esteemed for having "removed the high places" (2 Kgs 18:4). Recently, doubt has been cast on the cultic reforms of Hezekiah by L. K. Handy, "Hezekiah's Unlikely Reform," *ZAW* 100 (1988): 111–15; N. Na'aman, "The Debated Historicity of Hezekiah's Reform in the Light of Historical and Archaeological Research," *ZAW* 107 (1995): 179–95. J. Milgrom ("Does H Advocate the Centralization of Worship?," *JSOT* 88 [2000]: 59–76) departs from this view. Regarding Josiah, it is said that he repaired the high places that Solomon built (2 Kgs 13:13) and of course destroyed the high places at Bethel and Samaria.

18. See: Rehoboam, 1 Kgs 14:23; Azariah, 2 Kgs 15:4; Ahaz, 2 Kgs 16:4; Manasseh, 2 Kgs 21:3.

19. While the precise character of the high place is vague, it is clear that it served as a local place of worship, familiar both to Israel and its neighbors. Regarding the nature of these high places, see R. de Vaux, *Ancient Israel.* Vol. 2, *Religious Institutions* (New York: McGraw–Hill, 1965), 284–88. For further discussions of the high places, see Chapter 4 of the present study.

According to a report in the book of Samuel, even the prophet Samuel participated in a feast at a high place in the city of his birth, and brought with him Saul, who was anointed there by God (1 Sam 9:11–26). Solomon went up to sacrifice and YHWH revealed himself to him at Gibeon, which is described in the text as a "great high place" (1 Kgs 3:4). The high places were considered illegitimate only after Solomon built the Jerusalem Temple (1 Kgs 8).[20] Following the consecration of the Jerusalem Temple, all the other temples, including the high places, were viewed as illegitimate. The Deuteronomist began, of course, to assess the kings of Judah based on their negative or positive approach to the high places. This is the result of the Deuteronomist's interpretation and his exploitation of Deuteronomistic constitution (Deut 12:1–14) to promote cultic unity.[21] In other words, the Deuteronomist carried out the requirement of promoting cultic unity through the Jerusalem Temple.[22] Accordingly, all the other shrines, like the high places, are perceived by the Deuteronomist as direct violations of Deuteronomic law.

We now may properly conclude that the Deuteronomist's wish to promote cultic unity is the hidden motive behind his condemnation of the calf image. As we have seen above, the Deuteronomist identified "Jeroboam's sins" with the "sin of the calf." He emphasizes the calf image particularly in order to critique the religious policies of Jeroboam, as outlined in 1 Kgs 12:26–32. However, when we consider 1 Kgs 12:26–32 together with 1 Kgs 13:1–10 and 2 Kgs 23:15–20, we discover that the real target in the indictment of "Jeroboam's sins" is the cultic site at Bethel. The polemic against the site is the result of the implementation of the Deuteronomic constitution, which determines the centrality of worship at the Jerusalem Temple. When the Deuteronomist condemns the

20. See P. D. Miller, *The Religion of Ancient Israel* (London: SPCK, 2000), 53.

21. Cultic unity formulas such as "to the place which YHWH your God shall choose out of all your tribes to put his name there" (v. 5), "it shall come to pass that the place which YHWH your God shall choose to cause his name to dwell there" (v. 11), and "in the place which YHWH shall choose in one of your tribes" (v. 14), are interpreted in two ways. The first is that the expression "the place which YHWH shall choose" refers to a single site. It is possible that this place was Jerusalem or even an earlier northern site. The second is that the same expression does not refer to a single place, but assumes the existence of a variety of temples. For a detailed discussion of this subject, see B. Halpern, "The Centralization Formula in Deuteronomy," *VT* 31 (1981): 20–38; compare A. Rofé, "The Strata of the Law about the Centralization of the Worship in Deuteronomy and the History of the Deuteronomic Movement," in *Congress Volume, Uppsala 1971* (VTSup 22; Leiden: Brill, 1972), 221–26.

22. The Deuteronomist is the one who clarifies that "the place" is Jerusalem in the books of Kings (1 Kgs 8:16; 11:32, 36; 14:21; 2 Kgs 21:7).

calf, he also intends to condemn worship at Bethel, and thus "kills two birds with one stone." To this end, he masters a sophisticated literary writing technique: (1) he uses the phrase "he went up to the altar" in v. 33 of ch. 12, which serves as a bridge between 1 Kgs 12:25–32 and 13:1–10; and (2) with this phrase he refers at once to "Bethel" and the "calves" (vv. 32 and 33); the personification of the altar in 13:2, and its association with Jeroboam, enable the calves and Bethel, which were built by Jeroboam and are linked to the altar in terms of the literary structure, to be condemned simultaneously.

Chapter 3

THE ANALYSIS OF THE TEXTS

1. *Exodus 32*

1.1. *Literary Analysis*

It has been contended that the narratives related to Sinai/Horeb have a complicated literary composition due to multiple expansions.[1] Hence, it is not surprising to find in Exod 32–33 a labyrinth of various different sources.[2] According to Losa, as a result of the different traditions in its various compositions, Exod 32 comprises one of the most difficult and complicated texts in the Torah.[3] Literary contradictions in Exod 32, which are the product of the different traditions and sources—and which are suggested by scholars as a basis for this claim—include the following: (1) the manner in which Moses learned of Israel's sin (vv. 7–14, 15–20)—in the first passage, he learns of it directly through the word of God, while in the second passage, he observes it personally in the fracas in the camp; and (2) Moses' involvement in the request for forgiveness (vv. 11–13 and 30–32) and the multiple and inconsistent punishments (vv. 20, 26–29, 35)—the absolution for which Moses intervenes is given in vv. 33–35, and the punishment is also two-fold (by way of water in v. 20 and plague in v. 35).[4] On the basis of these inconsistencies, the literary structure of Exod 32 can be broken down into the following verses: 1–6, 15–20, 21–25,[5] 26–29, 30–34, and 35.[6] However, it is

---

1. Noth, *Pentateuch*, 33.
2. See J. Vermeylen, "L'affaire du veau d'or (Exod 32–34)," *ZAW* 97 (1985): 1.
3. See Losa, "Exode xxxii," 31.
4. Childs, *Exodus*, 558; Beyerlin, *Origins*, 18–19; see also Noth, *Exodus*, 244ff.
5. Verse 25 can be seen as relating in terms of literary continuity to vv. 26–29, which deal with the story of the origins of the Levitical priesthood. However, v. 25 is more properly seen as a continuation of the negative depiction of Aaron in vv. 21–24, when considering the expression "for Aaron had let them loose for a derision among their enemies" in v. 25.
6. For the most part, it seems that the aforementioned units are uniform, but there is room to discuss whether they should be further broken down.

worthwhile investigating whether all the contradictions in fact derive from the different sources and traditions or if another factor is involved. The present chapter will examine to which source or sources each literary passage is ascribed, and whether there is inconsistency or contradiction between the passages.

Opinions are divided regarding the attribution of passages to various sources, and this is due to the lack of a clear criterion for classifying the sources in Exod 32. This creates great difficulty in determining whether the primary source is J or E.[7] Although some researchers ascribe part of Exod 32 to J,[8] Noth was the first to claim that the entire narrative in Exod 32 belongs to J.[9] The reason for attributing Exod 32 to J is that it was constructed as a literary supplement to the Yahwistic narrative, which was introduced into the extensive account of the pre-history and early history of Israel. This supplement was inserted by J in order to condemn the rites introduced by Jeroboam ben Nebat.[10] According to Noth, no part of Exod 32 can be attributed to E. Childs is wary of ascribing the narrative of the golden calf to J, and suggests leaving open the question of whether a certain passage should be attributed to J or E.[11] Zenger, as well, refers to major parts of Exod 32:1–4a as characteristic of J.[12] Coats attributes Exod 32 to J, except the additions (vv. 1–6, 21–29) and Dtr (vv. 7–14).[13] By contrast, Vermeylen sees Exod 32–33 as the product of successive phases of Deuteronomistic editing.[14]

7. Scholars have ascribed most of Exod 32–33 to J or E, although they disagree significantly regarding the sources of each passage.

8. J. Wellhausen, *Die Composition des Hexateuchs und der historischen Bücher des Alten Testaments* (Berlin: Reimer, 1889), 194; H. Holzinger, *Exodus* (Tübingen: Mohr Siebeck, 1900), 108; J. E. Carpenter and G. Barford-Battersby, *The Hexateuch* (London: Longmans & Co., 1900), 130–32; H. Gressmann (*Die Anfange Israels* [Göttingen: Vandenhoeck & Ruprecht, 1929], 64ff.) attributes vv. 1–4, 17–18, 21–24, 25–28, 30–33, and 35 to J, while he attributes vv. 4b–6, 15–16, and 19–29 to E.

9. Van Seters ("The Golden Calf," 205) has contended that most of Exod 32 should be ascribed to J, with the exception of vv. 9–14 and 25–29.

10. Noth, *Exodus*, 246; in another book (*Pentateuch*, 39; see also *Exodus*, 244), he asserts that passages such as 4b–6, 15–20, 30–33, 34aα, 34b, 25–29, 34aβ, and 35 are secondary additions to the original passages (1–4a, 21–24), while vv. 7–14 is a Deuteronomistic supplement. Lehming ("Versuch zu Ex. Xxxii," 17) adopts Noth's view, provided that the entire narrative is not considered a relatively late addition.

11. Childs, *Exodus*, 558–59.

12. E. Zenger, *Die Sinaitheophanie, Untersuchung zum jahwistischen und elohistischen Geschichtswerk* (Wurzburg: Echter, 1971), 180ff.

13. Coats, *Rebellion*, 188.

14. Vermeylen, "L'affaire," 1–23. In his opinion, there are significant correspondences between Deut 9–10 and Exod 32–34 in terms of their content and order, based on the following comparisons: Exod 32:7–8a / Deut 9:12; Exod 32:9–10a /

For all that, an increasing number of scholars tend to ascribe Exod 32 to E rather than J. In contrast to Noth, Beyerlin attributes the entire chapter to E. Waterman also notes that the parts clearly related to Aaron and the calf are ascribable to E.[15] However, most of the aforementioned scholars fail to provide convincing arguments in support of the attribution of Exod 32 to E. The first step in such an attribution, in my view, is finding a link between Exod 32 and other passages ascribed to an Elohistic source. In the same way that Eissfeldt discerns a link between the text and Exod 24:15a, on the basis of which he attributes Exod 32 to E,[16] it is advisable to try to distinguish the "literary flow"[17] between Exod 32 and another source among the array of sources that stood at the disposal of the author of ch. 32, in order to identify the primary source of the text. Therefore, the first thing needed is to locate the beginning of the literary sequence of ch. 32. For this purpose, it is best to start the work of reconstruction with ch. 19, in which the narrative of Mt. Sinai/Horeb opens. The sources of the narratives preceding Exod 32 can be reconstructed as follows:[18] 19:1–2a (P),[19] 2b–9a (E),[20] 9b–16a (J),[21] 16aβ–17

Deut 9:13–14a; Exod 32:15 / Deut 9:15; Exod 32:19a / Deut 9:16a; Exod 32:19b / Deut 9:17; Exod 32:20 / Deut 9:21; Exod 33:1, 4 / Deut 10:1–3; Exod 33:28b / Deut 10:4; Exod 34:29 / Deut 10:5. His argument is that the correspondence between the two texts is the result of editing by the Deuteronomist, who wrote Deut 9–10 first and only afterwards Exod 32–34. He claims that the anteriority of Deut 9–10 to Exod 32–33 is supported by the following: (1) the wording of Exod 32:7–10 is that of the Deuteronomist; (2) the style of calf condemnation (Exod 32:20) matches the Deuteronomist's stereotypical iconoclastic expressions; (3) the phrase "a great sin," which appears in Exod 32:30, 31 is identical to the phrase in 2 Kgs 17:21, and refers to Jeroboam ben Nebat (1 Kgs 12:26–32).

15. L. Waterman, "Bull Worship in Israel," *AJSL* 31 (1915): 229–30.

16. O. Eissfeldt, *Hexateuch-Synopse* (Leipzig: J. C. Hinrichs, 1929), 152ff. He considers vv. 9–14 and 35 to be later additions and vv. 17–18, 25–29 to be attributable to L (Layman source), as first presented by him. Yet, this is not plausible since the verses ascribed to L contain complex theological views, which would be difficult to attribute to a layman. G. Beer (*Exodus* [Tübingen: Mohr Siebeck, 1939], 153ff.) also analyzes these verses in a similar manner, and attributes the following to E: vv. 1–6, 15–16, 19–25, 35, while he fixes vv. 7–14, 30–35 in the secondary parts, and classifies vv. 17–18, 25–29 as J, which for him represents an L source. Thus, his suggestion is compatible with that of Eissfeldt.

17. Regarding this term, see B. Schwartz, "What Really Happened at Mount Sinai?," *BR* 13, no. 5 (1997): 25.

18. On the methodology of reconstructing narrative and source, and for a full analysis of the Mount Sinai narratives, see, ibid., 20–30, 46.

19. The name "Sinai" is characteristic of both J and P, but vv. 1–2a are attributed to P due to the use of "number," a characteristic device used by P (v. 1), and the continuity of literary flow.

(E), 18 (J),[22] 19 (E),[23] 20–25 (J);[24] 20:1–23:33 (E);[25] 24:1–2 (J),[26] 3–8 (E), 9–11abα (J),[27] 11bβ–15a (E),[28] 15b–18a (P),[29] 18b (E);[30] 25:1–31:18a (P);[31] 31:18b (E).[32] By this method, the sources in chs. 19–31 are

20. There is an inconsistency between v. 2a and v. 2b, since, according to the latter, "Israel encamped 'before the mount,'" while the former verse states that "they had pitched 'in the wilderness.'" Also, the phrase "And Moses told the words of the people to YHWH" in v. 9b is not a proper continuation of v. 9a, since Moses already conveyed the people's response to the suggestion of the covenant in v. 8 and there is no other question demanding a reply from the people. In light of this fact, vv. 2b–9a are attributed to another source, E, since in E it is said that God lives on the mount and never descends from the heavens (see v. 3).

21. Another source begins with v. 9b and ends with v. 16aα, in which the people rejoice at the revelation of YHWH, while in vv. 16aβ–17, the impression is given that the people were afraid, and that Moses brought them to the foot of the mountain not so that they could see, but rather that they could hear (see Schwartz, "What Really Happened?," 23).

22. Note the use of the term "Mount Sinai."

23. Note the use of the term "voice," by which E stresses that the people did not see YHWH but rather heard him. However, J uses such concrete terms as "fire" and "smoke"; see, for example, J's phrasing in v. 11b: "YHWH will come down in the sight of all the people upon Mount Sinai."

24. This is the continuation of v. 18.

25. This is the part dealing with the giving of the Ten Commandments and the Laws of the Covenant to the people, and is a continuation of E's words in ch. 19, since for E, the most important thing is that God asked the people to keep the covenant and the people gave an affirmative reply, while in J, the covenant is not mentioned in ch. 19.

26. This section is the continuation of vv. 20–25 in ch. 19, since according to v. 25, Moses came down from the mountain to the people, and hence God's command that Moses come up to him is logical. Yet, according to E, in chs. 20–23, Moses remains on the mountain.

27. The description according to which "Moses went up with Aaron, Nadab and Abihu, and seventy of the elders of Israel," is not compatible with E, but rather J, and is a continuation of vv. 1–2.

28. The phrase "and did eat and drink" in v. 11bβ is a description of the feast of the covenant, and hence is related to vv. 3–8, which tell of the covenant ceremony.

29. The fact that the phrase "went up into the mount" in v. 15a is repeated in v. 18a suggests the ascription of vv. 15b–18a to another source, since it does not make sense that the phrase "Moses went up into the mount" would appear twice without a phrase like "Moses went down from the mount" somewhere between them. The terms "covered" (כָּסָה) and "the glory of YHWH" (כְּבוֹד יְהוָה) are characteristic of P. See Exod 16:13; 40:34, 35, 36.

30. This is the continuation of v. 15a.

31. Here appear the instructions regarding the preparation of the Tent of Meeting and all the ritual utensils, and they are attributed to P.

reconstructed as follows: J = 19:9b–16aα, 18, 20–25; 24:1–2, 9–11abα;
E = 19:2b–9a, 16aβ–17, 19; 20:1–23:33; 24:3–9, 11bβ–15a, 18b; 31:18b;
P = 19:1–2a; 24:15b–18a; 25:1–31:18a. Considering 32:1a, in which it is
said that the people yearned to see Moses, E is associated with ch. 32 in
terms of literary continuity, since only E describes Moses' long stay on
the mountain,[33] the same stay that caused the people to become concerned[34] about the prolonged absence of their leader. Also, in terms of
content, it appears that ch. 32 is a sequel to E's earlier chapters (19–24).
According to the narrative beginning in ch. 32, the making and worship of the golden calf by the people is an act in which they strayed from
"the way" commanded by YHWH (v. 8a). Here "way" refers to the Ten
Commandments (specifically, the commandment "You shall have no
other gods before me").[35] In other words, the people violated the covenant. The smashing of the tablets by Moses, upon which are inscribed the
Ten Commandments,[36] signifies the breaking of the covenant between
YHWH and the people (v. 19). Therefore, the literary continuity of ch. 32
can only be linked to a source referring to the covenant. Of the three
sources, only E meets this condition, since it contains the following: (1)
YHWH's request to establish a covenant and the people's affirmative
reply (19:2b–9a, 16aβ–17, 19; (2) the people's acceptance of the Ten
Commandments and Book of the Covenant (20:1–23:33); (3) the
ceremony of establishment of the covenant (24:3–8); and (4) YHWH's
request to Moses to ascend the mount to receive the tablets and their
giving (24:11bβ–15a, 18b; 31:18b).

---

32.   This is a continuation of the phrase "and I will give you the stone tablets" in
24:12b, while the term "tablets of the testimony" (לוּחֹת עֵדֻת) is ascribed to P, since
the term "testimony" (עֵדֻת) belongs to the general literary style of P.

33.   See the phrase "forty days and forty nights" (24:18b).

34.   The verb בוֹשֵׁשׁ in 32:1a, "And when the people saw that Moses delayed to
come down from the mount," which is a form of בּוֹשׁ ("to be ashamed, afraid"),
literally means to "cause shame" (see U. Cassuto, *A Commentary on the Book of
Exodus* [trans. I. Abrahams; Jerusalem: Magnes, 1967], 411; J. Durham, *Exodus*
[WBC 3; Waco, Tex.: Word, 1987], 416), but today it is associated with a root
bearing the meaning "to delay" or "to linger" (C. Houtman, *Exodus*, vol. 3 [Leuven:
Peeters, 2000], 631). It seems that the use of this word was meant to reflect the fear
and anger of the people caused by the long wait for Moses.

35.   See Cassuto, *Commentary*, 414.

36.   According to one hypothesis, the Torah and the commandments (מִצְווֹת) are
inscribed on the tablets (see 24:12b), but the general understanding is that the Ten
Commandments are inscribed upon them. Regarding the association of the words of
the covenant and the Ten Commandments, see Exod 34:28b.

Hence, it can be argued that in principle the literary sequence of ch. 32 flows according to the scheme of E. Moreover, the attribution of ch. 32 to E is further reinforced by the use of the word "Elohim" (אֱלֹהִים, twice in v. 16). In this context, one should remember that the cultic formula "This is your God, O Israel, who brought you up out of the land of Egypt" (v. 4b) is incompatible with the worldview of J, who emphasizes the theology of Zion and kingdom rather than the tradition of Moses.[37] The Exodus tradition was the basis for the religious history of northern Israel.[38] Further cause can be found for ascribing Exod 32 to E, namely, the role of intercessor that Moses assumes between God and his people (vv. 7–14, 30–34). The Elohist emphasizes the distance between God and human beings. God himself does not speak directly to his people (see Exod 20:18, 21). Thus, for example, it is an angel of God that calls to Abraham from the heavens (Gen 20:11), and God reveals himself to Abimelech in a dream at night (Gen 20:3, 6). Likewise, we should not overlook the thematic parallel between Exod 32 and the words of the northern prophet Hosea, who was active in the eighth century B.C.E. (a contemporary of the Elohist) and scathingly attacked the golden calf. First, the expression "My anger (אַפִּי) is kindled against them" (Hos 8:5) matches Exod 32:10–12, as a constant part of the motifs of heresy narratives. The word אַף is a term used frequently by Hosea to describe God's fury (11:9; 13:11; 14:5), usually with the first person suffix, such as in Hos 8:5: חָרָה אַפִּי בָּם. This expression appears to be a literary equivalent of "My wrath may wax hot against them" (יִחַר אַפִּי בָּהֶם) in Exod 32:10.[39] Second, Hosea contradicts the statement "This is your God, O Israel" (Exod 32:4, 8) with an antithesis: "it is not God" (Hos 8:6). It is likely that, for Hosea, the calf was not considered a footstool of YHWH. In Hosea's thinking, the calf is no longer a trait of YHWH, in the time when there was absolute identification of YHWH with Baal, whose symbol was the bull. Accordingly, calf worship in Hosea's view is the only evidence that the covenant was violated, and the parallel between Exod 32 and Hos 8 confirms the link between v. 1b and v. 5 in Hos 8.[40] This being the case, the thematic parallel between Exod 32 and Hosea's polemic against the golden calf corroborates the ascription of Exod 32 to E.

---

37. Mettinger, "Elusive Essence," 399; Albertz, *Israelite Religion*, 227.

38. See Albertz, *Israelite Religion*, 227.

39. See H. W. Wolff, *Hosea* (trans. G. Standsell; Philadelphia: Fortress, 1974), 141.

40. Ibid., 156.

It seems that the main source of Exod 32 is E. Now we will examine whether all of the passages in ch. 32 can be attributed to E in terms of literary continuity.[41] If there are no inconsistencies or contradiction between one passage and the other, the attribution of both of them to E will be reinforced. However, if we do find inconsistencies or contradiction between the passages—even one passage—then we can assume that there was another hand involved in the text other than that of the Elohist.

Verses 1–6 are usually considered a single unit ascribed to a basic source, which comprises the narrative core of Exod 32.[42] Some scholars have dissected vv. 1–6 according to terminology, style,[43] or other aspects,[44] but their views are unconvincing. Verses 1–6 are not only a single unit but also a pivot point for all of the narratives in Exod 32–34.[45] Yet, regarding the previous question, we should examine an argument made recently by White.[46] He suggests that vv. 1–6 be divided into two parts: 1–4a and 4b–6. The first part, which includes the polemic against Aaron, is ascribed to E, while the second part is the result of the "attack on Bethel" by the Deuteronomist.[47] According to White, the Deuteronomist, who was an ally of the Zadokite priests, added vv. 4b–6 to the

---

41. The aim of the "literary analysis" in this section is the identification of sources. Other than determining specific sources, terminology and meaning of words will not be considered.

42. S. R. Driver, *The Book of Exodus* (Cambridge: Cambridge University Press, 1953), 347–50; Beyerlin, *Origins*, 18–22; Hyatt, *Exodus*, 301–4; Childs, *Exodus*, 558–62.

43. Lehming, "Versuch zu Ex. Xxxii," 21–24, 50.

44. Noth, *Exodus*, 244–45.

45. Cf. Aberbach and Smolar, "Aaron, Jeroboam," 135–40.

46. M. White, "The Elohistic Depiction of Aaron: A Study in the Levite–Zadokite Controversy," in *Studies in the Pentateuch* (ed. J. A. Emerton; VTSup 41; Leiden: Brill, 1990), 149–59.

47. Ibid., 153–56. His idea is based on a number of premises. First, the Deuteronomistic Historian in fact intervened in the first four books of the Torah. He was an ally of the Zadokite priests, and of course had access to the epic compiled and edited by J and E, which almost certainly was held in the archives of the Temple. Second, the close parallels between Exod 32:4–5 and 1 Kgs 12:28, 32–33 suggest that the Deuteronomist did have a hand in the shaping of Exod 32. Third, Exod 32:1–6 and Gen 37:1–4 are mirror reflections of each other. Fourth, following Jenks's argument, the Elohist lived most likely in the late tenth century B.C.E., under the rule of Jeroboam ben Nebat. Fifth, the Elohist was Jeroboam's court scribe, whose duty was to promote the interests of the northern kingdom, including the superiority of Bethel and the exclusive legitimacy of the Levitical priesthood. Hence, the Elohist did not attack Bethel, but rather defended it (ibid., 151ff.).

tradition, rather than deleting Aaron,[48] since the story of Aaron's apostasy was already well known and well established. By adding vv. 4b–6, the Deuteronomist took the Elohist's polemic against the Zadokites and aimed it back at Bethel.[49] Yet, where and how can we discern the "attack on Bethel"? In this sense, one should question whether v. 6b reflects a situation later than that of vv. 1–6a. Most scholars interpret v. 6b as describing the orgies associated with the Canaanite fertility cult.[50] In order to confirm this interpretation, we must take into account three components related to the interpretation of the term צִיחֵק, since the key point in the interpretation of v. 6b turns upon it. First, one must confirm whether it can properly be said that the term צִיחֵק was employed by the Elohist in order to describe the normal cultic practices of Israelite religion. Second, the interpretation of v. 6b must be made while examining other verses, such as v. 18, which describe the calf cult. Third, if the term צִיחֵק is to be related to the fertility cult, two conditions must be present: (a) the verb צִיחֵק must carry the connotation of sexual activity; and (b) if it is agreed that the verb is used in this sense, then one must determine if this activity is part of the fertility cult, or is rather the product of euphoria and wantonness as a result of drunkenness. However, this is not the proper place to discuss this matter further.[51]

There are, anyhow, some points that are flawed in White's argument. First of all, his major claims should be summarized:[52] the Elohist, in his opinion, was Jeroboam's court scribe during the tenth century B.C.E. and

---

48. White contends that the Elohist inserted Aaron into the tradition of the golden calf and made him responsible for the idol, in order to denounce the sons of Zadok for the crime of apostasy (ibid., 155). However, Aaron was not inserted by the Elohist into the tradition of the golden calf, as his name was already associated with the Sinai tradition before the calf image was entered into the Yahwistic cult.

49. Ibid., 156.

50. A number of scholars support the view that the sexual orgies of the Canaanite fertility cult are described in v. 6: Cassuto (*Commentary*, 413–14) states: "But the people, who had already broken down every barrier, were beyond control…and the people sat down…to play (לְצַחֵק), in accordance with the custom obtaining at the feasts of the peoples addicted to the worship of the gods of fertility and the inchastity connected therewith." Noth (*Exodus*, 248) states: "Special emphasis is laid on the extravagant celebrations at the cult feast…(v. 6). True, eating (and drinking) form part of the rite of the communal sacrifice. Here, however, they are expressly mentioned with a purpose: 'and rose up to play,' doubtless refers to sexual orgies (see Gen 26:8) such as played a part in the Canaanite fertility cults." Hyatt (*Exodus*, 305) states: "This suggests a fertility ceremony, probably with obscene rites. In Gen. 26:8; 39:14, 17 the verb ṣāḥaḳ (*piel*) has a sexual connotation."

51. We will discuss these matters in §3.1.2 in Chapter 3.

52. See White, "Elohistic Depiction," 149–59 (esp. 151–55).

backed Jeroboam's cult at Bethel; according to E, the northern kingdom
planned to establish Bethel as an alternative to Jerusalem; the apostasy
story in Exod 32:1–4a was created as a polemic against the Zadokite
priests in Jerusalem; and Aaron in the narrative represents the Zadokite
priests. Yet, White offers no evidence that the Elohist was in fact a court
scribe to Jeroboam. Were there such evidence, we would be left with no
choice but to infer from his argument that the story in Exod 32:1–4a is
not a polemic against Bethel but rather an attack on the Zadokite priests
in Jerusalem. However, does Aaron in fact represent in Exod 32:1–4a the
Zadokite priests in Jerusalem? Although there is controversy regarding
Zadok's membership in Aaron's tribe,[53] in my opinion, Olyan's argument,[54] based on 1 Chr 12:25–30, that vv. 28–29 are an authentic source
for historical reconstruction, and show that Zadok was not an independent leader, but rather subordinate to Jehoiada, is more convincing.
When Levites from the sons of Aaron and from the family of Jehoiada
came to David, Zadok was already among the sons of Aaron. However,
while I accept Zadok's membership in Aaron's tribe, the weakest point
of White's argument is when he links the apostasy narrative related to
the calf with the Zadokite priests in "Jerusalem." If we assume, as White
contends, that in order to attack "the Zadokite priests in Jerusalem" the
Elohist invented the story, according to which Aaron made the golden
calf, who among the readers of the story would imagine that "Aaron" in
the narrative belongs to "the Zadokite priests in Jerusalem"? In my view,
no one! There is no connection between the calf and the Zadokite priests
in Jerusalem; there is no basis whatsoever for such a link. White's argument that the Elohist in the tenth century B.C.E. fabricated the story in
Exod 32:1–4a so as to revile the Zadokite priests in Jerusalem is unper-
suasive. Another weak point in White's account is that he does not offer
a literary explanation for the incoherence between vv. 1–4a and vv. 4b–6,
assuming that vv. 4b–6 are supposed to be a Deuteronomist addendum.
Above all, evidence that vv. 4b–6 are not a Deuteronomistic addition is
provided by the fact that Deuteronomistic theology is not interested in

53. Regarding the argument supporting Zadok's association with the sons of
Aaron, see M. Haran, "Removal of the Ark of Covenant," *Yediot Hahevra lehakira
Eretz Israel* 25 (1961): 211–23 (Hebrew), and Cross, *Canaanite Myth*, 206–15. On
the Jebusite theory regarding Zadok's ancestry, see H. H. Rowley, "Zadok and
Nehushtan," *JBL* 58 (1939): 113–41, and "Melchizedek and Zadok," in *Festschrift
Alfred Bertholet* (ed. W. Baumgartner et al.; Tübingen: Mohr, 1950), 461–72;
C. Hauer, "Who was Zadok?," *JBL* 82 (1963): 89–94; R. Rosenberg, "The God
Sedeq," *HUCA* 36 (1965): 161–77.
54. S. M. Olyan, "Zadok's Origins and the Tribal Politics of David," *JBL* 10
(1982): 177–93.

cultic activities.[55] Therefore, there is no need to discuss the claim that the Deuteronomist added vv. 4b–6 to 1–4a in order to divert the attack on "Aaron," meaning the "Zadokite priests in Jerusalem," to Bethel.

This being the case, as previously mentioned, the passage comprised of vv. 1–6, in its entirety, stands as a continuation of E = 19:2b–9a, 16aβ–17, 19; 20:1–23:33; 24:3–8, 11bβ–15a, 18b, and is directly linked to 31:18b.

Regarding the continuity between vv. 1–6 and 7–14, dispute remains. Some argue that inconsistency exists between vv. 1–6 and 7–14, as well as between vv. 7–14 and 15–20. As stated above, in vv. 7–14 Moses learns of the sin of the calf directly from God, while in vv. 15–20 he sees it for himself in the uproar in the camp. The reason for the inconsistency between the passages is the addition of vv. 7–14 by the Deuteronomist.[56] The basis for this claim is the fact that vv. 7–14 seem to reiterate Deut 9:12–19, 25–29 in quite similar words. But this fact is insufficient in order to attribute the entire passage to Deuteronomistic editing. This is the place to confirm the ascription of vv. 7–14 to E. Because Moses is depicted here as performing the role of a prophet in intercession between God and his people, vv. 7–14 should be attributed to E. As is well known, the Elohist particularly emphasizes the role of the mediator between God and his people: in E, God is linked to his people through the prophets;[57] he does his will through the prophets; Moses is known as the greatest intercessor between God and man, as messenger and prophet (compare Exod 3:10, 12; 20:19, 21; 32:7–14, 30–34). It should also be recalled that the term "My wrath may burn" (יְחַר אַף, vv. 10–11) is characteristic of the Elohist.

---

55. See M. Weinfeld, *Deuteronomy 1–11* (AB 5; New York: Doubleday, 1991), 37–44 (esp. 37, 40).

56. On the scholars who take vv. 7–14 to be an insertion, see Losa, "Exode xxxii," 32. Scholars who defend the Deuteronomistic editing of vv. 7–14 include Noth, *Pentateuch*, 33 n. 113, and *Exodus*, 244; C. A. Simpson, *The Early Traditions of Israel* (Oxford: Blackwell, 1948), 204–9; Lehming, "Versuch," 16–50; Hyatt, *Exodus*, 306; Childs, "Etiological Tale," 558; E. Aurelius, *Der Fürbitte Israels: Eine Studie zum Mosebild im Alten Testament* (Stockholm: Almqvist & Wiksell, 1988), 41–44. In P. Weimar's view ("Das Goldene Kalb: Redaktionskritische Erwägungen zu Exod 32," *BN* 38–39 [1987]: 60–117 [esp. 151–55]), this text (excluding vv. 9, 13) belongs to DtrN.

57. The Elohist emphasizes God's distance from people who are easily led into sin. This is the reason why the Elohist's God is not supposed to speak directly to people (see Exod 20:18, 21) but rather via an angel of God (Gen 22:11) or dreams (Gen 20:3, 6), with the exception of prophets.

It can be inferred from the above that the golden calf narrative in Exodus preceded that in Deuteronomy, as becomes clear when focusing on Moses' plea to God in Exod 32:7–14. A comparison of the version of Moses' plea in Exod 32:11–13 with that in Deut 9:26–29[58] reveals a number of key differences.

First, a number of expressions that appear in Deuteronomy, such as "your people and your inheritance" (עַם וְנַחֲלָה, Deut 9:26, 29)[59] and "redeemed" (פָּדָה, Deut 9:26),[60] expressions which we might consider characteristic of Deuteronomy, are not found in Exod 32:11–13.

A second difference can be found between Exod 32:13 and its counterpart in Deuteronomy: God's oath to the Patriarchs (Abraham, Isaac, and Israel), mentioned by Moses in his plea to God in Exod 32:13, is not mentioned in his plea in Deut 9. In other words, the אֲשֶׁר clause (Exod 32:13) is absent in Deut 9:27. In this context, it is important to note Greenberg's hypothesis.[61] In his opinion, the אֲשֶׁר clause specifies God's vow to the Patriarchs.[62] Moses' plea in this clause is meant to remind God of his oath to the Patriarchs. He argues that if God could not reconsider destroying the people who had sinned based on their own merit, then he should do so for the sake of his loyal servants, the Patriarchs, to whom he swore that they would be the fathers of a great nation. This is the basis of the dispute between God and Moses, whose aim is to cause God to desist from his plan to annihilate the "stiff-necked" people who sinned against him, and to establish "a great nation" through Moses (Exod 32:10). Yet, Deut 9:27—"Remember your servants, Abraham, Isaac, and Jacob; do not look at the stubbornness of this people, at their wickedness, or at their sin"—without the אֲשֶׁר clause, is liable to be read

---

58. In light of D's reliance upon Exod 32 in composing the golden calf story, it makes sense that Deut 9:26–28 follows vv. 13–14. The content of Moses' plea in Deut 9:18–19 does not match its parallel in Exod 32:11–33. Moreover, it is in discord with the current text, since the delay of forty days between the smashing of the Tablets of the Covenant (v. 17) and the destruction of the calf (v. 21) seems implausible. In any case, the Deuteronomic narrator altered the existing text regarding the calf image in Exod 32, and wrote Deut 9:9–10 while employing his own literary rhetoric and theological inclinations.

59. See Deut 4:20; 1 Kgs 8:51, 53 (Weinfeld, *Deuteronomic School*, 328).

60. See Deut 7:8; 13:6; 16:15; 21:8; 24:18; 2 Sam 7:23 (ibid., 326).

61. M. Greenberg, "Moses' Intercessory Prayer," *Tantur Yearbook 1977–1978* (1978): 21–36.

62. The אֲשֶׁר clause may be considered a direct object of the verb "remember" (זְכוֹר). The term ... זְכוֹר לְ is different from...זְכוֹר אֵת. The former is connected to someone (indirect object), while the latter to something (direct object). The אֲשֶׁר clause in Exod 32:13 is equivalent to the "direct object" of the verb זָכַר (ibid., 27–28).

as follows: God should consider his loyal followers, Abraham, Isaac, and Jacob; and he should ignore the people's obstinacy. In eliminating the אֲשֶׁר clause, gone is the motif of God's promise to the Patriarchs to make a great nation, and hence, the meaningful name "Israel" does not appear in the book of Deuteronomy. In Moses' plea in Deut 9:27, there is direct reference to the rights of the Patriarchs, a request from God to disregard the evilness of his people, while considering the meritorious Patriarchs, but not because of God's vow to them. I will now examine the exceptional differences between these two passages. Notably, Moses' plea in Exod 32 is understood as "Turn from your fierce wrath, and have mercy on your people," while in Deut 9 it is understood as "Remember your servants, Abraham, Isaac, and Jacob; do not look at the stubbornness of this people or at their wickedness or their sin!" In the Exodus version, there is no reference to the sins of the people; it is merely a plea of intercession. Why, then, is there such a disparity between the two versions? The reason is that in Exodus, Moses' plea is described by the Elohist as prophetic intercession, while in Deuteronomy it was adapted to fit the Deuteronomist's theoretical intentions. In Exodus, when Moses hears of the people's transgressions and the death sentence that YHWH has decreed for them, he attempts through his plea to temper YHWH's flaring anger. He does this by freezing the moment, so as to buy time to operate, and then asking for a pardon on behalf of his people. By contrast, the plea in Deut 9:26–29 appears only after Moses has descended from the mountain and has smashed the Tablets of the Covenant and the golden calf. In Deuteronomy, the impression is not created that the people's fate is at stake, or that they are on the verge of destruction. Hence, it seems that Moses' plea in Deuteronomy is not meant to stay God's burst of rage, expressed in the proposed annihilation of Israel. One can assume that Moses' plea in Deuteronomy is an adaptation of that in Exodus designed to meet the Deuteronomist's intention.

Finally, a third difference between the two versions can be explained as follows: in Exodus, the center of the plea is a reminder of the potential damage to YHWH's good name should he wipe out the people he liberated from Egypt—"Why should the Egyptians say, 'With evil intent he brought them out, that he might kill them in the mountains and exterminate them from the face of the earth'?" (Exod 32:12). By contrast, the exhortation in Deuteronomy is twofold: "lest the land from which you brought us out say, 'Because YHWH was not able to bring them into the land which he had promised them, and because he hated them he had brought them out to slay them in the wilderness'" (Deut 9:28). The first among the two exhortations in this verse—YHWH's impotence—is lacking in Exodus, but it is not genuine to Deuteronomy.

It appears in Moses' plea when YHWH condemns the people and voices his intent to exterminate them because they lost faith in him after the report from the spies, which deterred the people from going up and conquering the Land of Israel. Moses raises again the matter of YHWH's reputation: "If you kill this people as one man, then the nations who have heard of your fame will say, 'Because YHWH was not able to bring this people into the land which he swore to them, therefore he slaughtered them in the wilderness'" (Num 14:15–16). This motif, which belongs to the spy episode in Num 14, was added to Moses' plea by the Deuteronomistic editor following the sin of the golden calf.

All of these characteristics point to the secondary and unoriginal nature of the version in the book of Deuteronomy. This version is not an adaptation of an earlier formulation in the book of Exodus; it is different, rewritten and redesigned stylistically in order to fit new circumstances. Therefore, the claim that vv. 7–14 were inserted by the Deuteronomist between vv. 1–6 and vv. 15–20 is unconvincing. The fact that vv. 15–20 are a direct continuation of vv. 7–14 is confirmed by the literary framework of E: the site of the events "on the mount" and "at the foot of the mount" appear one after the other. In other words, the oscillation from one arena to the other—one high and one low—is the literary schema of the Elohist, which is meant to express his theological intent: "at the foot of the mount" (19:2b–9a)—the people's vow to keep the covenant; "on the mount" (24:18b; 31:18b)—the giving of the tablets as the Law of the Covenant; "at the foot of the mount" (32:1–6)—the violation of the covenant; "on the mount" (32:7–14)—YHWH's declaration of the nullification of the covenant and intent to destroy the people, and Moses' plea against the weight of the punishment; "at the foot of the mount" (32:15–20)—Moses' confirmation of the nullification of the covenant by smashing the tablets, which are the sign of the covenant.[63] Therefore, all the stages of events appear in correct sequence, in one elaborate composition by the Elohist.[64]

---

63. In Akkadian legal phraseology, "to smash the tablet" (*tumppam hepu*) means nullification or repudiation of a document or agreement (N. M. Sarna, *Exploring Exodus* [New York: Schocken, 1986], 219).

64. One suggestion explains the disorder of the text in vv. 15–20. According to D. Frankel ("The Destruction of the Golden Calf: A New Solution," *VT* 44 [1994]: 330–39), v. 20a was written as a response to Deut 7:5, 25—"and burn their graven images with fire"—and originally comprised an addition at the end of the verse. In this case, v. 20b should have come after v. 19, which ends with the smashing of the tablets by Moses. In other words, what was burned, ground, and sprinkled over the water was not the golden calf but the stone tablets. The expression "and burnt it with fire" (32:20a) was inserted at the beginning of v. 20 instead of at the end. Apparently,

In the opinion of some scholars, vv. 21–25 comprise an addition to the original (J or E).[65] They believe that the aim of this supplement was to elucidate Aaron's role in the construction of the golden calf and to justify his actions, thereby restoring his status. However, it seems that the excuse that the author puts in Aaron's mouth in response to his interrogation by Moses regarding the calf does not work to exonerate, but rather to condemn, him. The description of the calf emerging from the fire of its own accord ("and I cast it into the fire, and there came out this calf," 32:24b) is not a myth of divine self-creation,[66] but rather a satire, meant to scorn the wretched leadership of Aaron as compared to the exemplar leadership of Moses.[67] In fact, there is no reason to interpret this as an addition, since there is no inconsistency or contradiction between this passage and those preceding. The ascription of the passage to E is corroborated by the expression אַף חָרָה יִ ("anger burns hot," 32:22a), which is characteristic of the Elohist.

Verses 26–29 are an independent portion, which is unrelated to the calf narrative. Apparently, this passage was originally part of the story pertaining to investiture of the Levites to the priesthood. A glance at the passage shows that it is related to Deut 33:8–11, in which Moses praises the Levites. Therefore, some attribute both passages to a common source.[68] It may be possible to attribute Deut 33:1–8 to E based on the following argument: in order to find the source of Deut 33:8–11, first of all, one should check which priesthood the writer is alluding to in the passage. One hint is found in the phrase "whom you tested at Massah, with whom you contended at the waters of Meribah" (Deut 33:8). Considering that the waters of Meribah incident[69] is mentioned in Ps 81,

the process of destroying the golden calf idol, especially the order of actions taken by Moses, is illogical, but that is no reason to conclude that the episode is illogical, or that the text is faulty. Even the author of Deut 9:21 left the text as is, although he knew it was out of order. Regarding the meaning of the destruction of the golden calf, there is disagreement. This matter will be discussed below (in §2.2.2.3 in Chapter 3).

65. Those claiming that it was an addition to a J source include Noth, *Exodus*, 244–45, and Childs, *Exodus*, 569–70, and those arguing that it was an appendage to an E source include Beyerlin, *Origins*, 20, and Hyatt, *Exodus*, 309.

66. Thus argues S. E. Loewenstamm, "The Making and Destruction of the Golden Calf," *Bib* 48 (1967): 487–90.

67. Simpson, *Early Traditions*, 205; Hyatt, *Exodus*, 309; Durham, *Exodus*, 431.

68. Beyerlin (*Origins*, 132) typically attributes the two passages to the same source.

69. The description of the waters of Meribah incident in Num 20:2–12, which is normally attributed to P, is later than that in Ps 81 in terms of its origin, considering

which is attributed to a northern source,[70] it can be assumed that Deut 33:8–11 comprises an etiology of the Levite priesthood in northern Israel. Moreover, when we take into account the fact that these passages are meant to enhance the legitimacy of the ancient Levite priesthood, through the evocation of Moses' name,[71] the impression is created that the priesthood granted legitimacy in Deut 33:8–11 is the Levite priesthood of Dan. Judges 18:30 testifies to the fact that the Levite priesthood of Dan descended from Moses' grandson.[72] Therefore, grounds exist for ascribing Deut 33:8–11 to E. Such an attribution gains further reinforcement considering the number of blessings given to Joseph (vv. 13–17), which are more numerous and superlative than those given to Judah (v. 7). However, the following question arises: Could Deut 33:8–11 truly be the source for Exod 32:26–29? That is to say, given that Deut 33:8–11 is attributed to E, should Exod 32:26–29 also be attributed to E? Despite the similarity between them in terms of the zeal of the Levites for YHWH, it can be inferred that this similarity does not necessarily stem from the same source but rather from the mutual influence of two sources or alterations resulting from the fact that one source re-edited the other, which was pre-existent, or made use of the same material used in the other source.[73] Therefore, one can find the stylistic characteristics in the verses

the antiquity of Moses' blessing of Levi in Deut 33, which refers to the waters of Meribah incident. According to A. Rofé (*Introduction to Deuteronomy* [Jerusalem: Magnes, 1988 (Hebrew)], 234–49 [esp. 243]), Moses' blessing in Deut 33 is dated to the end of the Judges period. Eissfeldt ("El and Yahweh," *JSS* 1 [1956]: 226–31) dates Deut 32 to the eleventh century B.C.E.; and ascribes Deut 33, together with Deut 32, to E.

70. According to M. D. Goulder ("Asaph's History of Israel [Elohist Press, Bethel, 725 B.C.E.]," *JSOT* 65 [1995]: 71–81), Ps 81 is ascribed to E along with the other Psalms of Asaph, which are considered a single unit (Pss 73–83). This ascription is based on the fact that they call "the people of God" "Joseph" five times (once Ephraim, one Benjamin and once Manasseh); in these psalms (the Psalms of Asaph), the divinity is not termed "YHWH" or "Elohim" but rather the "God of Jacob," and often "El"; they refer repeatedly to the covenant, and to God leading his flock; they often contain historical references, especially to the exodus from Egypt.

71. For example, Moses' blessing in Deut 33 (also Moses' ordaining of the Levites into the priesthood in Exod 32:26–29).

72. M. D. Goulder, *The Psalms of the Sons of the Korah* (JSOTSup 20; Sheffield: JSOT, 1982), 57–59.

73. Several changes can be found between the two versions: (1) in Exod 32:26–29, the place in which the Levites slew their brothers, companions, and neighbors is not mentioned; (2) the two passages use different verbs to describe the Levites' zeal (Exod 32 uses the verb הָרַג, "slay," while Deut 33 has רָאָה, "see"; הֵכִיר, "recognize"; and יָדַע, "know"; (3) the objects of the verbs are different (Exod 32 has אָחִים,

of Exod 32:26–29 that form the basis for ascribing them to E. However, the stylistic characteristics for attributing Exod 32:26–29 to J are also found and these include: (1) the phrase מִי לַיהוָה אֵלַי ("Who is on the LORD's side," v. 26); (2) the expression כֹּה אָמַר יְהוָה אֱלֹהֵי יִשְׂרָאֵל ("Thus says the LORD, the God of Israel," v. 27);[74] (3) the slaying of the children of Israel by the Levites in Exod 32:26–29, which demonstrates their zeal for YHWH,[75] is reminiscent of the story of the killing of Hamor and Shechem by Levi in revenge for the rape of Dinah in Gen 34. This narrative, which is ascribed to J,[76] reinforces the argument for attributing the passage to J. It turns out that vv. 26–29 are rightly ascribed to J, and they were likely inserted by the late editor of the Torah in the current place.

Finally, vv. 30–35 are also attributed to E, in light of the fact that their content meets the expectations arising from the earlier verses ascribed to E. If so, we should recall the content of the sin of the golden calf prior to these verses, and take into account what is still to be anticipated. The story of the golden calf in Exod 32 is the work of the Elohist included in Exod 33–34, but it can be considered a single unit. It begins with the absence of the leader, and the people's demand for a substitute (v. 1). As a result, Aaron fabricates the golden calf in collaboration with the people, and the people themselves worship the calf (vv. 2–6). These

---

"brothers"; רֵעִים, "companions"; and קְרֹבִים, "neighbors"; while Deut 33 has אָב וָאֵם, "father and mother"; and בָּנִים, "children"). Apparently, the focus of the description of the Levite priesthood is different in the two passages: Exod 32:26–29 is related to the story of the creation or origin of the Levite priesthood (see the expression "Consecrate yourselves today to YHWH" in v. 29), while Deut 33:8–11 focuses on the devotion of the Levites to the Covenant of YHWH (his Torah).

74. See Exod 3:15; 4:22; 5:1; 7:17, 26; 8:16; 9:1, 13; 10:3; 11:4.

75. See the expression מִי לַיהוָה אֵלַי ("Who is for YHWH?") in v. 26.

76. Gen 34 is composed of two layers, one J and the other E. In particular, contradictions are apparent in vv. 25–31: according to vv. 25–26, Simeon and Levi alone attacked the city, while in vv. 27–29 the sons of Jacob pillaged the city; yet, in vv. 30–31, Jacob only rebukes Simeon and Levi. Hence, it emerges that Gen 34 was constructed through the merging of two narratives, namely, in one narrative the act is carried out by all of Jacob's sons, while in the other it is carried out by Simeon and Levi alone. The verses attributed to E are vv. 1–2a, 3–4, 6, 25 (other than the phrase "that two of the sons of Jacob, Simeon and Levi, Dinah's brethren, took each man his sword"), vv. 27–29, while the verses attributed to J are vv. 2b, 5, 7, 25 ("that two of the sons of Jacob, Simeon and Levi, Dinah's brethren, took each man his sword"), 26, 30–31. For a thorough discussion of Gen 34, see Y. Zakovitch, "Assimilation in Biblical Narrative," in *Empirical Models of Biblical Criticism* (ed. J. H. Tigay; Philadelphia: University of Pennsylvania Press, 1985), 175–96.

activities so enrage YHWH that he intends to annihilate his entire people, but Moses' intercession calms his fury (vv. 7–14). The narrative turns now to a description of the steps taken in dealing with the sin of the calf: (1) the smashing of the tablets, which symbolizes the breaking of the covenant between YHWH and the people (vv. 15–19); and (2) the destruction of the calf—the fountainhead of the sin—and the command for the people to drink the remains of the calf after it had been burnt, ground into a powder, and sprinkled over water (v. 20).[77] This is what has been told up to this point regarding the sin of the calf. That being the case, what else is to be expected?

According to the narration thus far, two crises have occurred among the people as a result of the sin of the calf. One is YHWH's threat to wipe them out. The other is the severance of the covenant-relationship between YHWH and the people, which finds expression in the smashing of the tablets. The first crisis is resolved by Moses' intercession. However, the second one is not yet solved. Verses 30–35 suggest that the solution to this crisis is also Moses' plea. The angel of God sent to the people (v. 34a) can be interpreted as YHWH's reply to Moses' plea for forgiveness of the people's sin. This is indicated by YHWH's desire to re-establish the covenant that had been violated with his people,[78] which is expressed in the reconstruction of the tablets (Exod 34:1, 4, 28), and even offers a solution to the issue of the leader, which served as the stimulus for the sin of the calf in the first place. It can be inferred from such that vv. 30–35 are linked to earlier passages: (1) vv. 1–6 deal with the leader; (2) vv. 7–14 are related to Moses' intercession;[79] (3) vv. 15–19 show the break in the covenant with God in wake of the sin of the calf, as mentioned above; (4) vv. 20–26 are related to the people's "great sin," for which Moses wished to atone (v. 30), and of which he has already reminded Aaron (v. 21).

---

77. Opinions are divided regarding the meaning of this act. It seems to me that this is a kind of "ordeal of an unfaithful wife" (סוֹטָה), as in Num 5:11–31. This matter will be discussed thoroughly in §2.2.2.3 in Chapter 3.

78. However, what is meant is not YHWH's expiation of the sins of the entire people, as is evidenced in such expressions as: "Whosoever has sinned against me, I will blot him out of my book" (v. 33b) and "nevertheless in the day when I punish, I will punish them for their sin" (v. 34b). YHWH's words in v. 34 can be interpreted in the sense that YHWH will restore the violated covenant (v. 34a), while he will save the punishment for another time in the future (v. 34b).

79. Incidentally, the aim of each of Moses' intercessions is different: in vv. 11–13 he intends to stop YHWH from exterminating the people, while according to vv. 30–32, his intent is to atone for the sins of the people, that is, to win forgiveness.

1.2. *Traditio-Historical Analysis*

1.2.1. *Affirmative Tradition Regarding the Calf Cult.* The attitude to the image of the golden calf in all of these passages in Exod 32 is negative. Yet, if we remove vv. 1–6 from a narrative context and discuss them as an isolated fragment, a positive attitude can be discerned alongside the negative one. First of all, it seems that the phrase עֲשֵׂה לָנוּ אֱלֹהִים ("make us a god") expresses the negative approach. One could very well agree with the interpretation that the people's request to make them אֱלֹהִים ("gods"/"god") does not refer to an image of other god as a substitute for YHWH, but rather to a tangible replacement for their leader Moses who had disappeared.[80] However, it does not appear that this was the Elohist's intention. How could the Elohist's intent—to condemn the calf image—with the expression עֲשֵׂה לָנוּ אֱלֹהִים be the same as that of the people he condemns for the calf image? Undoubtedly, for the Elohist, the term אֱלֹהִים in עֲשֵׂה לָנוּ אֱלֹהִים carries a negative meaning, that is, it refers to other god, in light of the expressions "they have turned aside quickly out of the way[81] which I commanded them" (v. 8) and "and have made a god of gold for themselves" (v. 31b). In other words, the Elohist, who condemns the golden calf as a violation of the commandment "You shall have no other gods before me" (Exod 20:3), uses the word אֱלֹהִים here in the sense of "other god."[82] However, we must note that a positive attitude to the golden calf is also latent in vv. 1–6. As mentioned in Chapter 1, אֱלֹהִים, appearing in the formula relating to Israel's exodus from Egypt, refers only to YHWH. Hence, אֱלֹהִים in the cultic formula, אֵלֶּה אֱלֹהֶיךָ יִשְׂרָאֵל אֲשֶׁר הֶעֱלוּךָ מֵאֶרֶץ מִצְרָיִם ("This is your God, O Israel, who brought you out of the land of Egypt," v. 4b), is also referring to YHWH alone. One may say, then, that in the same way that אֱלֹהִים in the phrase of עֲשֵׂה לָנוּ אֱלֹהִים ("make us a god," v. 1) refers to other god from the Elohist's perspective, אֱלֹהִים in the cultic formula (v. 4b) also refers to other god. It is true that when we read the cultic formula (v. 4b) alongside the phrase עֲשֵׂה לָנוּ אֱלֹהִים ("make us a god") in v. 1b, אֱלֹהִים in v. 4b could be identified easily with the אֱלֹהִים referred to in עֲשֵׂה לָנוּ אֱלֹהִים ("make us a god"), namely, other god. However, if we consider the expression עֲשֵׂה לָנוּ אֱלֹהִים ("make us a god") alongside Aaron's

---

80. J. Plastaras, *The God of Exodus: The Theology of the Exodus Narratives* (Milwaukee: Bruce, 1966), 228–39; M. Haran, *Temple and Temple-Service in Ancient Israel* (Oxford: Clarendon, 1978), 29 n. 28; G. W. Coats, *The Moses Tradition* (JSOTSup 161; Sheffield: JSOT, 1993), 125–34 (esp. 126).

81. The "way" refers to the Ten Commandments and particularly the first commandment (see Cassuto, *Exodus*, 414).

82. For a thorough discussion of this matter, see §2.2 of the present chapter.

proclamation חַג לַיהוָה מָחָר ("tomorrow is a feast to YHWH") in v. 5b, a
contradiction arises, since in the former expression the golden calf refers
to other god, while in the second it is linked ostensibly to YHWH. How
is it that two contradictory positions regarding the golden calf are
expressed in the same chapter? The answer to this question is related to
the following question: Is the cultic formula here the one that was
invented by the Elohist or the one that already existed in the cult of the
calf image which was regarded as affirmative, before the Elohist wrote
the narrative of the golden calf in Exod 32 in order to condemn it?

If we assume that the cultic formula in v. 4b is that which was
invented by the Elohist in order to denounce the golden calf, then we
must ask why Aaron does not utter the words חַג לָאלֹהִים ("feast to god")
but rather חַג לַיהוָה ("feast to YHWH"). If the phrase used were חַג
לָאלֹהִים, then it would be clear throughout that the reference is to other
god, given the fact, which we have already noted, that אֱלֹהִים in עֲשֵׂה לָנוּ
אֱלֹהִים ("make us a god") means other god. In such a case, the Elohist
would have been able clearly to decry the golden calf as such. However,
the fact that the Elohist has Aaron utter the words "feast to YHWH"
teaches us that the cultic formula is not that invented by the Elohist, but
rather that which already existed before him. Apparently, the reason that
the Elohist included the earlier cultic formula in his work is that he was
unable to achieve his objective in his polemic against the golden calf
without "handling" the cultic formula that was intended for YHWH, in
which the cult of the calf image was perceived in a positive light. In
other words, it seems that the Elohist could not effectively condemn the
cult of the calf image without changing contemporary public opinion,
which identified "God" (אֱלֹהִים) in the cultic formula with YHWH, and
YHWH with the golden calf, before which they proclaimed the cultic
formula "This is your God, O Israel, who brought you up out of the land
of Egypt" (32:4b).

The means used by the Elohist to alter public opinion is a demon-
stration of the gravity of the sin of the golden calf: it arouses the fury of
God, who decides to destroy his people (v. 10); it is considered the thing
that brings about the severance of the covenant between the people and
YHWH (v. 19); and above all, the golden calf bears no relation to YHWH
but rather to other god ("a god of gold," אֱלֹהֵי זָהָב, v. 31), and therefore,
is to be destroyed (v. 20). For those reading (or listening to) the Elohist
exposing the terrible sin of the golden calf, a disassociation is made
between the cultic formula, the expression "feast to YHWH" (חַג לָאלֹהִים),
and YHWH himself.

Assuming that the cultic formula antedates the Elohist, where and when can we find its origin? Can we assume that Jeroboam himself invented the cultic formula in the tenth century B.C.E., and that afterwards, in the eighth century B.C.E., the Elohist used it to condemn worship of Jeroboam's golden calves? Or did the golden calf cult already exist in the system of confederacy, while Jeroboam merely breathed new life into it, as previously mentioned?

Here we should recall the claim that whereas Aaron made only one golden calf, the cultic formula is expressed in the plural.[83] This shows that the cultic formula as expressed in Exod 32:4b refers to the two golden calves of Jeroboam ben Nebat.[84] To this argument one could reply that the grammatical plural could have been in the sense of "plural of majesty to YHWH," and that despite the existence of two temples (Bethel and Dan), there was only one calf image in one temple.[85] Therefore, one cannot say that the plural form of the cultic formula was originally that of Jeroboam. Furthermore, the phrase "who brought you up out of the land of Egypt" is relevant to Aaron's calf image in any event, but is relevant to Jeroboam's calves only on the assumption that the latter reproduced an ancient custom, while imitating Aaron's actions.[86] One can deduce from such that the cultic formula in Exod 32:4b originated at least sometime before the reign of Jeroboam ben Nebat. However, the opinion that the formula did not originate with Jeroboam, but rather in an earlier period, does not rule out the argument that the golden calf

83. See the Hebrew words, הֶעֱלוּ‎ ,אֱלֹהִים‎ ,אֵלֶּה‎.

84. Noth, *Exodus*, 246ff., and *Pentateuch*, 157ff.; Lehming, "Versuch," 49; Ringgren, *Israelite Religion*, 37; Fohrer, *Israelite Religion*, 82; Van Seters, "The Golden Calf," 300.

85. M. Buber, *Moses* (New York: Harper, 1958), 148 n. 177.

86. Regarding the anteriority of Exod 32 to 1 Kgs 12:26–33, see Childs (*Exodus*, 560), who offers several proofs that the Deuteronomist, who composed 1 Kgs 12:26–33, relied on the existent narrative, and adapted it to the polemic against Jeroboam: (1) Exod 32 is well constructed in a sin–forgiveness structure together with chs. 33 and 34 and because these chapters contain many pre-Deuteronomistic tokens, it appears that ch. 32 is also such; (2) in Exod 32 there are several contact points with the larger framework, which attests to an earlier phase of the tradition. On the basis of the comparison between Exod 32 and Deut 9, Losa ("Exode xxxii," 6) argues that the latter is based on the former. Cassuto (*Commentary*, 409) also thinks that the declaration "This is your God, O Israel, who brought you up out of the land of Egypt" is more appropriate to the period immediately after the exodus from Egypt than the period of Jeroboam, and therefore, the tradition of Aaron's calf cult was already well known at the time of the division of the kingdom. See also Aberbach and Smolar, "Aaron, Jeroboam," 129–40; Beyerlin, *Origins*, 128–29; Albright, *Stone Age to Christianity*, 300ff.

narrative in Exod 32—which was formulated in the eighth century
B.C.E.—was aimed against Jeroboam's calves, since the drawing of a
similarity[87] between the narrative of Aaron's calf and the description of
Jeroboam's calves was intended to denounce the latter. In the following
section, I will inquire into the origin of the cultic formula and the background to its production.

1.2.2. *Aaron, Bethel, and the Calf Image.* The cultic formula in v. 4b and
the phrase "feast to YHWH" in v. 5b attest not only to the positive public
opinion regarding the calf cult, but also to the fact that Aaron is depicted
as its founder. Here a question arises: Was there a priesthood honoring
Aaron as the progenitor of the priesthood before the Elohist's time? In E,
Aaron is not the priest. In the view of Simpson,[88] the Aaronite priesthood
became legitimate and pre-eminent in Judah only after the exile, and as a
result of the Priestly adaptation of the Torah (P) in the fifth century B.C.E.
The appearance of the Aaronite dynasty was, therefore, a result of the
new claim of P in the fifth century B.C.E. However, it seems that these
facts actually do not imply that the name of Aaron and the Aaronite
priesthood were not known before this period, but that during this period
the Aaronite priesthood came to the climax of its power. If this is the
case, where do we find evidence of the Aaronite priesthood before this
period? In order to answer this question, it is worth looking at Judg
20:27b–28a.

In Judg 20:27b–28a, we learn that the Ark of the Covenant stood at
Bethel, and that priests from the house of Aaron served there. A few
scholars question the historicity of these verses, since they appear to be a
later addition.[89] Yet, on the basis of the fact that the verses were inserted

---

87. Some similar elements are as follows: (1) golden calves were made by Aaron
and Jeroboam respectively; (2) in both descriptions, the cultic formula is expressed
in almost the same words—"This/Here is your god, O Israel, who brought you up
out of the land of Egypt"; (3) in both stories, altars were built and sacrifices offered
to the golden calf (Exod 32:6; 1 Kgs 12:32); (4) Aaron and Jeroboam are condemned
in the current texts; (5) the names of Aaron's sons, Nadab and Abihu, are almost
identical to the names of Jeroboam's sons, Nadab and Abijah. For a more detailed
examination of the characteristics common to the two narratives, see Aberbach and
Smolar, "Aaron, Jeroboam," 129–34, 140.

88. Simpson, *Early Traditions*, 387.

89. According to the majority of scholars, vv. 27b–28a are a priestly addition.
Yet Haran argues that they are Deuteronomistic, or a combination of Deuteronomistic and priestly sources, on the basis of the fact that in P the term "ark of the
covenant of God" (אֲרוֹן בְּרִית הָאֱלֹהִים) does not appear at all (it instead uses "ark of
testimony," אֲרוֹן עֵדוּת), while the expression "stood before it" (עוֹמֵד לְפָנָיו) is quite
rare in the style of P (see Haran, *Temple and Temple-Service*, 199 n. 16).

by a later editor, one cannot conclude that they do not include historical facts, since even a later editor could have added elements that the original author omitted. It is worthwhile checking the historicity of the text in two ways, asking: (1) Was there a temple at Bethel that housed the Ark of the Covenant? And (2) were there Aaronite priests at Bethel?

The evidence that there was a temple at Bethel and that cultic activities were carried out there is found in the expression "before YHWH" (20:23, 26). This expression is considered an indication of the existence of a temple there, since it stems from the basic view regarding the temple, which was the place where the Divine Presence resided. Actually, this expression was technical terminology of the temple.[90] The expression sometimes refers to "before the ark,"[91] sometimes to "the holy place before the curtain (פָּרֹכֶת)," sometimes to "the courtyard in front of the Tent of Meeting," and sometimes to "the courtyard of the Temple." The phrase was used in connection with the Ark even when it is outside of the Temple (such as 2 Sam 6:5, 14, 16–17, 21).[92] Subsequently, the expression "before YHWH" in Judg 20:23, 26 is an alternative term for "before the Ark of the Covenant." It also shows us that the phrase "went up and came to Bethel" means "went up to the Bethel temple where the Ark of the Covenant was housed."[93] Moreover, the hypothesis that the Ark of the Covenant was placed in the Bethel temple is further reinforced by the fact that the Bethel temple was the central one of the tribal confederacy. As Kraus[94] claims, the narrative in Judg 20:17–28 supplies evidence for the fact that, contemporaneously, Bethel was the central holy place of the tribal confederacy, in light of the report in Judg 20:18, and particularly 20:26,[95] suggesting that the Bethel temple held the utmost cultic importance for the entire tribal confederacy.[96]

90. Ibid., 26 and n. 24.

91. See Exod 16:33–34; Num 17:19, 22.

92. For the meaning of the technical term, see N. Rabban, "Before the Lord," *Tarbiz* 23 (1952): 1–8 (Hebrew).

93. Bethel had been a sacred place since the people's entrance into Canaan. This is clear not only from the tradition that the site was sanctified through God's revelation to Jacob (Gen 28), but also from the attitude toward Bethel in relation to other holy places, as written in 1 Sam 7:16.

94. H.-J. Kraus, *Worship in Israel* (trans. G. Buswell; Oxford: Blackwell, 1966), 147ff.; see also Albright, *Archaeology*, 103ff.

95. Judg 20:26 reads: "Then all the sons of Israel and all the people went up and came to Bethel and wept; thus they sat there before YHWH and fasted that day until evening. And they offered burnt-offerings and peace-offerings before YHWH."

96. Kraus, *Worship*, 147ff.

It is difficult to prove the authenticity of the report in Judg 20:28a, according to which Phinehas, Aaron's grandson, ministered at the temple of Bethel, since the reference to "Phinehas, the son of Eleazar, the son of Aaron" in v. 28a is attributed to a Priestly addition of the fifth century B.C.E.,[97] while in J and E there is no reference to the descent of the priesthood from the sons of Aaron.[98] However, it can be inferred that v. 28a is reliable in an indirect way. Its authenticity derives from answers to the following questions: (1) Why is there no reference to the priesthood in J and E? And (2) why did the Deuteronomist, the original author of Judg 20–21, fail to mention the Ark of the Covenant and the Bethel temple? In order to answer the first question, it is essential to understand the difference between the temple as the house of God and the altar. A house of God was a building, an edifice with a roof, while an altar, upon which sacrifices were offered, was found only in the open. There was also a functional difference between the two. Since the temple was perceived as the place in which the Divine Presence resides, it was equipped with fixtures and accessories (including the Ark, the cherubs, etc.) and cultic objects. In contrast, nothing was placed on the altar but sacrifices. Every temple would be accompanied by an altar placed in the adjoining court, but not every altar would necessarily need a temple. Only officials or functionaries of the priestly families ministered in the temple, or at the altar attached to it, while every Israelite could serve at the altars separate from the temple.[99] The narratives in J and E deal, therefore, with the altars that were located at a distance from the temple. Thus, these sources (J and E) bear a non-priestly character.[100] One must assume that had the Yahwist and the Elohist belonged to the priestly group, they would have referred to the temple and the priests. However, it appears that the reason that their work is disinterested in priestly rules

97. Even if the vv. 27b–28a are seen as a combination of Deuteronomistic and Priestly additions, the reference to "Phinehas, the son of Eleazar, the son of Aaron" appears to be a Priestly addition.

98. Since Wellhausen, there has been general agreement that the Aaronite priesthood is not mentioned in J and E. In the opinion of scholars who have followed Wellhausen, in these sources all of Israel is considered worthy of the priesthood. The Book of the Covenant (which is attributed to E) clearly shows how all of Israel is entitled to offer sacrifices at the altar, and there is no reference in it to any priesthood whatsoever. There is no reference to priests in either source. If Aaron is mentioned (e.g. Exod 15:20; 24:9; Num 12:1–6), his name appears not because of his role as priest, but rather as a prophet or one of the elders of Israel (see Haran, *Temple and Temple-Service*, 63–64).

99. See ibid., 15–16.

100. Ibid., 65.

and regulations in the temple is found in the fact that such rules and regulations were not sufficiently clear to those who were not priests.[101] Another hypothesis is that, historically speaking, there was no temple in Israel until after the settlement in Canaan, while before and during settlement in Canaan there were only solitary altars.[102] As a result, in J and E there is no reference to the temple or the Aaronite priesthood.

Yet the fact that the Aaronite priesthood is not referred to in these sources is insufficient cause for ruling out its existence at the very least during the Judges period. Although E does not describe Aaron as a priest, because of the two reasons noted above, in Exod 4:13–16, 27–31, and Deut 33:8–11, which are ascribed as aforementioned to E,[103] one can find clues to the fact that even E indirectly admits the existence of the Aaronite priesthood. Exodus 4:13–16, 27–31 describe how Aaron was appointed Moses' spokesperson. Here one should pay attention to the term "the Levite" used in reference to Aaron ("Aaron the Levite"). Certainly, "the Levite" does not signify "priest" in E. The meaning of the name becomes clear in light of the literary tradition regarding Levi and the Levites: the term "Levites" is associated with membership in a group of people appointed by the leader of the group, "Levi," with a special status and function in the tribal confederacy.[104] However, when we unite "the Levite," the epithet of Aaron, with Deut 33:8–11, which is attributed to E and describes the origin of "the Levite priesthood," we can find the Elohist's allusion to the Aaronite priesthood. In other words, the Levites are priests and Aaron also is a priest because he is a Levite. The statement in Deut 10:6, that after Aaron's death Eleazar ministered as priest in his place, may be decisive evidence of the way of thinking of the non-priestly sources regarding the figure of Aaron, and this is fundamentally no different from the way in which P conceives of him.[105] Moreover, according to the Deuteronomist, Eleazar, son of Aaron, as a priest, collaborated with Joshua when he divided the Land of Canaan (Josh 14:1; 19:51). This Deuteronomistic report precedes at the very least that of P, as Num 34:17 parallels Josh 14:1 and 19:51. Eleazar was buried "at the hill of Phinehas his son, which was given him in the hill country of

---

101. Ibid.
102. Ibid.
103. See the expression יִחַר אַף ("the anger of the LORD was kindled," Exod 4:14), הַר הָאֱלֹהִים ("the mountain of God," 4:27) as examples of the Elohistic style in Exod 4:13–16 and 27–31. Regarding the attribution of Deut 33:8–11 to E, see §1.1 in Chapter 3.
104. Ibid.
105. See ibid., 69–70.

Ephraim" (Josh 24:33). Phinehas, son of Eleazar, was a priest when the tribes on the east side of the Jordan planned the establishment of a separate altar (Josh 22:13, 30, 32). Thus, the family tree of the Aaronite priesthood is reconstructed based on the non-priestly sources: Aaron–Eleazar–Phinehas. If this is the case, it turns out that the lack of reference to the Aaronite priesthood and the temple in E does not indicate a denial of their existence.

The fact that the Tribe of Benjamin twice defeated all of the other tribes (Judg 20:17–25) shows how powerful this tribe was during the Judges period. This fact implies that the central temple[106] of the tribal confederacy was located in the territory of Benjamin. If this is so, where among the towns of the Benjamin region was the temple located? One can assume that it was Bethel, with its ancient history of divine revelations to the Patriarchs (Gen 28). It is probable that the Ark of the Covenant was kept at the Bethel temple, as we saw above, based on the expression "before YHWH" and the centrality of the temple. If this is the case, which priesthood ministered there? Based on the above reconstruction of the genealogical tree of the Aaronite priesthood, the priest was Phinehas, son of Eleazar, Aaron's grandson, at least after the people's entry into the Land of Canaan. Can another group be identified as a candidate for the Bethel priesthood? It seems not, even if Phinehas himself was not the priest at the time of the war of the Tribe of Benjamin, as argued by the priestly editor of Judg 20:28b. It appears that the Deuteronomist intentionally omitted the reference to Bethel and the Aaronite priesthood due to his theology. In accordance with this theology, which denied the existence of any temple other than the Jerusalem Temple, the Deuteronomist did not wish to refer to Bethel and the Ark of the Covenant, so much the more the priesthood that ministered there. Moreover, considering the fact that the Bethel temple was the strongest rival to the Jerusalem Temple throughout the period of the division of the kingdom and even after the exile of the southern kingdom of Judah,[107] the

106. Here the term "central temple" is not used in the Deuteronomistic sense, but rather in reference to the most important temple among those existing during the period of the tribal confederacy.

107. According to archaeological surveys conducted recently, Jerusalem and its environs lost most of its population in the sixth century B.C.E. Following the destruction of Jerusalem in 587 B.C.E., it appears that the population center moved from Judah to Benjamin (see O. Lipschits, "The History of the Benjamin Region under Babylonian Rule," *Tel Aviv* 26 [1999]: 179–85). After the fall of Jerusalem, there was naturally a need for an alternative cultic center. Bethel, which was almost certainly affected by the Babylonian conquest of Judah, could have assumed most of the functions and status of Jerusalem (ibid., 159–65).

Deuteronomist undoubtedly would have avoided reference to the Bethel temple.

Based on the above, the credibility of the report in Judg 20:27b–28a, that the Ark of the Covenant stood at Bethel and that the Aaronite priesthood ministered there, is verified. I will now consider how the calf cult at Bethel came about. Regarding this matter, we should first of all examine the transfer of the Ark of the Covenant to Shiloh. The Ark was at Bethel, under the charge of Phinehas. Yet, in 1 Sam 3:3 we find detailed information on its presence in another place: Shiloh. Why and when was the Ark moved from Bethel to Shiloh? One possible reply is that as a result of the downfall of the Tribe of Benjamin in the war against the other tribes of Israel, as reported in Judg 20, the tribe was separated politically from the rest of the tribes of Joseph; as a consequence they reasoned that it was not appropriate to leave the Ark at Bethel, which stood on the territorial border of the Tribe of Benjamin. Hence, it was moved to Shiloh.[108] It is possible that in the eyes of the priests at Bethel, the Ark served as a cultic object in the worship of YHWH, in the sense of a throne or footstool of YHWH.[109] It can be assumed that the safeguarding of the Ark by the priests at Bethel gave them special privileges and authorities that were greater than those of priests in other places. When the Ark was taken from them, these privileges and authorities were nullified, and one can assume that this caused them great frustration; when the Ark was taken from them, the priests were forced to seek out an alternative item, upon which the invisible YHWH could be represented as king. They found this in the calf image, which carried YHWH on its back. This tradition was not foreign to them, or was perhaps well known in those days.

Although there are no direct references to the calf cult prior to the time of Jeroboam ben Nebat, we can find a significant hint of such a tradition in the poetic language of Num 24:8 (as well as 23:22).[110] Actually, the poetic language in the Torah provides information on ancient cults of cattle images. For example, in the blessing of Balaam in Num 23:22 (// 24:8) we read: אֵל מוֹצִיאָם מִמִּצְרָיִם כְּתוֹעֲפֹת רְאֵם לוֹ, a verse which is

---

108.   See Eissfeldt, "Lade und Stierbild," 198ff.

109.   There are two layers to the story of the Ark. According to P, the Ark is a chest containing the tablets of the testimony (Exod 25:21; 40:3, 20). The Deuteronomic and Deuteronomistic tradition also sees the Ark as a receptacle for the tablets of stone (Deut 10:1ff.; 1 Kgs 8:9). On the other hand, ancient traditions from Shiloh and Jerusalem describe the Ark as a divine throne, upon which is enthroned the invisible YHWH (1 Sam 4:4; 2 Sam 6:2; 2 Kgs 19:15; Jer 3:16–17).

110.   The poetic language is usually considered an ancient element.

interpreted as follows: "God who brought them forth out of Egypt is like
the horns of the wild-ox." Coats suggests that the רְאֵם was an animal that
served as a symbol of Moses' leadership in the exodus from Egypt, and
that the symbolism of this ox retained its positive and original connotation in the prophecies of Balaam.[111] According to Coats, the term עֵגֶל
("calf"), which is used to denote the man-made animal figure in Exod 32,
is a contemptuous substitute for רְאֵם ("wild ox").[112] While the term "calf"
may be interpreted as derogatory,[113] one cannot separate the association
of רְאֵם with Moses and the clear association of רְאֵם with YHWH. This
association is just as apparent in the prophecies of Balaam as it is in Ps
22. As Coats shows, the phrase וּמִקַּרְנֵי רֵמִים עֲנִיתָנִי in Ps 22:22b is
interpreted as: "You (YHWH) answered me from the horns of the wild
ox."[114] Thus, in these references, a traditional link is evident between
YHWH and the wild ox, and particularly its horns. The image that comes
into focus, then, is that of YHWH being enthroned upon the horns of a
wild ox, which is similar to the alternative iconographic tradition of
YHWH being enthroned on the backs (or between the wings) of the
cherubs.

   In turn, we can assume that the exodus tradition, which depicted
YHWH's redemption through the metaphor of the strength of a bull, was
known to the Bethel priesthood. Although the tradition in Num 23:22
(// 24:8a)[115] does not describe what happened at Mount Sinai, it can be
assumed that the calf was known as a symbol, at least prior to the
establishment of the kingdom of Israel, as was the Ark, which served as a
stand or pedestal for YHWH, who brought Israel out of Egypt. The
possibility should be considered that the priesthood at Bethel used this

   111.   Coats, *Moses Tradition*, 129.
   112.   Ibid., 129–30. However, see J. W. Davenport, "A Study of the Golden Calf
Tradition in Exodus 32" (Ph.D. diss., Princeton Theological Seminary, 1973), 68–
70. Even if one accepts Coats' claim that the term "calf" was used by the Elohist as a
derogatory substitute for "wild ox," the cultic formula regarding the calf image
(Exod 32:4b) was associated with YHWH who "brought Israel up out of Egypt," as
previously mentioned.
   113.   According to M. Dahood ("Hebrew–Ugaritic Lexicography X," *Bib* 53
[1972]: 402–3), in Ugaritic, *ʿgl* ("calf") is similar to *ṯr* ("bull") in *KTU* 1.4 VI 41–42;
also *KTU* 1.22.12–13. See L. R. Fisher, *Ras Shamra Parallels: The Texts from
Ugarit and the Hebrew Bible*, vol. 2 (Rome: Pontifical Biblical Institute, 1972), 382.
In Hebrew, the same pair of words (עגל/שׁור, "bull/calf") is used in Ps 106:19–20,
where the text deals with the apostasy represented by the idol made at Horeb.
   114.   Coats, *Moses Tradition*, 131.
   115.   As we can see here, instead of a calf, appears the name רְאֵם, whose Akkadian root is *rimu*, which is a common epithet for god in Mesopotamia.

tradition as a basis for uniting the cult of YHWH, who took Israel out of Egypt, with the calf image. However, it is difficult to accept the opinion that the calf at Bethel represented YHWH,[116] since the priests only wanted to find a substitute to compensate for the loss of the Ark that had been taken away from them. Since the Ark of the Covenant was a mobile seat of honor or footstool for the invisible YHWH, it is reasonable to assume that a similar use was made of the calf image. The Bethel priesthood replaced the Ark with the calf image, and attempted to reinforce its authority in the worship of YHWH by linking this image with Aaron, the progenitor of the same priesthood. That is how Aaron became the revered founder of the priesthood of Ephraim, and the traditional authorizer of the calf cult.[117]

It is possible that the Bethel priesthood initiated the use of the cultic formula "This is your God, O Israel, who brought you up out of the land of Egypt" (32:4b). This formula is similar in character to that which Moses cries out when the Ark starts to move: "Rise up, O YHWH, and let your enemies be scattered; and let them that hate you flee before you" (Num 10:35). It is similar too to the words Moses uses when the Ark comes to rest: "Return, O YHWH, to the ten thousands of the families of Israel" (10:36). When Moses directs his speech to the Ark, he is actually addressing the invisible YHWH, who stands upon the Ark as if it were a footstool. Likewise, the word "Elohim" (אֱלֹהִים) in the cultic formula initiated by the Bethel priesthood is not directed to the calf image itself, but rather to the invisible YHWH standing upon its back. Thus, in the same way that the Ark did not represent YHWH, neither did the calf image represent YHWH.

Apparently, the Bethel priesthood determined this formula in order to bolster the calf, as part of the priesthood's desire to reassert the calf's authority. In other words, they tried to anchor the present cult of the golden calf in the earlier sources pertaining to the giving of the Torah at Mount Sinai and the exodus from Egypt. Jeroboam ben Nebat, who inherited the Bethel cult, and transformed it into the official national form of worship, used this cultic formula in the tenth century B.C.E., as seen in 1 Kgs 12:28. However, when the realization was made that the common people had forgotten the original meaning of the calf image as a footstool of YHWH, and had begun to perceive it as representing YHWH himself, the Elohist in the eighth century B.C.E. began to criticize it. As previously mentioned, he could not effectively criticize the calf image without dealing with the positive connotation of the cultic formula.

116.   For a detailed discussion, see §3 in Chapter 1.
117.   T. J. Meek, *Hebrew Origins* (New York: Harper, 1960), 136.

While writing his critique against the calf image, the Elohist introduced a negative slant into the cultic formula by adding the phrase "Come, make us a god (אֱלֹהִים) who shall go before us" (Exod 32:1b) before the cultic formula "This is your God (אֱלֹהִים), O Israel, who brought you up out of the land of Egypt" (32:4b). As a result, the "Elohim" (אֱלֹהִים) in the cultic formula became the calf image itself, namely, the image of other god.[118]

In sum, the origin of the cultic formula in Exod 32:4b and 1 Kgs 12:28 is in the calf cult at Bethel. It was not invented by the Elohist in order to denounce the calf cult, and even Jeroboam ben Nebat was not the first to formulate it. Therefore, the same cultic formula did not originate in an interdependence between the two texts, or a preference for one over the other, but rather in the same cultic background.

2. *The Analysis of Deuteronomy 9:1–10:11*

2.1. *The Compositional Analysis*

Deuteronomy 9:1–10:11 is a separate unit, which comes after 8:1–20[119] and before 10:12–12:32.[120] The central claim expressed by the present text is that the people inherited the Promised Land not by virtue of their righteousness, since, from a historical perspective, they immediately defied God. Among the sins of the Israelite people in the wilderness that are surveyed in this context, the sin of the golden calf is the gravest; notwithstanding that fact, God allows the people of Israel to inherit the Land. In order to express this argument, the current passage is largely composed of two topics: the first is the exhortation against the people's entry to the Promised Land, and the second is the admonition for the sin of the golden calf. The core verses comprising the first topic are 9:1–6. If vv. 7–8 are read as a continuation of v. 6, which deals with the misdemeanors of the people, then vv. 7–8 also belong to the first part.[121] However, according to Weinfeld, vv. 9–21 describe the sin of the golden calf, and are framed with a framework beginning with vv. 7–8 and

---

118.   See Loewenstamm, *Evolution*, 52.

119.   B. Peckham, "The Composition of Deut 9:1–10:11," in *Word and Spirit* (ed. J. Plernik; Willowdale, Ont.: Ontario, 1975), 3. On such delimitation, see G. Seitz, *Redaktioinsgeschichtliche Studien zum Deuteronomium* (Stuttgart: Kohlhammer, 1971), 79–81; A. D. H. Mayes, *Deuteronomy* (NCBC; London: Marshall, Morgan & Scott, 1991), 189.

120.   Peckham, "Composition." See also Mayes, *Deuteronomy*, 207.

121.   See N. Lohfink, *Das Hauptgebot: Eine Untersuchung literarischen Einleitungsfragen zu Deut 5–11* (Rome: Pontifical Biblical Institute, 1963), 290.

ending with vv. 22–24.[122] Consequently, 9:9–21 clearly refer to the sin of the golden calf. Yet, there is some doubt regarding the internal continuity of 9:9–21, since vv. 22–24 are not directly related to the sin of the golden calf. Should vv. 22–24 be seen as an addition? It seems that the discord between vv. 22–24 and the story of the sin of the golden calf is not the result of their insertion here, but rather the appraisal of the sin of the golden calf in connection with acts of rebellion among the people in the wilderness (namely, on the way to the Promised Land). Verses 10:6–9 also deal with the path of the Israelite people's journey, the death of Aaron, and the tribe of Levi, subjects that are not directly related to the golden calf. If we assume that textual editing in 9:1–10:11 is responsible for its internal inconsistency, based on the clear incongruity between 9:22–24 and 10:6–9, we should first review some opinions related to such editing.

According to Seitz, internal contradictions, disharmony between sentences, and inconsistency are all evident in Deut 9:9–10:11.[123] To begin with, (1) there are repetitions: the giving of the tablets of the Covenant, which appears twice in 9:10–11 ("And YHWH delivered to me the two tablets of stone..."/"YHWH gave me the two tablets of stone..."); YHWH's accusation of the Israelites is noted in vv. 12 and 13; Moses' intercession is reiterated again and again throughout ch. 9 (in v. 18, "And I fell down before YHWH, as at the first, forty days and forty nights..."; v. 20, "and I prayed for Aaron also the same time..."; v. 25, "So I fell down before YHWH the forty days and forty nights that I fell down..."), and is heard again in this context in 9:19b and 10:10; the phrase "forty days and forty nights" is used five times (9:9, 11, 18, 25; 10:10). In addition, (2) the continuity of the text is disrupted also by references to Aaron (9:20; 10:6–7) and incidents of uprising and rebellion (9:22–24). Furthermore, (3) inconsistency is also pronounced in 10:5, 11: according to v. 5, Moses came down from the mountain, but according to v. 11, he is still on the mountain; the intercession in 9:26–29 is answered only in 10:10, and so it appears that vv. 10:1–9 are out of place; it seems that 9:26–29 and 10:10b should come immediately after 9:13–14 (paralleling Exod 32:9–14).

Seitz attributes these problems to the editing of two layers (the Deuteronomic layer and the Deuteronomistic layer), the fusion of the two layers by the editor, and a series of later additions. According to Seitz, originally there was a Deuteronomic layer composed of 9:1–7a ("Hear, O Israel! You are to pass over the Jordan this day... Remember, do not

---

122. Weinfeld, *Deuteronomy 1–11*, 407.
123. Seitz, *Deuteronomium*, 51–69.

forget, how you provoked YHWH your God to anger in the wilderness"),
vv. 13–14 ("YHWH spoke to me, saying: 'I have seen this people, and,
behold, it is a stiffnecked people; let me alone, that I may destroy them,
and blot out their name from under heaven...'"), vv. 26–29 ("And I
prayed to YHWH..."), 10:10b ("and YHWH listened to me at that time
also and decided not to destroy you"), in which the speaker addresses his
listeners in the singular.[124] Afterwards, the Deuteronomistic layer was
added, which includes 9:9 ("When I went up the mountain to receive the
tablets of stone...then I stayed on the mountain forty days and forty
nights..."), v. 11 ("At the end of forty days and forty nights, YHWH gave
me the two tablets of stone, the tablets of the covenant"), v. 12 ("And
YHWH said to me: 'Arise, go down quickly from here, for your people
that you have brought out of Egypt have become corrupt...they have
made for themselves a molten image'"), vv. 15–17 ("So I turned and
came down from the mountain... And I looked and saw that you had
sinned against YHWH your God; you had made for yourselves a molten
calf... And I took hold of the two tablets, and threw them out of my two
hands..."), v. 21 ("And I took your sin, the calf which you had made, and
burnt it with fire...and I threw the dust into the brook..."), and 10:1–5, in
which the Ark is discussed, and 10:11 ("And YHWH said to me: 'Arise,
go before the people, so that they may enter in and possess the land...'").
Here the speaker addresses his listeners in the plural.[125] The above two
layers were then stitched together, and the "sutures" are evident in verses
such as 9:8 ("At Horeb you provoked YHWH that he was angered with
you to destroy you"), v. 25 ("I lay prostrate before YHWH the forty days
and forty nights"), and 10:10b ("Now I had stayed on the mountain, as at
the first time, forty days and forty nights").[126] Finally, a later addition was
inserted into the final text: Deut 9:7b ("From the day you came out of the
land of Egypt until you arrived in this place, you have been rebellious
against YHWH"), vv. 22–24 ("At Taberah, and at Massah, and at Kibroth-
hattaavah, you provoked YHWH to anger. And when YHWH sent you
from Kadesh-barnea, saying, 'Go up and possess the land which I have
given you'...you neither believed him nor listened to his voice... You
have been rebellious against the LORD from the day that I knew you"),[127]
v. 20 ("And YHWH was very angry with Aaron to destroy him, but at that
time I prayed for Aaron too"), and 10:6–9 ("And the children of Israel

124.   Ibid., 54, 56.
125.   Ibid., 55, 56.
126.   Ibid., 56.
127.   According to Seitz, both (vv. 7b and 22–24) are relevant to each other in
light of the parallel between these verses in words and content.

journeyed from the wells of Jaakites [Beeroth Bene-jaakan] to Moserah. There Aaron died... From there they journeyed to Gudgod, and from Gudgod to Jotbathah, a land of brooks of water... At that time YHWH set apart the tribe of Levi... For this reason, Levi has no portion nor inheritance with his brethren...").[128] Seitz offers, therefore, a solution to the problem of inconsistency in the passage 9:9–10:11, by claiming that it is composed of several layers. Mayes takes a position similar to that of Seitz. He too argues that the passage includes a Deuteronomic layer and a Deuteronomistic layer. He attributes 9:9–12, 15–19, 21, 25; 10:1–5 to the Deuteronomic layer.[129] However, his understanding of the relation between the Deuteronomic and Deuteronomistic layers differs from that of Seitz; he does not see them as two parallel layers that were sewn together by an editor, but rather claims that the Deuteronomist worked on the basis of the Deuteronomic description and included it in an artistic scheme.[130]

However, there is difficulty in linking 9:1–7a to 9:13–14 ("...I have seen this people, and, behold, it is a stiffnecked people. Let me alone, that I may destroy them and blot out their name from under the heaven...") if 9:1–7a, 13–14, 26–29, 10:10b are attributed to the Deuteronomic layer, as Seitz claims, since in 9:1–7a there is no reference whatsoever to an act of rebellion for which the people deserve to be destroyed, as proclaimed in v. 14. Therefore, when ascribing textual inconsistency and mismatch to the result of the editing of the different layers, it is necessary to identify an earlier layer between the two assumed layers in the passage between 9:7b–12 and 9:1–7a. This is because the former, disconnected from part of the latter or all of it, does not form a meaningful narrative.[131]

In contrast to the positions of Seitz and Mayes, Lohfink[132] contends that the majority of passage 9:9–10:11,[133] which is almost considered a

128. Ibid., 57.
129. Mayes, *Deuteronomy*, 42, 195.
130. Ibid., 196.
131. Peckham (*Hebrew Origins*, 3–59) divides 9:1–6 into two parts (vv. 1–3 and vv. 4–6). In his view, the first is linked to a Deuteronomistic layer 1 (Dtr1) composed of 9:7–12, 14–17, 21–26, 28–29; 10:1–5, 8–11, and the second to a Deuteronomistic layer 2 (Dtr2), composed of 9:13, 18–20, 27. Yet his analysis of the composition of 9:1–10:11 does not provide a satisfactory solution to the problem of discontinuity and inconsistency in this text, since the Dtr1 layer is included in the verses that cause such discontinuity and inconsistency, such as 9:7–8, 22–24; 10:8–9.
132. Lohfink, *Das Hauptgebot*, 200–218, 289–92.
133. According to Lohfink (ibid., 214–15), the golden calf narrative in Deut 9–10 actually begins in 9:9, since the golden calf narrative was adapted by the author in the framework of the phrase "forty days and forty nights." This phrase appears for the first time in v. 9.

Deuteronomistic text, as Seitz and Mayes phrase it, belongs to a single layer. In other words, according to Lohfink, this is actually a single basic text formulated by a single author that includes Deut 9:9–19, which describe the sin of the making of the golden calf by the people and YHWH's forgiveness of them, v. 21, which provides an account of the destruction of the calf, vv. 25–29, which describe Moses' intercession, 10:1–5, which report the making of the Ark, vv. 10–11, which tell of YHWH's reply to Moses' intercession in 9:25–29.[134] Deuteronomy 9:9–10:11, the basic text, according to Lohfink, is equal in terms of content to the third of Seitz's phases, in which the Deuteronomic and Deuteronomistic layers were edited together and "stitched" by the editor. It is also equal to Mayes' Deuteronomistic text, which is the product of an adaptation of an earlier Deuteronomic text. If this is the case, the basic text, according to Lohfink, is equal to the texts suggested by Seitz and Mayes, before 9:20, 22–24, and 10:6–9 were added to them. However, contrary to Seitz and Mayes, Lohfink does not distinguish between different stages in the basic text, but rather sees it as a whole. It seems that he does not attribute the discontinuity and inconsistency in Deut 9:9–10:11 to the editing of different layers but rather to the literary technique of the author, who adapted the text of Exod 32 in accordance with his theological intentions. Consequently, by comparing our text with the parallel text in Exod 32, Lohfink claims that the author of the golden calf in Deuteronomy did not describe his narrative in accordance with the literary flow of the narrative. Therefore, the disorder of the narrative does not necessarily indicate disunity,[135] and the repetitions in the text are structural markers that help to delineate literary units within a single text. The repetition of the expression "forty days and forty nights" (9:9, 11, 18, 25; 10:10), together with the references to "fire" (9:10, 15, 21; 10:4), basically indicate the beginning and end of these stylistic units respectively. This basic text includes five units: (1) 9:9–10, the making of the covenant; (2) 9:11–17, the violation of the covenant; (3) 9:18–19, 21, steps toward atonement; (4) 9:25–10:5, renewal of the covenant; and (5) 10:10–11, the results of the renewal of the covenant.[136] To the basic text (9:9–19, 21, 25–29; 10:1–5, 10–11) were added 9:1–8, 22–24.[137]

---

134. Ibid., 210–12, 215.

135. For example, it appears that the smashing of the calf in 9:21, which takes place at the foot of the mountain, disrupts Moses' second sojourn on the mountain, which begins in 9:18–19 and continues in 9:25–29. Also 10:3–5, which describes his third sojourn on the mountain, comes before Deut 10:10–11, which refers to Moses' second sojourn. See ibid., 213.

136. Ibid., 212–16.

137. Ibid., 290.

Clearly, 9:7 and 9:22–24 are attributed to the same layer in terms of the parallels in phraseology between them.[138] Deuteronomy 9:22–24 brings a detailed list of provocations against YHWH, thus elaborating on the abstract statement in 9:7. Deuteronomy 9:7 goes, therefore, with 9:6, and 9:23 with 9:1–2, since both are related to the spying affair.[139] Thus, claims Lohfink, 9:1–7, 22–24 belong to the same phase; 9:8, which is a heading to 9:9–19, is the product of the author of vv. 1–7, since it parallels 9:22 in its use of the expression "and at..." (...בְּ) before the name of the place.[140] Moreover, Deut 9:1–8, 22–24 are obviously attributed to a different stage than that of the basic text (Deut 9:9–19, 21, 25–29, 10:1–5, 10–11), since Deut 9:1–8, 22–24 are in tension with the internal structure of the basic text regarding the violation of the covenant and its renewal at Horeb.[141] Finally, Lohfink holds the same position as Seitz and Mayes in claiming that Deut 9:20; 10:6–7, 8–9 are comments added to the text at later stages.[142]

We have now reviewed the opinions of Seitz, Mayes, and Lohfink regarding the lack of continuity and consistency in Deut 9:7 (or, for some, 9:8) and following. In sum, Seitz and Mayes contend that it results from an integration of various layers, while Lohfink attributes it not to a combination of layers, but rather to the author's deliberate, theologically based scheme, as well as editorial additions. The main difference between their views has to do with the position that within the narrative of the golden calf in Deut 9:7 (or 9:8) and following there is a layer related to 9:1–6 (or 9:1–7), which refers to the exhortation against the people's entry to the Land of Israel. However, as we have seen above, when we link Deut 9:13–14, 26–29, and 10:10b[143] to Deut 9:1–7a, we actually cannot find literary continuity between them.[144] Therefore, Seitz and Mayes' argument is unconvincing, and Lohfink's opinion seems

138.   Ibid., 210. The parallels are: "how you provoked YHWH your God to wrath," v. 7a // "you provoked YHWH to wrath," v. 22; "you have been rebellious against YHWH," appearing in vv. 7b, 24; "from the day," 7b // "from the day," v. 24b.

139.   Ibid., 200, 211.

140.   Ibid., 211, 217. In v. 8, "and at Horeb," and in v. 22, "And at Taberah, and at Massah."

141.   Ibid., 217.

142.   Ibid., 290.

143.   These verses, according to Seitz, were united originally with Deut 9:1–7a of the Deuteronomic layer.

144.   Recall that, as previously mentioned, there is difficulty connecting 9:1–7a to 9:13–14 if 9:1–7a contain no reference to an act of rebellion for which the people are deserving of annihilation by God.

preferable. We can conclude, then, that the content of the admonition against the people entering the Land was not inserted into the narrative of the sin of the golden calf.

If this is so, may we conclude that originally the narrative of the sin of the golden calf was separate from the exhortation against the people's entry into the Land? May we infer that Deut 9:1–10:11 was formed from two different compositions, each written by a different author, that is, one author wrote the admonition against the entry into the Land, and the other wrote the narrative of the golden calf, and at some point in time the two were stitched together? Of course, one could also surmise that Deut 9:1–10:11 was written by one author dealing with the people's offenses, based on the fact that both the admonition against the people's admittance to the Land and the description of the sin of the golden calf condemn the people's behavior. However, in order to support this claim, one would have to establish the fact that the depiction of the sin of the golden calf is also a Deuteronomic (Dtn) composition, since the description of the people's entrance into the Land is attributed as such.[145] Yet, in my view, the narrative of the sin of the golden calf in Deuteronomy must be ascribed to the Deuteronomist (Dtr).[146] Furthermore, it can reasonably be assumed that the account of the sin of the golden calf was originally not linked to the exhortation against the people's entry into the Land, since there is no connection between the Elohistic version of the golden calf narrative, which is the source for the version of the sin of the golden calf in Deuteronomy, and the description of the people's admittance into the Land.

If this is the case, it appears that the lack of continuity and consistency in Deut 9:9–10:11 is primarily the result of the adaptation of the Elohistic version of the sin of the golden calf in accordance with the theological intentions of the author. The text describing the sin of the golden calf in Deuteronomy is an adaptation of the Elohistic version. Although controversy remains regarding the anteriority of the Elohistic version to that in Deuteronomy,[147] one could determine the anteriority of

145. The Land is actually central to the Deuteronomic theologies. See Mayes, *Deuteronomy*, 78–81.

146. For a detailed discussion of the attribution of the description of the sin of the golden calf to Deut or to Dtr, see the following §2.3 in Chapter 3.

147. While most scholars argue for the dependence of the version in Deuteronomy upon the Elohistic version in Exod 32 (see Greenberg, "Moses' Intercessory Prayer," 21–36; C. T. Begg, "The Destruction of the Calf [Exod 32,20/Deut 9,21]," in *Das Deuteronomium: Entstehung, Gestalt und Botschaft* [ed. N. Lohfink; Leuven: Leuven University Press, 1985], 208–51), others claim the opposite (e.g. Vermeylen,

the E version to that in Deuteronomy based on the following arguments. First, some contend that the compatibility between the two texts results from the editing of the Deuteronomist, who first composed all of Deut 9–10, and afterwards Exod 32–33 as well.[148] Yet, as I have shown above, a comparison of the text of Exod 32:7–14 with that of Deut 9:12–19, 25–29 points to the fact that the latter relies precisely upon the former. However, the most decisive evidence of the fact that the version in Deuteronomy is dependent upon the Elohistic one is found in Deut 9:20. There is no reference to Aaron in the book of Deuteronomy prior to this verse, meaning that such a reference is odd here, unless we assume that the author of this verse was familiar with the tradition linking Aaron with the sin of the golden calf. It is entirely incomprehensible why suddenly, in the middle of the narrative, there is a reference to Aaron, who up to this point has not appeared, unless we assume that his involvement in the narrative preceded its incorporation into Deuteronomy. Aaron's role in the sin of the golden calf is noted in Exod 32:1–6, 21–24, in which he is portrayed as playing a major role in the act of betrayal (vv. 1–6), while afterwards, he is required by Moses to explain the incident (vv. 21–24). This proves that there is no basis for the presence of this verse in Deuteronomy unless we assume prior knowledge of Aaron's role in Exod 32. From this perspective, it can be seen that the shift between the singular and the plural in Moses' speech does not reflect different layers, but rather different nuances, and the reiteration of words or expressions is not the result of the editing of the different layers, but rather comprises a literary technique fitting the theological position of the author.[149]

"L'affaire," 1–23; J. Van Seters, "Law and the Wilderness Rebellion Tradition: Exod 32," *SBLSP* 27 [1990]: 583–91, and "The Golden Calf," 290–318).

148. See Vermeylen, "L'affaire," 1–23. It also emerges from a study by Shalom-Guy, who attributes Exod 32 to the work of the Deuteronomic school, that the version of the sin of the golden calf in Deut 9 predates that in Exod 32, although Shalom-Guy does not make such a claim explicitly (see H. Shalom-Guy, "Between the Description of Jeroboam's Reforms and the Golden Calf Episode," *Shnaton Leheqer Hamiqr'a Vehamizrach Haqadum* 16 [2006]: 15–27 [Hebrew]).

149. On the contrary, in some cases the shifts from singular to plural and vice versa can be indicative of different layers (e.g. compare Deut 12:1–12 with 12:13–25), and, in general, such shifts from singular to plural are considered stylistic alternations (see Weinfeld, *Deuteronomy 1–11*, 15–16). J. A. Fitzmyer shows that the shift from plural to singular and vice versa was also found in treaty documents of the ancient Near East (*The Aramaic Inscriptions of Sefire* [Rome: Pontifical Biblical Institute, 1967], 96–100). Other studies examining the alternation between singular and plural include: C. T. Begg, "The Significance of the *Numeruswechsel* in Deuteronomy: The Pre-history of the Question," *ETL* 55 (1979): 116–24, and "The

Apparently, Lohfink's view with respect to Deut 9:1–10:11 is based on this perspective. Therefore, his opinion, that the discontinuity and inconsistency in the text of 9:1–10:11 result from a literary design in accordance with the author's theological beliefs, is usually quite convincing.

In general, I accept Lohfink's analysis. In his opinion, the layer of the admonition against the entry of the people into the Land (9:1–8,[150] 22–24) was added on to the layer of the description of the sin of the golden calf, which begins with 9:9 and ends with 10:11. In other words, the description of the sin of the golden calf is divided into five units by the structural marker "forty days and forty nights,"[151] and is therefore comprised of 9:9–19, 21, 25–29; 10:1–5, 10–11.

However, there are several weak points in Lohfink's analysis. First of all, he includes 10:11, which is part of the exhortation against the entry of the people into the Promised Land, in the basic text. According to Lohfink's analysis, this exhortation appears in 9:1–8, 22–24, while the story of the golden calf and Moses' task are included in 9:9–19, 21, 25–29; 10:1–5, 10–11. Yet, he seems to have failed to notice the logical contradiction in his argument, since he links 10:11, which describes the entry of the people into the Land, with the text relating the sin of the golden calf, while he attributes the passage related to the admonition against the people's entry into the Land (9:1–8, 22–24) to a text postdating the basic text.[152] When reading 9:1–10:11 in sequence, it appears that the sin of the golden calf, described from 9:9ff., was edited as one among a number of other incidents of revolt by the people in the

Literary Criticism of Deut 4,1–40," *ETL* 56 (1980): 10–55; D. L. Christensen, "The Numeruswechsel in Deuteronomy 12," in *A Song of Power and the Power of Song: Essays on the Book of Deuteronomy* (ed. D. L. Christensen; Winona Lake, Ind.: Eisenbrauns, 1993), 61–68; N. Lohfink, "Zum '*Numeruswechsel*' in Deut 3,21f," *BN* 49 (1989): 39–52; and H. Ausloos, "The Risks of Rash Textual Criticism Illustrated on the Basis of the '*Numeruswechel*' in Exod 23, 20–33," *BN* 97 (1999): 5–12.

150.   According to Lohfink (*Das Hauptgebot*, 211, 217), v. 8 is attributed to the author of vv. 1–7, 22–24. This seems unlikely, since the content of v. 8 does not pertain to the people's entry into the Land. This matter will be discussed more fully below. In the meantime, I will leave the issue of v. 8 as argued by Lohfink.

151.   As previously mentioned, in accordance with the structural marker "forty days and forty nights" (9:9, 11, 18, 25; 10:10), the basic text of the golden calf narrative is divided into five units: (1) 9:9–10, the establishment of the covenant; (2) 9:11–17, the violation of the covenant; (3) 9:18–19, 21, steps toward atonement; (4) 9:25–10:5, renewal of the covenant; and (5) 10:10–11, the results of the renewal of the covenant (see Lohfink, *Das Hauptgebot*, 212–16).

152.   See ibid., 200, 211, 290. According to Seitz (*Redaktioinsgeschichtliche*, 46, 54), however, 9:1–7 antedates 9:9ff. Mayes (*Deuteronomy*, 146) thinks the same.

wilderness, and is thematically interlinked with 9:1–8, 22–24, in which Moses shows that the people's entry into the Land is not due to their righteousness. However, considering the fact that the admonition belongs to a layer other than that of the sin of the golden calf, Deut 10:11, which is part of the admonition, is entirely unrelated to the sin of the golden calf narrative. The verse is nothing but a "blind motif"[153] in this context.

If this is the case, why is 10:11 positioned in its current place? This question can be answered from three directions. The first is to suggest that the exhortation against the people's entry into the Land and the description of the sin of the golden calf belonged to the same layer (or tradition), namely, all of the text of 9:1–10:11 was written by a single hand. Yet, this suggestion is implausible, since it cannot account for the textual discontinuity. The second is to suggest that the verse was originally linked directly to 9:1–7. This idea is also hard to accept since a logical connection between 9:7 and 10:11 is lacking. In other words, if 9:7, which speaks of the people's rebellion in the wilderness, is not followed by the forgiveness for such rebellion, then 9:7 is not directly linked to 10:11, where YHWH grants the people permission to enter the Land. The third direction is that the verse was added at the end (10:10) by the editor,[154] who combined the exhortation against the people's entry into the Land and the sin of the golden calf narrative.[155] This suggestion is convincing, and corrects the major weak spot in Lohfink's analysis. By adding 10:11, the description of the sin of the golden calf was incorporated into the admonition against the people's entry into the Land. This literary structure shows that the admittance to the Land was allowed as a fulfillment of God's promise to the Patriarchs, in spite of the people's insurrection, and particularly in spite of the sin of the golden calf.

Another weak point in Lohfink's stance is his contention that 9:8 belongs to the same layer as that of 9:1–7, 22–24.[156] In his view, 9:1–8, 22–24 belong to the same layer, and were written by one author.

---

153.   Van Seters uses this term in connection with a similar context. Such a context presupposes that the author knew of a tradition (or layer) in which the motif appeared, and that he decided to insert it here. On this term, see J. Van Seters, *Abraham in History and Tradition* (New Haven: Yale University Press, 1975), 163, 183.

154.   When assuming that the present text of 9:1–10:11 is composed of two layers, we must admit the existence of an editor who made a compilation of them. However, at this stage, it is too early to discuss the identity of the editor. I will deal with this matter after an examination of the components of each layer and of its author.

155.   Namely, 9:1–19, 21–29; 10:1–5, 10.

156.   Lohfink, *Das Hauptgebot*, 211, 217.

However, 9:8 serves as a preface to the sin of the golden calf narrative and, therefore, it is unreasonable to assume that it was written by the same author who composed 9:1–7, 22–24, the content of which is the admonition against the people's entry into the Land. Apparently, the editor, who compiled[157] the admonition layer (9:1–7, 22–24) and the sin of the golden calf layer (9:9–19, 21, 25–29; 10:1–5, 10), added 9:8 as a suture between the two layers, in the same manner that he added 10:11. The term "in Horeb" indicates the place where the sin of the golden calf occurred, as described in 9:9ff. The verbs הִקְצִיף ("provoked") and הִשְׁמִיד ("destroyed") in v. 8 are central terms that serve to express YHWH's rage in vv. 9–21.[158] Verse 8 is almost identical to v. 19a: "…you provoked YHWH's wrath so that he was angry enough to destroy you" (9:8)/ "…YHWH was angry against you to destroy you…" (9:19a). It seems that the editor contrived v. 8 on the basis of the expressions in vv. 9ff. and added it between vv. 7 and 9, not just as a suture between the two layers, but also as a prelude to the sin of the golden calf narrative. At this point, we should discuss 9:20. According to Lohfink, Seitz, and Mayes, this verse is an addition made during the final stage of editing as a comment, together with 10:6–7, 8–9. It is plausible that 9:20 is a later addition, based on the fact that up until this point in the text, there is no reference to Aaron and to his involvement in the sin of the golden calf, and the sudden appearance of the phrase "And YHWH was very angry with Aaron to destroy him" is illogical. Yet it appears to me that this verse is not a later addition, that is, it was not added at a stage following the compilation of the two layers, but rather was added together with v. 8 by the editor, for v. 20 is very similar to v. 8.[159] It seems that this view can be strengthened through an understanding of the editor's intent. In Exod 32:1–6, 21–24, Aaron is described as having played a leading role in the sin of the golden calf. However, in Exod 32–34, there is no reference whatsoever to Aaron's punishment or forgiveness, while in Exod 32:35, there is reference to a plague as the people's punishment. When the editor saw the text before him, which lacked any reference to YHWH's forgiveness toward Aaron for the golden calf affair, but included the

---

157.   According to Lohfink, the editor "added" 9:1–8, 22–24 to the "basic text," that is, 9:9–19, 21, 25–29; 10:1–5, 10–11, because he thinks that the latter precedes the former (see ibid., 290). Yet, in the meantime, before determining anteriority between the two layers, I prefer to use the term "compile" instead of "add."

158.   See vv. 14 and 19.

159.   Compare the two verses: "YHWH was very angry…to destroy him" (הִתְאַנַּף יְהוָה מְאֹד לְהַשְׁמִידוֹ, 9:20a) and "and YHWH was angry enough to destroy you" (וַיִּתְאַנַּף יְהוָה בָּכֶם לְהַשְׁמִיד אֶתְכֶם, 9:8b).

phrase "But again YHWH listened to me..." (Deut 9:19), expressing forgiveness toward the people who had been punished (Exod 32:35), he probably reasoned that inserting a verse expressing forgiveness toward Aaron was not only essential, but also coincided with the aim of the editing,[160] since Aaron's responsibility for the making of the golden calf was well known.

When attributing 9:20 to an editorial addition, it appears that 10:6–7 too was added by the same editor. When the layer of the admonition against the people's entry into the Land[161] is attached to the golden calf layer[162] through the addition by the editor of 9:8, 20, and 10:11, a general picture of the fulfillment of the promise of the Israelite people's entry into the Land (9:1; 10:11) emerges. In the framework of this picture, the impression is created that Aaron, as priest, is going with the people toward the Promised Land. Given the sense that Aaron has been exonerated from the sin of the calf, as depicted in 9:20, the narrating of Aaron's death in 10:6–7 while on his way to the Promised Land, and of Eleazar's inheritance of the priesthood is quite striking. Therefore, it can reasonably be assumed that 10:6–7 presuppose the existence of 9:19–20, and its insertion by the same editor who also inserted 9:20.

Accordingly, when we overcome Lohfink's weak points, it becomes possible to arrange the composition of Deut 9:1–10:11 as follows (for convenience, I will call the admonition layer "L–1" and the golden calf layer "L–2"):

L–1: 9:1–7, 22–24
L–2: 9:9–19, 21, 25–29; 10:1–5, 10
Editor's addition: 9:8, 20; 10:6–7, 11
Comment regarding the Levite priesthood: 10:8–9

Then, to whom (or to which school) should L–1 and L–2 be attributed? Who was the editor[163] of Deut 9:1–10:11, and when did he edit it? In

---

160. One can infer what the aim of the editor was from the theme of the text in 9:1–10:11, since almost the entire text was created through the work of the same editor. The theme is that despite the great sin of the people in worshiping the golden calf, in addition to other transgressions in the wilderness, their misconduct is forgiven, and they enter the Promised Land thanks to God's promise to the Patriarchs. I will discuss the editor's aims in detail in the following section.

161. Deut 9:1–7, 22–24.

162. Deut 9:9–19, 21, 25–29; 10:1–5, 10.

163. Henceforth, "the editor" refers to the one who compiled L–1 and L–2. Here, it should be mentioned that the terms "editor" and "author" can be used interchangeably and, accordingly, the editor was not limited to the role of collecting and editing materials, but also added words and phrases, or revised existing texts. On the

order to answer these questions, we should clarify the theological position from which the author of L–2 denounced the calf image. This
position, which served as a criterion for the author of L–2 in his criticism
of the calf image, will also allow us to determine the identity of the
author of L–2. It seems, incidentally, that this position can be elucidated
by way of a comparison of L–2 with Exod 32. Yet, before doing so, we
should briefly examine the relationship between the two texts, since a
comparison of the two presupposes a close relationship between them.

2.2. *The Observation of the Theological Position of L–2 through a Comparison of Exodus 32 and Deuteronomy 9:9ff.*

The description of the sin of the golden calf in Deut 9:9–19, 21, 25–29;
10:1–5, 10 (L–2) presupposes Exod 32, and from a literary point of view,
even relies upon it. This means that the former is an adaptation of the
Elohistic original by the author of L–2. Even scholars who contend that
the golden calf narrative in Exodus is not Elohist, but rather a Deuteronomistic fiction referencing 1 Kgs 12:26–32, admit that Deut 9:9ff. are
dependent upon Exod 32.[164] Van Seters, on the other hand, argues that
the golden calf narrative in Deuteronomy predates that which appears in
Exodus.[165] His explanation is that Exod 32 is a pure fiction, written by a
post-Deuteronomistic Historian, based on the story of Jeroboam's golden
calves in 1 Kgs 12, and even the latter, argues Van Seters, is wholly
fabricated.[166] However, this claim is unconvincing, and can be refuted as
follows. First, Van Seters does not consider the fact that Jeroboam's
golden calves were presented as a reconstruction of the calves at Bethel,
as we have already seen. Second, it can be shown that the current text of
Exod 32 is not pure fiction, created out of the polemical attitude toward
Jeroboam's golden calves, but rather an adaptation of the tradition
related to the golden calf cult at Bethel. As aforesaid, the two golden calf
narratives in Exod 32 and 1 Kgs 12 share a common background. An
additional, and very important, argument regarding the link between
Deut 9:9ff. and Exod 32 is that of Losa, according to which Exod 32 was
influenced by Deuteronomistic editing.[167] The basis for this claim is

interchangeability of the terms "editor" and "author," see J. T. Willis, "Redaction
Criticism and Historical Reconstruction," in *Encounter with the Text: Form and
History in the Hebrew Bible* (ed. M. Buss; Philadelphia: Fortress, 1979), 83–89.
    164.   Hoffmann, *Reform*, 307–9.
    165.   Van Seters, "The Golden Calf," 301.
    166.   Ibid., 299.
    167.   Losa, "Exode xxxii," 32. Researchers who defend the Deuteronomistic
depictions in vv. 7–14 include: Noth, *Pentateuch*, 33 n. 113, and *Exodus*, 244;
Simpson, *Early Traditions*, 204–9; Lehming, "Versuch," 16–50; Hyatt, *Exodus*, 306;

found in the fact that Exod 32:7–14 is very similar in its phrasing to Deut 9:12–19, 25–29. Indeed, it seems that the phrases in Exod 32:7–14 are reiterated quite literally in Deut 9:12–19, 25–29. Yet this fact is not sufficient ground for attributing the former to Deuteronomistic editing. The reasons for attributing Exod 32:7–14 to the Elohist were discussed above, and there is no need to repeat them.

2.2.1. General Survey of the Differences between Exodus 32 and Deuteronomy 9:9ff. It appears that the differences between the two texts, revealed through their comparison, stem from the different points of view of their authors, who were influenced by different historical and religious circumstances. The critical difference between the two authors is the means by which they condemned the calf image. This means is the word "way" (דֶּרֶךְ). As aforementioned, the word "way" in the phrase "they are quickly turned aside out of the way which I commanded them" (Exod 32:8; Deut 9:12) refers to the Ten Commandments. However, it seems that the word "way" is interpreted differently by the two authors in accordance with their historical and religious circumstances. In other words, to which commandment did each author refer when he defined the sin of the calf as a violation of the Ten Commandments?

In order to answer this question, it is worthwhile to compare the differences between the two texts. Following such a comparison, I will focus on the key differences revealed, with the aim of clarifying which commandment each author used in his critique of the calf image.

Table 1. *A Comparison of the Sin of the Golden Calf in Exodus and Deuteronomy*[168]

Exodus (24:12–14, 18; 31:18; 32:1–20)	Deuteronomy (9:7–10:5)
Chapter 24	*Chapter 9* (7) *...from the day that you left the land of Egypt, until you came to this place, you have been rebellious against YHWH.* (8) *At Horeb you provoked YHWH so that YHWH was angry enough to destroy you.*

Childs, "Etiological Tale," 558; Aurelius, *Der Fürbitte Israels*, 41–44. For Weimar ("Das Goldene Kalb," 60–117 [esp. 151–55]), this text (with the exception of vv. 9 and 13) belong to DtrN (a "nomistic" phase in Deuteronomistic Historiography).

    168.   The verses not included in L–2 of Deut 9:7ff. are italicized.

(12) And YHWH said to Moses: "Come up to me on the mountain and be there, and I will give you the tablets of stone, and the law and the commandment, which I have written for their instruction
(13) ...and Moses went up to the mountain of God.

(18) ...and Moses was in the mountain forty days and forty nights.

Chapter 31
(18) And he gave to Moses...the two tablets of the testimony, tablets of stone, written by the finger of God.

Chapter 32
(1) And when the people saw that Moses delayed to come down from the mountain, the people gathered around Aaron, and said to him: "Come, make us a god who will go before us"...

(4) ...and they said: "This is your God, O Israel, who brought you out of the land of Egypt."
(5) ...and said: "Tomorrow shall be a feast to YHWH."
(6) And the next day they rose early and offered burnt-offerings, and brought peace-offerings; and the people sat down to eat and to drink, and rose up to make merry (לְצַחֵק).

(9) When I went up the mountain to receive the tablets of stone, the tablets of the covenant which YHWH made with you,

I stayed on the mountain forty days and forty nights; I ate no bread and drank no water.

(10) And YHWH gave me the two tablets of stone written by the finger of God; and on them was written according to all the words, which YHWH spoke to you on the mountain out of the midst of the fire on the day of the assembly.
(11) And at the end of forty days and forty nights, YHWH gave me the two tablets of stone, the tablets of the covenant.

(7) Then YHWH said to Moses, "Go down, for your people, whom you brought out of the land of Egypt, have become corrupt.

(8) they have quickly turned aside out of the way which I commanded them; they have made them a molten calf, and have worshipped it, and have sacrificed to it, and said, "This is your God, O Israel, who brought you out of the land of Egypt."

(9) And YHWH said to Moses, "I have seen this people, and, behold, it is a stiffnecked people.

(10) Now let me alone, that my wrath may burn against them, and that I may consume them; and I will make you a great nation."

(11) And Moses entreated YHWH his God,

and said: "YHWH, why does your wrath burn against your people, whom you brought out of the land of Egypt with great power and with a mighty hand?"

(12) "Why should the Egyptians say, saying, 'With evil intent he brought them out to kill them in the mountains and to exterminate them from the face of the earth'? ..."

(13) Remember Abraham, Isaac, and Israel, your servants, to whom you swore by your own self, and said to them: "I will multiply your descendants as the stars of heaven, and all this land of which I have spoken I will give to your descendants, and they shall inherit it forever."

(12) And YHWH said to me: "Arise, go down quickly from here, for your people whom you have brought out of Egypt have become corrupt; they are quickly turned aside out of the way which I commanded them; they have made for themselves a molten image."

(13) And YHWH spoke to me, "I have seen this people, and, behold, it is a stiffnecked people;

(14) let me alone, so that I may destroy them, and blot out their name from under heaven; and I will make you a nation mightier and greater than they."

(25) So I fell down before YHWH... because YHWH had said he would destroy you.

(26) And I prayed to YHWH, and said: "O YHWH God, do not destroy your people and your inheritance, that you redeemed by your greatness, that you brought out of Egypt with a mighty hand.

(28) lest the land from which you brought us will say, "Because YHWH was not able to bring them into the land which he promised them, and because he hated them, he brought them out to slay them in the wilderness.

(27) Remember your servants, Abraham, Isaac, and Jacob. Look not upon the stubbornness of this people, nor their wickedness and sin.

(29) Yet they are your people and your inheritance, that you brought out by your great power and by your outstretched arm."

(14) So YHWH relented in the punishment he had threatened to inflict on his people.

(15) Then Moses turned and came down from the mountain with the two tablets of the testimony in his hand...

(15) So I turned and came down from the mountain, and the mountain burned with fire; and the two tablets of the covenant were in my two hands.

(16) And the tablets were the work of God...

(17) And when Joshua heard the noise of the people shouting,...

(18) And he said: "It is not the sound of the cry of triumph..."

(19) As he drew near the camp, he saw the calf and the dancing;

(16) And I looked, and, behold, you had sinned against YHWH your God; you had made for yourselves a molten calf: you had turned aside quickly out of the way which YHWH had commanded you.

and Moses' anger burned, and he cast the tablets out of his hands and shattered them at foot of the mountain.

(17) And I took hold of the two tablets and cast them out of my two hands, and broke them before your eyes.

(18) And I fell down before YHWH, as at the first, forty days and forty nights; I did neither eat bread nor drink water, because of all your sin which you had committed, in doing what was evil in the sight of YHWH, to provoke him.

(19) For I dreaded the anger and wrath of YHWH, for he was angry enough with you to destroy you. But YHWH listened to me at that time also.

(20) *With Aaron YHWH was deeply angry enough to destroy him, but I prayed for Aaron also at that time.*

(20) And he took the calf which they had made, and burned it with fire, and ground it to powder, and scattered it on the water, and made the children of Israel drink it.	(21) And I took your sin, the calf which you had made, and burned it with fire, and I crushed it and ground it well to powder, until it was as fine as dust, and I cast the dust into the brook that flowed down the mountain.
	(22) *And at Taberah, at Massah, and at Kibroth-hattaavah, you provoked YHWH to anger.* (23) *And when YHWH sent you from Kadesh-barnea, he said, "Go up and possess the land which I have given you." But you rebelled against the commandment of YHWH your God, and you did not believe him or listen to his voice.* (24) *You have been rebellious against YHWH from the day that I knew you.*
(21–24)	
(25–29)	
	10:1–5
(34–35) ...nevertheless in the day when I punish, I will punish them for their sin." And YHWH smote the people, because they made the calf, which Aaron made.	(1–5) (11) And YHWH said to me, "Arise, go before the people, that they may enter in and occupy the land which I swore to their fathers to give them."

The following twelve important differences can be noted:

(1) *Exod 24:12; 31:18 / Deut 9:10–11*. The tablets of stone in Exod 24:12 and 31:18 are defined as the Tablets of the Covenant in Deut 9:10–11. That which is told in Deut 9:11 is not a reiteration of 9:11 but rather emphasizes the fact that the stone tablets are the Tablets of the Covenant, and the day on which Moses received them was the same day that the people "turned aside out of the way" of YHWH, and committed the sin of the golden calf. Another phrase that is noteworthy in Deut 9:10 is "out of the midst of the fire," which calls for an examination of the sin of the golden calf from the angle described in Deut 4–5.

(2) *Exod 32:1–6 / No parallel in Deuteronomy; Exod 32:8 / Deut 12*. The author of L–2 omitted Exod 32:1–6, since for D, the main point of concern in the sin of the golden calf is the making of the golden calf, rather than its worship. For him, the most grievous part of the sin is the sculptural representation of the calf image, a topic I will discuss in

Chapter 4. The details regarding the worship of the calf are noted in Exod 32:8, and they too were omitted from the parallel narrative in Deut 9:12.

(3) *Exod 32:7 / Deut 9:12*. In Deut 9:12, Moses receives the order "go down quickly from here," while in Exod 32:7, he is simply told "go down." This difference leaves the impression that in Deuteronomy, Moses is commanded with great urgency to descend from the mountain, while in Exodus the order is less emphatic. In Exod 32:7, Moses is depicted as a person who pleads with God, in an effort to placate him and assuage his fury, while in Deuteronomy Moses seems to be thrust hastily by God down the mountain in order to confirm the people's sin.

(4) *Exod 32:10 / Deut 9:14*. The phrase "and blot out their name from under heaven" appears in Deut 9:14, while it is absent from Exod 32:10. This fact is probably indicative of the greater tendency in Deuteronomy to emphasize YHWH's rage and his threat to wipe out the people than that in Exodus.

(5) *Exod 32:11 / Deut 9:25–26*. The parallel version of Exod 32:11, which describes Moses' intercession on behalf of the people, is found in Deut 9:25–26. In Deut 9:25, YHWH's threat is re-emphasized through the use of the verb הִשְׁמִיד ("destroy").

(6) *Exod 32:13 / Deut 9:27*. In Moses' intercessional speech in Deut 9:27, which parallels Exod 32:13, the content regarding the promise to the Patriarchs, which is found in the passage following the conjunction אֲשֶׁר in Exod 32:13, is omitted. In its stead is Moses' plea to God not to turn his back on the people's hardship and their misconduct. This change has a paradoxical effect, one which serves to stress the sinfulness and evil of the people.

(7) *Exod 32:15 / Deut 9:15*. In describing Moses' descent from the mountain, the author of L–2 adds the expression "and the mountain burned with fire" to the original "the mountain" in Exod 32:15: "So I turned and came down from the mountain, and the mountain burned with fire…" This phrase also appears in Deut 4 when the making of graven images in the worship of YHWH is forbidden, since when the people stood at the foot of the mountain burning with fire, they could see no image of YHWH within the fire.

(8) *Exod 32:19 / Deut 9:16*. The עֵגֶל ("calf") in Exod 32:20 is described as a sin in Deut 9:21. The idea is that the author of L–2 emphasizes that the "molten calf" itself is a sin.

(9) *Exod 32:19 / Deut 9:17*. In Exod 32:19, Moses smashes the tablets in a fit of rage,[169] but in Deut 9:17, he destroys the tablets before the eyes of the people as a calculated measure rather than offhandedly. It appears

---

169.   See the expression "and Moses' anger waxed hot."

that a certain message is being conveyed by the author within this deliberate act.

(10) *No parallel verse in Exod 32 / Deut 9:18–19.* No parallel is found in Exodus to Moses' plea in Deut 9:18–19. What was the author of L–2's intention, then, when he wrote these verses? Apparently, they treat forgiveness as the first step in the renewal of the covenant. Yet it is probable that they also were aimed at emphasizing the severity of the people's sin: severe words are used in these verses to describe the people's sin, such as חַטָּאת ("sin"), הָרַע ("evil"), הִכְעִיס ("to anger," "to provoke to anger," "to provoke"), אַף ("anger"), חֵמָה ("hot displeasure"), קֶצֶף ("wrath"), and הִשְׁמִיד ("to destroy"); Moses' plea is described in harsh words—combined with puzzlement over the fact that the people's sin was so grave that because of it Moses had to pray forty days and forty nights. Nowhere else in the Bible is there mention of a collective sin other than this one in Deut 9:18–19, which demands the intervention of the leader by his fasting and praying for forty days and forty nights.

(11) *Exod 32:20 / Deut 9:21.* Deuteronomy 9:21 emphasizes that the people's sin is the calf image itself. In contrast to the Elohistic version, which is Exod 32:20, the author of L–2 deliberately inserts here the pronoun אֹתוֹ ("it") as a direct object of the verbs שָׂרַף ("burned") and כָּתַת ("pounded"), in order to stress the destruction of the calf image. The act of destroying the calf is described differently in each of the texts: in Deuteronomy, the calf is ground to dust, which is then cast into the brook flowing down from the mountain, while in the Exodus version the people are forced to drink of it.

(12) *No parallel verses in Exod 32–33 / Deut 10:1–5.* The ark of wood in Deut 10:1–5 is related to the sin of the calf. However, it is not mentioned in connection with the golden calf narrative in the book of Exodus.

The aforementioned differences can be summarized as follows: (1) in Deuteronomy, the sin of the calf is described in harsher terms than in Exodus (see 4, 5, 6, and 10, above), and especially noteworthy is the treatment of the dust of the calf image that was burnt and ground (see 8 and 11); (2) the author of L–2 is not interested in the reports of cultic activities that appear in Exodus (see number 2); (3) the author of L–2 interprets the stone tablets as the Tablets of the Covenant, and describes Moses' smashing of them as an intended action, rather than one improvised (see 1 and 9); (4) the phrase "the mountain burned with fire" in Deut 9:15 appears in relation to the prohibition of images in the worship of YHWH in Deut 4 (see 7); and (5) it is worthwhile studying why the "ark of wood" is referred to only in the version of the golden calf narrative written by the author of L–2, while there is no mention of it in E (see 12).

2.2.2. *Differences in Theological Tendencies and Emphases*. The word
"the way" in the phase "they have quickly turned aside out of the way
which I commanded them" (Exod 32:8; Deut 9:12b) apparently refers to
the Ten Commandments.[170] However, given the different theological tendencies of their authors, it seems that the word "the way" does not refer
to the same commandment in each of the texts. What is clear is that the
sin is related either to the first commandment ("You shall have no other
gods before me") or the second commandment ("You shall not make for
yourself a graven image").[171] A thorough examination of some of the
differences between the texts noted above could explain which commandment the people violated according to each of the texts.

2.2.2.1. *The Meaning of "Become Corrupt"* (שָׁחַת) *and "Turn Aside"*
(סור).

Exodus 32	Deuteronomy 9
(7) Then YHWH said to Moses, "Go down, for your people, whom you brought out of the land of Egypt, have become corrupt.	(12) And YHWH said to me: "Arise, go down quickly from here, for your people whom you have brought out of Egypt have become corrupt;

---

170.   Cassuto, *Commentary*, 414; Mayes, *Deuteronomy*, 199. In Deuteronomy,
to follow the words of YHWH, or his ways, means to keep his commandments
(Weinfeld, *Deuteronomy 1–11*, 391).

171.   The content of the first and second commandments changes according to
the manner in which the "ten" are counted. In the ancient Jewish tradition, there was
no fixed method of dividing the Ten Commandments, though there was a common
tendency to see the oneness of God and the prohibition of graven images as a whole
unit. Catholics and Lutherans follow this method. However, the Ten Commandments
are best divided into two parts, based on the criterion of the appearance of the
expression "YHWH your God" in the commandment (see Weinfeld, *Deuteronomy
1–11*, 245). Following this method, the first part of the Ten Commandments is
comprised of precepts including this expression, and these appear to be related to
divine injunctions, particularly in reference to the people of Israel. On the other
hand, the commandments that do not include this expression tend to concern human
and social obligations, which apply to all of humanity. In turn, the first part is comprised of the following five commandments: the prohibition against worshiping gods
other than YHWH, the prohibition against making graven images, the prohibition
against vain oaths, the instruction to keep the Sabbath, and the instruction to honor
one's parents. According to such a distribution, the first commandment is the prohibition against worshiping other gods, as established in Exod 20:3 and Deut 5:7, and
the second commandment is the prohibition against graven images or likenesses, as
delineated in Exod 20:4 and Deut 5:8.

(8) they have quickly turned aside out of the way which I commanded them; they have made for themselves a molten calf, and have worshipped it, and have sacrificed to it, and said, 'This is your God, O Israel, who brought you out of the land of Egypt.' "	they have quickly turned aside out of the way which I commanded them; they have made for themselves a molten image."

Despite the verbal similitude between the two texts, their theological emphases are quite different. It is important to examine the use of two verbs "turn aside" (סור) and "become corrupt" (שָׁחַת) in order to distinguish the nature of the difference between the texts. Both verbs are used to accuse the people of sinfulness. However, despite the superficial similarity in usage of the two verbs in the two texts, they actually mean different things. What, then, do the verbs "turn aside" and "become corrupt" mean in Exod 32 and Deut 9 respectively? In Exod 32, they refer to the fact that "they have made for themselves a molten calf, and have worshipped it, and have sacrificed to it, and said, 'This is your God, O Israel, who brought you out of the land of Egypt,'" while in Deut 9, they refer only to the fact that "they have made for themselves a molten image." The most conspicuous difference between Exod 32:7–8 and Deut 9:12 is found in the phrase "and have worshipped it, and have sacrificed to it, and said, 'This is your God, O Israel, who brought you out of the land of Egypt'" (Exod 32:8b). This serves as an explanation of v. 8aα, "they have made for themselves a molten calf," and is related in content to Exod 32:1, "Come, make us a god who will go before us; for as for this Moses, the man who brought us up out of the land of Egypt, we don't know what is become of him." Here, the calf is referred to as אֱלֹהִים. Also in Moses' words to God in Exod 32:31,[172] "Oh, this people have sinned a great sin, and have made for themselves a god of gold," the calf is identified as אֱלֹהִים. By contrast, in Deuteronomy the calf is neither called אֱלֹהִים nor identified with אֱלֹהִים. These facts show that for the Elohist, the author of Exod 32, the calf image was considered a god, that is, other god, different from YHWH. We may conclude, then, that in Exod 32, the making of the molten calf is associated with the worship of other gods, and hence a violation of the first commandment (32:8b and 31).[173]

172. This version is alluded to in Exod 20:23: "You shall not make *other gods* besides me; gods of silver or gods of gold, you shall not make for yourself." Although there are debates surrounding the meaning of the prohibition, but it appears that it contains a certain reference to gods of silver and gold.

173. E. Hadad, "The Sin of the Calf," *Magadim* 21 (1994): 29–36 (Hebrew).

However, it seems that Deut 9 emphasizes a new aspect of opposition to the golden calf. In Deut 9:12, "turned aside" and "become corrupt" refer to the making of a molten image. In other words, the author of L–2 emphasizes the sin of the golden calf as an illustration of the violation of the second commandment, the prohibition of the image. In Deuteronomy, the verb שָׁחַת ("become corrupt") appears four times in the context of idolatry, and is directed specifically against the sin of making an image, rather than the worship of pagan gods.[174] In Deut 4:16, clear use of the verb שָׁחַת is made in connection with the idea of making graven images: "lest you become corrupt and make a graven image for yourselves in the form of any figure, the likeness of male or female." This verse warns against making an image of any form, since YHWH did not reveal himself in any form "out of the midst of the fire" at Horeb (4:15); if this is the case, then the image referred to here is intended for the worship of YHWH, and not other gods, who would serve as a substitute for him. Through the use of the same expressions "out of the midst of the fire" and "burned with fire"[175] in Deut 4, the author of L–2 stresses that making an image is nothing other than making an image of YHWH.

2.2.2.2. The Destruction of the Tablets.

Exodus 32:19	Deuteronomy 9:16–17
As he drew near the camp, he saw the calf and the dancing;	(16) And I looked, and, behold, you had sinned against YHWH your God; you had made for yourselves a molten calf: you had turned aside quickly out of the way which YHWH had commanded you.
and Moses' anger burned, and he cast the tablets out of his hands and shattered them at the foot of the mountain.	(17) And I took hold of the two tablets and cast them out of my two hands, and broke them before your eyes.

Deuteronomy 9:9–10, the "verses of the tablets," are ascribed to the Elohistic traditions of Exod 24:12–14, 18b, and not 18a. However, when we compare Exod 24:12, "Come up to me on the mountain and remain there, and I will give you the stone tablets," with Deut 9:9, we find that the author of L–2 added to "tablets of stone" the definition "tablets of the

---

174.   Deut 4:16, 25; 9:12; 31:29.

175.   The expressions "out of the midst of the fire" (9:10) and "burned with fire" (9:15) in Deut 9 appear in chs. 4 and 5 (see "out of the midst of the fire," 4:12, 15, 33, 36; 5:4, 22, 24, 26, and "burned with fire," 4:11; 5:23). The implication seems to be that the message that the author of L–2 wished to convey through the sin of the golden calf is closely related to the prohibition of the image in chs. 4 and 5.

covenant" (see Deut 4:13; 9:11; 1 Kgs 8:9), in precisely the same way that the Priestly original defines the tablets as " tablets of the testimony."[176] Why did the author of L–2 add this description? Apparently, it stems from one of his theological tendencies, namely, the emphasis on aniconism.[177] The common people are liable to misinterpret the "tablets of stone" as a kind of pillar, the use of which was customary and widespread in the Yahwistic cult, and was considered a symbol of the divine presence, prior to the Deuteronomic reforms initiated by Hezekiah.[178]

The tendency of the author of L–2 to aniconism is evident upon comparison of his description of the destruction of the tablets with that of the Elohist. In Deuteronomy, Moses smashes the tablets in the sight of the people ("and broke them before your eyes"), while in Exodus, he destroys them apparently out of the view of the people ("and broke them at the foot of the mountain"). The Elohist stresses that the act of breaking the tablets was not meant to be seen by the people; the act of destruction is not a form of reprimand toward the people, but rather an emotional act on the part of Moses, who was alone by himself, at the foot of the mountain.[179] This interpretation is corroborated by the verse detailing the reason for the destruction of the tablets, "and Moses' anger burned," which is not mentioned in Deuteronomy. Moses unintentionally smashes the tablets, out of rage against the Israelites, as suggested in Nahmanides' interpretation, "and he could not restrain himself." In Deuteronomy, by contrast, the expression "before your eyes" implies a calculated act carried out in view of the people, in order to teach them a lesson. Evidence in support of such an interpretation may be provided by the addition in Deuteronomy, "And I took hold of the two tablets." This

176. Exod 31:18a; 32:15a, and 34:29 are attributed to P in terms of literary continuity and the Priestly phraseology as exemplified by the word "testimony" ("עֵדוּת"). See B. J. Schwartz, "The Priestly Account of the Theophany and Lawgiving at Sinai," in *Texts, Temples, and Traditions: A Tribute to Menahem Haran* (ed. V. F. Michael et al.; Winona Lake, Ind.: Eisenbrauns, 1996), 112–16.

177. See Deut 7:5 etc. Regarding iconoclasm as a religio-historical phenomenon, see H. Cancik, "Ikonoklasmus," in *Handbuch religionswissenschaftlicher Grundbegriffe*, vol. 3 (Stuttgart: Kohlhammer, 1993), 217–21. Cancik defines iconoclasm "as active opposition to images and figures prohibited by religion…(a) (in the explicit sense) the prohibition of the creation and worship of images related to religion…within a specific religion, in addition to the destruction of such images…; (b) (in the broader sense) destruction or damage of images… related to another religion…" (pp. 217–18).

178. On the subject of the legitimate use of a "pillar" (מַצֵּבָה) as a place of dwelling for the divine presence, see Mettinger, *No Graven Image*. The "pillar" will be discussed in Chapter 4.

179. See Hadad, "Sin of the Calf," 31.

expression points to a stage prior to the casting of the tablets, that is, it reflects preparation and premeditation. The tablets in Deuteronomy are deliberately smashed, so that the Israelites will take notice and reach the proper conclusions.[180]

In Deuteronomy, the description of the breaking of the tablets refers to the prohibition of the image. Therefore, their premeditated destruction by Moses attests to the fact that the tablets themselves are not holy: stone tablets are unlike the "pillar" (מַצֵּבָה). If the people were to accept the tablets as a gift from YHWH, they would perhaps serve as a substitute for the golden calf; if the calf, the handiwork of men, were regarded as sacred, then all the more so the tablets, which were God's handiwork! For this reason, Moses smashes the tablets in front of their eyes. Even if the people realize that the tablets are not an icon intended for the worship of YHWH, but rather surfaces upon which were written YHWH's instructions and precepts, the people must be denied the possibility of using them in the worship of YHWH. Moses destroys the tablets in the sight of the people in order to show them that if the tablets are off-limits in the worship of YHWH, then the calf figure is all the more so.[181] Had the tablets been given, it would have been forbidden to hold them up exposed before the people; they would have had to be concealed. This is the reason that the "ark of wood" is mentioned in Deut 10:1–5, in which is described the giving of the newly created tablets.[182]

In sum, the theological conception of the author of L–2, which is reflected in the manner in which Moses handles the tablets, is that all concrete images related in any way to the worship of YHWH are forbidden.

2.2.2.3. The Destruction of the Calf Image.

Exodus 32:20	Deuteronomy 9:21
And he took the calf which they had made, and burned it with fire, and ground it to powder, and scattered it on the water, and made the Israelites drink of it.	And I took your sin, the calf which you had made, and burned it with fire, and I crushed it and ground it well to powder, until it was as fine as dust, and I cast the dust into the brook that flowed down the mountain.

180.   Ibid., 32.

181.   Ibid., 33.

182.   In Deuteronomy, the "ark of wood" is unrelated to the presence of God. Its function is only as a receptacle for the tablets, which represent the covenant. Hence, in D the "tablets of stone" mean the "tablets of the covenant" (see Deut 9:9, 11). Perhaps this was meant to distinguish them from pillars, which were associated with the worship of YHWH.

After he smashes the two tablets to pieces, Moses continues his destruction of the calf image: he burns it, grinds it, and sprinkles the dust upon the water.[183] Yet the description of the destruction of the calf is different in the two texts, particularly with respect to the final stage of the destruction (the forcing of the people to drink the water mixed with the powdery remains of the calf versus merely casting the ashes of the calf into the flowing brook). Weinfeld contends that the two accounts of the destruction of the calf image derive from two different Ugaritic sources.[184] In other words, he explains that the different versions of the destruction of the calf are based on two versions of the destruction of Mot. According to one version (*KTU* 1.6 II 30–36),[185] after he is burned and ground, Mot is eaten by birds, while the second (*KTU* 1.6 V 13–19)[186] describes Mot's remains being scattered upon the sea. According to Weinfeld's line of reasoning, the Exodus version could have preserved the image of "being eaten," while the Deuteronomic version maintained the image of "scattering." Yet it is difficult to accept the idea of this parallelism between the biblical narrative concerning the golden calf and the Ugaritic narrative concerning Mot, as even Weinfeld himself admits.[187] Furthermore, even if we assume that the two narratives are

183. It has been suggested that the description of the destruction of the calf image is similar to that of the destruction of Mot in Ugaritic writings. Loewenstamm ("Golden Calf," 481–90) called attention for the first time to the treatment of Mot in Ugaritic (see C. H. Gordon, *Ugaritic Textbook* [Rome: Pontifical Biblical Institute, 1965], 2, 30ff.). Notable among the supporters of Loewenstamm's view is Childs ("Etiological Tale," 569, 572 n. 20). However, Frankel ("Destruction," 330–39 [esp. 333]) opposes Loewenstamm's suggestion, and proposes that Exod 32:20a was written as a comment in response to Deut 7:5, 25—graven images must be burned with fire—and is originally an addendum to the end of the verse. In such a case, Exod 20a would have to have appeared immediately following Exod 32:19, which concludes with Moses throwing the tablets from his hands and shattering them at the foot of the mountain. In other words, the stone tablets, not the molten calf, are crushed and the ashes strewn over the water. Moreover, he suggests that the author of Deut 9:21 deliberately adopted this ostensibly distorted text of Exod 32:20. Yet, perhaps it is unlikely that the author of Deut 9:21 would intentionally adopt a distorted text.

184. Weinfeld, *Deuteronomy 1–11*, 411–12.

185. *KTU* 1.6 II 30–36 reads: *tiḫd bn ilm mt b ḥrb tbqʿnn b ḫtr tdrynn b išt tšrpnn b rḥm tṯhnn b šd tdrʿnn širh l tikl ʿṣrm*, "He seized Mot, cut him to pieces with a sword, sifted him in her sieve, burned him with fire, ground him as grain in the handmill, and cast the remains out in the fields for birds to eat."

186. *KTU* 1.6 V 13–19 reads: *ʿlk pht šrp b išt ʿlk* [pht ṯḥ]*n brḥm...ʿlk pht drʿ b ym*, "Because of you I endured burning with fire, because of you I endured grinding in the handmill...because of you I endured scattering upon the sea."

187. Ibid., 412.

related to the versions of the destruction of Mot in the Ugaritic texts, it is difficult to believe that the biblical authors adopted the Ugaritic texts without their own theological motives. That is to say, it is more probable that the Elohist and the author of L–2 intended to portray the destruction of the calf image in light of their own theological motives and emphases. What is the peculiar emphasis of each of them?

Two key points emerge from the description of the destruction of the calf image in Deuteronomy: (1) the calf is referred to as a "sin," as seen in 9:16,[188] and (2) all of the objects ("sin," חַטָּאת; "calf," עֵגֶל; "it," אוֹתוֹ; [twice]; and "dust," עָפָר) of the verbs ("make," עָשָׂה; "take," לָקַח; "burn," שָׂרַף; "crush," כָּתַת; "grind," טָחַן; "cast," שָׁלַךְ) related to the destruction of the calf are mentioned, while in the Elohist description only one direct object is noted ("the calf," הָעֵגֶל) for six verbs ("take," לָקַח; "make," עָשָׂה; "burn," שָׂרַף; "grind," טָחַן; "scatter," זָרָה; "drink," שָׁקָה). By emphasizing these points, the author of L–2 means to stress that the destruction of the calf image is intended to entirely liquidate the sin associated with it. All of the acts of destruction and liquidation of the calf, which go as far as grinding it to dust and scattering the dust into the brook, are meant to blot out its existence completely.[189] This tendency is evident also in the addition of the verb "crush" (כָּתַת) and the emphasis on grinding it "well to powder as fine as dust" (הֵיטֵב עַד אֲשֶׁר דַּק לְעָפָר).[190] In sum, Deuteronomy, as opposed to Exodus, emphasizes the total denial of the existence of the calf image.

188. The Deuteronomist uses the word "sin" (חַטָּאת) in the context of the golden calf (1 Kgs 12:30; 13:34; 14:16; 15:3, 26, 30, 34 etc.) and it is an expression which characteristically refers to Jeroboam's sin, which caused the downfall of the northern kingdom (1 Kgs 14:15–16; 2 Kgs 17:22).

189. See Hadad, "Sin of the Calf," 34. The description of the obliteration of the calf image in Deuteronomy is verbally comparable to that in the books of Kings: "and cast the dust of them into the brook Kidron" (2 Kgs 23:12); "and cast the powder upon the graves of the common people" (2 Kgs 23:6); and "Asa cut down her image, and burnt it at the brook Kidron" (1 Kgs 15:13). Therefore, the similarity between the description of the destruction of the calf in Deuteronomy and Kings reinforces the view that the author of Deut 9–10 was affiliated with the same school as that of the author of the books of Kings, namely, the Deuteronomist.

190. In Deuteronomy the phrase appears as "and crushed it and ground it well to powder, until it was as fine as dust," while Exod 32:20 states, "and ground it to powder"; this method of destroying idolatrous/pagan objects—grinding to dust—is found in the account of Josiah's reforms in 2 Kgs 23: "and burned it…and ground it to powder" (23:6); "and he burned the high place and crushed it small to powder, and burned the Asherah" (23:15). See Weinfeld, *Deuteronomy 1–11*, 412.

2.2.2.4. The Ark of Wood in Deuteronomy 10:1–5. The passage describing the ark of wood (10:1–5) is usually structured as part of the narrative of the sin of the golden calf. This account of the making of the new tablets, and the preparation of an ark for them, is partially dependent on Exod 34:1–4, but not in its entirety. The fabrication of the ark is not mentioned in this passage. According to P, the ark was constructed by Bezalel after Moses descended from the mountain (Exod 37:1–9), and not before he went up again, as told in Deuteronomy (10:3).[191] The account of the ark in Deuteronomy is inserted after the sin of the calf, but is not mentioned at all in the story of the calf in Exodus, and is not related to it. Here arises the question: Why did the author of L–2 add the reference to the ark to the narrative of the golden calf?

We saw earlier that in Deuteronomy Moses feared that the tablets would become a new icon in the worship of YHWH. In such a case, they could have served as the basis for a misguided cult, in which the stones would be seen as representing YHWH's presence. Only after the sin of the golden calf, when it is already clear that the Israelites are liable to sin in such a manner, does Moses give the order to make an ark of wood in which the tablets are to be placed.[192] In other words, the ark is designed to prevent the tablets from being used as an image for the worship of YHWH. The author of L–2 emphasizes the negation of the icon. In his eyes, then, the ark itself need not be considered something that represents YHWH's splendor; it is merely a receptacle for the tablets. For this reason, the ark in Deuteronomy is made of simple wood. The author of L–2 attempts to extricate the ark from its traditional image as a symbol of YHWH's presence. Thus, according to the theology of the author of L–2, the ark lost its traditional character as a signifier of the Divine Presence[193] or as a seat of honor for God,[194] and through a process of

191.   Rashi was correct in saying that the ark in Deut 10:1 was not prepared by Bezalel: "This is not the ark made by Bezalel…and this is the one that went out with them to war."

192.   Hadad, "Sin of the Calf," 35.

193.   The Ark is the most important cultic object before the monarchical period. In the pre-monarchical period, the theory was formulated according to which the Divine Presence is always associated with the Ark. Each time the Ark was lifted, Moses said "Rise up, O YHWH," and when it was lowered, he said "Return, O YHWH" (Num 10:35–36). The same idea is expressed in 1 Sam 4:6–7: "…When they knew that the Ark of YHWH had come into the camp…they said, 'A god has come into the camp'…" In both texts, the language serves to emphasize the close relation between YHWH and the Ark, while the conceptual distinction between YHWH and his cultic symbol is preserved. It can be assumed that the Ark was considered a mobile throne of the unseen God, and represented his active power and presence, which was

rationalization, its function was reduced merely to that of a receptacle for the Tablets of the Covenant.[195] This is the reason why there is no mention in Deut 10:1–5 of the cover (כַּפֹּרֶת) of the ark or the cherubs, which gave the ark the appearance of a heavenly chariot or throne.[196]

Now we should examine the intent of the author of L–2 in adding the account of the ark of wood to the Elohist's narrative of the sin of the calf. The reference in L–2 to the ark in the context of the golden calf story implies obliquely that the calf image paralleled the ark in its function. In general, scholars accept the analogy between the ark with the cherubs in the Jerusalem Temple and Jeroboam ben Nebat's calves at Bethel and Dan, in terms of their function.[197] Thanks apparently to this function, the calf image was not subjected to criticism before the eighth century B.C.E. In any case, there was probably a specific reason why the author of L–2 added the account of the wooden ark. It appears that by refuting the function of the ark as a symbol of the Divine Presence or as a seat of honor, the author of L–2 attempted to diminish the significance of the calf image, which was likened to the ark in terms of its function. He had to refuse any analogy between the ark and the calf, deny its mythological character, and rationalize the function of the ark.[198] He reduces its function merely to that of a receptacle for the tablets. His addition of the account of the ark to the sin of the golden calf seems to have an effect that negates the distinction of the calf as a symbol of YHWH or his presence.

In sum, as far as the author of L–2 is concerned, the wooden ark as a container for the tablets of stone serves not only to protect the tablets from misjudgment on the part of the people, but also to negate indirectly the perception of the calf image as analogous to the ark.

---

expressed particularly in times of battle (Num 10:35–36). On the theology of the Divine Presence, see W. Zimmerli, *Studien zur alttestamentlichen Theologie und Prophetie* (Munich: Kaiser, 1974), 249–50.

194.   According to Haran, the seat of honor is composed of two parts: the divine throne, as represented by the cherubs, and the footstool, as represented by the Ark itself (Haran, "Ark and the Cherubim," 30–39, 89–94).

195.   See 1 Kgs 8, in addition to Deut 10:1–5.

196.   Compare with Exod 25:10–22.

197.   Those biblical scholars who have followed H. Th. Obbink ("Jahwebilder," 264–74), and who have gained support especially from Albright (*Stone Age to Christianity*, 299ff.), contend that the calf image represents the footstool of the invisible YHWH (see Loewenstamm, *Evolution*, 53). For a detailed discussion of the similarity between the ark and the calf image, see §3 in Chapter 1.

198.   On the negation of the mythology of the Holy Ark, see G. von Rad, *Studies in Deuteronomy* (trans. D. Stalker; London: SCM, 1963), 40.

2.2.3. *Summary: The Theological Proposition of the Author of L–2.* It seems that the Elohist and the author of L–2 both view the sin of the golden calf as a violation of the Ten Commandments.[199] However, they hold different positions regarding which commandment the calf image violates. A comparison of each of the texts shows that the author of L–2 regards the sin of the calf as a violation of the commandment "You shall not make for yourself a graven image," while the Elohist sees it as an infraction of the commandment "You shall have no other gods besides me." In other words, the polemical approach of the author of L–2 toward the calf image presupposes the commandment forbidding the image, while the polemical approach of the Elohist sees the calf as other god.

2.3. *The Authors of L–1 and L–2 and the Editor of Deuteronomy 9:1–10:11*

In order to make a determination regarding the question of which author (Deuteronomic or Deuteronomistic) the two layers (L–1 and L–2), should be attributed to, one must first of all understand the theological attributes of "proto-Deuteronomy" or the "original Deuteronomy" and its scope and content. It is probable that the "original Deuteronomy" became involved in the religious reforms of King Josiah.[200] According to 2 Kgs 22–23, these reforms began with the discovery of "the book of the Law" (סֵפֶר הַתּוֹרָה), which scholars usually identify with the earliest form of the book of Deuteronomy.[201] The main problem with the link between the Deuteronomic author and Josiah's reforms concerns the historicity of 2 Kgs 22–23.

There are some biblical scholars who deny the historicity of Josiah's reforms, arguing that there is a lack of archaeological data establishing the occurrence of such reforms.[202] However, Dever has recently claimed

---

199. As aforementioned, the word "way" in the phrase "they have turned aside out of the way which I commanded them" (Exod 32:8; Deut 9:12b) refers to the Ten Commandments.

200. It is very likely that Josiah's reforms began after the death of Ashurbanipal, the last important Assyrian king, in 626 B.C.E. and ended in 622 B.C.E.

201. The link between 2 Kgs 22–23 and Deuteronomy is accepted by scholars as an immutable "cornerstone"; see R. E. Clements, *Deuteronomy* (Sheffield: JSOT, 1989), 71. Reuter has dealt with this link and argues that the book referred to in connection with Josiah's reforms was the Book of the Covenant (Exod 20:22–23:33); see E. Reuter, *Kultzentralisation: Entstehung und Theolgogie von Deut 12* (Frankfurt: Anton Hain, 1993), 58–243. However, this thesis is implausible, as there is no direct link between Exod 20:22–23:33 and the narrative in 2 Kgs 22–23, which is clearly suggestive of Deuteronomy.

202. See S. Herrmann, *A History of Israel in Old Testament Times* (Philadelphia: Fortress, 1975), 36 n. 25; J. M. Miller, *The Old Testament and the Historian*

that archaeological discoveries illuminating folk religion in Judah during the seventh century B.C.E. verify the text.[203] Moreover, although it is accepted that Josiah's reforms did not stem from religious but rather political motives, namely, the desire for Judean independence during the decline of the Assyrian Empire, there is no need to deny the connection between the "original Deuteronomy" and Josiah's reforms. In other words, although the view that the reforms were planned and implemented as part of a political program is plausible, it appears that among the steps taken was the elimination of the cult of the state gods of Assyria from the Temple of Jerusalem.[204] It is possible that the "Book of the Law" was found at the Temple of YHWH when the cultic objects used in the worship of the Assyrian god were removed (2 Kgs 22:8). However, there is also an argument stating that the motif of the discovery of the book in the Temple of YHWH was a common literary technique in ancient times that was intended to grant divine legitimacy to recently composed texts.[205] However, this claim is implausible. On the basis that documents were stored in the Temple due to their importance (Deut 31:26; 1 Sam 10:25; 2 Kgs 19:14), it is more likely that the discovery was made of a book that had been deposited and preserved at the Temple of YHWH.[206] Accordingly, one must recognize the close link between the religious reforms of Josiah and the "Book of the Law," regardless of whether Josiah's reforms were initiated as a result of the discovery of the book or whether the book was just another means or part of political reforms. The first version of the book can possibly be dated to some time before Josiah's reign based on the following: the account in Prov 25:1, in which we learn that the books were edited during the time of Hezekiah; the fact that the Northern Israelite tradition, found in Deuteronomy, is well explained by the hypothesis that most of the refugees from Northern Israel fled to Judah, taking with them their traditions from the days of

(Philadelphia: Fortress, 1976); R. Rendtorff, *The Old Testament: An Introduction* (Philadelphia: Fortress, 1983), 2; H. N. Rösel, *Israel in Kanaan: Zum Problem der Entstehung Israels* (New York: Lang, 1992), 74.

    203. W. G. Dever, "The Silence of the Text: An Archaeological Commentary on 2 Kings 23," in Coogan et al., eds., *Scripture and Other Artifacts*, 143–68.

    204. Fohrer, *Introduction*, 168. The policy against Assyria began in the days of Hezekiah, during a time of national reawakening, and was renewed by Josiah. See M. Weinfeld, "The Emergence of the Deuteronomic Movement and its Antecedents," in Lohfink, ed., *Das Deuteronomium*, 90–91.

    205. B. J. Diebner and C. Nauerth, "Die Inventio des ספר התורה in 2 Kön 22: Struktur, Intention und Funktion von Auffindungslegenden," *DBAT* 18 (1984): 95–118.

    206. Fohrer, *Introduction*, 169.

Hezekiah.[207] Therefore, it is plausible that this book was composed in the time of Hezekiah, abandoned at the Temple of YHWH in the days of Manasseh as a result of his religious persecutions, and subsequently readopted under the rule of Josiah, thus influencing his reforms.

Therefore, in order to distinguish the scope and content of the original Deuteronomy within the book of Deuteronomy, we should first examine Josiah's religious reform program, as outlined in 2 Kgs 23, alongside the verses in Deuteronomy that parallel the reforms, based on the following criteria: the means taken to achieve cultic unity (vv. 8–9, 19); elimination of the symbols of the cult of Asherah (vv. 4, 6); elimination of the houses of the קְדֵשִׁים[208] (v. 7); elimination of the cultic articles for the heavenly host, such as sun and stars (vv. 11–12); prohibition of human sacrifice (children) (v. 10); expulsion of the mediums and spiritists (v. 24). The verses in Deuteronomy that parallel the reform program of Josiah in 2 Kgs 23 are suggestive of the direction of the "original Deuteronomy." These verses are as follows:

207. The flow of migration from the northern kingdom to Jerusalem and Judah during the period of Hezekiah is archaeologically confirmed. See M. Broshi, "The Expansion of Jerusalem in the Reigns of Hezekiah and Manasseh," *IEJ* 24 (1974): 21–26. On the Northern origins of the major traditions in Deuteronomy, see de Vaux, *Ancient Israel*, 338; H. H. Rowley, *Worship in Ancient Israel* (London: SPCK, 1967), 106ff.; O. Eissfeldt, *The Hebrew Kingdom* (Cambridge: University Press, 1965), 172ff.; Bright, *History of Israel*, 319ff.; N. Lohfink, "Culture Shock and Theology: A Discussion of Theology as a Cultural and Sociological Phenomenon Based on the Example of Deuteronomic Law," *BTB* 7 (1977): 12–22; Weinfeld, "Emergence of the Deuteronomic Movement," 76–98 (esp. 85), *Deuteronomy 1–11*, 44–54. The Northern origin of the traditions of the Deuteronomic author can be traced through his skeptical view of the kingship, his connections with Hosea, and his use of the term "love" (אַהֲבָה) instead of the term associated with the Jerusalem tradition. On the argument of the first version of the Deuteronomic author, in particular, who was supposed to have originated from the North, see Lohfink, "Culture Shock and Theology," 12–22, and Weinfeld, *Deuteronomy 1–11*, 44–55. However, according to other scholars, the Deuteronomic author was one of Josiah's supporters and composed a propaganda document in support of his reforms (see Clements, *Deuteronomy*, 71, and Y. Suzuki, "A New Aspect of the Occupation Policy by King Josiah," *AJBI* 18 [1992]: 31–61).

208. The term קְדֵשִׁים has generally been translated as "male cult prostitutes" or "male shrine prostitutes" (see NAB, NAS, NIV etc.). However, such translations are to be reconsidered in light of the etymological study of its cognate words in Ugarit and Akkadian documents. For a detailed study of the words קְדֵשָׁה and קָדֵשׁ, see §2.3.2.2.3 in Chapter 4.

	2 Kings 23	Deuteronomy
Cultic unification	8–9, 19	12:13–18
Elimination of symbols of the cult of Asherah	4, 6, 14	12:3
Elimination of cultic articles for the heavenly		
host (sun and stars)	11–12	17:3
Prohibition of human sacrifices (children)	10	18:10
Expulsion of the mediums and spiritists	24	18:11–12
Elimination of the houses of the קְדֵשִׁים	7	23:18

It may be said that a central theological theme reflected in both texts is the emphasis on the exclusive worship of YHWH, and an elimination of all non-Yahwistic components (namely, pagan gods, foreign religious customs, and folk cults influenced by foreign customs).[209] In other words, Josiah's religious reforms are the realization of the program of the "YHWH alone" theology.[210] The aniconic actions within the general reform can be attributed to the "YHWH alone" movement. The prohibition of other gods accompanies the prohibition of the images of other gods (in the spectrum of the worship of YHWH alone), since all of the deities in the ancient East were represented by symbols or icons.[211]

This is the place to discuss the scope of the proto-Deuteronomic movement, which is assumed to have served as a model for Josiah's reforms. In order to understand this phenomenon, it should be noted that 2 Kgs 22:8 terms the book found at the temple "the Book of the Torah" (סֵפֶר הַתּוֹרָה), which suggests less of a narrative content than Deut 1–11, 27–33.[212] From this, we can infer that the body of the book was formed out of the laws, which appear in Deut 12–26, namely, the code of the laws. It is beyond the scope of the current study to deal with the entire content of the proto-Deuteronomic book in Deut 12–26, as we are primarily concerned here with whether the commandment prohibiting the image can be found in it.[213] It turns out that this law cannot be found

209. Regarding the claim that cultic unification was not at the center of Josiah's reforms, see L. J. Hoppe, "Jerusalem in the Deuteronomistic History," in Lohfink, ed., *Das Deuteronomium*, 107–10.

210. Actually, Hosea was the initiator of the "YHWH alone" movement, which permeated Judah at the end of the eighth century B.C.E., and influenced the formulation of the first version of Deuteronomy. Hosea's "YHWH alone" movement will be discussed in Chapter 4.

211. See Weinfeld, *Deuteronomy 1–11*, 288; Morenz, *Egyptian Religion*, 150–56; according to J. Faur ("Biblical Idea of Idolatry," *JQR* 69 [1978–79]: 6–7), the essence of paganism or idolatry is the identification of the god with its image or sculptural representation.

212. Fohrer, *Introduction*, 169.

213. The law prohibiting images was formulated mainly in reference to the making of visual or sculptural representations of YHWH. The prohibition of idols or

anywhere in Deut 12–26.[214] Consequently, the law forbidding the image was not included in the "Book of the Torah" mentioned in 2 Kgs 22:8, namely, the proto-Deuteronomic book, which served as a model for Josiah's reforms. The fact that there is no law prohibiting the image in the laws contained in Deut 12–26, which includes within it the body of the proto-Deuteronomic text, allows us to determine which parts of Deut 1–11, 27–33 belong to the introduction of proto-Deuteronomy and to its conclusion. That is to say, the passages or verses related to the law prohibiting images do not belong to them. According to the aforementioned criterion, L–2, in which its author condemns the calf image on the basis of the law forbidding the image, is not attributed to the Deuteronomic layer, but rather to the Deuteronomistic one (Dtr).

Unfortunately, however, apart from the law prohibiting the image, there is no other unequivocal criterion for determining the scope of the proto-Deuteronomic composition in Deut 1–11, 27–33. There is controversy, in particular, surrounding the scope of the preface to Deuteronomy. The text of Deut 1–11 is comprised of two prefaces (1:1–4:40, and 4:44–11:32). According to Noth, Deut 1–3(4) did not serve as a preface to the Deuteronomic law (chs. 12–26), but rather as an introduction to the whole of Deuteronomistic History.[215] In other words, in Noth's view, Deut 1–3 was compiled together with chs. 31 and 34 by the Deuteronomist in the framework of Deuteronomistic History as a whole. This argument arouses much controversy, which persists due to the complex character of the book of Deuteronomy. Notable among those opposing Noth's contention is Mayes, who thinks that the work of the Deuteronomist in Deut 1–3 is not directly continued in Deut 31, when considering of some materials in chs. 5 and 9–11 which must be assigned to his hand.[216] Also Westermann states, in response to Noth's aforementioned

icons of pagan gods is already subsumed within the prohibition of worship of other gods, as every god in the ancient Near East had an image or icon associated with it. In Chapter 5 (§1.2), I will discuss in detail the fact that the prohibition of the image in the Bible refers to images of YHWH.

214. It can be argued that the law forbidding the image could have been included in the proto-Deuteronomic introduction or conclusion. However, the hypothesis that a law that was not included in the body of law termed "the Book of Torah" would be inserted into its introduction or conclusion is not reasonable. The order to destroy the pillars, burn the Asherah, and cut down the statues in Deut 12:3, is interpreted from the perspective of the ban on the worship of other gods, which is commanded in Deut 12:2.

215. M. Noth, *The Deuteronomistic History* (JSOTSup 15; Sheffield: JSOT, 1981), 33.

216. See A. D. H. Mayes, *The Story of Israel between Settlement and Exile* (London: SCM, 1983), 23–24.

theory, that the Deuteronomistic editing cannot be appraised as a single unit. Westermann thinks that Noth's argument, that Moses' speeches in Deut 1–3 represent the beginning of a comprehensive history, and are aimed at preparing Israel for their entry into the Land and life within it (Deut 1–3[4]) until the Babylonian exile, when the comprehensive history comes to an end, is a fundamental error.[217] I agree with Westermann that there is insufficient cause for removing Deut 1–3 from the totality of the proto-Deuteronomic book. Nevertheless, we should begin here to trace the general scheme of the proto-Deuteronomic book: Deut 4:44–28:68.[218] Within this gamut, the passages and verses concerning the promise and conquest of the Land are ascribed to the Deuteronomic layer (Dtn).[219] Therefore, L–1 may be attributed to the Deuteronomic layer (Dtn).

From this, I conclude that L–1 can be dated to the period of Hezekiah, considering the fact that this layer is attributed to the original Deuteronomic author. If so, when was L–2 composed? Can any clues be found in the text of Deut 9–10 regarding the time in which L–2 was written? Who was the Deuteronomist? Are we dealing with a single editor (or author), several editors, or a school? When we ascribe L–2 to the Deuteronomist, was he the author who wrote the "Deuteronomistic History," that is, the author referred to by Noth? And who edited and joined the two layers (L–1 and L–2) to form the present text of Deut 9:1–10:11? In order to provide answers to these questions, we should first summarize the attributes of the Deuteronomist referred to by Noth. Noth contends that the books of the "first prophets," Joshua, Judges, Samuel, and Kings, make up a sequential history characterized by basic uniformity of language, style, and content.[220] The Deuteronomist, according to Noth, unified the Deuteronomic law within his work, namely, the Deuteronomistic History, while framing it first in Moses' speeches.[221] The Deuteronomist also added other sources, such as the stories of conquest and settlement of the Land, prophetic narratives and speeches, annals, and lists. He arranged these sources, shaped them, constructed a unique chronology of his own design, and inserted his own comments (sometimes putting them in the mouths of lead characters) during critical

---

217.   C. Westermann, *Die Geschichtsbücher des Alten Testament: gab es ein deuteronomistisches Geschichtswerk?* (Gütersloh: Kaiser, 1994), 39–40.

218.   See Weinfeld, *Deuteronomy 1–11*, 10. It is understood that the verses related to the law prohibiting the image are not included in this text, as aforementioned.

219.   See Mayes, *Deuteronomy*, 78–81.

220.   Noth, *The Deuteronomistic History*, 17–26.

221.   Ibid., 27–33, 45–60.

moments in the history.[222] The Deuteronomist was not only the editor, but also the author of the history that he gathered from diverse sources and traditions, and arranged according to his own program and discretion. Therefore, his work is uniform in both form and content.[223] The Deuteronomistic History was probably composed in the middle of the sixth century B.C.E. by a single author.[224] His attitude regarding the future of the people of Israel is pessimistic: in his work he expresses despair and hopelessness with respect to the future of this now exiled and dispersed people, and their chances of one day being gathered together and returning to the Land.[225]

Noth's theory was so convincing that it was accepted by the majority of scholars.[226] Nevertheless, there were many disputes surrounding his assertions. The common denominator of those who oppose his theory is a questioning of the contention that the Deuteronomistic History was written by one author at a given time in the period of the Babylonian exile. Although this is not the place to deal with all of the debates, one theory that cannot be ignored is that of the double-redaction, which was proposed by American scholars,[227] following Cross's[228] work on the Deuteronomistic History. According to these scholars, the first Deuteronomistic layer (Dtr1) is dated to the period of Josiah, prior to his death in 609 B.C.E., and the second (Dtr2) to the period of the Babylonian exile. Their assertion is that the two editing layers were not executed by two authors with different theological backgrounds, but rather by one school, based on the same theology. Therefore, the Deuteronomist carried out his work in the time of the exile from a similar perspective and theological

222. Ibid., 118–21, passim.
223. Ibid., 20, 24, 26.
224. Ibid., 27, 35, 122.
225. Ibid., 142–43.
226. According to Knoppers (*Two Nations under God*, 1–56), almost all scholars view the books of the first prophets, Joshua, Judges, Samuel, and Kings, as a single extensive corpus.
227. Such scholars include: J. Levenson, "Who Inserted the Book of the Torah?," *HTR* 68 (1975): 203–33; B. Halpern, *The First Historians: The Hebrew Bible and History* (San Francisco: Harper & Row, 1988), 107–21, 207–40; R. Nelson, *The Double Redaction of the Deuteronomistic History* (JSOTSup 18; Sheffield: JSOT, 1981); H. Tadmor and M. Cogan, *2 Kings* (AB 11; Garden City, N.Y.: Doubleday, 1988); I. Provan, *Hezekiah and the Books of Kings: A Contribution to the Debate about the Composition of the Deuteronomistic History* (BZAW 172; Berlin: de Gruyter, 1988); S. L. McKenzie, *The Trouble with Kings: The Composition of the Book of Kings in the Deuteronomistic History* (VTSup 42; Leiden: Brill, 1991).
228. Cross, *Canaanite Myth*, 274–89. As a result, they are called "the Cross school."

orientation to those of the first author, in the time of Josiah, and did not challenge or contradict him.[229] He continued to use the terms, expressions, words, and style of the first version.[230] Both layers (Dtr1 and Dtr2) belonged to one school, and perhaps even one family.[231] The relevant differences between the two Deuteronomists are not perceptual or conceptual, but rather historical. In other words, the creation of the second Deuteronomistic version (Dtr2) was a response to new historical circumstances.[232] Although there are those who will refute the existence of a Deuteronomistic school or movement,[233] this argument has its merits: not only is it capable of explaining the remarkable consistency throughout the Deuteronomistic History, but it can also resolve a problematic point in Noth's argument. His claim that all of the Deuteronomistic History was written by one author during one period has an advantage in that it explains its consistency. However, it appears that Noth is unable to explain the inconsistency or discontinuity in this work. His reply to this problem is that the Deuteronomist incorporated disharmonious sources and refrained from processing or adapting them, with the aim of objectively transmitting the history of the people of Israel.[234] Yet this explanation is incompatible with his earlier claim that "Dtr was not merely an editor but the author of a history which brought together material from highly varied traditions and arranged it according to a carefully conceived plan... Dtr apparently arranged the material according to his own judgment."[235] However, if the author of the Deuteronomistic History was really one person, it is hard to believe that a historian (and not a collector of historical sources!) would incorporate contradictory sources into his work with no adaptation or processing. Therefore, Noth's assertion that the Deuteronomistic History in its entirety was composed by one author at one point in time is unconvincing.

229.   R. E. Friedman, "From Egypt to Egypt: Dtr1 and Dtr2," in *Traditions in Transformation* (ed. B. Halpern and J. D. Levenson; Winona Lake, Ind.: Eisenbrauns, 1981), 185–92, and "The Deuteronomic School," in *Fortunate The Eyes that See* (ed. A. B. Beck et al.; Grand Rapids: Eerdmans, 1995), 74; Cross, *Canaanite Myth*, 287–89.

230.   Friedman, "From Egypt to Egypt," 185–86.

231.   Ibid.

232.   Ibid., 186.

233.   For example, see N. Lohfink, "Was There a Deuteronomistic Movement?," in *Those Elusive Deuteronomists* (ed. L. S. Schearing and S. L. McKenzie; JSOTSup 268; Sheffield: Sheffield Academic, 1999), 36–66.

234.   Noth, *Deuteronomistic History*, 120, 128ff.

235.   See ibid., 26.

Freedman, and even other representatives of the "Cross school," have not offered an alternative analysis of the Deuteronomistic History in Deuteronomy or in other books, as Römer contends.[236] However, it cannot be denied that their argument regarding the existence of a Deuteronomistic school could overcome the weak spot in Noth's theory. Freedman's suggestion that discrepancies or differences in the Deuteronomist History stem from the responses of the second Deuteronomist (Dtr2) to new historical circumstances is convincing.[237]

The issue in L–2 that can be resolved through the hypothesized existence of a Deuteronomistic school is the attribution of Deut 9:21. The close link between Deut 9:21 and 2 Kgs 23:4–6, namely, the use of the same terms and phrases in both texts is undeniable. In other words, the terms and phrases, such as "burn" (שָׂרַף), "fire" (אֵשׁ), "fine" (דַּק), "dust" (עָפָר), "into the brook" (אֶל נַחַל), and "cast" (שָׁלַךְ), which are used in the description of the destruction of the cultic objects (altars, *asherahs*, pillars, and graven images) in the framework of Josiah's religious reforms appear also in Deut 9:21 in connection with the destruction of the golden calf.[238] Therefore, Freedman attributes Deut 9:21 to the Josiah version of the Deuteronomistic History (Dtr1).[239] However, as I claimed above, Deut 9:21 is included in L–2, which deals with the law prohibiting the image. The verse cannot be detached from L–2 and attributed to Dtr1. Yet the proto-Deuteronomy did not espouse the law forbidding images and his text served, as aforesaid, as a guide in the reforms of Josiah. For this reason, it is hard to believe that the Josiah version of the Deuteronomistic History (Dtr1) presupposed the law prohibiting the image.[240] And therefore, it is not likely that Deut 9:21, which presupposes

236. T. Römer, "The History of Israel's Traditions," in *The History of Israel's Traditions* (ed. S. L. McKenzie and M. P. Graham; JSOTSup 182; Sheffield: JSOT, 1994), 188–89.

237. Against this argument, see R. Albertz's thesis ("In Search of the Deuteronomists: A First Solution to a Historical Riddle," in *The Future of the Deuteronomistic History* [ed. T. Römer; Leuven: Leuven University Press, 2000], 1–17), which claims that there were two families in the Deuteronomistic school, the Hilkiah and Shaphan families.

238. For a comparison of the terms and phrases in 2 Kgs 23:4 and Deut 9:21, see Begg, "Destruction of the Calf," 236–38.

239. Friedman, "From Egypt to Egypt," 191.

240. According to Rose, the Josiah phase in Deuteronomy reflects a monolatric perspective, since pagan gods comprised a real threat to Israel. In the exilic phase of the Deuteronomistic editing (esp. Deut 4), a clear monotheistic disposition is apparent, which is reminiscent of that of the Second Isaiah. See M. Rose, *Der Ausschliesslichkeitsanspruch Jahwes: Deuteronomische Schultheologie und die Volksfrömmigkeit in der späten Königszeit* (Stuttgart: Kohlhammer, 1975), 185ff. See also

the law prohibiting the image, is attributable to Dtr1. Accordingly, L–2, which includes Deut 9:21, should be ascribed to the Exilic version of the Deuteronomistic History (Dtr2). The author of Dtr2 adapted and reinterpreted the Elohistic version of the sin of the golden calf in accordance with the situation in the period of exile, during which the law prohibiting the image was crystallized. In his work, he continued to use terms and phrases that were found in the Josiah version, which was composed by his predecessor in the same school.

Apparently, the editor who compiled the two layers (L–1 [Dtn] and L–2 [Dtr2]) was also a member of the Deuteronomistic school. Hence, it is worth examining Deut 10:6–7, which correspond to Num 33, which is attributed to P.[241] These verses, in which the names of Aaron and Eleazar are mentioned as priests, and which tell of the people of Israel's journey in the wilderness, were added by the editor. However, the description of the journey in Deuteronomy is different from that in Num 33 in several ways:[242] (1) the version in Deuteronomy is written in the style of E (also J) ("From there they journeyed," see Num 21:12–13), rather than the style of P ("And they journeyed…and pitched in…," see Num 1–49); (2) the order of the camps is different (in Num 33, the order is Moserah, Bene-jaakan, Hor-haggidgad, and Jotbathah, while in Deuteronomy, the order is Bene-jaakan, Moserah, Gudgod, and Jotbathah); (3) there are slight variations in the names of places; (4) according to Deuteronomy, Aaron dies and is buried at Moserah, while according to P, he dies and is buried at Mount Hor (Num 33:37–38). Clearly, the description of the journey in Deuteronomy is independent of that in Num 33. It appears that the former is based on an Elohistic source, and was inserted in Deuteronomy due to the information on Aaron and Eleazar, who were the first Levites dedicated to the priesthood.[243] Hence, it is reasonable to assume that the editor who combined the two layers was also a member of the school of the second Deuteronomist, which found itself in different circumstances some time after the composition of L–2.

A. Rofé, "The Monotheistic Argumentation in Deuteronomy IV 32–40: Contents, Composition and Text," *VT* 35 (1985): 434–45.

241.   The Torah, in general, was not created by a single process of integration of all the pre-existing layers and sources. It was created through gradual processes of editing. P, the final source, occasionally served as a framework for editing the pre-existing sources, such as in the story of the flood, the history of the nations, the description of the oppression in Egypt, and the narrative of the calling of Moses (see Fohrer, *Introduction*, 190–91).

242.   Weinfeld, *Deuteronomy 1–11*, 419.

243.   Ibid. Regarding the non-Priestly source, which describes Aaron and Eleazar as Levites, see Exod 4:14; Josh 24:33.

3. *The Polemical Points*

As stated above, the Elohist and the Deuteronomist both constructed descriptions of the sin of the golden calf from the perspective that it was a violation of the Ten Commandments, but are divided on the question of just which commandment is violated by the calf image. A comparison of the texts shows that the Elohist understands the sin of the calf as a breach of the commandment "You shall not have other gods besides me," while the Deuteronomist in Deuteronomy sees it as an infringement of the commandment "You shall not make for yourself a graven image."

3.1. *The Polemic of the Elohist*
3.1.1. *The Polemic Against the Calf Image Itself.* As was noted above, through an analysis of Exod 32, and a comparison between it and Deut 9:7–10:11, the primary motive for the negative position of the Elohist toward the calf image is related to his view that it represents a pagan god.

When the Elohist began to deal with the polemic against calf worship, he already had before him a cultic formula with respect to it. He could not have criticized the calf without dealing with the cultic formula that was used in a positive sense, that is, in connection with the worship of YHWH. For this reason, he inserted the expression "make us a god (אֱלֹהִים)" within his polemic against the calf cult, in order to transform the positive image in the cultic formula into a negative one. As a result, the אֱלֹהִים in the cultic formula was turned into the image of the calf itself, namely, the image of other god.

3.1.2. *The Polemic Against the Calf-Image Cult.* It appears that the Elohist's condemnation of the calf image is accompanied by a condemnation of its cult. As long as the Elohist sees the calf image as a pagan god, one would not expect him to describe its worship in a positive light.

Nevertheless, in order to understand the cultic state of affairs described in Exod 32, it is worth exploring the meaning of the term צִחֵק in v. 6b, namely, the central expression used to depict the worship of the calf image. However, because there is disagreement regarding the meaning of this term, besides an examination of the uses of the term in the Bible, we must take into account the following two aspects: (1) if the term לְצַחֵק is related to descriptions of joy during feasts, festivals, or religious events (such as the offering of a sacrifice and the like), an understanding of the content and scope of the "joy" involved in the cultic activities in the Bible will help us to comprehend the meaning of the term לְצַחֵק; and (2) a consideration of other terms related to the description of the cultic situation in Exod 32 is essential to an understanding of the term לְצַחֵק.

First of all, I will examine the uses of the term לְצַחֵק in the Bible, and reveal its possible meanings. לְצַחֵק is the Piel form of the verb צָחַק ("to laugh"). The Piel form of צָחַק appears six times in the Bible in addition to Gen 32:6, namely: Gen 19:14; 21:9; Judg 16:25; Gen 26:8; 39:14, 17. In the first three instances (Gen 19:14; 21:9; Judg 16:25), the term probably does not have a sexual connotation. In Gen 19:14, Lot has a hard time convincing his sons-in-law of the sincerity of his intentions: וַיְהִי כִמְצַחֵק בְּעֵינֵי חֲתָנָיו ("but he seemed to his sons-in-law as one that jested"). To his sons-in-law, Lot seems to be "jesting" or "mocking" them.[244] In Gen 21:9, Sarah's fears are described, when she notices Hagar's son, Ishmael, מְצַחֵק. In this case, מְצַחֵק is interpreted as "laughing at,"[245] "mocking,"[246] or "making sport."[247] In Judg 16:25, the verb צִיחֵק, which corresponds to the verb שִׂיחֵק ("to play"), may be interpreted as "he performed gymnastics."[248] Accordingly, in these verses (Gen 19:14; 21:9; Judg 16:25), the conclusion is that the verb צִיחֵק suggests something in the manner of "to make sport," "to joke," "to amuse or entertain."[249] In the three other cases (Gen 26:8; 39:14, 17), the verb צִיחֵק may be interpreted as implying sexual exaltation. In Gen 26:8, the verb צִיחֵק may have the connotation of sexual play or foreplay. Some commentators have interpreted מְצַחֵק here in a non-sexual way.[250] However, if Isaac is only engaging in an amusing conversation with Rebecca, why did the king of Gerar determine that they were actually husband and wife?[251] Another instance of לְצַחֵק that is interpreted as describing sexual activity is found in Potiphar's wife's accusation that Joseph tried to rape her (Gen 39:14–18). According to the text, Potiphar's wife claims that her husband brought Joseph to their house in order to לְצַחֵק בָּנוּ (39:14), and afterwards to לְצַחֵק בִּי (39:17). What exactly does she mean when she uses the expression לְצַחֵק here? It should be noted that here the word is synonymous with לִשְׁכַּב ("to lie with"). Sasson's determination[252] that

---

244. So RSV; JPS; J. Skinner, *Genesis* (ICC; Edinburgh: T. & T. Clark, 1951), 308.
245. So ESV.
246. So ASV, KJV, NAS, NAU, NIB, NIV.
247. So JPS. J. Sasson supports this interpretation; see his "The Worship of the Golden Calf," in *Orient and Occident: Essays Presented to C. H. Gordon* (ed. H. A. Hoffner; AOAT 22; Neukirchen–Vluyn: Neukirchener Verlag, 1973), 155.
248. Ibid., 154.
249. So ESV, NAS, NAU.
250. JPS and KJV translate it "Isaac was sporting with Rebekah"; Sasson ("Worship of the Golden Calf," 155) supports this interpretation.
251. V. P. Hamilton, *The Book of Genesis: Chapters 18–50* (Grand Rapids: Eerdmans, 1995), 195–96.
252. Sasson, "Worship of the Golden Calf," 151–59.

the accusation of sexual harassment is found in the statement בָּא אֵלַי
לִשְׁכַּב עִמִּי ("he came in to me to lie with me")[253] rather than לְצַחֶק בָּנוּ
("to mock us") is unconvincing, since in v. 17 Potiphar's wife accuses
Joseph of making sexual advances to her by the exclusive use of the term
לְצַחֶק. What act of betrayal could have caused Potiphar to incarcerate
Joseph, his most loyal servant, if לְצַחֶק does not signify sexual activity,
but rather only making sport, insulting, or mocking? The fact that
Potiphar's wife uses the term לְצַחֶק in the sense of sexual assault is
reinforced by her claim that "I lifted up my voice" (39:18, also 14),
which immediately follows לְצַחֶק. Here, the meaning of the scream is
that she was sexually assaulted.[254] That is to say, the expression "raised
her voice" supports the suggestion that לְצַחֶק clearly denotes sexual
activity. Therefore, from the biblical narratives, one can suggest two
general meanings of the verb צִיחֵק: (1) "to joke, mock, amuse, entertain,
and make sport"; (2) "to engage in sexual relations." Here, the image that
is evoked by these meanings is "joy or merriment."

It is worth examining the content and scope of the "joy" expressed in
connection with common worship in the Israelite religion. According to
Deuteronomy, every time that a sacrifice or an offering from the flock or
field is brought to the Jerusalem Temple, and every time that the people
assemble after the harvesting of the crops, in order to celebrate Shavuot

---

253.   Since the expression בָּא אֵלַי לִשְׁכַּב עִמִּי, "he came in to me to lie with me"
is read in the Septuagint as εἰσῆλθεν πρός με λέγων κοιμήθητι μετ᾽ ἐμοῦ, that is, בָּא
אֵלַי לֵאמוֹר שְׁכָבִי עִמִּי, "he came to me to say (or saying) 'lie with me'." The Greek
version could be explained in two ways, both of which are plausible, although the
first possibility that follows seems more likely. The first possibility is that λέγων
("saying") could have been unintentionally omitted from the text due to its earlier
appearance in the passage (haplography). In such a case, the imperative (שְׁכָבִי, "lie
with!") is accepted as an infinitive (לִשְׁכַּב, "to lie with"). The nuance of MT (as
reflected in the LXX) can be taken as "he came to me demanding to lie with me" (see
H. M. Orlinsky, "Critical Notes on Gen 39:14, 17; Jud 11:37," *JBL* 61 [1942]: 87–
90). A second possibility is to understand the -לְ in לִשְׁכַּב as an abbreviation of לֵאמוֹר
in a *Vorlage* (see P. Katz, "*Katapaúsai* as a Corruption of *katalýsai* in the Septuagint," *JBL* 65 [1946]: 324; Allen, *Greek Chronicles, Part II: Textual Criticism*
[VTSup 27; Leiden: Brill, 1974], 86).

254.   See Deut 22:23–27. Of course, it is almost impossible to cite Deuteronomic
verses in order to corroborate the story of Joseph (J). Nevertheless, it is correct that a
woman's screams are heard when she is being raped or sexually assaulted. The lack
of a scream during sexual activity in a populated area leads to the conclusion,
according to Deuteronomic law, that the sex act was consensual (Deut 22:23–24).
The absence of such a cry when talking about a married or engaged woman in an
unpopulated area does not comprise incriminatory evidence against her, as there may
have been no one close enough to have heard her cry (Deut 22:25–27).

or Succoth, the following words appear: "and you shall eat there before
YHWH your God, and you shall rejoice."[255] In the book of Deuteronomy
"joy" is in principle a given religious phenomenon before YHWH, one
experienced while eating and drinking at a sacrificial feast.[256] It seems to
me that in regular worship in the Israelite religion, "joy" is associated
with eating a sacrificial meal and singing. In Deuteronomy, the connection between the sacrificial meal[257] and rejoicing before YHWH is unmis-
takable,[258] while in other texts "joy" is described in terms of singing. In
Nehemiah's dedication ceremony for the wall of Jerusalem, Levites are
brought to Jerusalem "to keep the dedication with gladness, both with
thanksgivings, and with singing" (Neh 12:27). In some verses in Psalms,
singing (songs of praise) is understood as a standard ritual practice (Pss
27:6; 54:6; 107:22; 141:2).[259]

At this point, in order to understand the scope of the description of
"joy" expected in normal worship of YHWH, it is worth examining the
prophetic texts that date to the period before the Exile, or Deuteronomy,
in which expressions with the root שׂמח are used to describe religious or
cultic rejoicing. Three texts will be examined here: Hos 9:1; Isa 22:13,
and Isa 30:29. According to Braulik, reflected in these texts is the perverted cultic reality of Israelite religion, due to which the Deuteronomic
command was resolved to rejoice before YHWH during every ritual
activity.[260] Scathing condemnation of the people of Israel is found in Hos
9:1 regarding their celebration of the harvest and autumn festival
(Succoth),[261] "the feast of YHWH" (Hos 9:5; cf. Judg 21:19–21; Deut
16:13–15; Lev 23:39–43). Ecstatic rejoicing characterized this festival.[262]

---

255.   Deut 12:7 (pl.), 12 (pl.), 18 (pl.); 14:26; 16:11, 14; 26:11.
256.   See G. Braulik, *The Theology of Deuteronomy* (trans. U. Lindblad; N.
Richland Hills, Tex.: Bibal, 1994), 27ff.
257.   Usually, a sacrificial meal means a feast including the drinking of wine.
Ritual eating is discussed in detail in §2.3.2.2 in Chapter 4.
258.   See Deut 14:26; 16:11, 14–15; 26:11; 27:7.
259.   M. Greenberg, "On the Refinement of the Conception of Prayer in the
Hebrew Scriptures," *AJSR* 1 (1976): 60. According to Westermann and Kugel,
sacrificing and singing songs of praise are analogous activities; see C. Westermann,
Praise and Lament in the Psalms (Atlanta: John Knox, 1981), 28–29, 76; J. Kugel,
"Topics in the History of the Spirituality of the Psalms," in *Jewish Spirituality:
From the Bible Through the Middle Ages* (ed. A. Green; New York: Crossroad,
1986), 125–27.
260.   Braulik, *Theology of Deuteronomy*, 36–37.
261.   J. L. Mays, *Hosea: A Commentary* (London: SCM, 1969), 125; Wolff,
Hosea, 153; A. A. Macintosh, *Hosea* (ICC; Edinburgh: T. & T. Clark, 1997), 337.
262.   Mays, *Hosea*, 125.

Hosea, then, commands Israel not to rejoice: "Do not rejoice, O Israel, with exultation like the peoples!" (Hos 9:1). Why? In this context, the word "peoples" (עַמִּים) is interpreted as gentiles or idolaters.[263] As Mowinckel[264] contends, the festival was Canaanite in origin and was adopted by Israel after their settlement in the Land. Likewise, Rudolph suggests that Israel's joy in their festival deteriorated to that of Canaanite ecstasy, and that their uncontrolled joy and shouts came from the Canaanite rite.[265] Hence, even though it is a "feast of YHWH" (vv. 4, 5), Hosea sees it as an expression of Israel's heresy and godlessness. In their exultation they behaved like pagans. Given these views, Hosea's prohibition of rejoicing is justified. Since in this context the term שִׂמְחָה corresponds to גִיל ("joy, gaiety"), which in Barth's view is "an act of expressing joy in spontaneous, enthusiastic cries,"[266] it appears that this word too means "cries of joy."

Isaiah 22:13 laments the "inopportune exultation" of the population of Jerusalem, when they are expected to repent.[267] The climate in the city is not marked by sorrow or regret over Hezekiah's surrender to the Assyrian king Sennacherib.[268] Instead of remorse and lamentation, the people rejoice in a ritual celebration including the eating of meat and the drinking of wine.[269]

The prophecy of the downfall of Assyria causes the people to sing "as in the night when a feast is hallowed," and to be with "gladness of heart, as when one goes with the pipe to come into the mountain of YHWH, to the Rock of Israel" (Isa 30:29). It is not clear which feast or festival is being referred to here. The word "night" seems to imply Passover, since

263. Wolff, *Hosea*, 154.

264. See S. Mowinckel, *The Psalms in Israel's Worship* (2 vols.; New York: Abingdon, 1962), 1:130ff.

265. W. Rudolph, *Hosea* (Gütersloh: Mohn, 1966), 175.

266. C. Barth, "גיל gyl, גִילָה gîlāh," *TDOT* 2: 471; Wolff, *Hosea*, 153.

267. See v. 12: "And in that day did YHWH, the GOD of hosts, call to weeping, and to lamentation, and to baldness, and to girding with sackcloth." The terms "weeping," "lamentation," "baldness," and "sackcloth" mark the ritual of repentance; see H. Wildberger, *Isaiah 13–27* (trans. T. H. Trapp; CC; Minneapolis: Fortress, 1997), 372.

268. Apparently, Isa 22:12–13 refers to the situation described in 2 Kgs 18–19, and Isa 36–37; see J. D. Watts, *Isaiah 1–33* (WBC 24; Waco, Tex.: Word, 1985), 284.

269. This situation can perhaps be explained as follows: if the future is not clear or optimistic, then one should live for the moment (see Wildberger, *Isaiah 13–27*, 373–74). See Eccl 5:17: "Behold what I have seen to be good: it is comely for one to eat and to drink, and to enjoy pleasure for all his labour, in which he labours under the sun, all the days of his life which God has given him; for this is his portion."

Deut 16:6–7 mentions a nocturnal celebration only in connection with this event. However, it is hard to conclude that the simile used in Isa 30:29 refers to Passover in Jerusalem during the time of Hezekiah's reforms, since we have no information in our possession regarding the celebration of Passover during the time of Hezekiah, other than 2 Chr 30, which is regarded as ahistorical. Thus, most scholars think that this is the autumn festival, Succoth,[270] considering the fact that all the Israelite feasts begin in the evening after sundown.[271]

"Joy" (שִׂמְחָה) especially in ritual practice, is a given religious phenomenon. However, it seems that the pre-Deuteronomic passages do not characterize regular Yahwistic worship in terms of שִׂמְחָה. Hosea 9:1 demands that Israel refrain from rejoicing. Isaiah 22:13 describes a joyful celebration that deteriorates into an unrestrained eating and drinking binge. Isaiah 30:29 compares the people's rejoicing to a gleeful march marking the night before a festival. Usually, the religious or ritual rejoicing mentioned in the biblical texts "does not refer to a sustained emotion, a state, but to joy expressed spontaneously and fundamentally."[272] So the most fundamental expression of joy is the cry of joy that contains only very few or almost no verbal elements.[273] This gaiety results in many forms of noise, gesticulation, clapping of hands, shouting, music, and dancing, which escalate to the point of madness. This characterization is especially pronounced when the people are intoxicated by wine (Isa 22:13).[274]

At this time, in order to clarify the meaning of the term צִחֵק in Exod 32:6b, it is worth analyzing other words referring to cultic practice surrounding the calf image in Exod 32. Verses 17–18 describe Joshua and Moses' responses to the sounds they hear coming from the camp of the Israelites, as they descend from the mountain. The main difficulty in discerning the cultic nature of the goings-on in the camp lies in the interpretation of the verb עָנָה; in v. 18, the verb appears twice in the Qal infinitive form (עֲנוֹת) and once in the Piel infinitive form (עַנּוֹת). The question of the root and meaning of the word raises quite a few difficulties, and accordingly, many attempts have been made to resolve them. At least four meanings for the root עָנָה are known in biblical

270. See H. Wildberger, *Isaiah 28–39* (trans. T. H. Trapp; Minneapolis: Fortress, 2002), 199.

271. J. N. Oswalt, *The Book of Isaiah: Chapters 1–39* (Grand Rapids: Eerdmans, 1986), 567.

272. E. Ruprecht, "שמח to rejoice," *TLOT* 3:1273.

273. Ibid., 1274.

274. Ibid.

Hebrew:[275] (1) עָנָה I, "to answer, reply"; (2) עָנָה II, "to be occupied, busied with"; (3) עָנָה III, "to be bowed down, afflicted"; and (4) עָנָה IV, "to sing." First, a determination of which of the above meanings is appropriate to v. 18 will help us to understand Joshua's response to the sound in the camp. The prelude to this poem (v. 17) attests to the fact that Joshua interpreted the sounds as a war cry. In the military context, the verb לַעֲנוֹת, which appears in the first two lines of the poem, means "to sing," in accordance with the custom common throughout the ancient East of emphasizing military activity through dancing and singing.[276] However, Moses rejects Joshua's interpretation. Why does he do so? Does he mean that the sound is not a war song, but rather one relating to a festival? It is quite reasonable to interpret it this way. If so, the Piel form of עָנָה (עִינָה) can be interpreted as "to sing a song distinctly."[277] Yet, did the narrator (the Elohist) have cause to use עִינָה instead of עָנָה, if both essentially mean "to sing a song"? It seems that if there were actually no difference between the two forms, there would be no reason to use עִינָה instead of עָנָה. Verse 18 takes the following form: "It is not A, but rather B" (אֵין קוֹל עֲנוֹת...וְאֵין קוֹל עֲנוֹת, "It is not the sound of עֲנוֹת...but the sound of עֲנּוֹת"). If this is the case, we have sufficient basis to assume that the latter (Piel) form carries a different meaning than the former (Qal) form.[278] What is this difference? As I hypothesized above, the latter refers to singing a ritual song, while the former refers to singing a war song. However, there are no instances known to us in which the verb עָנָה refers to a war song, while the verb עִינָה is indeed used in reference to ritual songs. Accordingly, it is unconvincing to claim that the first means simply "to sing," while the second is "to emphasize the

275. BDB, 772–77.
276. See R. M. Good, "Exodus 32:18," in *Love and Death in the Ancient Near East: Festschrift M. H. Pope* (ed. J. H. Marks and R. M. Good; Guilford, Conn.: Four Quarters, 1987), 137–42 (esp. 140). If so, the first two lines of the poem may be translated as follows: "It is not the sound of the cry of triumph, nor is it the sound of the cry of defeat." However, the reading in Targum Onkelos (לא קל גיברין דנצחין בקרבא/ואף לא קל חלשין דמתברין) omits the meaning of עֲנוֹת in the first two lines.
277. BDB, 777.
278. Even if we ignore the Masoretic vocalization, the context (v. 17) and the poem (v. 18) themselves imply that the third instance of עֲנּוֹת is supposed to be different in meaning from the first two, as suggested above. It would be more accurate to say that the Masoretic vocalization suggests that the third instance of the verb has a meaning other than "song" or "cries," which is the clear meaning of the first two. In this sense, it is implausible to read all three as Piel, as does Albright (*Yahweh*, 43–44), whose reading harmonizes the text with the Greek and Syriac versions.

antiphonal or responsive quality of the chant."[279] Although the possibility exists that עַנּוֹת in the last line (infinitive of the verb עִינָה) signifies
"ritual song,"[280] we cannot escape the suspicion that the Elohist had a
special reason for using the verb עִינָה instead of עָנָה. It seems that we can
offer two possibilities with respect to the meaning of עִינָה. One is that
עִינָה refers not only to a simple ritual song, but even to a joyful cry, since
the cultic rejoicing described in the pre-exilic (or pre-Deuteronomic)
texts entailed cries of joy. Another possibility has been suggested by a
number of scholars, such as Deen, Morag, and Hacham. According to
Deen,[281] the verb עִינָה presupposes another, more conventional, meaning of the verb form, which is "to bend," "torture," or "cause suffering."
In Hebrew, the most common usage of the verb עִינָה is "to torture," or
"torment,"[282] with a narrower definition being "to rape" or "to ravish," a
meaning which appears both in legal contexts[283] and narrative passages in
the Bible.[284] The verb עִינָה (the Piel form of עָנָה), which carries the
meaning "to rape, to force a woman to have sexual relations," is related
to the meanings of the verb עָנָה, "to make love" and "to have consensual
sexual relations."[285] Yet, according to Morag[286] and Hacham,[287] the verb
עִינָה does not necessarily denote non-consensual sexual relations, but
rather relations between men and women that violate accepted norms and
conventions (see Deut 21:14; 22:23–24; Judg 19:24; Ezek 22:10–11).
The passage in Deut 22:23–24 supports the view that עִינָה does not carry
the meaning "to rape," but rather "to engage in consensual sexual

---

279.　Even Sasson ("Worship of the Golden Calf," 157) does not distinguish
between the two when he interprets them as "'antiphonal' singing."

280.　See F. I. Andersen, "A Lexicographical Note on Exodus xxxii 18," *VT* 16
(1966): 108–12.

281.　A. Deen, "The Goddess Anath and some Biblical Hebrew Cruces," *JTS* 23
(1978): 25–30.

282.　See Gen 16:6; Deut 8:16; Num 29:7; Isa 3:4.

283.　Deut 21:12; 22:24, 29. Weinfeld (*Deuteronomic School*, 268) argues that
עָנָה, even in the Piel form, does not necessarily imply rape. He notes that Targum
Jonathan and Rashbam interpret אנתא in Deut 21:14 as "since you've already had
sex with her."

284.　Gen 37:2; Judg 19:24; 20:5; 2 Sam 13:12, 14, 22, 32; Ezek 22:11; Lam
5:11.

285.　This meaning of the Qal form of עָנָה III is based on the fact that the Piel
conjugation has the causative and factual meaning of the matching Qal form. On the
causative meaning of Piel, see GKC §141.

286.　S. Morag, "Question of the Uniqueness of Hosea's Language: Semantic
and Lexical Traits," *Tarbiz* 53 (1984): 489–510 (esp. 497 n. 31) (Hebrew).

287.　N. Hacham, "'anna," *Tarbiz* 69 (2000): 144–45 (Hebrew).

relations."[288] Therefore, the verb עִינָּה can be translated literally as "having sexual relations."

Here, the word עַנּוֹת (the last instance, the Piel form of עָנָה) in Exod 32:18 can be interpreted in two ways: "to sing (a kind of joyful cry)" and "to have sexual relations."[289] In light of these data, taking into consideration the verb צִיחֵק, we can describe the cultic phase in the golden calf narrative in a number of ways: (1) cultic athletics/dancing and singing (cries of joy); (2) engaging in sexual relations; or (3) an event combining ritual singing and dancing and sexual activity. Sasson claims that the cultic affair depicted in Exod 32 fits the first definition. In asserting that ancient Near Eastern cultic practice included (ritual) meals, followed by athletic activities, pantomime, and antiphonic song, he suggests that the cultic festivities in Exod 32 were an "orderly ritual."[290] However, the weak point in his argument is that while he views the cultic scene in Exod 32 as an "orderly ritual," he fails to present evidence or examples from biblical sources in support of this contention, and cites only ancient Near Eastern texts, such as documents from Akkad and Mari. Moreover, if we truly were talking about an "orderly ritual" to YHWH, there would be no cause for the narrator (the Elohist) to include v. 25: "And when Moses saw that the people were broken loose—for Aaron had let them loose for a derision among their enemies." What factor here would subject Israel to "derision" by its enemies? We could perhaps attribute it to the construction of the golden calf by the Israelites. And yet cultic idols were very common in the nations surrounding Israel, and could not have been the reason for such derision. A more plausible reason might be related to the people's behavior in relation to the calf image, in light of the expression פָּרוּעַ הוּא ("broken loose," "wild," "out of control," "unbridled"). The adjective פָּרוּעַ is the active present participle of the verb פָּרַע which means "to let loose," or "let unbridled." Thus, the

288. In these verses, the young woman is stoned to death because she did not turn the incident into a rape but rather cooperated ("because she cried not, being in the city"). See ibid. (esp. 442).

289. Other attempts have been made to explain the third עַנּוֹת. R. Edelmann ("To *ʿannôt* Exodus xxxii 18," *VT* 16 [1966]: 355) prefers to see it not as a verb, but rather a vocalization error in writing the name Anath, the Canaanite goddess. He is supported in this view by Whybray ("ענות in Exodus xxxii 18," *VT* 17 [1967]: 122), who claims that the pronunciation of עַנּוֹת, as it appears in the place name Beth Anoth in Josh 15:59, can be considered an idiomatic variant of Anath. However, this suggestion is not particularly convincing, since the cult of the goddess Anath is barely acknowledged in the Bible, and it is highly implausible that the sound heard by Moses and Joshua would be the voice of the goddess Anath.

290. See Sasson, "Worship of the Golden Calf," 151–59 (esp. 152).

expression פָּרוּעַ הוּא refers to lawless, uninhibited or wild behavior. For this reason, Moberly claims that Exod 32:6b depicts an orgiastic fertility cult:[291] "If the people cast off restraint in the presence of an image which was the symbol of fertility, the implications are obvious."[292] However, Moberly's suggestion that the people's misbehavior in the presence of the calf image obviously points to a fertility cult is unlikely, unless we also assume that the sexual activity was engaged in as part of a fertility cult that was known to exist in Israel or Canaan. We need to determine whether the sexual activity referred to took place in an atmosphere of sexual licentiousness, induced by intoxication, or rather in the context of ritualism intended to ensure fertility. For the time being, the only thing we are sure of is that the cultic affair depicted in Exod 32, as inferred from the use of the word פָּרוּעַ ("uncontrolled") differs from the practice of the normal Yahwistic cult.

It was the Elohist who condemned the calf image and its worship. Yet the polemic surrounding the calf image did not begin before the end of the ninth century B.C.E. As far as we know, the prophet Hosea, who was active during the eighth century B.C.E., was the first to criticize the calf cult, as we have found no evidence of anyone who indulged in polemics against it before him, not even Elijah or Jehu. This fact allows us to infer that, at the very least, there was a neutral or positive attitude toward the cult of the calf image. This inference is accordant with the analysis that Exod 32:4b–5 reflects the positive attitude toward the calf cult that prevailed at Bethel in the time of the Elohist. If this is the case, what caused the Elohist and Hosea to take up a negative attitude toward the calf cult? What was the background of the change from the positive image of the calf to the negative one of a pagan god? If, indeed, sexual relations were engaged in during worship, did this take place as part of a fertility cult?

In the next chapter (Chapter 4), I will deal with these concerns via an analysis of those texts in the book of Hosea that are relevant to the polemic surrounding the calf image and its cult.

3.2. *The Polemic of the Deuteronomist*
The Elohistic version of the polemics surrounding the calf image was altered by the Deuteronomist. Based on what we have seen above, the Deuteronomist reinterpreted the Elohist's account from his theological

291.   R. W. L. Moberly, *At the Mountain of God* (JSOTSup 22; Sheffield: JSOT, 1983), 46. This argument was advanced previously by scholars such as Noth, *Exodus*, 248; Cassuto, *Commentary*, 413–14; and Hyatt, *Exodus*, 305.
292.   Moberly, *Mountain of God*, 196 n. 7.

perspective. However, in contrast to the Elohist, whose critique of the calf image was carried out on the basis of the aspiration to "exclusive worship of YHWH," namely, the wholesale rejection of other gods and the prohibition of their worship, the Deuteronomist embarks upon a polemic against the golden calf from an aniconic point of view, which insists on the prohibition of the making of images.

If for a particular reason the calf image, which started out as a pedestal of YHWH, became an image (or representation) of YHWH or of other god, which god did it represent? YHWH or a pagan god? According to the Elohist, who derides the calf image from the perspective of the prohibition of the worship of other gods, the calf was a representation of a pagan god. However, when the Deuteronomist comes to denounce the calf from the perspective of the law forbidding the image, the image that he wishes to prohibit is that of YHWH, as we have seen the above sections (§§2.2.2.1–4). In other words, for him the calf image is considered a representation of YHWH. In Chapter 5, this fact will be reinforced through an examination of Deut 4–5, which are linked to L–2.

In any case, it appears that the Deuteronomist's critique of the calf image is closely related to the historical background of the crystallization of the law prohibiting the image. In Chapter 5, I will investigate this motive through an examination of the nature of the commandment forbidding the image and the historical background to its crystallization.

Chapter 4

HOSEA AND THE CALF IMAGE

The calf image in Israel had its origins in the cult at Bethel, where it served as a cultic appurtenance in the worship of an aniconic YHWH, that is, it served as the pedestal of the invisible YHWH. However, the Elohist, who wrote the narrative of the golden calf, criticized the calf image and its cult as a violation of the injunction prohibiting the worship of other gods. I have already deduced from such that the calf image was perceived by the Elohist as representing a foreign god. What, then, was the factor that caused him to judge the calf image as such? In order to provide an answer to this question, we should first of all direct attention to the fact that the Elohist attributes the fall of the northern kingdom in Exod 32:35 to the sin of the golden calf.[1] Also from the perspective of the Deuteronomist in the books of Kings, Jeroboam's sin of the golden calf is regarded as a religious factor in the demise of the northern kingdom of Israel.[2] According to 1 Kgs 16:33, King Ahab committed a sin greater than all the kings of Israel before him, including undoubtedly Jeroboam ben Nebat. His sin, of course, was worshipping Baal (v. 32). It is logical, therefore, that the Deuteronomist would blame him for the downfall of Israel. To this assumption one could respond that Baal worship was eradicated by Jehu (2 Kgs 10:18–28), and that therefore the Deuteronomist did not attribute responsibility to it and Ahab for the demise of Israel. However, there is some doubt regarding the account in 2 Kgs 10:28, according to which Baal worship was wholly abolished by Jehu. Such an account seems naïve. Apparently, Jehu's reforms were not as systematic as portrayed in the text, and he did not totally root out Baal worship.[3] Religion is not an entity that can be cut down once and for all

---

1. The word וַיִּגֹּף ("struck [with a plague]," from the root נָגַף) in v. 35 hints at the punishment for the sin of the calf image, namely, the fall of the northern kingdom of Israel. See H. D. Preuss, *Old Testament Theology*, vol. 1 (trans. L. G. Perdue; Edinburgh: T. & T. Clark, 1996), 77–78.

2. See 2 Kgs 17:12–23 (esp. 16, 21–23); 2 Kgs 10:29. See also §1 of Chapter 2.

3. Smith, *Early History of God*, 73. On the political circumstances surrounding Jehu's reforms, see H. Donner, "The Separate States of Israel and Judah," in *Israelite*

through political repression. This view is corroborated by archaeological evidence: the names Baal[4] and YHWH appear in the same group of texts in the Kuntillet ʿAjrud inscriptions, which are attributed to the northern kingdom of Israel in the eighth and ninth centuries B.C.E.[5] These findings attest to the fact that Baal worship persisted in Israel even after Jehu's revolution.[6] Also the fact that the prophet Jeremiah attributes the fall of northern Israel to the sin of Baal worship (Jer 23:13)[7] reinforces the credibility of the evidence.

and Judaean History (ed. J. H. Mays and M. M. Miller; Philadelphia: Westminster, 1977), 407–13; G. W. Ahlström, "The Battle of Ramoth-Gilead in 841 B.C.," in *"Wünschet Jerusalem Frieden": Collected Communications to the 12th Congress of the International Organization for the Study of the Old Testament, Jerusalem 1986* (ed. M. Augustin and K. D. Schunk; New York: Lang, 1988), 157–66.

4. For example, "Baruch Baal" (ברכ בעל).

5. In the beginning, some scholars, including Meshel, who was the first to conduct a dig at Kuntillet ʿAjrud (see Z. Meshel, *A Religious Centre from the Time of the Judaean Monarchy on the Border of Sinai* [Israel Museum Catalogue 175; Jerusalem: Israel Museum, 1978]), thought that the site belonged to the Kingdom of Judah due to its location some 50 kilometers south of Kadesh-Barnea. However, today almost all of the prominent scholars, and even Meshel himself ("Two Aspects in the Excavation of Kuntillet ʿAjrud," in *Ein Gott allein?* [ed. W. Dietrich and M. A. Klopfenstein; Göttingen: Vandenhoeck & Ruprecht, 1994], 99–104), support the attribution of the inscriptions to Israel in the eighth and ninth centuries B.C.E., based on the following considerations: (1) -יו, a theophoric component of all the first names in the Kuntillet ʿAjrud inscriptions, is a form characteristic of the north, as opposed to -יהו, which was common in Judah (see Meshel, "Two Aspects," 101–2; B. A. Mastin, "Yahweh's Asherah, Inclusive Monotheism and the Question of Dating," in *In Search of Pre-Exilic Israel: Proceedings of the Oxford Old Testament Seminar* [ed. J. Day; JSOTSup 406; London: T&T Clark International, 2004], 330–32); (2) the inscription יהוה שמרנ (YHWH of Samaria) in a blessing on a jar indicates that the blessing was written by a person who worshipped YHWH in Samaria (Mastin, "Yahweh's Asherah"; Meshel, "Two Aspects," 101); (3) according to Ahituv, the ascription of the site to Israel accords well with the biblical tradition of Elijah's journey to Horeb (see S. Ahituv, *Handbook of Ancient Hebrew Inscriptions from the Period of the First Commonwealth and the Beginning of the Second Commonwealth [Hebrew, Philistine, Edomite, Moabite, Ammonite and the Bileam Inscription]* [Jerusalem: Mosad Bialik, 1992], 152). Meshel (ibid., 103) suggests that the inscriptions were written around 800 B.C.E., during the reign of Jehoahaz, the king of Israel who defeated Amaziah, king of Judah (2 Kgs 14:1–16; 2 Chr 25:1–24).

6. On this point, Y. Kaufmann's claim (*The Religion of Israel* [trans. M. Greenberg; Chicago: University of Chicago Press, 1960], 368–71) that the "Baalim" (or "Baal") in Hos 1–3 refer to those before Jehu, and therefore that Hos 1–3 has no connection to the historical situation in the eighth century B.C.E., is unconvincing.

7. See Smith, *Early History of God*, 75. Cf. n. 87 on Jer 23:13 in §4 of Chapter 1.

If this is the case, why does the Deuteronomist create the impression that Baal worship was totally eradicated only in the northern kingdom by not mentioning Baal worship in northern Israel after the days of Jehu (2 Kgs 11–17),[8] despite the fact that Baal worship was also suppressed in Judah (2 Kgs 11).[9] Apparently, this account is related to the special intent of the Deuteronomist that is suggested in 2 Kgs 10:29: "However, he did not turn away from the sins of Jeroboam the son of Nebat, which he had caused Israel to commit, the golden calves that were in Bethel, and that were in Dan." This verse implies that the reason why the Deuteronomist portrays Jehu as the one who utterly abolished Baal worship, but left the golden calves of Jeroboam, is his desire to emphasize that the fall of Israel came not as a result of Baal worship, but rather Jeroboam's calves. In other words, it seems that when the Deuteronomist described the reason for the downfall of Israel in theological terms in 2 Kings, he stressed the sin of the golden calf, rather than Baal worship. It is possible that the real reason behind the Deuteronomist's attribution of the demise of Israel to the sin of the calf is his desire to condemn Jeroboam for causing the division of the united kingdom of Israel and the disintegration of cultic unification.

If the Baal cult was not fully eradicated by Jehu but rather continued after him, it clearly could have influenced religious life among the people to such an extent that the prophet Jeremiah viewed it as a major factor leading to the fall of the Kingdom of Israel, as indicated in Jer 23:13. Therefore, it appears that the Baalism had an influence on the people, and caused them to view the calf not as a pedestal of YHWH, but rather as an image of God (or a god) himself. Hence, the origin of the Elohistic polemic around the calf image and its cult is located here. One can, then, inquire into the polemic of the Elohist against the calf image and its link to the cult of Baal through an examination of the verses dealing with the calf image in the book of Hosea. These verses include criticism of both the cult of Baal and the calf image. Before looking at these verses, however, we must first answer the question of whether the book of Hosea includes the messages of the historical Hosea of the eighth century B.C.E., and examine the relationship between the Elohist and Hosea; a consideration of the fundamental motive behind the Elohist's polemic against the calf image through the book of Hosea presupposes that there is a close relation between them.

---

8. For example, Kaufmann, *Religion of Israel*, 369.

9. For accounts indicating that Baal worship continued in Judah after the destruction of the Baal temple administered by the priest Jehoiada, see 2 Kgs 21:3; 23:4–5.

1. *The Essential Considerations for Arguments in the Chapter*

1.1. *The Authenticity of the Book of Hosea*

The majority of the book of Hosea, it appears, contains Hosea's prophecies or those of his disciples. However, many scholars claim that the later
additions were inserted by the Deuteronomists who copied and edited
Hosea's original words, and even incorporated into them new ideas that
matched the period and the atmosphere in which they lived. In the opinion of Fontaine,[10] the words of the prophet were collected and preserved
by his disciples who fled to Judah when the Assyrians destroyed their
capital, Samaria, and exiled the nobility of Israel. It is also possible that
his prophecies were reorganized, and that prophecies were added to them
by the Deuteronomistic editors even at the beginning of the seventh
century B.C.E. and during the Babylonian exile, when Hosea's words
became especially relevant to those who wished to understand the
meaning of Judah's suffering. Therefore, it is difficult to reconstruct
Hosea's original utterances.

Our main interest here is in clarifying whether the messages in the
book of Hosea reflect the religious setting in the eighth century B.C.E.,
and whether their original source is from Hosea, the prophet who lived
during that time. I will argue that the book of Hosea's messages, and
above all its criticism of Baal worship at the time, should be attributed to
Hosea himself, while not denying that the book of Hosea underwent
editing processes. The view that the book of Hosea should not be
ascribed to the prophet himself is based on the supposition that the book
was composed by two authors who lived during different periods.
According to this view, the book of Hosea was formed in different units.
To a large extent, scholars divide the book into two parts: (1) chs. 1–3;
and (2) chs. 4–14.[11] According to Kaufmann, this division is based on

10. C. R. Fontaine, "Hosea," in *A Feminist Companion to the Latter Prophets*
(ed. A. Brenner; Sheffield: Sheffield Academic, 1995), 40–69 (esp. 40–41).

11. Wolff (*Hosea*, xxix–xxxii), along with other scholars such as Andersen and
Freedman, subdivide the second part into 4:1–11:11 and 12:1–14:10. Kaufmann
(*Religion of Israel*, 368–71) and H. L. Ginsberg ("Hosea, Book of," *EncJud* 8:1010–
24) claim that chs. 1–3 are the work of various prophets from the ninth century
B.C.E.; Kaufmann (*Religion of Israel*, 368–77) even went as far as to term chs. 1–2
"First Hosea" and chs. 4–14 "Second Hosea." F. I. Andersen and D. N. Freedman
(*Hosea* [AB 24; Garden City, N.Y.: Doubleday, 1980], 61–64) argue that chs. 1:2–
3:5 have a different literary-historical background; they hypothesize that there was
another hand involved that dealt with collecting and compiling, based on the
statistical data related to the use of prepositions (especially in the case of 2:2–23, in
which there is a large number of prosaic prepositions).

the literary difference between the two units, which were written by two different authors (First Hosea and Second Hosea).[12] As Kaufmann suggests, chs. 1–3 describe a series of events, while in chs. 4–14 there is no chronological chain, but rather an accumulation of fervid condemnations, arguments, threats, revisions, and hopes.[13] The reason that Kaufmann attributes chs. 1–3 to First Hosea and chs. 4–14 to Second Hosea is located in the assumption that Baal worship existed in the time of First Hosea but not in the time of Second Hosea. According to this method, while Baal worship is described in chs. 1–3 as a contemporary sin, in chs. 4–14 it is described as a sin of the past (9:10; 11:2; 13:1). In Kaufman's view, Baal worship was eradicated "once and for all" in the time of King Jehu (2 Kgs 10:28),[14] that is, prior to the middle of the ninth century B.C.E. Hence, for Kaufmann "Ephraim," who is described with the words "but when he became guilty through Baal, he died," in Hos 13:1, refers to the dynasty of Ahab, which was annihilated by Jehu (2 Kgs 9–10).

However, the name Ephraim, which appears 35 times in Hosea, never refers to a specific dynasty, but rather always serves to represent the northern kingdom of Israel,[15] or as a name for Samaria, which represents the northern kingdom of Israel (7:1) or the region of the tribe of Ephraim in the land of Israel (5:9; 11:8). Therefore, the phrase "(Ephraim)…he died" is interpreted as "(Ephraim)…was considered as good as dead," in the words of Ibn Ezra.[16] Furthermore, it is illogical to interpret Ephraim as the Ahab dynasty since, in such a case, he could not have existed after Jehu, and could not have comprised the subject of the sentence "And now they sin more and more, and have made them molten images of their silver," in 13:2. That is to say, the implication of "he died" is not the final eradication of "Ephraim," because the "and now" in 13:2 presupposes Ephraim's existence. Accordingly the dynasty of Ahab, which was ostensibly annihilated by Jehu, cannot be "Ephraim." Therefore, we can conclude that Ephraim here refers to the remnants of the northern kingdom of Israel after the attack of Tiglath-pileser in 733 B.C.E.[17] In turn, we may infer that Baal worship persisted in the northern kingdom of

---

12. See Kaufmann, *Religion of Israel*, 368–77.

13. Ibid., 368–69.

14. See ibid., 369.

15. For example, 5:3, 5, 12, 14; 6:4; 10:11, etc.

16. Related to this point, it is worth mentioning Andersen and Freedman's (*Hosea*, 630) interpretation that "to say that Ephraim 'died,'…could mean that they received the death sentence."

17. See Wolff, *Hosea*, 91.

Israel even after the reign of Jehu. Archaeological evidence[18] supports the hypothesis that Baal worship was not wholly eradicated by Jehu and that it continued long after his time.

Recently, Yee has suggested that the history of the composition of the book of Hosea is more complex.[19] Yee thinks that Hosea complained only of the political alliances of the northern kingdom with its neighbors. It is her contention that Hosea imagined the immoral behavior of leaders, such as the priests, the king, and the princes, as embodied in the personage of Rachel. What Hosea describes as Rachel's harlotry is the alliances that the northern kingdom established with foreign forces, and the schemes that accompanied such alliances. A collector[20] gathered together the prophecies of Hosea (probably after the fall of Samaria in 721–722 B.C.E., during the time of Hezekiah's reforms), and reinterpreted them; he added ch. 1, along with a number of comments to ch. 2. As a result of his editing, Rachel was transformed from the Israelite matriarch to the unfaithful wife of Hosea, Gomer, and Rachel's children from the ten tribes of Israel into the three children of Hosea. Thus the collector created a metaphor of marriage between God and Israel, with all its associated imagery. After the collector, the first redactor (R1—who must be dated to the period of Josiah's reforms in Judah), who was steeped in Deuteronomistic theology, was deeply interested in cultic practice and customs. He reinterpreted the "harlotry" of the people (which referred to alliances with foreigners in the original tradition of Hosea), and turned it into a sinful cult. The Baalim (הַבְּעָלִים), rather than the foreign nations, became the elicit lovers of the mother. The second redactor (R2),[21] who was responsible for the final version of the book of Hosea, was a Deuteronomist. He was concerned about the disastrous event of the exile. He reformulated the tradition, revised the work of the first redactor (R1), and introduced into the text for the first time the motif of the journey, so as to fit the people's repentance and their return to the Land from exile.[22] In sum, according to Yee, the redactors of the book of Hosea gave a crude

---

18. In the following section I will examine in detail the archaeological evidence, which shows that Baal worship continued in Israel after King Jehu.

19. See G. Yee (*Composition and Tradition in the Book of Hosea* [Atlanta: Scholars Press, 1987], 305–17) for a summary and conclusions.

20. Yee (ibid., 112) terms the author of First Hosea "collector." According to Yee, the author of First Hosea fulfilled an important role in the literary construction of the book of Hosea.

21. According to Yee, the second redactor is close to the second Deuteronomist (Dtr2) during the exile.

22. Ibid., 129–30.

religious interpretation to the original message of the prophet who, as aforesaid, dealt exclusively with political life in the northern kingdom.

However, the assertion that Hosea originally directed the word זְנוּת ("harlotry") against politics rather than religion in the kingdom, based on Hos 8:9–10, is a baseless theory. Also groundless is the claim that Hosea personified in the figure of Rachel the harlotrous character of the leadership. Not a word regarding זְנוּת appears in the verses suggested by Yee, and in them the leaders' character is condemned.[23] Moreover, if the first redactor really was steeped in Deuteronomistic theology, it is implausible that he would transform Hosea's political prophecies into descriptions of cultic practices, since Deuteronomic/Deuteronomistic theology was not interested in cultic practices.[24] Therefore, Yee's view that the book of Hosea in its present form is the result of the distortions of redactors from the Deuteronomistic theological school is unconvincing.[25]

I will now examine the verses and expressions that scholars attribute to the redactors of the book of Hosea from Judah (or to the Deuteronomists). The verses are as follows: (1) references to the unification of the kingdoms in 2:1–3 (EV 1:10–2:1) and 3:5, which in the opinion of scholars were added in the days of Josiah as a result of the expansion of the northern kingdom (2 Kgs 23:15–20); (2) elaboration of the redemption oracles introduced by the expression "in that day" in 2:18–22 (EV 16–20), 23–25 (EV 21–23); (3) references to the redemption of Judah (1:7) and condemnations of it (5:5; 6:11; 8:14), which were added in order to apply Hosea's words to life in Judah during the seventh century B.C.E.; and (4) the title (1:1) and the proverbial epilogue (14:9, 10). However, we find some grounds that these verses are not to be attributed to redactors from Judah.

First, there is no reason to view that the prophecies regarding the unification of the two kingdoms emanated from Judah. Instead, they call for the wellbeing of all the people of God who came out of Egypt, journeyed through the desert, and conquered the Land (2:16–17 [EV 14–15]; 9:10; 12:14; 13:5).[26] In these prophecies (2:1–3 [EV 1:10–2:1]; 3:5), there is a repetition of Hosea's vision that the end will be like the beginning, only

---

23. The priests: 5:1; 6:9; the king: 7:3, 5; 8:10; the princes: 7:3, 5; 8:10.

24. See Weinfeld, *Deuteronomy 1–11*, 37–44 (esp. 37, 40). As we saw in the comparison of the texts of Exod 32 and L–2 (in Deut 9:7–10:11), the Deuteronomist removed all of the expressions (such as "bowed" and "sacrificed") and verses (1–6, 17–18) related to cultic practices from the original text, namely Exod 32.

25. Yee does not identify the editors of the book of Hosea with the Deuteronomists (Dtr1 and Dtr2), but claims that the first was influenced by the theology of the Deuteronomistic school.

26. See D. A. Hubbard, *Hosea* (Leicester: Inter-Varsity, 1989), 31.

better. The use of the term "return" (שׁוּב, 2:9 [EV 2:7]; 3:5; 14:2–3) suggests such a connotation. The expression לֹא עַמִּי ("not my people") in
1:9–2:1 (EV 1:10) points, already at the outset of the book, to the
concepts of judgment and redemption that shape it as a whole. If the
Israelites reunite, and return to the way as they were in the beginning,
they will have a leader—"one head" (2:2 [EV 1:11); this "one head"
cannot be forged on the model of Jeroboam ben Nebat and his heirs, who
supported the mode of worship rejected by Hosea. "David," then, was the
only worthy model (3:5).[27] Moreover, the view that 2:1–3 (EV 1:10–2:1)
and 3:5 are original depends on the argument that the thought included in
these verses is consistent with views expressed in other places by Hosea.[28]
Indeed, the verses constitute a summarization of YHWH's judgment, as
declared by Hosea: Israel's growth, in accordance with the growth of
their sin, will cease (4:10; 9:12, 16; 14:1 [EV 13:16]); the covenant will
be nullified; the Syro-Ephraimite war is an event that attests to YHWH's
wrath (5:8–14); and even the Land will become infertile (2:11 [EV 2:9],
12 [EV 10], 14 [EV 12]; 4:3).[29]

Secondly, it appears that the unit 2:18–25 (EV 16–23) is related to
2:16–17 (EV 14–15) for the following reasons: (1) the orientation of both
passages is toward the future; (2) in both passages, the Baalim and
YHWH's new name אִישִׁי ("my husband," 2:18 [EV 16]) are mentioned,
and are undoubtedly a continuation of 2:4–15 (EV 2–13); (3) in both
passages an entering into a covenant with animals is described (2:20 [EV
18]), which is the opposite of the threats mentioned in 2:14 (EV 12) and
4:3; (4) the final restoration, described in 2:23–25 (EV 21–23), uses the
themes of YHWH's gifts to Israel (2:10–11 [EV 8–9]), of the effect of
Israel's response to YHWH's courting of them (2:16 [EV 14]), and of the
names of Hosea's children (1:2–9; 2:3 [EV 1]). The passage 2:18–25 (EV
16–23) is related to 2:4–17 (EV 2–15) and 1:2–9. It is similar in content
and style to the biographical section in 1:2–9. On the assumption that
such a link exists between 2:18–25 (EV 16–23) and 1:2–9, a basis is
established for attributing the first text to Hosea himself or his disciples.
God's revelation and words to Hosea in 1:2–9 are best understood as a
reflection of Hosea's experiences related to his marriage and the names
of his children.[30] This marriage comprises a parable of the people's
infidelity to YHWH, and the names of Hosea's children serve as messages

27. See G. I. Emmerson (*Hosea: An Israelite Prophet in Judean Perspective*
[Sheffield: JSOT, 1984], 98–113) for arguments relating to structure, language, and
contents that show that 3:5 "belongs to the primary stratum of materials" (p. 113).
28. See Rudolph, *Hosea*, 56.
29. See Macintosh, *Hosea*, 34.
30. Ibid., 9.

to the nation, as in the case of the prophet Isaiah (Isa 7:3; 8:3). However, the description of Hosea receiving YHWH's message written in the third person might imply that 1:2–9 was composed by his disciples.[31]

Thirdly, we find in Hosea verses referring to Judah (1:1, 7, 11; 4:15; 5:5, 10, 12, 13, 14; 6:11; 8:14; 10:11; 12:1, 3). Undeniably, among the verses there are some that are supposed to be a comment or addendum by the Judean editor.[32] However, this is insufficient cause for claiming that all of the verses are the result of later editing, or for ruling out the hypothesis that Hosea himself was interested in Judah and its future relations with Israel. And it is quite possible that some of the references to Judah could have come from the prophet himself.[33] Hosea's commitment to the covenant, which he sees as relevant to all of YHWH's people, should have caused him to apply its judgments and blessings to Judah as well as to the tribes of northern Israel from which he came.[34]

Fourthly, the heading (1:1) suggests that it is probably an addition of the Judean editor, since in the list of kings related to the period of Hosea's activity, the Judean kings are given preference. Finally, that the general messages in the book of Hosea were of Hosea himself could be ascertained through the message in the prologue and epilogue of the book: the message begins with wordplay on Jezreel[35] and ends with the

---

31. Mays, *Hosea*, 47, states: "The skillful way in which the material is ordered… suggests that the work was done by a contemporary disciple, if not by the prophet himself." Emmerson (*Hosea: An Israelite Prophet*, 21–40) claims that the salvation speeches came originally from Hosea (or from a close disciple), and are not a product of editing in Judah after Hosea's time. The arrangement of the sayings, in any case, points to the Judean editor, who sought to emphasize national repentance more than divine sovereignty. See also D. J. A. Clines ("Hosea 2; Structure and Interpretation," *StudBib* 1 [1978]: 83–103).

32. In 1:1; 4:15; 5:6; 6:11; 10:11, the term "Judah" does not fit the context.

33. For a discussion of this question, see R. E. Clements, "Understanding the Book of Hosea," *RevExp* 72 (1975): 417–19.

34. Emmerson (*Hosea: An Israelite Prophet*) comes to the conclusion that the references to Judah's salvation in 1:7 (p. 95), 1:11 (p. 98), and perhaps 12:1 (pp. 115–16) are attributable to Hosea, as well as references in the context of the Syro-Ephraimite war (Israel–Assyrian coalition against Judah) in 5:10–14 (p. 70), and the pronouncement of the judgment in 8:14 (p. 77). She reads the name "Judah" in 6:4 and 12:3 as a scribal substitute for "Israel" (pp. 65, 71) and is uncertain about the judgment threat in 6:11. She attributes 4:15 (p. 80) and 5:5 (p. 67) to the Judean editor's reaction on the basis of their structure, and arrives at the conclusion that one aim of the Judean editing was to condemn Judah for imitating the sins of Israel.

35. See 1:4; 2:2 (EV 1:11), 24–25 (EV 22–23). Hosea's wordplay on the name Jezreel (יִזְרְעֶאל), a name derived from the verb זָרַע ("to scatter, to sow") and thereby

metaphor of the fruitful cypress tree (14:9 [EV 8]). Hosea reminds Israel, in numerous prophecies, that YHWH is the only source throughout their lives, and therefore the use in the epilogue of the image of fertility to describe YHWH's authority provides support for those who insist on the uniformity of the book. Regarding the proverbial epilogue, it should be noted that Hosea uses proverbs to stress or encapsulate his message at critical points.[36] Verse 10 (EV 9) is not an exception to this rule, and serves as a final emphasis and recapitulation of the words of prophecy. Hence, the epilogue in 14:10 is merely a final accentuation regarding the "knowledge of God," and the main point that he attempts to elucidate here is the spiritual blindness of the Israelites.[37]

The above observations may lead to the conclusion that most of the messages in the book of Hosea are those of the prophet Hosea, and therefore, in my opinion, one should read the book as reflective of the historical situation prevailing during the days of the prophet himself. The book of Hosea comprises a testimony to the actions and statements of Hosea, the prophet of the eighth century B.C.E. The religious and cultic environment depicted in the book is also dated to this period. It can be assumed that others played a role in the editing process leading to the final text, but I cannot concur with Fontaine or Yee in their attribution of the message of the book to the work of the final editor. I find myself in agreement with Jeremias that (1) the message of the book of Hosea was basically complete before it was reinterpreted for the public in Judah; and (2) this reinterpretation did not alter the book (or the message) in substance.[38]

1.2. *Hosea and the Elohist*

Hosea was one of the prophets of the eighth century B.C.E. from the northern kingdom of Israel. The references to Jeroboam ben Joash in 1:4 show that Hosea began to preach no later than 745 B.C.E. The list of the kings of Judah, and especially the reference to King Hezekiah (715–687 or 725–697) in 1:1, suggest that Hosea was active until the final years

linked to the Exile (i.e. God's scattering the Israelites to foreign countries), predicts God's impending judgment on northern Israel in the prologue.

36. See 4:9, 11, 15; 8:7.

37. Hosea features not only the basic principle of religious corruption, but also the idea that redemption from corruption depends on "knowledge of God." Regarding the former, see 2:10 (EV 8); 4:1, 6; 5:4; 11:3; and regarding the latter 2:20; 6:3, 6; 8:2; 13:4; 14:10.

38. See J. R. Porter ("The Supposed Deuteronomistic Redaction of the Prophets," in *Schöpfung und Befreiung* [ed. R. Albertz et al.; Stuttgart: Calwer, 1989], 69–78 [esp. 71–76]), who asserts that, in Hosea, the verses attributed to Deuteronomistic editing reflect their proto-deuteronomistic character.

prior to the fall of Samaria.[39] Jeroboam ben Joash (787–747 B.C.E.) was a very dominant king: he recovered the territory lost by his predecessors in Transjordan (2 Kgs 25–28), and his reign is presented in the Bible as a period of security and prosperity (Amos 3:15; 5:11; 6:1, 4–6, 13). Yet, in spite of his notable accomplishments—which included military and diplomatic successes outside of his country,[40] security, stability, and domestic prosperity—he failed to escape furious attacks by the prophets Amos and Hosea due to his religious and social misdeeds.[41] Unlike Amos, who places emphasis on the disparity between the covenant's requirements in the socio-economic sphere and their actual implementation (see Amos 2:6–15, as well as a number of other verses in the book), Hosea speaks passionately about religious obligation and cultic practices, and denounces what he sees going on around him in his day as idolatry and acts of heresy, which are undoubtedly the product of syncretism with the Baal worship.[42] Although Amos probably implies the calf image,[43] we should actually focus on Hosea in this matter, since he was the one who seemingly initiated the condemnation of the calf image, whose worship he perceived as a violation of Israel's covenant with YHWH. In other words, Hosea condemns the calf image from a religious perspective. According to Hosea, the syncretism of the worship of YHWH with that of Baal is the basic reason why the calf image is transformed into Israel's sin.

---

39. G. I. Davies, *Hosea* (NCBC; London: Marshall Pickering, 1992), 24–25. Andersen and Freedman (*Hosea*, 35) argue rather unconvincingly that the central themes of the book of Hosea and most of his religious sermonizing match approximately the decade 750–740 B.C.E., or perhaps more roughly the period between 755/50–745/40, during which the first major crisis occurred in the northern kingdom. This claim may be refuted (see Wolff, *Hosea*, 21) not only due to the tremendous political difficulties that occurred after the fall of the dynasty of Jehu (1:4; 3:4), but also due to Hosea's words related to the critical events of the Syro-Ephraimite war (5:8–11), and the conquest of vast territories in Israel by Tiglath-pileser III in 733 B.C.E. (5:14; 7:8–12).

40. During the reign of Jeroboam ben Joash, Israel enjoyed the advantages of the power of the Assyrian Empire, mainly because the Assyrians, under Adad Nirari III, stopped the advancement of the Aramaeans (Syrians) from Damascus resulting in their weakening. As a consequence, Israel expanded territorially, which enabled military and economic development.

41. One could argue that both prophets attack a flagrant violation of the covenant.

42. Andersen and Freedman, *Hosea*, 38.

43. The phrase שֹׁמְרוֹן אַשְׁמַת ("the guilt of Samaria") in Amos 8:14 is interpreted as the "sin" (JB), "shame" (NIV), or "idol" (NAB) of Samaria, and certainly refers to the calf of Samaria. Other verses mention Bethel (Amos 4:4; 5:5; 7:9; 8:14), where the assumption is that the reference is to the calf at Bethel.

Why did this prophet oppose calf worship? My view is that his opposition stemmed from his affinity with the prophetic traditions of Mosaic
religion and law, as preserved within the ancient tribal confederacy. On
this subject, Hosea is traditional: he regards himself as an heir to the
earlier prophets, a link in the chain of YHWH's messengers, extending all
the way back to Moses. Hosea explicitly describes Moses as a prophet in
12:13: "And by a prophet YHWH brought Israel up out of Egypt, and by a
prophet was he kept";[44] the emphasis that he places on the covenant (Hos
2:20 [EV 18]; 6:7; 8:1; also 4:2 and 8:12), as well as the content of the
Ten Commandments and the Law, situates him in the same northern
tradition represented by the narratives of Elijah and Elisha.[45] The Elohist
was also close to the prophetic tradition. For the Elohist, God commu-
nicates with his people through his prophets;[46] through them he expresses
his will. Moses in particular was the great intercessor, who was sent as a
prophet (see Exod 3:10, 12; 20:18, 21; 32:1–14, 30–34). It turns out that
Hosea has a lot in common with the Elohist: period of activity (the eighth
century B.C.E.), land of origin (the northern kingdom of Israel), and theological orientation[47] (rooted in Mosaic Law and the prophetic tradition).

In addition, it appears that Hosea had an idealized image of the priesthood, according to which its essential role was to preserve and teach the
Law of God.[48] *Torah* in the Bible always means "instruction, guidance,"
even when it includes laws.[49] Yet Hosea perceives the Torah not as

44. Jenks, *Traditions*, 113.
45. Ibid., 114.
46. The Elohist emphasizes the distance between God and human beings, who
are liable to fall into sin. For this reason, in his view, God himself is not supposed to
speak with his people directly (see Exod 20:18–20) but rather through prophets,
angels of God (Gen 22:11), or dreams (Gen 20:3, 6). Regarding the theological
characteristics of the Elohist, see Fohrer, *Introduction*, 155–58.
47. Jenks (*Traditions*, 112–17) argues the theological affinities between Hosea
and the Elohist epic as follows: Jacob, Moses, the Covenant, the Golden Calf, the
Wilderness, and the kingship; Hos 4:2 (Exod 20:1–17) / 8:4–5; 10:5–6 (Exod 32;
1 Kgs 12:25–33; 13) / 8:12 (Exod 24:1–3, 11bβ, 12–15α, 18b; 31:18; 32:15–16;
Deut 31:9–11) / 8:13; 9:3; 11:5 (Exod 13:17; 14:12; 17:3; Num 11:20; 14:3; 4) / 9:10
(Num 25:1–5) / 12:3–7, 13 (Gen 15:22–26; 27:43; 28:10–12, 17–18, 20–22; 29:18–
20; 30:31; 31:20) / 12:14 (Exod 3:1–15; 4:10–31; Num 12; Deut 34:10).
48. The teaching of the Torah was the most essential function of the priesthood
(see G. von Rad, *Old Testament Theology*, vol. 1 [trans. D. M. Stalker; Edinburgh:
Oliver & Boyd, 1967], 243ff.; W. Zimmerli, *Old Testament Theology in Outline*
[Edinburgh: T. & T. Clark, 1978], 93–99).
49. See B. J. Schwartz, "Torah from Zion: Isaiah's Temple Vision (Isaiah 2:1–
4)," in *Sanctity of Time and Space in Tradition and Modernity* (ed. A. Houtman, M.
Roorthuis, and J. Schwartz; Leiden: Brill, 1998), 17 n. 13; H.-J. Fabry, "תורה *tôrâ*,"

personal instructions given by the priest, but rather "the entire disclosure of YHWH's will."[50] Accordingly, for Hosea, the Torah mediates between people and the full "knowledge" of God (4:6). Hence, we can say that Hosea expresses for the first time a comprehensive knowledge of Torah, which afterwards becomes a basic assumption in Deuteronomy (17:19; 31:9–12; and cf. 1:5).[51] In Hos 4:4–8, YHWH announces his central indictment against the priesthood. What is the priesthood's transgression? Their sin is that they destroyed the people of YHWH by "rejecting knowledge" and "ignoring the law of their God" (v. 6). "Knowledge" is an abbreviated form of "knowledge of God." The parallel expression with Torah in v. 6 clearly points to its content. For the Israelites, the Torah provided divine guidance on how to conduct one's life, and so the lack of Torah led to the destruction of the covenant people.[52] Therefore, according to Hosea's view of the priesthood in Israel, its primary role was to transmit and teach the Torah.[53] In turn, the priest was accused of neglecting his main duty. Here, accordingly, it is assured that Hosea held a very high view of the priesthood. It appears that this concept of the priesthood, which had its origins in the tribal confederacy, was maintained among the Levitical circles in the north during Hosea's time.[54] It is possible that this group, to which Hosea seemed closely affiliated, comprised a sort of opposition party that was set against the syncretistic cultic practices in the north.[55] This circle probably had a close connection with the prophetic traditions mentioned above. This relationship between the Levites and prophets accounts for Hosea's expertise regarding a large number of the ancient Israelite traditions.[56] In particular, the description of the Levites in Deut 31:9–13 and 33:8–10 hints at this prophetic-Levitical group's affiliation to the Elohist in the polemical narrative of the golden calf, as it is now presented in Exod 32.[57] If Hosea indeed

TDOT 15:609–46 (esp. 611); G. Liedke and C. Peterson, "תורה *tôrâ* instruction," *TLOT* 3:1415–22.

50. Wolff, *Hosea*, 138.
51. Ibid.
52. Mays, *Hosea*, 69.
53. Ibid.
54. Ibid. The priests' monopoly on Torah teaching did end with the Exile (De Vaux, *Ancient Israel*, 354f.).
55. Davies, *Hosea*, 79.
56. Wolff, *Hosea*, 162ff., 172, 196, 234ff.
57. The Elohistic tradition brings the importance of Moses to the fore, and has a close relation to the prophetic tradition (Fohrer, *Introduction*, 156). Eissfeldt (*Hebrew Kingdom*, 203), in particular, notes that Amos, Hosea, and other prophets functioning in northern Israel had an intimate relationship with the Elohistic

belonged to this group, it may be assumed that he had influence on the Elohist and/or was influenced by the Elohist who made the polemical narrative of the golden calf, as it appears in the current text of Exod 32.

2. Baalism and the Calf Image

2.1. Baalism and Yahwism Affected by Baalism
As I contended above, Baalism was the decisive component of the negative image of the calf image in northern Israel in the eighth century B.C.E. The book of Hosea clearly refers to Baal worship in a number of passages. Hosea 2:15 (EV 13) speaks of "the days of the Baalim, when she made sacrifices smoke to them." These festival days are contrasted to the sacred festival days of Israel, such as "her new moons, and her sabbaths, and all her appointed seasons" (2:13 [EV 11)].[58] Although it is possible that Israel's own festivals are included in the expression "days of the Baalim," it is more likely that these were festivals specific to the worship of Baal,[59] held outdoors, in high places, and under "oaks and poplars and terebinths" (4:13).[60] Above all, the references to Baal (2:10 [EV 8], 18 [16]; 13:1) and Baalim (2:19 [EV 17]; 11:2) provide further evidence of the existence of Baal worship in the time of Hosea.

At this point, in order to understand the influence of Baal worship on the Israelite religion, and thereby Hosea's polemical attitude to the calf image, one must compare the text to evidence from archaeological excavations in Israel pertaining to the period of the divided kingdom,

---

tradition. In a comparison of the Elohist source (E) and Hosea, Jenks points out that it may not be concluded that they directly influenced each other, but that the thoughts of both were indeed linked to the northern tradition. Specifically, he argues that the similarity between the two can be found in the prophetic tradition and God's punishment, and that the Elohistic source in fact reflects the early circumstances of the northern tradition, while the book of Hosea reflects the later situation (Jenks, *Traditions*, 117).

58. The word מוֹעֵד indicates a selected time or place. Apparently, in Hos 2:13 (EV 11) the word is generally used to indicate national festivals, such as Passover (Feast of Unleavened Bread), Shavuot, and Succoth. Although there is no mention of Passover or Shavuot in the book of Hosea, it can reasonably be assumed that these festivals were celebrated in the time of Hosea, in light of the references to Succoth (12:10) and the commandment "Three times you shall keep a feast to me in the year" (Feast of Unleavened Bread, Feast of Harvest, and Feast of Ingathering) in Exod 23:14–17 (E). For more information on these festivals, see K. R. Joines, "Feasts and Festivals," *MDB*: 297–98.

59. Cf. 9:5. In Akkadian, *Um ili* means "feast, festival"; cf. *ANET* 434:16.

60. Wolff, *Hosea*, 40.

that is, Iron Age II. The Samaria Ostraca[61] provide evidence attesting to the existence of Baal worship during this period.[62] Among these sherds from the eighth century B.C.E. (that is, more or less contemporary with Hosea), are eleven proper names compounded with YHWH, eight with Baal.[63] It can be argued that Baal names from the Samaria Ostraca should not be used as evidence of the existence of Baal worship, since the name "Baal" could be considered an appellation of YHWH.[64] However, in truth, the distinction between "Baal" as the name of a deity and "baal" as an epithet of YHWH is meaningless when it comes to the situation of syncretism between YHWH and Baal. Hosea 2:18 (EV 16) plays on the term "baal" as an epithet of YHWH and indicates that northern Israelites made no distinction between YHWH and Baal.[65] The verse says: "And in that day, declares YHWH, that you shall call me אִישִׁי ('my husband'), and shall call me no more בַּעְלִי ('my baal,' i.e., 'my lord')."[66] What is peculiar about this verse in contrast to the rest of the book of Hosea is that it implies that YHWH was worshipped as Baal. This is another matter entirely from the prophetic accusations that Baal was worshipped instead

61. These inscriptions—clay sherds, inscribed with ink—were found in 1910 in debris that had been leveled out in order to install a floor for two long storage rooms in the immediate environs of Omri's palace, in the fortress area of Samaria.

62. Miller, *Religion of Ancient Israel*, 57.

63. See A. Lemaire, *Inscriptions hébraiques* (Paris: Cerf, 1977), 55; I. T. Kaufman, "The Samaria Ostraca: An Early Witness to Hebrew Writing," *BA* (1982): 229–39; J. H. Tigay, *You Shall Have No Other Gods: Israelite Religion in the Light of Hebrew Inscriptions* (Atlanta: Scholars Press, 1986), 65–66; J. D. Fowler, *Theophoric Personal Names in Ancient Hebrew* (JSOTSup 49; Sheffield: JSOT, 1988), 54–63, 338; G. I. Davies et al., *Ancient Hebrew Inscriptions: Corpus and Concordance* (Cambridge: Cambridge University Press, 1991), 39–57.

64. Cf. O. Keel and C. Uehlinger, *Gods, Goddesses, and Images of God in Ancient Israel* (Minneapolis: Fortress, 1998), 204–5. Actually, it has long been accepted that "baal" in the biblical onomasticon may have been an epithet of YHWH, synonymous with אָדוֹן ("lord"). See G. B. Gray, *Studies in Hebrew Proper Names* (London: Black, 1896), 141–46; S. R. Driver, *Notes on the Hebrew Text and the Topography of the Books of Samuel* (Oxford: Clarendon, 1960), 253–55.

65. See Andersen and Freedman, *Hosea*, 278–79.

66. According to Wolff (*Hosea*, 49), both אִישִׁי and בַּעַל can have the meaning "husband." Nevertheless, אִישִׁי is probably a term of affection; the husband as one who belongs to, but also enjoys deep personal relations with the wife; see especially Gen 2:23; 3:6, 16. On the other hand, בַּעַל also means "owner," "possessor," or "proprietor," and tends to emphasize the legal position of a husband as lord over his wife (see legal texts such as Num 21:3, 22; Deut 24:4; 32:22). The former definition is more intimate, personal, and general; it indicates the way in which Israel will surrender to YHWH in the fullest sense, like a lover, and not only as a husband to whom she is legally bound.

of YHWH or alongside him; that is, this verse describes a syncretistic cultic practice, in which the two gods were identified with each other, almost as if they were one.[67] In fact, Hos 2:18 (EV 16) is interpreted as meaning that in the time of renewal, that is, in the time of YHWH's judgment or salvation, Israel would neither confuse YHWH with Baal nor turn to the Canaanite deities. Conversely, this verse explains the religious reality in Hosea's time, when Israel confused the two deities.[68] So it is assured that Hos 2:18 (EV 16) is concerned with the use of Baal as an epithet of YHWH in the very dangerous syncretistic state. This is the reason, as is evident in the following verse (2:19 [EV 17]), for the prophet Hosea's appeal for the omission of the name of "Baal" from the Israelite vocabulary, thereby eradicating the worship of all other gods who might bear the name "Baal," as well as the false worship of the one true God, YHWH.[69]

Therefore, the interpretation of the onomastic element בַּעַל in the Samaria Ostraca as an epithet of YHWH cannot be the grounds for denying the Baal cult in the time of Hosea. The name בַּעַל, as embedded in the names inscribed on the Samaria Ostraca, serves as evidence of the existence of Baal worship in Hosea's time. As mentioned by Zimmerli,[70] the Israelites served both YHWH and Baal during the period of the Judges and the early monarchy.[71] In other words, two religions coexisted in the

---

67. Ibid., 82.

68. Ibid., 49; however, according to Mays (*Hosea*, 48), the answer to the question of whether the word בַּעַל was used as an epithet of YHWH, in the sense of "Lord" or rather as the name of the Canaanite god, is unclear; apparently both are correct.

69. Andersen and Freedman, *Hosea*, 279.

70. W. Zimmerli, "Das Bilderverbot in der Geschichte des alten Israel: Goldenes Kalb, Eherne Schlange, Mazzeben und Lade," in *Studien zu Glaube und Geschichte Israels. A. Jepsen zum 70 Geburtstag* (Stuttgart: Calwer, 1971), 56.

71. The Gideon narrative (Judg 6:11–32), which seems to represent the clearest account of the conflict between the devotees of Yahwism and Baalism during the time of settlement, may be acknowledged by almost all as Deuteronomistic material. There are undoubtedly two compositions in Judg 6:11–32 that have been interwoven. The account in 6:11–24 depicts Gideon as a deliverer liberating his people from a foreign oppressor, the Midians, while the narrative of 6:25–32 shows Gideon struggling openly against Baal worshippers. Therefore, Bentzen determines that "a section like 6:25–32 clearly points to a period, characterized by an especially acute contest with Baal-worship, presumably the time of Elijah" (A. Bentzen, *Introduction to the Old Testament*, vol. 2 [Copenhagen: Gad, 1952], 91). In contrast to Bentzen and many other scholars, M. S. Smith (*Early History of God*, 13–14) offers a fascinating interpretation of the Gideon narrative. In his view, the original traditions of Gideon do not speak of a choice between YHWH and Baal, such as that seen in the

life of the Israelites. Such a coexistence of the two religions may cause the people to be free in their use of the name Baal as an epithet of YHWH.[72] The coexistence of the two religions and a custom of free use of the word Baal as an epithet of YHWH could be two sides of the same coin; therefore, in fact, it is hardly possible to decide whether the use of names with the onomastic element בעל and the Yahwistic element יה or יו within the same family points to an epithet of YHWH or to the god Baal.[73] If this is so, names containing the onomastic element בעל may indicate that in Israelite society, including some royal circles, Baal worship was viewed as legitimate. What is certain is that the inclusion of the word בַּעַל into the Israelite cultic jargon, as an epithet of YHWH, contributed to the acceptance of Baal worship, along with its associated practices.

It seems that such syncretistic phenomena among the Israelites were strengthened[74] after the royal court circles of Samaria fell under the influence of Jezebel, the Sidonian queen, who officially imported Baal worship to Israel.[75] The Israelites were inclined toward syncretism and syncretized the Yahwistic cultic practices with those of the Canaanite

period of Elijah, for the name "Jerubbaal" (ירובעל, Judg 6:25–32) is unlikely to be interpreted "Let Baal contend against him," since there is rarely a name that contains a statement directed against its bearer. He, therefore, suggests a very relaxed situation: "Joash" (יואש), who carries a YHWH name, has an altar dedicated to Baal while his son, who carries a Baal name, builds an altar to YHWH. In other words, he sees a coexistence of two religions rather than a conflict.

72. Even in the same family the onomastic elements יה or יו and בעל occur together. For instance, two of Saul's sons were named "Yonathan" (יונתן, 1 Sam 13:16) and "Eshbaal" (אשבעל, 2 Sam 2:8); among David's sons there were "Adoniyah" (אדניה) and "Shephatiah" (שפטיה, 2 Sam 3:4) together with "Beeliada" (בעלידע, 1 Chr 14:7; cf. 2 Sam 5:16).

73. Smith (*Early History of God*, 14–15) suggests three possibilities: an epithet of YHWH, the acceptance of a god, or both.

74. The syncretism of Yahwism and Baalism in Canaan has traditionally been understood as a movement involving only a minority of the Israelites (F. E. Eakin, "Yahwism and Baalism before the Exile," *JBL* 84 [1965]: 407). Also, see Albright, *Stone Age to Christianity*, 281.

75. The fact that Solomon's temple was designed by a Canaanite architect implies that the worship of YHWH could be easily blended with Baalistic cults. Archaeological excavations at Kuntillet ʿAjrud reveal that toward the end of the ninth century also there was a flourishing cult of YHWH, which included the use of the term *baʿal* as an alternative name for YHWH (Andersen and Freedman, *Hosea*, 49). The fact that Elijah stood alone as a Yahwist, without contemporary support (1 Kgs 18–19), shows how syncretism between Yahwism and Baalism, under the royal leadership, prevailed in the ninth century B.C.E.

religions. However, the clear contest between these two ideologies did not come to the fore until the appearance of Elijah, the zealous devotee of YHWH, during the period of the Omri dynasty. In the main, the Israelites ignored this consciousness, even though Eljah declared the absolute separation of the worship of YHWH from the worship of Baal. So the distinction between the two must have been rather blurred.

However, one must admit that the syncretism of Yahwism with Baalism did not reach its culmination until the time of Hosea, who was the first prophet to condemn the calf image as an idol. That is to say, no one officially criticized the calf image before Hosea, not even the zealous Yahwists, Elijah and Jehu. This means that the recognition of the calf image as a pedestal of YHWH[76] was still alive among the Israelites during the time of Elijah and Jehu. Yet, as time went by, the Israelites went after the concrete representation of the deity. Eventually, syncretism in the Israelite religion increased and reached its culmination in the eighth century B.C.E. when the majority of the Israelites came to identify the calf image with the symbol of the deity.

2.2. *Texts Concerning the Calf Image*
In this section, using texts in which Hosea condemns the calf image, the relation between the criticism of the calf image and the syncretized Yahwism with Baalism will be examined.

2.2.1. *Hosea 8:4–6*. In this passage, after the indictment of the kings who were appointed and ruled against the will of YHWH ("They have set up kings, but not from me"),[77] and of the people's sins of idolatry (8:4),

---

76. As we saw in Chapter 1, the legitimacy of the calf image in the worship of YHWH derived from its identification as a pedestal of YHWH.

77. Some scholars think that the verb הִמְלִיכוּ ("crowned," 8:4) refers to the worship of a major deity (such as Baal or Molech); see H. Nyberg, *Studien zum Hoseabuche* (Uppsala: Almqvist & Wiksell, 1935), 39; H. Cazelles, "The Problem of the Kings in Osee, 8:4," *CBQ* 11 (1949): 14–25; G. Östborn, *Yahweh and Baal: Studies in the Book of Hosea and Related Documents* (Lund: Gleerup, 1955), 34. If this verb were followed by the words וְלֹא אוֹתִי ("and not me," direct object), instead of וְלֹא מִמֶּנִּי ("and not from me"), this interpretation could apply to Hos 8:4–11, in which there is no account of war, but rather worship of the calf of Samaria. However, the phrase "They have set up kings, but not from me" refers to the kings appointed against YHWH's will. Hosea condemns such idolatrous kings as being responsible for Israel's sins of idolatry. As aforementioned, in the Bible, the kings of Israel, including Omri and Ahab, did evil in the eyes of YHWH (1 Kgs 16:25, 30). This means that they had apostatized to Baal. Omri worshipped vain idols (1 Kgs 16:26), and Ahab built an altar to Baal and to Asherah in the temple of Baal in Samaria (1 Kgs 16:32–33). This king and his house are said to have abandoned

Hosea focuses on YHWH's wrath because of the idolatry and in particular the calf image in northern Israel (vv. 5, 6).

Verse 4b mentions the silver and gold used to manufacture idols. Hosea 2:10 (EV 8) accuses Israel of using "silver and gold…for Baal," and idolatry is a frequent topic in the following chapters of the book of Hosea.[78] The most famous examples of silver or gold figures were the golden calves of Bethel and Dan set up by Jeroboam ben Nebat. The calf in Hos 8:5 probably refers to that at Bethel.[79] Samaria in this passage may stand for the northern kingdom as a whole rather than the place itself, as in 1 Kgs 13:32. In light of doubt concerning the existence of the calf image in Samaria, Hos 10:5 appears to indicate that the inhabitants of Samaria are represented as worshippers of the calf at Bethel.[80] Accordingly, "the calf of Samaria" should be regarded as the calf of Bethel (= Beth-Aven, in 10:5), where the "king's sanctuary" (see Amos 7:13) resided. But 8:6, "and it is no god," implies that the Israelites regarded the calf as a divine entity. These words suggest that the syncretism that identified Baal with YHWH also identified the silver and gold idol of Baal with the golden calf, which had been considered the pedestal of YHWH. Thus, the fusion of the worship of YHWH and the worship of Baal comprises the starting point for Hosea's scorn toward and condemnation of the calf image.

2.2.1.1. עֲצַבִּים *(8:4),* זָנַח עֶגְלֵךְ שֹׁמְרוֹן *(8:5).* The phrase, זָנַח עֶגְלֵךְ שֹׁמְרוֹן ("cast away your calf, O Samaria"), is an admonition addressed to the Israelites (in Samaria), and explains how they need to deal with their calf, while the verb זָנַח ("cast away") should be read in the imperative form, according to LXX.[81] The meaning conveyed here, then, is "Cast

---

YHWH and served the Baals (1 Kgs 18:18). Regarding King Joram of Judah, we read that he walked in the way of the kings of Israel (2 Kgs 8:18). According to 2 Kgs 10:21, there was a temple of Baal in Samaria during Ahab's time.

78. See 10:5–6; 11:12; 13:3, 8; see also 4:12, 17.

79. Cf. 10:5: "The inhabitants of Samaria shall be in dread for the calves of Beth-Aven." As will be discussed in detail below, Beth-Aven is a derogatory term for Bethel. The calf of Dan was likely destroyed after the invasion by Tiglath-pileser III in 733 B.C.E. (see Wolff, *Hosea*, 140).

80. Albright, *Archaeology*, 160. Kraus (*Worship in Israel*, 152) notes, however, that according to this text, the calf image did exist in the Samaritan temple.

81. The reason for reading זנח in the imperative form is as follows: first, the verb זנח should be read as a transitive verb, in the same way that it functions in v. 3 as a transitive verb, given the symmetric relation between v. 3 and v. 5a (זָנַח, "cast away" = זָנַח, "cast away"; טוֹב, "good" = עֵגֶל, "calf"; יִשְׂרָאֵל, "Israel" = שֹׁמְרוֹן, "Samaria"). However, because the word "Samaria" does not serve as the subject, but rather as a

away your calf, O Samaria." Why is such an exhortation directed at
Samaria (the Israelites)? One possible answer is found in v. 5aβ: "my
anger burns against them." The ending of the sentence with the indirect
object in the third person plural (בָּם) assumes the foregoing word, עֲצַבִּים
("idols") mentioned in v. 4.[82] Accordingly, v. 5 can be read as "Cast
away your calf, O Samaria. (If not,) my anger will burn against it, as was
against them (עֲצַבִּים, 'the idols')." The term עֲצַבִּים is a neutral word for
"image," the root of which is עצב I, "to form." Yet usually it also contains an undertone of scorn, given its similarity in articulation to the root
עצב II: "to hurt, pain, grieve."[83] When Hosea speaks of idols (עֲצַבִּים) in
the plural (see also 4:17; 13:2; 14:9), he is probably thinking not only of
the calves at Dan and Bethel, but also other Canaanite idols (= other
gods).[84] For Hosea, Canaanite gods were designated as Baalim (בְּעָלִים),[85]
since Baal was probably considered in his eyes as representative of
Canaanite deities in general.[86] This inference is culled from the lamentation that we saw in v. 5b, עַד מָתַי יוּכְלוּ לֹא נִקָּיוֹן ("how long will they be
incapable of innocence?"),[87] which informs us that such cultic idols
(עֲצַבִּים), which were identified with idols of Baal,[88] influenced the worship of YHWH and polluted it. Therefore, it can be said that the polemic
nature of the calf image stems from its syncretistic characteristics, which
were influenced by the Canaanite religious context, namely, Baalism.

vocative case, the transitive verb זָנַח, "to cast away") as a command seems to take
עֶגְלֵךְ ("your calf") as its object. On the relation between vv. 3 and 5a, see Wolff,
Hosea, 140.

82. The plural suffix "them" in בָּם (= בְ + ם) is considered by Ibn Ezra to be a
reference to the calves of Samaria, and by Kimchi as a reference to the two calves or
to Israel, who made them; Macintosh (*Hosea*, 302) contends that since only one calf
is mentioned, the reference is clearly to the inhabitants of Samaria, but this claim is
unconvincing, since all of the verbs in vv. 4, 5a, and 6 are directed at idols (calf and
other idols), and so logically the verb חָרָה ("burns") is directed at idols and not
people (the inhabitants of Samaria).

83. See C. R. North, "The Essence of Idolatry," in *Von Ugarit nach Qumran* (ed.
J. Hempel; BZAW 77; Berlin: Töpelmann, 1958), 154.

84. Wolff, *Hosea*, 139.

85. The Baalim in the book of Hosea are discussed in detail below, §3.2.1.

86. Cf. 8:4b, "of their silver and their gold have they made them idols," with
2:10b (EV 8b), "and multiplied unto her silver and gold, which they used for Baal."

87. According to Rashi, the noun נִקָּיוֹן ("cleanliness," "innocence," "purity")
means "to clean oneself of filth." Thus, this lamentation can be understood as
follows: "How long will it be before they will be rid of the defilement of Canaanite
worship?"; the meaning of such will become clearer with the expounding of the
following phrase כִּי מִיִּשְׂרָאֵל in 8:6.

88. As aforementioned, 2:10 (EV 8) and 8:4b.

2.2.1.2. כִּי מִיִּשְׂרָאֵל *(v. 6)*. There has been an argument about the emendation of כִּי מִיִּשְׂרָאֵל into כִּי מִי שׁוֹר אֵל.[89] However, the word שׁוֹר ("bull") seems odd here, following the word עֵגֶל ("calf") in vv. 5a and 6b (unless Hosea intends the bull as a sacrificial animal; cf. 12:12). Also, the word אֵל as a proper noun is inappropriate to 2:1 (EV 1:10); 11:9, and 12:1, since for Hosea calf worship is associated with Baal (13:1–2).[90] In order to disclose the meaning of כִּי מִיִּשְׂרָאֵל, we must pay attention to the phrase וְהוּא. First, we will note that וְהוּא is related to כִּי מִיִּשְׂרָאֵל, because the Masoretic accentuation *zakeph qaton* (:), which is above וְהוּא, connects the pronoun הוּא with what comes before it. When we connect, then, כִּי מִיִּשְׂרָאֵל with וְהוּא, we may face another problem with how to deal with the conjunction -וְ. This difficulty seems to be solved as follows: the pronoun הוּא serves to emphasize עֵגֶל ("calf"), which is the subject of the noun-sentence, (כִּי) מִיִּשְׂרָאֵל.[91] If we take into account the fact that the conjunction -וְ can also serve as a mode of emphasis,[92] it is probable that the phrase וְהוּא serves to emphasize the subject עֵגֶל ("calf").

The cry כִּי מִיִּשְׂרָאֵל is syntactically linked to the lamentation עַד מָתַי לֹא יוּכְלוּ נִקָּיוֹן (8:5b). Probably, this lamentation can be understood as "How long will they (the inhabitants of Samaria) be incapable of innocence?" The lamentation, preceded by the phrase depicting God's fury over the calf, חָרָה אַפִּי בָם, emphasizes the extent to which the Israelites adopted the misperception of the calf as their god through their identification of YHWH with Baal. However, the following word in v. 6, כִּי, which is a conjunctive, alludes to a hope that Israel will repent of its submission to Canaanite influence, and thus avoid God's wrath, since here the conjunctive כִּי sets the two clauses in opposition in terms of their meaning. When the word כִּי is accompanied by a negative sentence, it is interpreted as "but."[93] In such a case, it will be followed by a clause whose meaning is opposite to that of the previous clause. If this is so, the reading of the phrase מִיִּשְׂרָאֵל as מִי שׁוֹר אֵל does not result in it having the opposite meaning to the previous clause, עַד מָתַי לֹא יוּכְלוּ נִקָּיוֹן. Now we can see how the Masoretic reading מִיִּשְׂרָאֵל ("[it-the calf-is] from Israel") implies a meaning opposite to that of the clause עַד מָתַי לֹא יוּכְלוּ נִקָּיוֹן: it appears that the lamentation עַד מָתַי לֹא יוּכְלוּ נִקָּיוֹן ("How long

89. N. H. Tur-Sinai, "Dunkele Bibelstellen," in *Vom Alten Testament. Festschrift K. Marti* (ed. K. Budde; BZAW 41; Giessen: Töpelmann, 1925), 277–80.

90. Wolff, *Hosea*, 141–42.

91. On the reinforcement or emphasis of the subject in the noun-sentence by adding a third person singular or plural pronoun, see GKC §141 g.

92. Cf. Gen 3:16; Isa 2:1. See GKC §154 a, n. 1.

93. Cf. BDB, 474; see also Gen 17:15; 24:3–4; 45:8; Exod 1:19; 15:8; Deut 21:16; 1 Sam 6:3; 27:1; 1 Kgs 21:15; Isa 10:7; 28:27; 29:23; 30:5.

will they be incapable of innocence?"), in tandem with the expression of God's anger חָרָה אַפִּי בָּם ("my anger burns against them"), describes a very hopeless state among the people of Samaria (namely, the Israelites) when speaking of God's judgment with regard to calf worship.

However, the conjunctive כִּי turns the situation of helplessness into one of hope; the phrase כִּי מִיִּשְׂרָאֵל וְהוּא indicates that it (the calf) is "indeed" from Israel.[94] In Israel, they could never even have imagined the image of YHWH without Canaanite influence. Indeed, the calf is from Israel, and it comes together with an aniconic tradition. It does not originate in Canaanite religion, which identified the deity with the image. In the beginning, the calf itself was not a revered idol nor was it an image of YHWH, but rather it transformed into something that was not properly understood, and thus became a deified figure, due to the fusion of the worship of YHWH with the worship of Baal, in which the god Baal was represented by the bull. The calf came from Israel, and never had anything to do with idols or icons of YHWH. Therefore, the cry כִּי מִיִּשְׂרָאֵל וְהוּא implies an appeal to Israel to abolish the influence of Canaanite religion, in which deities are represented through human-made images. There is hope for the inhabitants of Samaria (namely, the Israelites) if only they will understand that YHWH, the God of Israel, cannot be represented through a human-made image, in contrast to the Canaanite custom in which the calf image can serve as a deity. Thus, the calf image is indeed not a deity (לֹא אֱלֹהִים הוּא) (8:6a) and is no more than the pedestal of YHWH.

2.2.1.3. כִּי שְׁבָבִים יִהְיֶה *(v. 6)*. The calf is not a god (לֹא אֱלֹהִים הוּא) who can provide divine succor for man and be honored, for it was made with human hands. Ultimately, the calf of Samaria, which is regarded as a god based on the Canaanite belief that the craftsman-made idol is a god, shall be consigned to the flame (שְׁבָבִים, 8:6b),[95] to complete extinction. The

---

94. "Not imported from foreign peoples" according to Macintosh (*Hosea*, 303).

95. The word שְׁבָבִים is a *hapax legomenon*. It may be compared to the word שְׁבִיבִים, which means "sparks" or "flame" (cf. Job 18:5) (W. F. Albright, "Anath and Dragon," *BASOR* 84 [1941]: 17 n. 26). According to this approach, the meaning of the expression is that the calf will be consigned to the flames. Other interpretations have been suggested by reference to other words. First, one may view its root שׁוּב in its Polel form, the meaning of which is "to drive out, banish, expel" (Macintosh, *Hosea*, 311). In such a case, the phrase שְׁבָבִים יִהְיֶה עֵגֶל שֹׁמְרוֹן in v. 6b takes on the literal meaning "the calf of Samaria will be banished," that is, "will be ousted (deported)." Second, it could be that this word is related in its root to the Middle Hebrew word שָׁבַב ("to chop," "to cut"), and to its cognate, the Arabic word *sabba* ("to cut"), or *seība* ("chips," "splinters"), which presumably refers to wood chips or

word שְׁבָבִים here recalls Moses' burning of the golden calf, before grinding it to dust (Exod 32:20). Again, we find further confirmation that Hosea was affiliated somehow with the prophetic-Levitical group, which was associated with the Elohist, who composed the polemical narrative of the sin of the golden calf, namely, that which appears in Exod 32. Hence, we can assume that both Hosea and the Elohist were influenced by the prophetic-Levitical group, and it is very likely that they shared the same ideas regarding the destruction of the calf image, even though they used different terms to express them.

2.2.2. *Hosea 10:1–8.*

Verses 1–8 of ch. 10 comprise a single passage. Therefore, vv. 5–8—the attack on the cultic rites at Bethel—are needed in order to understand the whole context of vv. 1–8. Before Hosea criticizes the calf image at Bethel, he spells out the aspects of Israel's apostasy to YHWH (vv. 1–4): in spite of YHWH's great multiplication of the fruit of his land (v. 1a), Israel multiplied the pillars by the altars (v. 1b). In other words, while YHWH[96] was generous in bringing wealth and

splinters. In this case, the phrase just mentioned from 8:6b would take on the meaning "the calf of Samaria shall be cut into trifling pieces," namely, "it shall be nothing only trifling chips" (see Wolff, *Hosea*, 142). These views on the text can be properly evaluated by the conjunction כִּי in the present phrase. In general, the conjunction כִּי has the function of joining two separate phrases. Here, of course, כִּי is used to indicate that the current the phrase שְׁבָבִים יִהְיֶה עֵגֶל שֹׁמְרֹון has a certain relation to the one before it. What relation, then, is there between the first phrase and the second? According to BDB (pp. 471f.), the word כִּי is read as "because, that, when, because, but, for," and so on. Therefore, the phrase that follows כִּי expresses "reason, emphasis, time, contrast, and rhetoric" with respect to the word or phrase that precedes it. If so, in the case of the first option given above, the current phrase hardly relates in its meaning to the one that precedes it. This view comes from the parallelism between שְׁבָבִים יִהְיֶה and נָלָה מִמֶּנּוּ ("departed from it," 10:5), as Macintosh claims (p. 310). While in 10:5, "deportation" could be the reason for "mourning" (10:5), in 8:6 the meaning of "deportation" rarely makes sense in relation to the cry לֹא אֱלֹהִים הוּא ("It is not God," v. 6aβ). In the ancient Near East, the plunder of idols or images of a god did not denote the negating of the existence of a god (see 1 Sam 4:7–11). Here, the conjunction כִּי is used to introduce a statement with emphasis, like "yes, certainly, surely" (as in 1 Sam 17:25; Isa 32:13; Jer 22:22; Hos 6:9; 9:12; 10:3, and so on; see BDB, 472). Therefore, the present phrase is meant to stress the negation of the divinity of the calf. In this sense, the second view is also attractive. However, the view that interprets the word שְׁבָבִים in light of שְׁבִבִים is preferable rather than the view (2), since the former is more thoroughly emphasizing the negation of the divinity of the calf through interpreting שְׁבָבִים as burning of the calf image.

   96. In agreement with most scholars, the pronoun הוּא in v. 2 is identified as referring to YHWH. Verbs and nouns referring to the people of Israel are in the plural

prosperity to Israel, Israel abused his gifts in pagan rites; Israel repu-
diated YHWH as their king (vv. 2–3); they violated YHWH's covenant
(v. 4). Verses 5–8 describe the severe hardships that the national calf cult
at Bethel brought upon the people, and the despairing reaction to the
situation on the part of the population of Samaria.[97]

2.2.2.1. לְעֶגְלוֹת[98] בֵּית אָוֶן יָגוּרוּ...וּכְמָרָיו עָלָיו יָגִילוּ עַל כְּבוֹדוֹ *(v. 5)*. "Beth-
Aven" (בֵּית אָוֶן) is a derogatory term for Bethel (as it appears in 4:15).
For the first time in the Bible, Hosea terms the Bethel priests כְּמָרִים
(plural of כֹּמֶר). The word reappears later in Zeph 1:4 and 2 Kgs 23:5,
and is reserved for those who associated themselves with the worship of
Baal.[99] In addition, the verb אָבַל ("to mourn") could have referred mainly
to the Baalistic lamentation and mourning rituals, and even the ritual wail
over the death of Baal in the myth.[100] Therefore, the terms that Hosea
uses, such as כְּמָרִים and אָבַל, in reference to the calf figure, suggest that
during his time the calf figure apparently was identified with Baal.

2.2.2.2. נִדְמֶה שֹׁמְרוֹן מַלְכָּהּ כְּקֶצֶף עַל פְּנֵי מָיִם *(v. 7)*. It is unlikely that the
reference to the king of Samaria (מַלְכָּהּ) points to a human king. There
was no actual human king who was called the "king of Samaria" (yet cf.
Jonah 3:6). In v. 7, there is a thematic relation to v. 3, which suggests
that Israel abandoned the rule of YHWH, when it did not grant him the
title "king." In light of the rejection of YHWH as king, one can imagine
the positioning of a pagan god in his place, namely, the calf image in
v. 5f.[101] The title "king of Samaria" is the name given to the calf image,
which no longer comprises the footstool of YHWH, but rather is identified

form in this unit. These facts suggest that the subject of the singular verbs in v. 1 is
YHWH. Thus, YHWH is emphasized as he who brought about Israel's prosperity, a
point which Hosea tirelessly reiterates. The verb בּוֹקֵק in the factitive Polel conjugation, therefore, means "to make luxuriant" (see Andersen and Freedman, *Hosea*,
550).

97. Macintosh, *Hosea*, 400.

98. The noun עֶגְלוֹת, used uniquely here, appears to be in the form of a feminine
construct plural. Andersen and Freedman (*Hosea*, 554) suggest that it may denote
the name of the female counterpart of the "calf of Samaria" (עֵגֶל שֹׁמְרוֹן, 8:5, 6).
However, the third masculine singular pronouns—עָלָיו, עָמֹו, כְּמָרָיו and so on—
indicate עֶגְלוֹת and make it clear that עֶגְלוֹת does not denote עֶגְלָה as a counterpart
or consort of עֵגֶל but עֵגֶל itself. On this point, Rudolph's approach, whereby the
feminine plural ending is understood as an abstract plural and the word as denoting
the calf cult, is very convincing (see Rudolph, *Hosea*, 195).

99. Wolff, *Hosea*, 175.

100. Ibid.

101. Mays, *Hosea*, 142; Andersen and Freedman, *Hosea*, 518, 558.

with Baal. As was observed above, 8:6 attests to the fact that at this time the Israelites viewed the calf image as a god. The idea that the god is king of the city is common in Canaanite religion. According to an Ugaritic myth, after Baal's victory over Yamm the goddess Anath calls him "our king, mightiest Baal, our judge, over whom there is none."[102] Baal himself brags, "I alone am he who is king over the gods."[103]

If this is the case, "king of Samaria" points to the "calf of Samaria" in 8:5, which can be understood as the "calf" of Bethel, as we saw above.[104] Verse 7 is a figurative repetition of the future fate of the calf image, as described in 8:6: it will perish away (נִדְמֶה),[105] when the Assyrian forces come, like a splinter (קֶצֶף)[106] upon the water.

2.2.2.3. בָּמוֹת אָוֶן חַטַּאת יִשְׂרָאֵל *(v. 8)*. The word בָּמוֹת ("high places") indicates shrines with cultic accessories, including an altar, located mainly on high places, such as mountains or hills.[107] Hosea condemns the בָּמוֹת as the sin of Israel by attaching the derogatory term אָוֶן to בָּמוֹת. The question arises whether the pair of words בָּמוֹת אָוֶן refers to Beth-Aven, namely, Bethel. It seems that the term אָוֶן in itself becomes a synonym for Bethel, when we examine it in the context of Jer 4:15.[108] However, the pejorative term אָוֶן is not reserved for Bethel alone (Hos 6:8; 12:12). Nevertheless, it appears that here syntactically it refers to the sins of

---

102. *KTU* 1.3 V 40–44, as translated in G. R. Driver, *Canaanite Myths and Legends* (Edinburgh: T. & T. Clark, 1956), 54. The statement regarding the superiority of Baal refers mainly to his rivalry with Yamm. The supreme god, El, still reigns over the divine realm, the context indicates. Line 44 refers to "El the king who installed him" (i.e. Baal) (see ibid.).

103. *KTU* 1.4 VII 49–50, as translated in Driver, *Canaanite Myths*.

104. See the interpretation of זֶנַח עֶגְלֵךְ שֹׁמְרוֹן (Hos 8:5) in §2.2.1, above.

105. The meaning of the verb נִדְמֶה is "to come to an end, to be ruined, to perish." Cf. Macintosh, *Hosea*, 406.

106. Regarding the meaning of the word קֶצֶף, a number of interpretations have been offered: its meaning as "foam" is based upon the verb קָצַף ("to be angry"); its meaning as a "chip of wood" can be inferred from Joel 1:7, and from the Arabic root. See ibid. It appears that both options are admissible. The expression עַל פְּנֵי מָיִם ("upon the water") recalls Exod 32:20.

107. The subject of בָּמוֹת will be discussed in detail in §2.3.2.2.

108. At this point, Jeremiah circumscribes northern Israel, when he says "For a voice proclaims from Dan and announces אָוֶן from Mount Ephraim," similar to the territorial horizon of the coming disaster in Jer 8:16. This figurative description is a multi-layered paraphrase of "from Dan to Bethel," similar to "from Dan to Beersheba" (see Z. Kallai, "Beth-el-Luz and Beth-aven," in *Prophetie und geschichtliche Wirklichkeit im alten Israel. Festschrift für S. Hermann* [ed. R. Liwak and S. Wagner; Stuttgart: Kohlhammer, 1991], 171–88).

Bethel, since, as we saw above, שֹׁמְרוֹן מַלְכָּה, that is, מֶלֶךְ שֹׁמְרוֹן (king of Samaria) in v. 7 refers to the calf image at Bethel (= Beth-Aven). Apparently, the expression בָּמוֹת אָוֶן, though it does not directly indicate Beth-Aven (= Bethel), does describe the "sanctuaries of wickedness," including that of Bethel.[109] In other words, Bethel was the primary example of wicked בָּמוֹת, which were found throughout the northern kingdom. I will discuss below the question of why בָּמוֹת אָוֶן were "the sin of Israel."

2.2.3. *Hosea 13:1–3.* There is a certain consistency between these three verses in terms of their content.[110] In view of the punishment imposed in the past on Ephraim (13:1),[111] a certain pattern of ongoing sin is distinguishable (13:2), one which leads to the prophecy foreseeing its end (13:3).

2.2.3.1. וַיֶּאְשַׁם בַּבַּעַל וַיָּמֹת *(v. 1).* In v. 1, Hosea speaks of Ephraim's superiority over the other tribes of Israel. However, for Hosea, Ephraim, which has long since ceased to mean the tribe, denotes the area of Mount Ephraim, where the royal residence of Samaria is located. From there, during the previous two decades, numerous political decisions were made that led to the "trembling" (רְתֵת)[112] of the other areas of the northern kingdom, and also Judah. It can be said, therefore, that there was a certain fear of Ephraim that prevailed. In its superiority, Ephraim brought guilt on itself because of Baal (וַיֶּאְשַׁם בַּבַּעַל). Namely, Ephraim worshiped Baal from whom it expected the fertility, and contaminated the YHWH cult.[113] As a consequence of its sin, Ephraim[114] was virtually rendered dead[115] in the wake of the campaign waged by Tiglath-pileser III

---

109. See Wolff, *Hosea*, 176; Mays, *Hosea*, 142.

110. Mays (*Hosea*, 171–73) divides them into past (13:1), present (13:2), and future (13:3).

111. Verse 1 refers to Hosea, who stands in the present ("now," v. 2), and looks back upon the guilt of Ephraim in the past (Wolff, *Hosea*, 225).

112. Until the discovery of the Qumran scrolls, this word was attested only in the Hebrew Bible. It means "terror, trembling, shuddering," and is used in 1QH 4.33.

113. Wolff, *Hosea.*

114. Of course, as we saw earlier, here "Ephraim" does not refer to the vestiges of the state that existed after 733 B.C.E. (see ibid., 91).

115. וַיָּמֹת does not mean the complete extermination of Ephraim, since עַתָּה ("now") in v. 2 presupposes its existence. Regarding this point, it is worth mentioning Andersen and Freedman's interpretation (*Hosea*, 630) "to say that Ephraim 'died' could mean that they received the death sentence. In this sence, the comment of Ibn Ezra is accepted, according to which Ephraim is considered 'as good as dead.'"

in 733 B.C.E.[116] And it is very likely that it was during that year that Hosea was looking back.

2.2.3.2. וְעַתָּה יוֹסִפוּ לַחֲטֹא *(v. 2)*. Despite the punishment suffered by Ephraim at the hands of Tiglath-pileser, they continue to sin (v. 2). That is, Ephraim continues to fail YHWH in its pagan worship. Some phrases show that the worship of the calf image actually reflects Baal worship. First, the phrase זֹבְחֵי אָדָם means "slaughterers of men," with the intent being human sacrifices.[117] According to Jer 19:5 and 32:35, the Baal worshippers sacrificed their children to this god.[118] If follows from such that although the intent of the calf image was to represent the pedestal of YHWH, it was now degraded to the rank of an apparatus for the worship of Baal as a result of the identification of YHWH with the latter. Second, the expression עֲגָלִים יִשָּׁקוּן conveys that those who were accustomed to Baal worship, like זֹבְחֵי אָדָם, for example, expressed their devotion and homage to the calves as they did to Baal (see 1 Kgs 19:18).

2.2.3.3. מַסֵּכָה *(v. 2)*. After the catastrophe that struck the northern king-dom in 733 B.C.E., the calf cult grew stronger, and merged with the cult of Baal. Verse 1 describes this growth with the increase in the number of calf images. מַסֵּכָה in v. 2a is the word used to denote the golden calf in Exod 32:4, 8; Deut 9:16; 1 Kgs 14:9; and 2 Kgs 17:16. Apparently, when Hosea used this term, the golden calf of Bethel stood before his eyes. If so, does the word עַתָּה ("now"), namely, after 733 B.C.E., signify the fact that the מַסֵּכָה has just been made for the first time? I assume not. What then is Hosea's intent when he says "now" they made a molten image? מַסֵּכָה is syntactically in apposition with עֲצַבִּים: although מַסֵּכָה is singu-lar, here it represents the calves in v. 2b.[119] Therefore, the meaning of the phrase וְעַתָּה...וַיַּעֲשׂוּ לָהֶם מַסֵּכָה is that the people commonly made calf images from silver, and not from gold, for personal use and public rites at the high places.[120]

116. Wolff, *Hosea*.

117. Ibn Ezra and Rashi argue that the expression זֹבְחֵי אָדָם refers to slaughterers of men and human sacrifices. For Rashi, the pagan priests believed that they alone were worthy to kiss the calves, since they sacrificed הַדּוֹרוֹן הֶחָבִיב (namely, "the dearest thing"). See also Andersen and Freedman, *Hosea*, 630; Wolff, *Hosea*, 219.

118. Cf. Lev 18:21; 20:2; 2 Kgs 23:10; Ezek 16:20–21; 23:37; Ps 106:37–39.

119. עֲגָלִים, accordingly, is syntactically identical to עֲצַבִּים, which usually con-tains an undertone of contempt, due to its similarity in vocalization to the words from the root עצב II, meaning "to pain, sorrow, grieve."

120. When Hosea speaks of idols (עֲצַבִּים) in the plural (also in 4:17; 8:4; 14:9 [EV 8]), he probably had in mind, in addition to the calf images, many other cultic idols for Canaanite gods (other gods). So both terms are here represented as מַסֵּכָה.

2.3. *Negative Impacts of Baalism on the Calf Image*

2.3.1. *The Bull of Baal and the Calf Image of YHWH.* The prophet Hosea

knowingly gives expression to the critique of "the calf of Samaria" (Hos
8:5) when he aims to represent the cultic practices that Jeroboam ben
Nebat instituted at the national sanctuary at Bethel (cf. 10:5).[121] Hosea's
cry "it is not God" (8:6) indicates that in his day the image was regarded
as a divine symbol. Hence, in his view, the calf image was essentially
degraded from the pedestal of YHWH to a symbol of divinity (YHWH or
Baal). As has already been observed in the texts of polemics against the
calf image, the main impetus for the polemic against it is related to the
syncretism between Yahwism and Baalism. That is to say, the essential
distinction between the actual deity, YHWH, and the golden calf, which
served as his pedestal, became increasingly blurred in the public consciousness by the assimilation of YHWH with Baal, whose symbol was
the bull.[122] If we accept the view that the primary motive for the polemic
against the calf image has to do with the syncretism between Yahwism
and Baalism, a question arises: Why is only the assimilation of YHWH
with Baal to be blamed for the polemic against the calf image, even
though YHWH was also assimilated with El, whose symbol was also a
bull? In order to answer this question, we first need to bear in mind that
Hosea's cry לֹא אֱלֹהִים הוּא ("it is not God," Hos 8:6) is the antithesis of
the cultic invocation אֵלֶּה אֱלֹהֶיךָ ("This is your God," Exod 32:4, 8) or
הִנֵּה אֱלֹהֶיךָ ("behold your God," 1 Kgs 12:28). In order to avoid mis-
interpretation of the original nature of the cultic invocation, we need to

---

121.   See the interpretation of Hos 8:5 in §2.2.1 and Hos 10 in §2.2.2.

122.   Originally, according to the Ugaritic myth, the title "bull" (*ṯr*) was given to
El (*Ilu*), the creator of the earth and the heavens. However, the Ugaritic texts
describe his most significant rival, Baal, who is younger than him, as a new face in
El's family (see M. S. Smith, *The Ugaritic Baal Cycle*. Vol. 1, *Introduction with
Text, Translation and Commentary of KTU 1.1–1.2* [VTSup 55; Leiden: Brill, 1994],
91–93). The passages *KTU* 1.10 III 5–7, and 1.11, 1.5 V 18–21 describe the aspi-
ration of Baal to supplant El and his efforts to seize the position of El as "bull" (see
H. Gese, *Die Religionen Altsyriens. Die Religionen Altsyriens, Altarabiens und der
Mandäer* [Die Religionen der Menschheit 10/2; Stuttgart: Kohlhammer, 1970], 129;
J. C. de Moor, *The Rise of Yahwism: The Roots of Israelite Monotheism* [Leuven:
Peeters, 1997], 74). Baal fights like a bull (*KTU* 1.6 VI 17–18) and he has bull horns
(*KTU* 1.101). In *KTU* 1.92, Baal is devoured as a bull by Astarte (Ashtoreth) (cf. B.
Margalit, "KTU 1.92 [Obv]: A Ugaritic Theophagy," *AuOr* 7 [1989]: 67ff.). In
Canaanite iconography, Baal is depicted with bull horns, and in Phoenician iconogra-
phy with a bull head (cf. W. Culican, "Melqart Representations on Phoenician
Seals," *AbrN* 2 [1960–61]: Plate I, Fig. 1; E. Gubel, "The Iconography of the Ibiza
MAI 3650 Reconsidered," *AuOr* 4 [1986]: Fig. 1 = Figs. 36 A–B).

note that the identity of אֱלֹהִים in it changes in accordance with the different stages in the story of the golden calf.

Before the polemic against the golden calf, which the Elohist expressed in his narrative, the calf image was associated with Elohim, who brought Israel out of Egypt, and this Elohim was identified with YHWH.[123] The prevailing view is that the relationship between YHWH and El existed mainly because YHWH originally had the same characteristics as the god El.[124] In spite of several opinions that object to this view,[125] it is clear that YHWH was equated with the El of the Patriarchs, who was none other than the supreme Canaanite deity described in the Ugaritic texts.[126] The Bible shows that there was no problem with the assimilation of YHWH

123. See H. Motzki, "Ein Beitrag zum Problem des Stierkultes in der Religions-geschichte Israels," *VT* 25 (1975): 470f. n. 10.

124. See Cross, *Canaanite Myth*, 44–75.

125. The reasons for the objections are as follows: (1) El's character, as conveyed in the Ugaritic texts, is uniformly benevolent, while YHWH has a fierce as well as a kind side; (2) in early poetic passages, such as Judg 5:4–5, YHWH is associated with a storm, a characterization which is inappropriate to El; (3) the cultic title of El—"El who creates hosts"—does not fit YHWH. YHWH is unlikely to mean "(he) creates," since Exod 3:14, in which YHWH calls himself "I AM THAT I AM," implies that it means "he is." Yet these are merely differences in interpretation, and could not be a decisive ground for argument that YHWH and El became identified after the Yahwistic group moved to Canaan, where El was being worshipped (Eissfeldt, "El and Yahweh," 33–37). Rather, it seems that to a certain extent the characteristics of YHWH that resembled those of the god El made it easier, among the Yahwistic group, to identify the two with each other. Accordingly, it appears that the view that claims that the assimilation of YHWH with El came about as a result of YHWH's El-like qualities, and the view that contends that such assimilation resulted from the migration of the Yahwistic group to Canaan, where El was being worshipped, should be integrated.

126. J. Day ("Yahweh and the Gods and Goddesses of Canaan," in Dietrich and Klopfenstein, eds., *Ein Gott allein?*, 182–84) suggests a number of points of equation of YHWH with El, the supreme Canaanite deity. First, YHWH, as an aged God, is derived from the entity El. In the Ugaritic texts, El is characterized as "the father of years" (*ʾab šnm*). The reference to YHWH's "years" appears in Job 36:26 and Ps 102:25, 27, and the name of the patriarchal deity El-Olam (אֵל עוֹלָם) in Gen 21:33 originally meant "El, the ancient one." Second, the idea of YHWH as creator also comes from El. Just as El is called *ʾl qn ʾrṣ* ("El, creator of the earth"), reflected in the Hittite–Canaanite name *Elkinirša*, so the Bible speaks of "El–Elyon, creator (קֹנֵה) of heaven and earth" (Gen 14:19, 22). Third, just as in the Hittite–Canaanite myth of *Elkinirša*, El's residence is the source of the River Euphrates, so in the Bible "the garden of YHWH" (Isa 51:3) is located at the source of the river Euphrates (cf. Gen 2:10–14). Fourth, the identification of YHWH with El naturally also carries with it an empyrean pantheon of subordinate gods.

and El. The god El, whom the Patriarchs worshipped, is described as the god who brought Israel out of Egypt. The book of Genesis and Exod 6 show signs of pre-Yahwistic worship among the pre-Israelite clans, including the worship of El, who is known as the god of the Patriarchs.[127] According to the Priestly source, the Patriarchs worshipped God under the name "El Shaddai" (Gen 17:1; 28:3; 35:11; 48:3; Exod 6:3).[128] The name YHWH was probably originally the cultic name of El, who was worshipped in the south.[129] Although the integration process of YHWH and El is not clearly known to us, it appears that it occurred when the Yahwistic group settled in the hill country, and established a symbiosis with the old pre-Yahwistic Israelite group of El worshippers, which included the clan of Jacob around Bethel and the clan of Israel around Shechem.[130] The divine designation "El Elohei Yisrael" (אֵל אֱלֹהֵי יִשְׂרָאֵל), which is associated with this pre-Yahwistic group in Canaan (cf. Gen 33:20), became "YHWH Elohei Yisrael" (יְהוָה אֱלֹהֵי יִשְׂרָאֵל; cf. especially Josh 24:2, 23; Judg 5:3, 5) as a result of this interfusion.[131] Therefore, the names and attributes of El were always openly associated with YHWH.[132] A significant number of El's traits and functions also appears as YHWH's traits and functions in the early traditions of Israel, including YHWH's role as judge in the court of El (Pss 82; 89:6–8) and in the general picture of YHWH at the head of the divine council; YHWH's kingship (Exod 15:18; Deut 33:15; Num 24:21); YHWH's wisdom, age,

---

127. The Patriarchs are associated with a series of deific entities with the name "El," for example, אֵל עֶלְיוֹן ("God Most High") in Jerusalem (Gen 14:19, 22); הָאֵל בֵּית אֵל ("God of Bethel," Gen 31:13; 35:7; cf. also 28:11–19); אֵל אֱלֹהֵי יִשְׂרָאֵל ("God, the God of Israel") in Shechem (Gen 33:20); אֵל עוֹלָם ("YHWH, the Everlasting God") in Beer Sheba (Gen 21:33); and אֵל רֳאִי ("The God of vision") of the Negev (Gen 16:13).

128. Albertz, *Israelite Religion*, 30.

129. There are poetic texts that can be described as "theophanies from the south," in which YHWH is referred to as going forth from Sinai, Seir, the steppe of Edom, Teman, and Paran (Deut 33:2–3; Judg 5:4–5; Hab 3:3; Ps 58:8–9) (see Axelsson, *Seir*, 48–65). To these biblical texts are now added material from Kuntillet ʿAjrud, where we find both *yhwh tmn/tymn*, "YHWH of Teman," and other theophoric expressions; cf. M. Weinfeld, "Kuntillet ʿAjrud Inscriptions and Their Significance," *SEL* 1 (1984): 121–30 (esp. 126).

130. Regarding both of these groups, see C. H. J. de Geus, *The Tribes of Israel* (Assen: Van Gorcum, 1976), 180.

131. E. Rössler, "Jahwe und die Götter im Pentateuch und im Deuterono-mistischen Geschichtswerk" (Ph.D. diss., Phil. Bonn, 1966), 36, 203ff.

132. Ibid., 2–3. For inscriptional evidence corroborating the identification of YHWH with El in pre-Exilic Israel, see P. D. Miller, "El, The Creator of Earth," *BASOR* 239 (1980): 43–46.

and compassion and, above all, YHWH as creator and father (Gen 49:25; Deut 32:6).[133] In sum, the Bible attests to the fact that YHWH and El were transformed in Israelite belief into a single entity by a complete assimilation between them.

Given this assimilation of YHWH and El, the term *ṯr* or *ṯwr* ("bull"), which serves as an epithet for El in Ugaritic texts, is also applied to YHWH. In the Balaam oracles, this assimilation is confirmed with a metaphor of the רְאֵם ("wild ox"):

> How can I curse whom El has not cursed?
> How can I denounce whom YHWH has not denounced? (Num 23:8)

> YHWH, his God, is with him…
> El brought him out of Egypt
> He is like the wild ox's horns to him (Num 23:21–22; cf. 24:8[134])

Since the Balaam oracles probably belong among the most ancient poetry in the Bible,[135] these formulations hold particular significance as a witness to how Israel spoke of the Exodus in the earliest period of its history.[136] The use of the several distinct designations in reference to the deity in the broader context in which these formulations appear indicates that the name "El" is being used as a proper noun in itself, and is not a generic appellative. The fact that in Num 23:8 "El" and "YHWH" are used as analogous terms, and that in 24:16 (cf. v. 4) three names of the deity—"El," "Elyon," and "Shaddai"—are used in the same sense, supports this assertion. Therefore, these texts show that at least some of

---

133.   Cross, *Canaanite Myth*, 72.

134.   Num 24:8 is different only in that the suffix of the object is in the third person masculine singular instead of third person masculine plural, as in 23:22.

135.   See the evidence of such in W. F. Albright, "The Oracles of Balaam," *JBL* 63 (1944): 208–11, and 216 n. 54; Albright, *Yahweh*, 1–46; D. N. Freedman, "Divine Names and Titles in Early Hebrew Poetry," in *Magnalia Dei. Festschrift G. E. Wright* (ed. F. M. Cross et al.; Garden City, N.Y.: Doubleday, 1976), 66–68; Cross, *Canaanite Myth*, 99 n. 30, and also p. 157.

136.   This claim, of course, assumes that Num 23:22 and 24:8 are integral and original to their context. For a convincing argument that states that Num 23:22 is integral to its context, see A. Tosato, "The Literary Structure of the First Two Poems of Balaam (Num xxiii 7–10, 18–24)," *VT* 29 (1979): 101–4. Similar arguments could apply to Num 24:8. This is a unique formula (since it is the only attestation of the Exodus formula using El as a divine name instead of YHWH in the Bible) located in a rather unlikely context (since the Balaam oracles say nothing else about the Exodus, nor do they develop themes likely to attract a statement about the Exodus into this context).Thus, it is unlikely that the formulas at Num 23:22 and 24:8 were introduced secondarily.

the Israelites in earliest Israel believed that it was "El" who liberated them from Egypt, and "El" was none other than YHWH.

"El" as "YHWH," who is compared here with the horns of the wild ox (רְאֵם), is associated in this text with the exodus from Egypt, in the same way that he is later associated with Jeroboam's calf image. The fact that the place in which Jeroboam installed the image bears the name "Beth-El" (בֵּית אֵל) is of primary importance in this context.[137] The cultic formula of the golden calf in 1 Kgs 12:28 shows that it is associated with "El," who brought Israel out of Egypt. Once again, it should be noted that in almost every place where this formula or a variation of it appears in the Bible, the god who brought Israel out of Egypt is identified as "YHWH."[138] From such, one may conclude, as does Donner,[139] that the formula in 1 Kgs 12:28 indicates that the golden calves of Jeroboam were also associated with YHWH.

We can answer, then, the question raised above as follows: the reason why the assimilation of "YHWH" and "El" did not cause a problem in relation to the calf image was their perfect integration. They had already long ago become a single entity with two different names. However, there was no complete integration of YHWH and Baal. When the call was made for the exclusive worship of YHWH, Baal was doomed to be criticized as other god. The calf image, which via the influence of Baal-ism came to be regarded as a divine symbol and not as YHWH's pedestal, was subjected to criticism as other god. Thus, Hosea's criticism "it is not God" (לֹא אֱלֹהִים הוּא) is not antithetical to the Yahwistic cultic formula with the calf image in the period when there was no polemic against it, but rather to the cultic formula of calf worship in the time of the polemical phase against it. Although originally Jeroboam's calves were linked to YHWH-El as his footstool, as time went on, they became increasingly linked to Baal. However, although the assimilation of YHWH and Baal was so profound that the masses confused the two deities, there is no

137. Bethel was closely associated with the clan of Jacob (Gen 28:10–22; 31:13; 35:7). It is interesting to note that we encounter the expression אֲבִיר יַעֲקֹב ("mighty one of Jacob") as the name of a god that Jacob worshipped (Gen 49:24), a name that some scholars translate as "the bull of Jacob." The calf of Jeroboam can be found in אֲבִיר יַעֲקֹב. For a discussion of the term אֲבִיר יַעֲקֹב, see A. S. Kapelrud, "Abīr," *TDOT* 1:42–44. The instances in which it appears as a divine designation include: Gen 49:24; Ps 132:5; Isa 49:26; 60:16; cf. Isa 1:24.

138. See Exod 15:6; Deut 1:27; 6:12, 23; 7:8, 19; Judg 6:13; 1 Sam 12:6; 1 Kgs 7:36; 9:9; 2 Chr 7:22; Jer 15:14–15; 23:7–8.

139. H. Donner, "Hier sind deine Götter, Israel!," in *Wort und Geschichte: Festschrift K. Elliger* (AOAT 18; Neukirchen–Vluyn: Neukirchener, 1973), 45–50 (esp. 48).

evidence that there was complete unity between them. In the eyes of the observants (the prophets, for instance) of normative Yahwism, the assimilation of God and Baal was rather perceived as a state of confrontation.[140] Despite the fact that both of the deities shared a number of storm-god characteristics, they remained independent. Therefore, in the eyes of Yahwistic devotees, such as the prophets, Baal is none other than a separate god. As a result of the assimilation of YHWH with Baal, however, in the eyes of the populace, the calf image could have been viewed as a symbol of Baal or a representation of YHWH. Hosea's criticism "it is not God" also can be interpreted as a reproof toward the populace who came to venerate the calf image in two ways: on the one hand, as a symbol of Baal, and on the other hand, as an image of YHWH. Which did Hosea mean when he exclaimed "it is not God"? His words can be interpreted in light of the answer to the following question: Did Hosea criticize the calf image from a position that demanded the exclusive worship of YHWH, or rather on the basis of the law forbidding the use of an image in the worship of YHWH?

2.3.2. The Cult of YHWH Identified with Baal. It appears that when the identification of YHWH with Baal became so profound, there was almost no difference between the cult of YHWH and that of Baal. What, then, were the characteristics of the Baalized cult of YHWH? Through the book of Hosea we may get an idea regarding the characteristics of such a cult in the eighth century B.C.E.

It has been asserted that the sexual terminologies[141] in the book of Hosea, especially in chs. 1–4,[142] often refer to cultic prostitution and sexual rites in Canaanite fertility cults. However, fundamental questions have recently been raised regarding this interpretation: Were there really any sexual rites in Canaanite religion? Is there any evidence of initiation rites or any non-professional sexual activity? Is there proof of professional sexual activity in the framework of religious ceremonies, such as that termed "cultic prostitution" by scholars? In order to assess the conflicting views regarding the sexual terminologies in the book of Hosea, we I examine chs. 1–4. First of all, we will observe chs. 1–3, which are

---

140.   H. H. Rowley (*Unity of the Bible* [New York: Meridien, 1957], 24) notes "the uneasy syncretism of YHWH and Baal, which was always liable to break out into conflict in times of crisis."

141.   For example, אֵשֶׁת זְנוּנִים ("a wife of harlotry," 1:2); כִּי זָנְתָה אִמָּם ... כִּי אָמְרָה ("For their mother has played the harlot...for she said: 'I will go after my lovers,'" 2:7 [EV 5]).

142.   Hos 1:1; 2:4 (EV 2), 7; 3:3; 4:10, 12–14, 18. See also Hos 5:3, 4; 6:10; 9:1.

claimed to be metaphorical descriptions of Israel's religious reality, and afterwards we will turn to ch. 4, which is said to depict a reality characterized by sexual activity in the context of cultic practice.

2.3.2.1. אֵשֶׁת זְנוּנִים *in Hosea 1–3.* In Hos 1:2, YHWH calls upon his prophet to take an אֵשֶׁת זְנוּנִים.[143] What type of woman is meant here? According to Bird, the word זְנוּנִים is a plural abstract noun, one implying unconventional sexual behavior.[144] It is unlikely that this phrase simply refers to a prostitute, a woman given to prostitution.[145] If it were so, she should have been called אִישָׁה זוֹנָה instead of אֵשֶׁת זְנוּנִים. Nor is it an intensive form of זוֹנָה, for in the book of Hosea Gomer is never called a זוֹנָה ("prostitute"). Thus, it is not precise to claim that Hosea took a prostitute as his wife.

It was Wolff[146] who tied the expression אֵשֶׁת זְנוּנִים into the fertility cult hypothesis. He suggests that in the book of Hosea one should imagine a sexual rite practiced as part of Baal worship, in which Israelite women were asked to lose their virginity through sex with foreigners, with the expectation that in return they would gain the blessing of fecundity.[147] In

---

143.   In Hos 3:1, Hosea is commanded to "love a woman beloved of paramour and an adulteress" (3:1). So the conflicting accounts regarding Hosea's wife in chs. 1 and 3 have greatly troubled scholars. G. Nagy (*The Best of the Achaeans: Concepts of the Hero in Archaic Greek Poetry* [Baltimore: The Johns Hopkins University Press, 1979], 43) views the contradictions as resulting from changes that occurred in the oral tradition: "There may theoretically be as many variations on [the theme of Hosea's marriage] as there are compositions. Any theme is but a multiform, and not one of the multiforms may be considered a functional 'Urform.'" However, one cannot ignore the possibility of different modifiers for her. In any case, what is important is that the two descriptions of the woman intend to create the impression of the essential image of a wife whose sexual behavior is inappropriate.

144.   P. A. Bird, "'To Play the Harlot': An Inquiry into an Old Testament Metaphor," in *Gender and Difference in Ancient Israel* (ed. P. L. Day; Minneapolis: Fortress, 1989), 80. She presents the nuances of the various biblical terms for prostitute, harlot, and so on (ibid., 75–94).

145.   Josh 2:1; Judg 11:1. However, in the book of Hosea, Gomer is never called a זוֹנָה ("prostitute").

146.   Wolff, *Hosea*, xxii, 14–16, and also 86ff.

147.   Among the many modern scholars who support the hypothesis positing the existence of fertility rites in Canaan and Israel, are Albright (*Archaeology*, 75–77), G. von Rad (*Old Testament Theology*, vol. 2 [New York: Harper, 1965], 141–42), and K. Koch (*The Prophets*, vol. 1 [Philadelphia: Fortress, 1982], 81). Albright (*Archaeology*, 75–77) contends that "sacred prostitution was apparently an almost invariable concomitant of the cult of the Phoenician and Syrian goddess, whatever her personal name, as we know from many allusions in classical literature, especially

support of his argument, Wolff cites the well-known passage of Herodotus (1.199) in which it is reported that Babylonian women were ostensibly required, once in their lifetimes, to prostitute themselves to foreigners in honor of the goddess of love. He notes that similar rites are mentioned by Lucian (*De Syria Dea* 6), and St. Augustine (*De Civitate Dei* 4.10, with regard to the Phoenicians). Regarding the biblical case, Wolff claims that a similar sexual rite might have been practiced, based on Lev 29:29 and Prov 7:13–23, as well as the fact that in Deut 23:18 there is a reference both to professional prostitution and to a (single occurrence) sexual initiation rite. Like Rost,[148] Wolff supposes that these verses describe a rite of sexual initiation, since in Canaanite religion the ability to procreate was associated with the god Baal, and there was a widespread belief that the womb was opened in his temple. These considerations led Wolff to see אֵשֶׁת זְנוּנִים as a reference to "a…young woman ready for marriage who had submitted to the Canaanite bridal rite of initiation."[149] Her children are "children of promiscuity" (יַלְדֵי זְנוּנִים), since their mother participated in the sexual initiation rites before her marriage in order to acquire her ability to bear them.[150] Wolff claims, therefore, that there were few women who did not engage in the sexual rite. Gomer, אֵשֶׁת זְנוּנִים, whom Hosea is to marry, is not an exceptionally wicked woman; she is simply a representative of her contemporaries in Israel.

However, this supposition is based to a large extent on speculation. First of all, it should be noted that Herodotus speaks of Babylon, and not Syria or Israel. Herodotus does not even deal directly with a bridal ritual, but rather claims that women were required to prostitute themselves once in their lifetime. Another problem in using Herodotus' report as a source for these customs is the vast gap in time between the era when this custom was purported to have existed and when Herodotus' report was written.[151] Furthermore, many scholars at the beginning of the twentieth

---

in Herodotus, Strabo, and Lucian… [T]he erotic aspect of their cult must have sunk to extremely sordid depths of social degradation." Von Rad (*Old Testament Theology*, 2:141–42) identifies אֵשֶׁת זְנוּנִים whom the prophet Hosea marries with "a woman who took part in the Canaanite fertility rites."

148.   L. Rost, "Erwägungen zu Hos 4:13f.," in Baumgartner et al., *Festschrift Alfred Bertholet*, 451–61 (esp. 451).

149.   Wolff, *Hosea*, 15.

150.   Wolff (ibid., 88) expounds that "daughters" and "brides" in 4:13b could mean the more beautiful women among those who came to the initiation rites at the high places and went aside with priests into the forest.

151.   Herodotus was a close contemporary of Ezra and Nehemiah in the fifth century B.C.E.

century reached the following conclusions:[152] Herodotus could never have visited all of the places he claimed to have visited; his cultural analyses were superficial and relied heavily on his source, Hecataeus; Herodotus' knowledge of Mesopotamia was much less accurate and complete than his knowledge of Egypt; no cuneiform text supports the idea that Assyrian or Babylonian women engaged in this rite; Herodotus, like all the Greeks, wrote about the "barbarians" with the aim of demonstrating the superiority of the Greeks, and his texts are replete with accusations of cannibalism and rites of sexual lawlessness. In his accounts of barbarian sexual morality, Herodotus apparently tried to show the terrible results that could occur if decent women were not kept in isolation and guarded as they were in Greece.[153] Hence, his writings cannot be used as a reliable source with respect to Mesopotamia.

What is more, Wolff's suggestion has no biblical ground. There is no biblical trace hinting that sexual initiation rites existed for marriage in Israel. Proverbs 7:13–23 refers to a married woman, who is neither a virgin, a bride, nor a cultic prostitute engaging in any rite whatsoever. According to van der Toorn, female prostitution was engaged in to earn money for the payment of vows, and not as part of a fertility rite.[154] In Deut 23:18, there is no reference at all to sexual relations of the type implied by the notion of sexual initiation rites.[155] Moreover, Deut 22:23–24 dictates the punishment for a case of pre-marital loss of virginity; according to Wolff's theory, it might be expected that this legislation should have included an indictment of such initiation rites. In fact, there is no such thing. Deuteronomy 22:13–21 deals with the legal dictates regarding proof of virginity (when a husband has doubts regarding it): yet here as well there is no reference to sexual rites involving virgins.[156]

Therefore, the idea that the term אֵשֶׁת זְנוּנִים refers to a woman who participated in a marriage rite is implausible. It also does not refer to a professional prostitute. If not, then to whom does it refer? Truly the term is a vague one, unique to Hosea. The crux of the interpretation of the

152. W. Baumgartner, "Herodots babylonische und assyrische Nachrichten," in *Zum Alten Testament und seiner Umwelt* (Leiden: Brill, 1959), 282–331; particularly, see O. K. Armayor, "Did Herodotus Ever Go to Egypt?," *JARCE* 15 (1978): 59–73.

153. T. Frymer-Kensky, *In the Wake of the Goddesses: Women, Culture, and the Biblical Transformation of Pagan Myth* (New York: Maxwell Macmillan, 1992), 200.

154. K. van der Toorn, "Female Prostitution in Payment of Vows in Ancient Israel," *JBL* 108 (1989): 193–205.

155. The term קְדֵשָׁה will be discussed below, §2.3.2.2.3.

156. For a more detailed critique of Wolff, see Rudolph, *Hosea*, 44ff.

term is centered on the word זְנוּנִים. As an abstract plural noun,[157] the word זְנוּנִים refers to a personal attribute, and not to an activity. Hence, Bird's opinion that Hosea's use of this abstract noun may imply a tendency rather than a profession seems reasonable.[158] Therefore, the woman characterized as an אֵשֶׁת זְנוּנִים is a woman of loose sexual morals, whose promiscuous nature is exhibited in her "fornications" (זְנוּנִים).[159] This also has symbolic significance, as implied by other uses of the word זְנוּנִים in the book of Hosea. In Hos 4:12 and 5:4, the people are condemned for their estrangement from YHWH by a "spirit of whoredom" (רוּחַ זְנוּנִים). The use of the term זְנוּנִים here serves to express a certain state of alienation from God, which came about due to their following other gods (Baal). If this is the case, it seems that for Hosea the term זְנוּנִים serves to describe the religious condition in Israel. The reason that he uses the expressions אֵשֶׁת זְנוּנִים and יַלְדֵי זְנוּנִים is his desire to articulate the religious "adultery" that had spread across the Land: כִּי זָנֹה תִזְנֶה הָאָרֶץ מֵאַחֲרֵי יְהוָה ("the Land does commit great harlotry, departing from YHWH," 1:2). The implication here is clear: the Land has taken lovers other than YHWH. The logical assumption is that the "love affairs" are with other gods, notwithstanding the fact that Hos 1:2 does not identify the objects of Israel's affections. In any event, the message in this verse is that "the Land" is unfaithful to YHWH.[160] Not only is the Land referred to here as an אֵשֶׁת זְנוּנִים ("a woman of harlotry"), but its children are represented as יַלְדֵי זְנוּנִים ("children of harlotry"). This identification between the woman and the land, and the woman's children and the children of Israel, ultimately comes to light in ch. 2,[161] where the woman's pursuit of her lovers serves as a metaphor for the cultic practices of the general population, and of the men in particular. Therefore, it is important to remember that despite the use of female sexual imagery, Hosea addresses his prophecies precisely to his fellow citizens and the Israelite elite, rather than to the Israelite women.[162]

157.   GKC §124f. esp. 397.
158.   Bird, "To Play the Harlot," 80.
159.   Ibid.
160.   Ibid., 81.
161.   In 2:5 (EV 3), the mother and the Land are identified with each other.
162.   See P. A. Bird, "The Place of Women in the Israelite Cultus," in *Ancient Israelite Religion: Essays in Honor of Frank Moore Cross* (ed. P. D. Miller, P. D. Hanson, and S. D. McBride; Philadelphia: Fortress, 1987), 397–419. It should be noted that unlike other prophets—Amos (4:1) and Isaiah (3:16), for example—who directly blame Israelite women for their sins, Hosea blames the men of Israel for the sexual improprieties of the women. In Hos 4:14, God may even be excusing the Israelite women from any punishment for purported sexual crimes.

The placing of responsibility on the Land (that is, the people) in Hos 1:2, is elaborated in an extended allegory in ch. 2. In 2:7b (EV 5b), the charge is summed up as follows:

> For she said: I will go after my lovers, who give me my bread and my water, my wool and my flax, my oil and my drink.

It seems clear, from the nature of the gifts mentioned in 2:7 (EV 5), that they are related either directly or indirectly to the Land's products (see 2:10 [EV 8], 11 [EV 9], 14 [EV 12]), which depend on rain. Israel thinks the gifts come from her "lovers," whom she "goes after" (2:7 [EV 5], 9 [EV 7]), and she decorates herself in order to win their hearts (2:15 [EV 13]); but actually these gifts are from YHWH (2:10 [EV 8]), who will take them away from her, and strip her naked (2:11 [EV 9], 12 [EV 10], 14 [EV 12]; cf. 5 [EV 3]). The allegory is obvious: Israel has turned to Baal, the Canaanite weather god, abandoning her covenant Lord, YHWH, who is the true God of fertility.[163] Therefore, we can sum up and say that the sexual terms such as זוֹנָה and זְנוּנִים in Hos 1–3 suggest that Israel turned to Baals, and that Israel's act of "harlotry" with Baal is expressed in her worship of him (2:10 [EV 8], 13 [EV 11], 15 [EV 13]).

2.3.2.2. The Reality of the Perverted YHWH Cult in Hosea 4. Despite the metaphorical use of sexual terms in Hos 1–3 to describe the acts of infidelity in the Israelite religion, which abandoned YHWH and followed Baals, one can see that in ch. 4, in the context of the cult of Baal or the perverted cult of YHWH, those languages are no longer metaphorical.

Hosea 4 is composed of three sections, each of which comprises in effect a single composition: vv. 1–3; vv. 4–10; and vv. 11–19. Each section ends with a declaration of YHWH's visitation (vv. 3, 7–10, 19). In the introductory section, the basic tone toward Israel (the inhabitants of the Land) is contentious (vv. 1–2), and it includes a proclamation that the people's future is going to be the miserable state of languishment[164] (v. 3). The subsequent sections (vv. 4–10, 11–19) criticize Israel's failing relationship with God. The second section focuses on the guilt of the priests,[165] who failed to bring the people closer to (a knowledge of) God

---

163. Bird, "To Play the Harlot," 82.

164. In v. 3, the word אֻמְלָל, Pual of the root אָמַל, meaning "to be weak, languish," describes the miserable state of the inhabitants and animals due to YHWH's judgment in the form of a great drought (cf. BDB, 51; Wolff, *Hosea*, 68); it denotes first the withering of vegetation (Isa 16:8; Joel 1:12), but can also mean, in antithesis of "giving birth to children" (1 Sam 2:5), to become childless, barren (Jer 15:9).

165. The phrase וְעַמְּךָ כִּמְרִיבֵי כֹהֵן ("for your people are as they that contend with the priest") in v. 4b is corrupted, and thus it should be vocalized as follows:

(vv. 4–6), and ends with a pronouncement of their sentence for this crime (vv. 7–10).[166] The final section states that as a result of this cult, the priests and the people indulged in a perverted form of worship (vv. 11–18), and confirms that the inevitable exile[167] is the result of the perverted sacrificial rites that they engaged in (v. 19).[168]

The section consisting of vv. 11–19 can be divided into two parts: vv. 11–14 and vv. 15–19. While the first part focuses on the reality of and reason for the perverted cult, the second part confirms that such a cult is religious adultery, betrayal of YHWH, and apostasy, which finds expression in the following of other gods.[169] Verses 11–14 are framed by two verses (v. 11[170] and v. 14[171]) that are similar in tone and content: the

---

וְעַמְּךָ רִיבִי (הַ)כֹּהֵן (cf. the comment of *BHS*). The assumption is that the כ preceding מְרִיבֵי is a dittography, and therefore should be omitted. And the word כֹּהֵן is understood as a vocative and as a collective singular. Therefore, the phrase is interpreted as follows: "My contention is with you, O priest." It appears that in vv. 4–6 the primary responsibility for YHWH's impending wrath on the Land (4:3) is placed on the priests.

166.   In vv. 7–10, the form of speech changes from an indictment of the priests, addressed collectively in the second person singular, to judgment upon them for their misdeeds expressed in the third person plural. Since vv. 4–6 and 7–10 both tell of the guilt of the priests followed by the resulting judgment, there is no reason to doubt that the two passages belong to the same source. Grammatical changes in person are common among the prophets and not least in Hosea, where different themes are also artfully combined in a single discourage (see Macintosh, *Hosea*, 141).

167.   The phrase צָרַר רוּחַ אוֹתָהּ בִּכְנָפֶיהָ ("The wind has bound her up in her wings") metaphorically depicts Israel's fateful exile: it is understood that the enemy of Israel (a strong nation) metaphorically represented by a wind will sweep Israel into exile (see Macintosh, *Hosea*, 173).

168.   The phrase וְיֵבֹשׁוּ מִזִּבְחוֹתָם is interpreted as "and they shall be ashamed because of their sacrifices." The word זִבְחוֹת, which is the feminine plural of זֶבַח, appears only here, and may reflect northern dialectical usage (Macintosh, ibid.). Therefore, the phrase implies that Israel's shamefulness (exile) will come from their perverse cultic rites.

169.   The verb זָנָה in v. 15 serves to depict metaphorically the religious adultery of Israel; the verb סָרַר represents Israel's lack of obedience, rebellion, and betrayal; the phrase חֲבוּר עֲצַבִּים אֶפְרָיִם ("Ephraim is joined to idols") in v. 17 indicates that Israelites worshipped other gods embodied by idols (עֲצַבִּים).

170.   (לִשְׁמֹר) זְנוּת וְיַיִן וְתִירוֹשׁ יִקַּח לֵב ("[to take heed to] harlotry, wine, and new wine take away the heart"). In v. 11, the subject of the verb יִקַּח is the entire previous phrase beginning with לִשְׁמֹר at the end of v. 10. In defense of the verse division of MT, Rudolph (*Hosea*, 105) translated v. 10 in the following way: "They have ceased to take heed of YHWH." However, this view goes against the argument that the verb שָׁמַר is not used elsewhere with YHWH as its object. Usually, the verb שָׁמַר, commonly translated "to keep," denotes here "cleaving to," "devoting oneself to," and

people became addicted to promiscuity and wine, and hence lack awareness and sensitivity (v. 11);[172] they are undiscerning, and this will lead to their destruction (v. 14b).[173] These two verses are important to an understanding of the verses they enclose. Verse 11 presents a cause for the people's perverted cultic activities, which are described further on in the following verses (vv. 12–14a). In other words, the features of the perverted cult described in vv. 12–14 are actually a result of that which is said in v. 11 regarding the spiritual state of the priest and the people.[174] So, vv. 11–14 are structured in the following way:

> the cause *a* (v. 11)
>> the result (vv. 12–14a)
> the cause *a'* (the confirmation of cause *a*) (v. 14b)

In this manner, the structure of the text allows for a unified reading: vv. 11–14 are written in a critical tone, directed against the perverted cultic rites, which are a result of the people's stupidity, and which led to their destruction.

the usage is peculiar to Hosea (see Morag, "Uniqueness of Hosea's Language," 501f.). Elsewhere שָׁמַר is commonly used in the semantic field of ethics and religion when its objects are "instruction," "ways of YHWH," "words of YHWH," "statutes and ordinances," and so on. Here, however, its use is in the field of sexuality and sensual love (see 12:13), and therefore, its meaning is "love of" or "devotion of" (see Macintosh, *Hosea*, 148–49).

171.   Verse 14 reads: וְעָם לֹא יָבִין יִלָּבֵט ("and the people that does not understand will come to ruin").

172.   The word לֵב ("heart") in v. 11 symbolizes the place of thought and understanding (see Deut 29:3; Jer 5:21; Prov 7:7). So, those whose hearts were taken away became senseless and inconsiderate.

173.   The phrase עָם לֹא יָבִין is literally understood as "a people who do not discriminate (or understand)." The verb יִלָּבֵט is a deviation from נָדְמוּ in v. 6. See Andersen and Freedman, *Hosea*, 370. Ruin is the fate of the foolish talker in the two other places in which the verb יִלָּבֵט appears (Prov 10:8, 10).

174.   According to the LXX, עַמִּי ("my people") at the beginning of v. 12 is connected to the end of v. 11, and so v. 11 is read "Harlotry, wine, and new wine take away the heart (of my people)" (see Wolff, *Hosea*, 83; Andersen and Freedman, *Hosea*, 364). Furthermore, i-, the third masculine suffix in עֵצוֹ and מַקְלוֹ of v. 12, is of the (collective singular) people, while it is read in the plural. This fact indicates that vv. 12–14 should be read together with v. 11. If so, we will note that the spiritual state of the people, as articulated in the phrase "(to take heed to) harlotry, wine, and new wine take away the heart," is the main factor that leads to the people's perverted cultic practices (vv. 12–14a). The phrase וְעָם לֹא יָבִין יִלָּבֵט ("and the people that does not understand will come to ruin," v. 14b) confirms this suggestion in the same tone in v. 11.

I will now examine the practical features of the aforementioned cultic practices described in vv. 12–14a. Particular attention will be paid to the sexual language used by Hosea in the creation of metaphorical meanings, or in the depiction of practical sexual activity, in each individual instance.

2.3.2.2.1. *Verse 12.*

2.3.2.2.1.1. עַמִּי בְּעֵצוֹ יִשְׁאָל וּמַקְלוֹ יַגִּיד לוֹ *(v. 12a)*. The phrase בְּ...יִשְׁאָל is technical and denotes the seeking of oracles.[175] In normative Yahwism, it is YHWH himself who is the legitimate object of such inquiry.[176] In this verse, in any case, the people[177] are accused of turning to עֵצוֹ ("their stock") and מַקְלוֹ ("their staff").[178] What was the real reason for the criticism of the people with regard to the "stock" and "staff"? One view holds that "stock"/"staff" symbolize the male sexual organ.[179] Another suggests that "stock"/"staff" refer to divination methods involving the use of wooden rods.[180] The evidence suggested for such is as follows: the word עֵץ ("tree, wood") serves as a reference to the "tree oracles," such as the "oak of Moreh" and the "oak of Meonenim" (see Gen 12:6; Judg 9:37);[181] the word מַקֵּל[182] can denote a "staff" delivering the oracles of a tree.

However, it should be noted that the usual object of the verb שָׁאַל is a god; the usual subject of the verb הִגִּיד is a speaker.[183] Therefore, both words, עֵץ and מַקֵּל, in conjunction with these verbs seem to have something to do with the symbol of deity, perhaps Asherah, or a cult-pole (cf. Deut 16:21; Judg 6:25–26, etc.).[184] In this respect, it is implausible that

---

175.   Macintosh, *Hosea*, 151.

176.   See Judg 1:1; 1 Sam 2:1; Ezek 21:26.

177.   Although עַמִּי ("my people") is linked to v. 11, the subject of the verb יִשְׁאָל is עַמִּי, which is collective singular. Yet Andersen and Freedman (*Hosea*, 356) contend that the subject of the verb יִשְׁאָל must be the priest, based on the fact that the verb appears in the singular form.

178.   As mentioned above, ‑וֹ, the third masculine suffix in עֵצוֹ and מַקְלוֹ of v. 12, is of the (collective singular) people. It is, however, translated in plural in the LXX.

179.   H. L. Ginsberg, "Lexicographical Notes," in *Hebräische Wortforschung* (VTSup 16; Leiden: Brill, 1967), 74ff.; Bird, "To Play the Harlot," 83.

180.   See Macintosh, *Hosea*, 152.

181.   The oak tree is associated with the location of an oracle and the term מְעוֹנְנִים refers to diviners, soothsayers (cf. BDB, 47).

182.   In this context, the word מַקֵּל is understood simply to denote a "branch, small branch."

183.   The word מַקֵּל has no preposition unlike its parallel עֵצוֹ, so it appears that it is the subject (Andersen and Freedman, *Hosea*, 366).

184.   Ibid. The word עֵץ is also a derogatory term for a graven image or wooden idol of a god (see Jer 2:27; Hab 2:19; Isa 40:20; 44:13).

the two words עֵץ and מַקֵּל signify the male sexual organ or are suggestive of divining techniques.[185] The object of the attack here is the
people who do not inquire of YHWH (לֹא שׁוֹאֲלִים בַּיהוָה) but inquire of
other gods[186]; they place their trust in other gods and follow them. This
view is also supported by the sexual language זָנָה in the second part of
the verse.

2.3.2.2.1.2. כִּי רוּחַ זְנוּנִים הִתְעָה וַיִּזְנוּ מִתַּחַת אֱלֹהֵיהֶם *(v. 12b)*. While the verb
הִתְעָה allows for an abstract meaning in describing the people's ethical
aberration (Ps 5:4; Prov 7:25; 14:22), in its literary sense it is linked to
intoxication (Isa 19:14; 28:7; Job 12:25). The verb describes the uncon-
scious erring of the drunken person, and thereby his loss of reason.[187] The
phrase רוּחַ זְנוּנִים הִתְעָה ("the spirit of harlotry has caused [them] to err")
is parallel to the phrase לִשְׁמֹר זְנוּת וְיַיִן וְתִירוֹשׁ יִקַּח לֵב ("to take heed to
harlotry, wine, and new wine take away the heart") in its meaning.
Therefore, the phrase of v. 12b can be understood as follows: "the spirit
of harlotry has caused (them)[188] to err, and they have acted promiscu-
ously toward their God." The idiom זָנָה מִתַּחַת is strongly reminiscent of
the expression זָנָה מֵאַחֲרֵי in 1:2b. The verb זָנָה together with the com-
posite preposition מִתַּחַת[189] implies here "the rebellious betrayal of an
obligatory relationship of obedience and submission."[190] In other words,
the phrase זָנָה מִתַּחַת אֱלֹהֵיהֶם suggests that the people (including the
priests) became estranged from their God, and went whoring after other
gods.[191] In this phrase, as in 1:2b,[192] the use of sexual language, and

185. Macintosh, *Hosea*, 152.
186. In foreign religions in ancient times, gods and their symbols were completely identified.
187. The use of this verb in describing animals going astray (Exod 23:4; Isa
53:6; Job 38:41; Ps 119:176) suggests that a person who wanders astray (Gen 21:14;
37:15; Ps 107:4; Isa 47:15) or who is drunk (Isa 28:7) is like a brainless animal
(Andersen and Freedman, *Hosea*, 367).
188. עַם ("people") should be seen as the object of the verb הִתְעָה since the
subject of the following clause (...וַיִּזְנוּ) is syntactically related to the object of the
previous clause.
189. The preposition מִתַּחַת is comprised of תַּחַת, which implies subordination,
and the word מִן ("from, out of"), which has a privative force (see Macintosh, *Hosea*,
152).
190. See Wolff, *Hosea*, 85.
191. Hos 9:1, with the idiom זָנָה מִן, will help us to understand the phrase זָנָה
מִתַּחַת אֱלֹהֵיהֶם: it clearly has a female model in mind, although the verb appears here
in the masculine, as here, addressing collective Israel; the accusation of fornication
is immediately followed in 9:1 by further reinforcement—אָהַבְתָּ אֶתְנָן עַל כָּל גָּרְנוֹת
דָּגָן ("you have loved a harlot's earnings on every threshing floor"), which creates an

specifically the verb זָנָה is employed to depict the unfaithfulness of the people to their God (YHWH) due to their rebellious spirit (רוּחַ זְנוּנִים, "spirit of harlotry").

2.3.2.2.2. *Verse 13.*

2.3.2.2.2.1. עַל רָאשֵׁי הֶהָרִים. The phrase ...עַל רָאשֵׁי הֶהָרִים...וְעַל הַגְּבָעוֹת (וְעַל הַגְּבָעוֹת...תַּחַת אַלּוֹן וְלִבְנֶה וְאֵלָה ("Upon the tops of the mountains, and...upon the hills...under oaks and poplars and terebinths"), in Hos 4:13, recalls the Deuteronomic expression עַל הֶהָרִים הָרָמִים וְעַל הַגְּבָעוֹת וְתַחַת כָּל עֵץ רַעֲנָן ("upon the high mountains, and upon the hills, and under every green tree") in Deut 12:2,[193] and its variations,[194] which refer to the location of the illegitimate cult practices in the eyes of the Deuteronomic author. Considering that in Israel the hills and mountains were often sites for בָּמוֹת,[195] and even the verses in which such a phrase

impression of licentiousness, and reiterates other key terms (אָהַב, "to love"; דָּגָן, "grain") from ch. 2. I understand from such that collective Israel is personified as female in each of these uses of זָנָה and is accused of "acting like a promiscuous woman/prostitute" (see Bird, "To Play the Harlot," 83).

192.   Hos 1:2b reads: כִּי זָנֹה תִזְנֶה הָאָרֶץ מֵאַחֲרֵי יְהוָה ("for the land does commit great harlotry, departing from YHWH"). The Land in 1:2 is not only identified with a woman/wife ("wife of harlotry"), but also its inhabitants are identified with "children of harlotry." In 4:12, the subject of the promiscuity is the people instead of the Land.

193.   This expression has characteristically been referred to as a Deuteronomic set-phrase. See J. Bright, "The Date of the Prose Sermons of Jeremiah," *JBL* 70 (1951): 35. However, Hos 4:13 appears to have an original format, and Deut 12:2, on which other verses are dependent, seems to be a prosaic form of the former (Hos 4:13). The texts in Deuteronomy and Hosea share a form of expression in which appear the words הַר ("mountain"), גִּבְעָה ("hill"), and the name of a tree or related term. Furthermore, Hos 4:13 offers names for three trees (אַלּוֹן, "oak"; לִבְנֶה, "pop-lar"; and אֵלָה, "terebinth"). Deut 12:2 seems to have compressed these terms into כָּל עֵץ רַעֲנָן ("every green tree"). If this argument regarding the literary dependence between Hosea and Deuteronomy is valid, then we possess further evidence that Deut 12:12 is a more recent text than Hosea. For a detailed explication of the literary dependence between these verses, see W. H. Holladay, "On Every High Hill and Under Every Green Tree," *VT* 11 (1961): 170–76.

194.   1 Kgs 14:23; 2 Kgs 16:4; Isa 30:25; 57:5, 7; 65:7; Jer 2:20; 3:6; 17:2; Ezek 6:13; 20:28; 34:6; Hos 4:13; 2 Chr 28:4.

195.   It should be acknowledged that not all of the בָּמוֹת in Israel were located on high places. The בָּמָה at Topheth in Jerusalem was located in "the valley of the son of Hinnom" (Jer 7:31; 19:5–6; 32:25), and Ezekiel attacks the בָּמוֹת of the hills and ravines (Ezek 6:3). Therefore, while a reference to a בָּמָה may not necessarily indicate its location on a hill or mountain, the converse, a reference to a hill or mountain where cultic activities take place, certainly suggests a בָּמָה. What is important here regarding the בָּמוֹת is that the word בָּמָה denotes an object similar in

appears[196] explicitly indicate the high hills as a location for בָּמוֹת, it is certain that the cultic rites described in Hos 4 took place at בָּמוֹת.[197] As we saw above (§2.2.2), we may conjecture the cultic circumstance regarding the calf image at Bethel from an observation of the characteristics of the cultic rites in the high places, as they are described in Hos 4, since for Hosea Bethel is a primary example of the wicked בָּמוֹת that spread throughout the northern kingdom.

Hosea explicitly condemns בָּמוֹת as a sin (Hos 10:8), and describes the cultic activities at the בָּמוֹת with fury and disgust in 4:11–14. Undoubtedly, in the early period of the history of Israel, the בָּמוֹת were considered legitimate sites for the worship of YHWH. Samuel partook in a sacrificial meal at a high place in his hometown, and took with him Saul (1 Sam 9:11–26). Even the Deuteronomistic sources show that the בָּמוֹת were accepted as sites for the worship of YHWH prior to the construction of Solomon's temple:[198] Solomon offered sacrifices and YHWH revealed himself to him at the high place at Gibeon, described in the text as a בָּמָה גְדוֹלָה ("a great high place," 1 Kgs 3:4). The Deuteronomist notes their

structure to an altar, and identified in its function with an altar in Israelite religion, as evident in the pre-Deuteronomistic sources (1 Sam 9:12–25; 1 Kgs 3:4). See Haran, *Temple and Temple-Service*, 19–20.

196.   1 Kgs 14:23; 2 Kgs 16:4; 1 Kgs 11:7 (cf. also 2 Kgs 23:13).

197.   According to biblical reports, the בָּמָה is usually understood as an open-air ritual precinct situated in an elevated natural or human-made setting, while the cultic accessories associated with it usually include pillars, altars, and sacred trees or *asherim*. Some scholars (cf. W. B. Barrick, "What Do We Really Know about 'High-places'?," *SEÅ* 45 [1980]: 54; R. E. Stager and S. R. Wolff, "Production and Commerce in Temple Courtyards: An Olive Press in the Sacred Precinct at Tel Dan," *BASOR* 243 [1981]: 99; J. E. Catron, "Temple and *bāmāh*: Some Considerations," in *The Pitcher is Broken: Memorial Essays for Gösta W. Ahlström* [ed. S. W. Holloway and L. K. Handy; JSOTSup 190; Sheffield: Sheffield Academic, 1995], 150–65) report that some בָּמוֹת, such as that at Dan, had roofed buildings. However, such reports do not deny the existence of the בָּמָה as an open-air sanctuary, but instead affirm also the existence of a "house of bama" (בֵּית בָּמָה), that is, a בָּמָה with roofed buildings, which is mentioned in the Bible, too (1 Kgs 12:31; 13:32; 2 Kgs 17:29, 32; 23:19; cf. M. Haran, "Temples and Cultic Open Areas as Reflected in the Bible," in *Temples and High Places* [ed. A. Biran; Jerusalem: Hebrew Union College, 1981], 31–32). For a בָּמָה as a rustic open-air sanctuary from the Iron Age I, see A. Mazar, "Iron Age I," in *The Archaeology of Ancient Israel* (ed. A. Ben-Tor; New Haven: Yale University Press, 1992), 292–93; Mazar, "The 'Bull Site,'" 27ff.; W. G. Dever, *Recent Archaeological Discoveries and Biblical Research* (Seattle: University of Washington Press, 1990), 132–34; Haran, *Temple and Temple-Service*, 18–25.

198.   See Miller, *Religion of Ancient Israel*, 53.

continuation as sites of sacrifice by the people and their continued construction by kings:[199] the בָּמוֹת are similarly regarded as shrines of Yahwistic worship in 2 Kgs 17:25–29, where Aramaic peoples who "feared YHWH" appointed priests to serve him at the בָּמוֹת. Although Hosea, in northern Israel, vehemently condemned the high places as a sin (Hos 10:8), in Judah, Hezekiah was the first king to destroy the local shrines, namely, the בָּמוֹת (2 Kgs 18:4),[200] though Manasseh brought them back into use (2 Kgs 21:3), which persisted until Josiah's reforms (2 Kgs 23). Josiah recalled all of the Judean priests to Jerusalem and destroyed the local sanctuaries, that is, the high places (2 Kgs 23:5, 8–9). Apparently, he waged a more thorough reform than that of Hezekiah, which extended to the territories of the northern kingdom. In fact, it was Josiah who dismantled the בָּמוֹת at Bethel, even though Hosea was the first to condemned them (Hos 10:8).[201]

Why, then, were the high places, which had been accepted for the worship of YHWH, condemned in prophetic and official circles? At least in the case of southern Judah, it might be argued that the בָּמוֹת, the local sanctuaries, were eliminated by Hezekiah and Josiah in order to centralize worship at the temple (מִקְדָּשׁ) in Jerusalem. Yet this argument does not explain Hosea's delegitimization of the high places in northern Israel. It would be a mistake to insist on a fundamental difference between a high place and the temple (מִקְדָּשׁ) in Jerusalem.[202] It is correct that our biblical text supplies a clearer picture regarding popular religion in northern Israel than it does regarding southern Judah; one might suspect that the texts that dealt with southern Judah were redacted to conform to

---

199. Ibid.

200. In any case, it should be noted in this context that some scholars (e.g. H. Spieckermann, *Juda unter Assur in der Sargonidenzeit* [Göttingen: Vandenhoeck & Ruprecht, 1982; Grand Rapids: Eerdmans, 1989], 170–75, 195–99; Na'aman, "Debated Historicity," 179–95) attribute the accounts of the elimination of the high places and pillars in 2 Kgs 18:4 to Deuteronomistic redaction, and they seriously doubt that Hezekiah carried out a real cultic reform. However, Weinfeld ("Emergence of the Deuteronomic Movement," 85) postulates "an aniconic tendency originating in the North which pervaded Judah after the destruction of Samaria."

201. According to 2 Kgs 17:25–28, the בֵּית בָּמוֹת at Bethel was not destroyed in 722 B.C.E. by the Assyrians. The possibility that it was destroyed by Hezekiah seems to be meager, as his reform does not seem to be extensive and far-reaching, especially given the fact that his son restored the previous order. The prophetic oracle on the destruction of the Bethel altar, in the story of Jeroboam in 2 Kgs 13, could be interpreted as an insertion in reference to the reform of Josiah in 2 Kgs 23:15–20.

202. Regarding this matter, it is worth noting M. Haran, "The Divine Presence in the Israelite Cult and the Cultic Institution," *Bib* 50 (1969): 253f.

the norms at the time when the cult was unified and centralized to the temple (מִקְדָּשׁ) in Jerusalem, or limited to it. In northern Israel, in any event, the important holy places, including that of Bethel, were in effect בָּמוֹת. Therefore, it would not make sense to try to find a reason for the denunciation of the high places in northern Israel by way of contrasting the high place (בָּמָה) and the temple (בֵּית מִקְדָּשׁ). It seems that the reason for the polemical attitudes toward the high places in Hosea's case must be examined in light of the prevailing cultic attitudes toward the high places. In other words, it seems that the negative attitude regarding the בָּמוֹת developed because of the cultic activities performed on them. The cultic practice at the high places entailed the use of their basic appurtenances, namely, pillars (מַצֵּבוֹת) and sacred trees or *asherim* (אֲשֵׁרִים), which were related to other gods.[203] The pillars and the *asherim* could have been additional reasons for condemnation of the high places, other than the cultic rites held at them, as is evident in the polemical nature of the prophecies of Hosea, and the reforms of Hezekiah (2 Kgs 18:4) and Josiah (2 Kgs 23:5–14). Hosea clearly refers to the high places in 10:8. However, he condemns them only indirectly through criticism of the abominable cultic activities that took place "on the tops of mountains" (4:13), where the בָּמוֹת were located, as aforementioned. The disparagement of the high places as "the sin of Israel" (10:8) suggests that the cultic customs practiced at the high places were at the very least non-Yahwistic and reprehensible. It seems that Hosea's negative attitude toward the high places relates to the cultic rites associated with them, and the appurtenances of the בָּמוֹת, such as pillars and sacred trees or *asherim*, which represented other gods.

2.3.2.2.2.2. יְזַבֵּחוּ...יְקַטֵּרוּ. What exactly took place at the high places on the tops of mountains? Hosea makes use of the verbs לְזַבֵּחַ ("offer sacrifices") and לְקַטֵּר ("burn incense" or "make offerings by fire") in order to describe the cultic features happening there, namely, slaughtering of sacrificial animals and eating of their meat, as well as the smoke rising from the burning of incense or sacrifices.

---

203. All of the kings of northern Israel are condemned in the Bible (1 Kgs 12:26–33; 13–14; 15:25–26, 34; 16:2–4, 13, 19, 25–26, 30–33; 18–19; 21:20–26; 22:51–53; 2 Kgs 13:2–3, 11; 14:25; 15:9, 18, 24, 28; there is moderate condemnation in 2 Kgs 3:2–3; 10:18–31; 17:2). The reason for their condemnation is not the use of the high places, but rather the worship of pagan gods there, or worship of YHWH accompanied by Baalized cultic practices (2 Kgs 17:7–18). On appurtenances of the high places, see Exod 34:13; Deut 7:5; 12:3; 1 Kgs 14:23; 2 Kgs 21:3; 23:14; 2 Chr 14:2; 31:1; 33:3.

For Hosea, the verbs לְזַבֵּחַ and לְקַטֵּר signify the sacrifices offered to the Baalim, the Canaanite gods,[204] at the high places (בָּמוֹת, Hos 11:2). These two words appear sometimes in the Deuteronomistic History, mainly with regard to other gods.[205] The verb זִיבֵּחַ naturally presupposes as its object the זֶבַח ("sacrifice"), which is a general term for the sacrifices eaten at feasts.[206] Therefore, what is meant by the verb here is not only the slaughter of the sacrificial animal, but also, and especially, the eating of its meat (Hos 8:13).[207] According to BDB, the meaning of the Piel form of the root קַטֵּר is "to make sacrifice smoke; to send sacrifice in smoke; to offer sacrifice by burning."[208]

Since Hosea's time, the Piel form of קַטֵּר has often been used in the context of the worship of other gods.[209] The Piel form of קַטֵּר, which is the one used in Hos 4:13 (cf. Isa 65:3bβ), usually refers to offerings made by fire in honor of other gods or to the Baalized Yahwistic cult at the condemned high places. Therefore, the use of the Piel form of קַטֵּר in Hos 4:13 may indicate that the prophet is actually decrying the people offering sacrifices by fire to pagan gods.

2.3.2.2.2.3. עַל כֵּן תִּזְנֶינָה בְּנוֹתֵיכֶם וְכַלּוֹתֵיכֶם תְּנָאַפְנָה (*v. 13b*).[210] The question that arises related to this phrase is whether the sexual languages—זָנָה ("commit harlotry") and נָאַף ("commit adultery")—are metaphorical, or

---

204. Baal is representative of the Canaanite gods. This subject is discussed in detail in §3.2.1.

205. 1 Kgs 11:8; 22:24; 2 Kgs 12:4; 14:4; 16:4, 35; see also 2 Kgs 22:17.

206. BDB, 256. In the texts of the Holiness code and Priestly code, זְבָחִים are defined as זֶבַח שְׁלָמִים ("sacrifice of peace-offerings," Lev 3:1), but sometimes the word זֶבַח is used as a more general term for sacrifice (Lev 17:5, 7, 8; 19:6; 23:37; Num 16:3).

207. Wolff, *Hosea*, 86.

208. BDB, 882.

209. De Vaux, *Ancient Israel*, 438; Wolff, *Hosea*, 40; BDB, 882. The Piel form of the root קַטֵּר is normally used in reference to worship in places such as high places (1 Kgs 22:44; 2 Kgs 12:4; 14:4; 17:11; 23:5), hills (Hos 4:13), mountains (Hos 11:2; Jer 1:16), gardens (Isa 65:3), and so on. On the other hand, the Hiphil form of the verb, הִקְטִיר, which appears mainly in Leviticus, as aforementioned, is used in reference to worship of YHWH. For further distinction between the Piel and Hiphil forms of the root קַטֵּר, see J. Wellhausen, *Prolegomena to the History of Ancient Israel* (trans. J. S. Black and A. Menzies; 3d printing; Cleveland: World Publishing, 1961), 63 n. 2; see also K. Nielsen, *Incense in Ancient Israel* (VTSup 38; Leiden: Brill, 1986), 156.

210. Here, the speech shifts from the third person plural (4:13a) to the second person plural (4:13b). It appears that the shift was made in order to emphasize the consequences of the indictment against the listeners (the people) by addressing them

whether they indicate actual sexual activity. If they refer to actual sexual activity, another question must be added: Did such sexual activities take place in the context of cultic rites? In order to answer these questions, we should first of all remember that v. 13 is closely interrelated to its preceding and following verses, as we saw above (§2.3.2.2). Verses 11 and 12 show the people's spiritual status in terms of the cultic reality depicted in v. 13, and elucidated afterwards in v. 14.

The sacrificial cult described in v. 13a is the illicit one carried out at the high places (בָּמוֹת), as was observed above. Verse 13b opens with the adverb עַל כֵּן ("therefore"). This term[211] assumes that the present phrase (v. 13b) describes the consequences of the improper activities depicted in the preceding phrase (v. 13a). That is to say, a person's actions (v. 13a) have repercussions in the behavior of one's daughters (v. 13b). The cultic activities in v. 13a are described through the two verbs זִבַּח and קִטֵּר.[212] In particular, the activities associated with the verb זִבַּח include sacrificial meals, and seem to be related to the sexual language of זָנָה and נָאַף in v. 13aβ: after the offering of the sacrifice, under the shade of the trees, the participants in the cult partook of the meat, reserving, in the manner of זְבָחִים, the required portions for the altar and for the priests,[213] and drank wine.[214] In light of v. 11, and the comment on v. 12a, we can understand that the participants in the rites gorged themselves and became intoxicated with wine, which led to a loss of self-control, and a consequent laxity of their consciences and morals. Possibly, as a result of this, they indulged in sexual orgies. When we examine in this context the phrase in v. 13b, it becomes evident that the sexual language in the cur-

---

directly. Such a shift is "characteristic of Hosea's style" (see Mays, *Hosea*, 73). The shift to the second person plural may also have been made when the secondary statement regarding "no punishment" was added. Wolff (*Hosea*, 85) and Andersen and Freedman (*Hosea*, 369) note that in vv. 13b and 14aα reference is made to different groups. In my view, the indictment is addressed to the same group, whether directly or indirectly. בָּנוֹת ("daughters") and כַּלּוֹת ("daughters-in-law") are linked in order to create a poetic analogy. They should be understood as one class, that is, sexually mature young women.

211.   The expression עַל כֵּן introduces, "more generally than לָכֵן, the statement of a fact, rather than a declaration" (BDB, 487).

212.   As we saw earlier, the two verbs together assume the form Piel, which appears in the sources only in cases of illicit rites of worship of other gods (Wolff, *Hosea*, 35). This polemical form of the usage of Piel is characteristic of Hosea, who provides us with the earliest record of such usage; in fact, it is even possible that he invented it.

213.   Cf. de Vaux, *Ancient Israel*, 417ff.

214.   The sacrificial meal included the eating of meat and the drinking of wine (see Exod 32:6; Num 25:2; Deut 12:7, 8; 27:7; 1 Chr 29:22).

rent clause indicates actual sexual relations, and is not metaphorical.[215] If
this is so, a question arises: Were young women truly formally involved
in the sacrifice of their virginity, as part of a Canaanite fertility cult,
as asserted by Wolff? He claims that the description here refers to a
Canaanite bridal rite.[216] As has been observed above, the hypothesis
that such a "bridal rite" existed in the ancient Near East is merely an
unfounded allegation. Therefore, it is more reasonable to assume that the
phrase תִּזְנֶינָה בְּנוֹתֵיכֶם וְכַלּוֹתֵיכֶם תְּנָאַפְנָה ("your daughters play the harlot,
and your daughters-in-law are adulteresses") verifies incidental sexual
abandon during festivities. The important question that remains now is
whether there were other sexual fertility rites that professional cultic
functionaries carried out in the ancient world and in Israel. This issue
will be dealt with in v. 14aβ.

2.3.2.2.3. *Verse 14.*

2.3.2.2.3.1. כִּי הֵם עִם הַזֹּנוֹת יְפָרֵדוּ וְעִם הַקְּדֵשׁוֹת יְזַבֵּחוּ *(v. 14aβ)*. Usually it
is understood that this phrase spells out the cultic activities alluded to in
v. 13: (1) this phrase is related to v. 13b through the repetition of the
sexual term זָנָה (תִּזְנֶינָה, זֹנוֹת), which is highly important for understanding the two phrases (vv. 13b and 14aβ), and through the focus on paired
classes of women (זֹנוֹת and קְדֵשׁוֹת); and (2) it is linked to v. 13aα
through the primary repetition of the verb זִיבֵּחַ; with emphatic הֵם it
recommences to describe in detail the men's activity stated in v. 13a.
Thus, this phrase reveals in fact what lurks behind the cryptic references:
(1) they offered their "sacrifices" on mountaintops, and hills, and under-
neath trees with קְדֵשׁוֹת; and (2) those who offered sacrifices in those
places had sexual relations with prostitutes: עִם הַזֹּנוֹת יְפָרֵדוּ.[217] This all
suggests that sexual abandon and offering of sacrifices were part of a
full-scale cultic rite. From here, one may argue that this attests to a

---

215.   As far as I know, no one views the sexual language in this phrase as metaphorical.

216.   Wolff (*Hosea*, 86) contends that among the sexual rites, Hosea distin-
guishes between the cultic practices of the priests (v. 14aβ) and the customs of the
other participants in the cult (vv. 13b and 14aα). The latter, according to him, indicates the bridal rite, which is the initiation rite of a bride-to-be (virgin), in which she
engages in sex with a stranger in the sacred place.

217.   The verb יְפָרֵדוּ appears in the Piel form of the root פרד (there is also a Pual
form in Est 3:8). The verb פֵּירֵד usually is understood to denote "to isolate and seg-
regate oneself" (BDB, 825; see Wolff, *Hosea*, 72). Thus, the usual interpretation of
the phrase עִם הַזֹּנוֹת יְפָרֵדוּ is that the men isolate themselves and associate with the
prostitutes, which implies sexual intercourse with them. See Andersen and Freedman, *Hosea*, 370.

so-called fertility cult, based on the fact that the term קְדֵשׁוֹת is in apposition with זֹנוֹת, and that the act of sacrifice parallels sexual activity. This phrase has, in fact, provided decisive biblical grounds for many scholars to assert that there were sexual fertility cults in Israel. These scholars also have contended that the majority of the Israelite population engaged in fertility rites.

If this passage indeed condemns such fertility cults, then at least one of the types of women mentioned (זֹנוֹת and קְדֵשׁוֹת) could have been זֹנוֹת קְדֵשׁוֹת ("sacred prostitutes"). The term זֹנוֹת ("prostitutes") is the plural form of זוֹנָה ("prostitute"), which is the female form of the active present participle of the verb זָנָה.[218] From a sociological perspective, a זוֹנָה ("prostitute") is a woman whose profession is to provide sexual services in exchange for money.[219] Yet the verb זָנָה explicitly refers to indiscriminate and unlawful sexual activity, especially on the part of an unmarried woman, and the word זוֹנָה, the participle form of זָנָה, at times more broadly denotes a woman of promiscuous sexual practices or lewd behavior.[220] In Hebrew conception, therefore, prostitution (זְנוּת) carries a connotation of adultery, and applies to a promiscuous or unchaste woman, whose role and profession are defined in terms of her sexual activity with men with whom she has no marital relations.

The phrase here does not tell us unequivocally that the harlots (זֹנוֹת) are involved in the cultic activities as cultic functionaries. The Piel verb of פרד may help us to some extent to determine the role of the זֹנוֹת, as it is one in a series of polemical verbs in the Piel form,[221] and appears nowhere else in this vocalization or in connection with זֹנוֹת. Was its purpose to describe a cultic practice? Is cultic prostitution being hinted at via use of the word זֹנוֹת? If it might be proved that the קְדֵשׁוֹת, which are analogous to זֹנוֹת in this verse, were actually sacred prostitutes, then it can be assumed that the זֹנוֹת were also involved in cultic rites, and that the verb פִּירֵד alludes to cultic prostitution.

218. There is no masculine noun derived from this root, that is, there is no masculine equivalent to the word זוֹנָה. References in the Bible to male prostitution are extremely limited. The only such instance is perhaps the use of the term כֶּלֶב ("dog") in Deut 23:19.

219. J. H. Gagnon, "Prostitution," *IESS*, 592–98 (esp. 592).

220. See P. A. Bird, "The Harlot as Heroine in Biblical Texts: Narrative Art and Social Presupposition," *Semeia* 46 (1989): 119–39 (esp. 120–21).

221. As was observed above, זבח and קטר are both given an unusual vocalization (Piel) used elsewhere only of illicit cultic activity (Wolff, *Hosea*, 35). The polemical use of these verbs in the Piel form is the characteristic of Hosea, and may be his own innovation, as noted above.

2.3.2.2.3.2. Observations on the Term קְדֵשָׁה. It appears that the feminine noun קְדֵשָׁה denotes a woman who was consecrated as a functionary at the shrines. The word קְדֵשָׁה occurs five times in the Bible. The Hebrew usage is confined to three passages: Gen 38:21–22 (sg., 3 times); Hos 4:14 (pl.); Deut 23:18 (sg.).[222] The term קְדֵשָׁה very commonly has been assumed as "sacred prostitute" by modern scholars following the view of Frazer, who compiled a collection of texts from western Asia, in which customs of "sacred prostitution" are reported.[223] This assumption regarding the existence of "sacred prostitution" centers on the concept of divine copulation and its human representatives as an essential component of "fertility cult religion."[224] The primary basis for the assumption that קְדֵשָׁה is actually a "sacred prostitute" rests in the juxtaposition of the words זוֹנָה and קְדֵשָׁה in the Bible (Gen 38:15, 21–22, 24; Deut 23:18–19; Hos 4:14): this contiguity is manifested in a manner that the first term defines the second. That is to say, their argument is that there is parallelism between זוֹנָה and קְדֵשָׁה, and the interchange of the two terms in Gen 38 leaves no room for doubt that קְדֵשָׁה was a sacred prostitute akin to the hierodule in Greece.[225] It is of course the opinion of the supporters of this approach that such an institution existed in Israelite cults, and that it was influenced by other religions and mythologies in the ancient Near East.[226]

222. In the text of Deuteronomy, the word קְדֵשָׁה is complemented by the masculine term קָדֵשׁ. Five instances of the masculine form of the word קְדֵשָׁה appear in 1 Kgs 14:24; 15:12; 22:47; 2 Kgs 23:7; and in Job 36:14. Yet Bird refutes the existence of a קָדֵשׁ as a counterpart of the קְדֵשָׁה in Israel. See P. A. Bird, "The End of the Male Cult Prostitute: A Literary-historical and Sociological Analysis of Hebrew *QĀDĒŠ-QĔDĒŠÍM*," in *Congress Volume, Cambridge 1995* (VTSup 66; Leiden: Brill, 1997), 37–80.

223. J. G. Frazer, *The Golden Bough: A Study in Magic and Region* (New York: Macmillan, 1935). For a critique of the classical sources to which Frazer and others refer, see R. A. Oden, *The Bible Without Theology: The Theological Tradition and Alternatives to It* (San Francisco: Harper & Row, 1987), 137–52.

224. See Oden, *Bible Without Theology*, 138–40. According to P. L. Berger (*Social Reality of Religion* [Harmondsworth: Penguin, 1987], 41, 47), religion is one of the ways of granting legitimacy whereby a human world is elevated to an ultimate religious-sacred world, as if that world had been in existence from the beginning of time. In the very ancient religions (such as Canaanite religions), an analogy was made between the human world created through language and the religious–sacred world whose structure is reflected in the human world. An example of such an analogy is sexual intercourse that imitates the creation of the universe or the beginning of the seasons of growth. Berger describes this as follows: "Representation of human beings becomes mimesis of divine mysteries."

225. See M. C. Astour, "Tamar the Hierodule," *JBL* 85 (1966): 185–96 (esp. 185–86).

226. See K. van der Toorn, "Cultic Prostitution," *ABD* 5:510.

However, this common assumption has recently met with vehement opposition by some scholars.[227] They review carefully the evidence of the Mesopotamian and Ugaritic cognate terms to Hebrew קְדֵשָׁה. The Code of Hammurabi (§181) mentions the *qadištu* alongside two other classes of cult-related women, not prostitutes, but rather *nadītu* and *kulmašītu*, in an inheritance law treating the case of a daughter "given to a god" by her father.[228] In Old Babylonian texts, the *qadištu* are associated with giving birth to a baby (a "house" in which the midwife assists the woman in her labor pains is called *bīt qadišti*, "the house of *qadištu*"),[229] and wet-nursing (*VAS* 7 10 1–3; 37 13–17; Ana ittišu VII iii 11–14).[230] In the Standard Babylonian texts (Malqu III, 40–55; Šurpu III, 69, 116–17), the *qadištu* women are identified with witches or sorceresses.[231] In a Middle Assyrian text (*KAR* 154), the *qadištu*-woman performs a ritual with the SANGA-priest. In the ritual, the *qadištu*-women intone the chant, prolong the chant, and the SANGA performs a purification ceremony. And the *qadištu*-women partake of the sacrificial offering.[232] They are also associated with purification rites.[233] On the basis of these functions of the *qadištu*, it is argued that the *qadištu* should be acquitted of the charge of cultic prostitution. Furthermore, there is no evidence that the *qadištu* was a functionary of the cult of Ishtar, the goddess of erotic love.[234] Also in terms of the Ugaritic texts there is no evidence that the *qdšt* was a "sacred prostitute." Rather, the masculine term *qdš* seems to denote a "cantor" who sang during sacrifices (*KTU* 1.112),[235] while the feminine term *qdšt* (*KTU* 4.69) denotes personal[236] or clan names.[237]

---

227. M. Gruber, "Hebrew *qedešah* and Her Canaanite and Akkadian Cognates," *UF* 18 (1983): 133–48; J. G. Westenholz, "Tamar, Qedeša, Qadištu, and Sacred Prostitution in Mesopotamia," *HTR* 82 (1989): 245–65. See also Oden, *Bible Without Theology*, 140–47; van der Toorn, "Cultic Prostitution," 510–13; Frymer-Kensky, *In the Wake of the Goddesses*, 199–202; B. Schwartz, *The Holiness Legislation: Studies in the Priestly Code* (Jerusalem: Magnes, 1999), 155–62 (Hebrew).

228. Gruber, "Hebrew *qedešah*," 144.

229. Ibid., 143; Westenholz, "Tamar, Qedeša, Qadištu," 252.

230. Gruber, "Hebrew *qedešah*," 142–43; Westenholz, "Tamar, Qedeša, Qadištu," 252.

231. Gruber, "Hebrew *qedešah*," 145; Westenholz, "Tamar, Qedeša, Qadištu."

232. Gruber, "Hebrew *qedešah*," 139–40; Westenholz, "Tamar, Qedeša, Qadištu," 254.

233. Gruber, "Hebrew *qedešah*," 141; see also W. G. Lambert, *Babylonian Wisdom Literature* (Oxford: Clarendon, 1960), 160.

234. Gruber, "Hebrew *qedešah*," 146.

235. Westenholz, "Tamar, Qedeša, Qadištu," 249.

236. Gruber, "Hebrew *qedešah*," 147.

237. Westenholz, "Tamar, Qedeša, Qadištu," 250.

Westenholz hypothesizes that their function was similar to that of the
Levites in Israelite worship on the grounds that they were closely associated with priests in the administrative lists (*KTU* 4.36; 4.38; 4.69).[238] In
conclusion, the above scholars raise the argument that there is no cognate
evidence to substantiate the meaning or function of a "sacred prostitute"
in the Akkadian or Ugaritic literature; the function of women termed
qadištu or *qdšt* was as singers/chanters, midwives, wet nurses, or inter-
mediaries in purification rituals.

Since no proof has been found for cultic prostitution in Mesopotamia
and Ugarit, from where the institution of cultic prostitution was assumed
to flow to Israel, we can say with confidence that any link between
prostitutes and fertility rites is mere speculation. Subsequently, the קְדֵשָׁה
in the Bible should be cleared of all suspicion that she served as a
"sacred prostitute" in an Israelite fertility rite. Similarly, it seems implausible that the זֹנוֹת in v. 14 were perceived of as "sacred prostitutes," or
that the verb יְפָרֵדוּ implies cultic sexual relations. Nevertheless, could it
be that the word קְדֵשָׁה is completely free of any connotation of adultery
or prostitution? As van der Toorn[239] claims, the parallelism between the
קְדֵשָׁה and the זוֹנָה in Gen 38 and Deut 23:18–19,[240] in addition to Hos
4:14, lends preference to the view that the קְדֵשָׁה indeed was involved in
sexual activity of some kind. One trait that the זוֹנָה and the קְדֵשָׁה clearly
shared was that they were both women who lived outside of the family
structure, without a man to protect them. As such, the קְדֵשָׁה was vulnerable to sexual propositions, and as far as we know, she could have practiced sexual freedom, like the זוֹנָה.[241] In the light of such considerations,
the קְדֵשָׁה as a woman holding a non-priestly temple role performing
menial tasks might be relatively easily drawn into sexual relations,
especially in the sacred places (or high places) in rural areas, as seen in
Hos 4:12–14. Especially when inebriated with wine in the cult, as implied
in vv. 11–12, she would be more vulnerable to sexual profligacy and be
as good as a זוֹנָה.

238.   Ibid., 249–50.

239.   Van der Toorn, "Female Prostitution," 193–205. Although he admits that
the קְדֵשָׁה was involved in sexual activities, he strongly argues that "sacred prostitution" never existed as a magical rite in the context of fertility cults to secure
fecundity and fertility. Yet he holds that some "prostitution" may be called "sacred"
insofar as its revenues were spent in the payment of vows and were thus turned over
to the temple.

240.   Bird ("End of the Male Cult Prostitute," 47–51) contends that vv. 18 and
19 in Deut 23 are parallel in terms of both structure and content.

241.   Frymer-Kensky, *In the Wake of the Goddesses*, 201.

We come to the conclusion, therefore, regarding the verse examined here, that the apposition of הַקְּדֵשׁוֹת and הַזֹּנוֹת is not meant to condemn the former as cultic prostitutes, but rather the moral corruption of the people: the cult with הַקְּדֵשׁוֹת who were never mentioned in the normative Yahwistic religion alludes to a perverted rite of non-Yahwistic religion (or Baalized Yahwistic religion); the people are decried for offering sacrifices with קְדֵשׁוֹת who have become a type of זֹנוֹת who did their business with the cultic participants while drunk with wine in the rural sanctuaries. Hosea condemns the people for this. Thus, it seems clear that the drunken sexual activities of the קְדֵשׁוֹת had nothing to do with a fertility rite.

2.3.2.2.4. *Verse 10 and the Fertility Cult.* Scholars who have asserted the existence of sacred prostitution and fertility rites have not hesitated to draw a link between sexual profligacy and fertility rites. Hosea 4:10a is a decisive phrase for these scholars when they come to consider the possible existence of fertility rites in Israel: וְאָכְלוּ וְלֹא יִשְׂבָּעוּ הִזְנוּ וְלֹא יִפְרֹצוּ ("And they shall eat, and not have enough, they shall commit harlotry, and shall not increase").

The verb הִזְנוּ is the Hiphil form of the root זנה, but in v. 10 it has no causative and transitive meaning, in contrast to its normal usage as a transitive verb.[242] In Hosea, the Hiphil form of זנה seems to be used to denote the meaning of Qal when we note Morag's supposition that in northern Hebrew there was a confusion of Qal with Hiphil forms.[243] The verb פָּרַץ (v. 10), which is literally translated as "to break out/into/through," describes not only a violent act by God against humans or animals, but also an increase in the human or animal population, which bursts out in all directions.[244] If this is the case, what does the verb הִזְנוּ refer to when it comes before the verb יִפְרֹצוּ? Considering the fact that the verb הִזְנוּ is actually the cause for its following verb יִפְרֹצוּ, some scholars claim that the verb does not refer to extra-marital sexual relations, but to cultic sexual relations intended to guarantee fertility. If so, then as Andersen and Freedman contend, the general picture described in

242. Cf. Exod 34:16; Lev 19:29.
243. See Morag, "Uniqueness of Hosea's Language," 489–511 (esp. 500 n. 44). The use of the root זנה in the Hiphil form as a transitive verb is sometimes found (e.g. Lev 19:29). Yet its use as an intransitive verb, such as the Qal form of זנה, only appears in Hosea (other than in the present verse, see Hos 4:18; 5:3). Morag postulates that in the area of northern Israel (and also in Phoenicia) the past form of Hiphil was Yiphil, and afterwards there was a tendency to replace it (or Hiphil) with the Qal form, and thus essentially to confuse the two.
244. See Andersen and Freedman, *Hosea*, 337–38.

v. 10 reflects the "the magical character of contemporary Israelite religion." Therefore, they interpret the verse as follows: cultic eating, which is supposed to bring about an abundance of food, actually results in the opposite; cultic sexual intercourse, which is supposed to ensure fertility, ultimately fails.[245]

In contrast to this interpretation of Hos 4:10 as referring to a sexual fertility rite, Gruber reads the terms הִזְנוּ and יִפְרֹצוּ differently. He follows Ginsberg's translation of Hos 4:10: "Truly they shall eat, but not be sated; they shall swell, but not be satisfied."[246] Here Gruber translates הִזְנוּ as "swell," that is, "drink excessively." Such a translation is based on his expectation that "if the first clause speaks of eating, the second clause would speak of drinking," according to "the rules of biblical poetry."[247] However, this suggestion may be refuted by the argument that the appearance of "drinking" and "eating" together in the Bible is not a rule of biblical poetry,[248] but rather a recurrent motif throughout the Bible. To enumerate all the instances would be superfluous, yet we should take heed of the fact that there are a number of cases in which the verb אכל ("to eat") includes within its meaning the verb שתה ("to drink") as well: (1) in the description of the banquet (מִשְׁתֶּה) in Gen 19:3 only the verb אכל is used, while in Gen 26:30 (also in Job 1:4) it appears to describe a combination of eating and drinking; (2) at the covenant meal, "they ate and drank" (Exod 24:11), but in the description of the covenant meal between Jacob and Laban (Gen 31:6) only the verb אכל is used; (3) in certain places, the people are depicted as eating and drinking at sacrificial meals (Exod 32:6; 1 Chr 29:22), while in other places only the verb אכל appears, though the context seems to imply drinking as well (Num 25; Deut 12:7, 8; 27:7); (4) in sequential verses, the verb אכל suggests "eating and drinking" (Judg 19:4, 6, 8; 1 Sam 1:8, 9; 1 Kgs 19:5, 6, 7, 8; Prov 23:7, 8; Eccl 2:24, 25; cf. Gen 24:33, 54). Furthermore, the direct object of the verb אכל is תִּירוֹשׁ ("new wine") in Deut 12:17, even though תִּירוֹשׁ is a beverage, and thus ostensibly requires the verb שתה. In light of these examples, we may conclude that the verb אָכְלוּ in Hos 4:10a means eating the cultic meal, including the drinking of wine. There are no examples in the Bible in which the verb הִזְנוּ directly refers to drinking. Therefore, Gruber's interpretation is unconvincing.

245. Ibid., 362.

246. M. Gruber, "Marital Fidelity and Intimacy: A View from Hosea," in Brenner, ed., *A Feminist Companion to the Latter Prophets*, 172; Ginsberg, "Lexicographical Notes," 73–74.

247. Gruber, "Marital Fidelity," 172.

248. Gruber notes only two instances in biblical poetry: Prov 9:4 and Eccl 9:7.

To a certain extent, the meaning of v. 10 must be examined from the point of view of the textual structure. As we have seen above (§2.3.2.2), Hos 4 is composed of three parts: vv. 1–3, vv. 4–10, and vv. 11–19. Each part concludes with a declaration of YHWH's visitation that will be imposed because of the people's misdeeds (vv. 3, 7–10, and 19). Verse 10 should be understood according to this textual structure. First of all, it should be noted that v. 10 does not refer to YHWH's visitation on the perverted cult (vv. 12–14), but to the people's lack of knowledge of God and his Torah (vv. 4–6). Had v. 10 dealt with the perverted cult, it should have been placed after v. 14. Hence, this verse should be understood in the context of the second part (vv. 4–10). While the first half of the second part (vv. 4–6) incriminates the priests and places the responsibility for the people's ignorance of God on them,[249] the second half (vv. 7–10) claims that, as a result of that sin, the priests and the people will be condemned to the same punishment (v. 9), the content of which is proclaimed in v. 10. From the point of view of the content, the second part clarifies the first part (vv. 1–3), where the basic tone of the denunciation of the people (vv. 1–2) is focused on their ignorance of God (אֵין דַּעַת אֱלֹהִים, "there is no knowledge of God"), and thereby the miserable state of languishment (including drought and sterility) is proclaimed on Israel (v. 3). Accordingly, v. 10 is a confirmation and elucidation of the judgment that is described in v. 3. In other words, v. 10 is understood as a reiteration of v. 3, where it is proclaimed that YHWH will put an end to all the fertility and fecundity in the Land of Israel because of the people's evil deeds that resulted from their ignorance of the knowledge of God. Therefore, v. 10 can be understood as a proclamation of the judgment that the people's fertility and procreation will cease: they will have no more food,[250] and no more children.[251]

3. *Conclusion*

3.1. *The Cultic Reality Described in Exodus 32*
As was observed above, the explanations of the cultic practices described through the term צִיחֵק in Exod 32:6b are divided into two opposing views: one argues that the cult depicted in Exod 32:6b was actually an

---

249.   Cf. the comments in n. 165.

250.   The use of the phrase וְאָכְלוּ וְלֹא יִשְׂבָּעוּ is understood as being paradoxical for the severe hunger.

251.   The phrase הִזְנוּ וְלֹא יִפְרֹצוּ also expresses, in a paradoxical way, the severe barrenness: try as they might to conceive, even at the price of all kinds of extra-marital sexual relations (i.e. fornication, prostitution), they will fail to bear children.

"orderly ritual"; and the second contends that this represents the sexual fertility cult. Sasson[252] represents the first view, and Moberly the second.[253] The weak point in Sasson's position is that it fails to explain why the participants in the rite were criticized as being פָּרֻעַ ("wild," v. 25) if the cultic practice had been an orderly one. As has been observed above, the term פָּרֻעַ implies that the people's behavior in that cult deviated from the "orderly Yahwistic ritual"; that is, the phrase פָּרֻעַ הוּא hints at people's looseness and licentious behavior in regard to the cult. It seems that this observation superficially justifies Moberly's interpretation that Exod 32:6b describes an orgiastic sexual wantonness in the context of a fertility rite: "if the people cast off restraint in the presence of an image which was the symbol of fertility, the implications are obvious."[254] Nevertheless, Moberly's interpretation cannot be accepted without two key conditions being fulfilled: that sexual activity was part of a fertility cult, and that such a cult indeed existed in Israel (or Canaan) in the ninth–eighth centuries B.C.E. As observed above, however, the relevant sources regarding the so-called fertility cult from Mesopotamian and Ugaritic texts and the Bible do not afford any proof that there was in fact cultic sex, or that there were functionaries responsible for such a cult (i.e. the so-called sacred prostitutes).

If the cult described in Exod 32 did not meet the expectations of the normative Yahwistic cult, or even a sexual fertility cult, what actually was its nature? What was the term צִחֵק meant for? What was the practical feature of the cult described by the term צִחֵק in Exod 32:6?

My view is that it is possible to infer the implication of this term from the characteristics of cultic rites in the time of Hosea (the eighth century B.C.E.). This is because Hosea has some features in common with the Elohist, as observed above.[255]

As already observed, the perverted cultic features described in the book of Hosea can be summed up as follows: (1) the relevant texts in which Hosea criticizes the calf image show that the cult with regard to the calf image was directed to Baal or to Baalized YHWH; and (2) the examination of chs. 1–4 led to a rejection of the claim that the cult of Baal (or of Baalized YHWH) was a sexual fertility one: the sexual

252.   See Sasson, "Worship of the Golden Calf," 151–59 (esp. 152).

253.   See Moberly, *Mountain of God*, 46. His assertion was preceded by that of other scholars, including Noth, *Exodus*, 248; Cassuto, *Commentary*, 413–14; and Hyatt, *Exodus*, 305.

254.   Moberly, *Mountain of God*, 196 n. 6.

255.   For detailed information regarding the close relationship between the Elohist and Hosea, see §1.2 in Chapter 4.

language in Hos 1–3 is metaphorical. It describes Israel being drawn to other gods (i.e. בְּעָלִים); there is no account of a sexual initiation rite for intended brides, as Wolff argues; even the sexual language of Hos 4 (esp. vv. 13–14), which describes actual sexual activities, has nothing to do with sexual rites designed to ensure fertility. Such sexual activities are related to moral laxity induced by drunkenness.

It appears that the cultic features described in Exod 32 are similar to those of the rites mentioned in Hos 4 (especially vv. 13–14), rites which seem to involve general depravity and fornication resulting from revelry and wine-drinking during sacrificial festivities. As in Hos 4, the verb שָׁתָה in Exod 32:6b implies that the people were intoxicated with wine. Apparently, this freed them of (moral) inhibitions, as implied by the word פָּרוּעַ. Hence, from this we may deduce that the term צִיחֵק in Exod 32:6b describes sexual promiscuity, which occurred as a result of intoxication.

If this is the case, why did the Elohist not use a more straightforward verb, such as זָנָה, in order to describe sexual promiscuity? As observed above, the meaning of the term צִיחֵק is open to dispute. The nature of the calf cult that accompanied the sacrificial offering, which the term צִיחֵק in Exod 32:6 describes, is unclear, even when taking into account the term עַנּוֹת in Exod 32:18, the meaning of which is equivocal. Probably the Elohist deliberately employed ambiguous verbs to describe the cultic feature of his time. That is to say, it seems that he capitalized on the ambiguity of the verb צִיחֵק in order to depict comprehensively the cultic feature. As observed above, when the verb צִיחֵק appears alongside the term עַנּוֹת, the cultic feature could be imagined in several ways: (1) "to do cultic sport (dance) with singing," or (2) "to have sexual intercourse," or (3) a combination of cultic dance with singing (or cries of joy) and sexual intercourse. Considering the fact that the verb צִיחֵק is an obvious euphemism referring to sexual licentiousness in light of the cultic reality in the eighth century B.C.E. as described in Hos 4:12–14, we can reject Sasson's view that the meaning of צִיחֵק is limited to the first of the three definitions just indicated. Nevertheless, if we restrict the meaning of צִיחֵק to the second definition, we still would not understand precisely what the Elohist intended to express through this ambiguous term. What seems more probable is that he meant to describe a mixture of cultic singing and dancing, cries of joy, and sexual relations in a state of intoxication through the ambiguous term צִיחֵק. As far as the calf image is concerned, its cult could be portrayed as that of Baalism or some other religion in the ancient Near East: one could eat to satiety and drink one's fill, with song and dance contributing to the festive mood; under such circumstances one could easily lose one's sense of propriety and indulge in a type of behavior such as sexual promiscuity.[256] It seems that the Elohist intentionally used the vague term צִיחֵק in order to describe such a perverted cult in comparison to the normal Yahwistic one. Hence, the ambiguous term צִיחֵק was perhaps more appropriate as a description of the cultic reality characterized by wanton behavior than more concrete sexual terms, such as זָנָה and נָאַף. Nevertheless, we should re-emphasize that such sexual licentiousness is far from what is termed a fertility cult or ritually organized prostitution.

3.2. *Hosea and the Exclusive Worship of YHWH*

Hosea's exclamation לֹא אֱלֹהִים הוּא ("it is not God," Hos 8:6) is an antithesis to the cultic invocation אֵלֶּה אֱלֹהֶיךָ ("these are your gods," Exod 32:4b) or הִנֵּה אֱלֹהֶיךָ ("behold, your God," 1 Kgs 12:28). As observed above, however, it is worth reiterating that Hosea's criticism, לֹא אֱלֹהִים הוּא, against the calf image was an antithesis to the cultic invocation to the calf image, which at first had begun as YHWH's pedestal but was being considered as the symbol of other god under the influence of Baalism. In other words, this antithesis was formulated at least 200 years after the time of Jeroboam, and after the original nature of the calf image as a pedestal of YHWH had already deteriorated into a symbol of Baal or into the image of Baalized YHWH. If so, which god was identified with the calf image when Hosea denounced it? Was it Baal's symbol or YHWH's representation? Two possibilities are feasible. Hosea's cry לֹא אֱלֹהִים הוּא ("it is not God") directed against the calf image can be interpreted in two ways, namely, on the one hand, as an admonition toward the populace who revered it as an image of Baal and, on the other hand, as an exhortation toward those who saw it as the image of YHWH.[257] If we assume that Hosea's polemic against the calf image is based on the commandment "You shall not make for yourself a graven image," the deity identified with the calf image was YHWH, since this commandment is the injunction against the image of YHWH.[258] However, there is no evidence in the book of Hosea that he criticized the images on the basis of this commandment. If he was familiar with an early form of the Decalogue (cf. Hos 4:2), then it was undoubtedly a

256.   Van der Toorn, "Female Prostitution," 193–205 (esp. 202).
257.   As a result of the assimilation of YHWH and Baal, the calf image could have been perceived by the populace either as a symbol of Baal or a representation of YHWH.
258.   This will be discussed in detail in Chapter 5.

version that did not include the commandment "You shall not make for yourself a graven image." His anti-idolatry statements belong to the sweeping criticism of the syncretistic cult that resulted from the influence of other religions.[259] The elimination of other religious influences from the Yahwistic cult implies the rejection of gods from such religions. The rejection of other gods is directly related to the denial of their symbols or images.[260] That is to say, Hosea's polemic regarding cultic images does not stem from the commandment prohibiting images, but rather from the request for the exclusive worship of YHWH.

In fact, Hosea explicitly demands the exclusive worship of YHWH. He requires that the Israelites worship YHWH alone, and forsake all other gods: "Yet I am YHWH your God from the land of Egypt; and you know no God but me, and beside me there is no savior" (Hos 13:4). In this sense, the book of Hosea may be regarded as the earliest classical document of the YHWH-alone movement.[261]

Hosea's request to worship YHWH alone is well expressed through the marriage metaphor (chs. 1–3). Hosea describes the covenantal relationship between God and his people in terms of a marriage contract, that is, a monogamous relationship between a man and woman. This metaphor validates YHWH's claim to be the sole God of Israel. The covenant requires that Israel refrain from worshipping other gods, and even associating with those who worship them (Exod 20:2–3; Deut 5:6–7; and Exod 34:11–16; Deut 7:3–6). It is interesting to note that when the Israelites associate with other gods, the Bible denounces them by using the sexual term זָנָה. Just as a woman's sexual intercourse outside her marital relationship is criticized by the term זָנָה, so Israel's apostasy and her association with other gods are criticized figuratively by the term זָנָה. As we have already seen above, Hosea compares Israel in its deviation from YHWH to "a wife of harlotry" (אֵשֶׁת זְנוּנִים) and the children of Israel to "children of harlotry" (Hos 1:2; 2:6 [EV 4]). The "lovers" (in Hos 2:7 [EV 5]) whom this woman (namely, Israel) chases after represent other gods (אֱלֹהִים אֲחֵרִים, in 3:1). Hosea terms such gods בְּעָלִים. Here a question arises: What is the meaning of the term בְּעָלִים for Hosea? Is it a plural form of the god Baal, or a generic term for various gods?

259. Mettinger, *No Graven Image*, 180.
260. All of the foreign gods of the religions that were known to the Israelites had symbols (or images).
261. See B. Lang, *Monotheism and the Prophetic Minority* (Social World of Biblical Antiquity 1; Sheffield: Sheffield Academic, 1983), 30–31.

3.2.1. *Baal, Baalim, and Other Gods*. The term בַּעַל appears three times
in the plural form in the book of Hosea (2:15 [EV 13], 19 [EV 17]; 11:2).
This datum raises the question whether the term used by Hosea refers to
a specific deity, or whether it should be treated literally, as referring to a
plurality of deities. There are two possible answers to this question: the
first is that Hosea utilizes the term בְּעָלִים in reference to the multiple
local manifestations of the single Canaanite god Baal-Hadad,[262] and the
second is that Hosea could be referring to a plurality of different
Canaanite deities that were accorded the title בַּעַל.[263] However, in order
to understand the term בְּעָלִים better, we need to note that the term בַּעַל
underwent a complex development in its meaning. The term itself,
whether singular or plural, is a common noun meaning "lord," "owner,"
"husband," and the like. So the term בַּעַל could be developed in its
meaning and applied to the different entities, ranging from the god Baal,
through his manifestations at a variety of cultic sites, to various divine
"lords" or gods.[264]

Since Hosea uses both the singular and plural forms of בַּעַל,[265] we
should survey the range of meanings of these terms and references in the
book of Hosea, as well as in other books of the Bible. As we know from
Ugaritic texts and other sources, Baal, a chief among the Canaanite gods,
is the storm god Hadad.[266] The Baal of "Carmel" in 1 Kgs 18[267] and the
Baal condemned by Hosea were also storm gods, and perhaps one and
the same god.[268] Hosea plays on the relationship between the god Baal

---

262.   Mays, *Hosea*, 43; Andersen and Freedman, *Hosea*, 256–57; Wolff, *Hosea*,
38–39.

263.   These may include Baal (1 Chr 4:33), Baal-Gad (Josh 11:17; 12:7; 13:5),
Baal-Hamon (Song 8:11), Baal-Hazor (2 Sam 13:23), Baal-Hermon (Deut 3:9; Judg
3:3; 1 Chr 5:23), Baal-Lebanon (2 Kgs 19:23; Ps 29:5–6), Baal-Maʿon (Num 32:38;
1 Chr 5:8; Ezek 25:9), Baal Peor (Num 25:3; Deut 4:3; Ps 106:28; cf. Hos 9:10),
Baal-Perazim (2 Sam 5:20; 1 Chr 14:11), Baal-Shalisha (2 Kgs 4:42), and Baal-
Tamar (Judg 20:33).

264.   Smith, *Early History of God*, 47.

265.   For the former, see Hos 2:10 (EV 8), 18 (EV 16); 13:1.

266.   Baal Zaphon, an epithet of the storm god Hadad, appears in the Ugaritic
text (*KAI* 50:2–3; 69:1) and is also mentioned as the name of place in the Bible
(Exod 14:2; Num 33:7).

267.   Undoubtedly, the Baal in 1 Kgs 18 is a storm god, since the narrative
revolves around the competing gods' ability to generate rain. The competition is
decided by a bolt of lightning dispatched into the sky, and afterwards a great rain-
storm ensues. The Baal of Carmel surely was known in Tyre, as he was in Samaria
and Jezreel, and in fact in any place where Canaanite religion was practiced (see
Andersen and Freedman, *Hosea*, 257).

268.   Smith, *Early History of God*, 47.

and his manifestations in numerous cultic sites, as well as the generic use of his name, which refers to "lords" or other gods.[269] So, the בְּעָלִים in Hos 2:19 (EV 17) may refer to various manifestations of the god Baal, or to a generic use of his name for other gods. Yet it is probable that the term בְּעָלִים in Hos 2:19 (EV 17) is used in the first sense, since the בְּעָלִים in v. 19 (EV 17) are linked to בַּעַל in v. 18 (EV 16). As observed above, the proclamation of v. 18 (EV 16) reveals that in the time of Hosea the confusion of YHWH with the god Baal by the Israelites was grave. However, it appears that the term בְּעָלִים in Hos 11:2 tends toward the second meaning. The word פְּסִלִים ("graven images" or "idols") in this verse is paralleled to בְּעָלִים: "The more they called them, the more they went from them; they sacrificed to the בְּעָלִים, and offered (burning incense) to פְּסִלִים." Based on this Hebrew poetic parallelism, one may understand this verse as referring to two separate acts: one of offering a sacrifice, and the other of offering incense, both of which are cultic in nature, or as referring to a single act of sacrificing, in which case פְּסִלִים ("graven images" or "idols") would refer to בְּעָלִים. For Hosea, another term for idols is עֲצַבִּים. In contrast to פְּסִלִים, which were mainly made of wood and stone, עֲצַבִּים in the Bible were usually made of metal, particularly silver and gold.[270] While the term עֲצַבִּים in the book of Hosea is probably a derogatory appellative for calf images,[271] it seems that the term פְּסִלִים was used to imply idols of all the various gods. So, the term בְּעָלִים of Hos 11:2 refers to various gods. Hence, we can assume that the term בְּעָלִים in Hosea's time was already used to refer to various pagan gods and "lords." The evidence from the sixth and seventh centuries B.C.E., after the time of the prophet Hosea, reflects the broad generic usage of the term בְּעָלִים. Such evidence can be found in the book of Jeremiah. The singular form, בַּעַל (2:8; 7:9; 11:3, 17; 23:13; 32:29), in Jeremiah attests to the fact that the West Semitic storm-god, Baal, continued to be acknowledged as the god Baal in Israel.[272] Nevertheless, the fact that the term בְּעָלִים in Jer 2:23 is the equivalent of אֱלֹהִים in v. 28 shows that the term בְּעָלִים developed into a generic term denoting various gods. Likewise, the plural form בְּעָלִים could be developed from numerous manifestations of the god Baal at various cultic sites into a profusion of

269. B. Halpern, "'Brisker Pipes than Poetry': The Development of Israelite Monotheism," in *Judaic Perspectives on Ancient Israel* (ed. J. A. Neusner et al.; Philadelphia: Fortress, 1987), 77–105 (esp. 84, 92–94).

270. See Hos 4:17; 8:4; 13:2; Ps 135:15. On the meaning of עֲצַבִּים, see the interpretation of Hos 8:4–6 in §2.2.1.

271. See the interpretation of Hos 8:4–6 in §2.2.1.

272. Smith, *Early History of God*, 48.

various gods with different cults and identities.[273] As a result of such a development, the original deity, the god Baal, came to be perceived as a different god depending upon the variety of special practices and characteristics found at a given local shrine.[274] Thus, the distinctive features of the worship of the god Baal in one place may, through a process of localization, have become different from those practiced in another location despite the fact that they may originally have been the same deity.

In sum, Hosea's opposition to Baal is not only directed toward Baal-Hadad (the Phoenician god), but also to all of his local manifestations. In other words, the demand to worship YHWH alone required the wholesale rejection of the Baal cult wherever it occurred, and regardless of whether such cults were addressed to Baal-Hadad or any other בְּעָלִים. Apparently, this opposition extended to deities who do not belong to the Baal type, for example, the female deities.[275]

3.2.2. Hosea 14:9 (YHWH and Asherah). Is there an allusion to the existence of a goddess that Hosea takes aim at as part of his demand to worship YHWH alone? On the face of things, no such goddess is mentioned in the book of Hosea. However, part of what is written in the book may attest to the fact that there was such a goddess (or goddesses), and that Hosea opposed her (them).

The key text implying the existence of such a goddess is found in Hos 14:9, in which Hosea has YHWH proclaim: אֶפְרַיִם מַה לּוֹ[276] עוֹד לָעֲצַבִּים אֲנִי עָנִיתִי וַאֲשׁוּרֶנּוּ אֲנִי כִּבְרוֹשׁ רַעֲנָן מִמֶּנִּי פֶּרְיְךָ נִמְצָא ("Ephraim! What more has he to do with idols? I have humbled him, but I will prosper him. 'I am like a luxuriant cypress'—From me comes your fruit!"). The daring comparison here of YHWH to a tree, which is the only such instance in the Bible, and which appears alongside condemnations of Israel's idolatry, has led many scholars to suggest that Hosea is indulging in polemics here against Israel's idolatry, which is connected to the fusion of the worship of YHWH with the Canaanite tree symbolism. Could it be then that this was a polemical attack on the *asherah*/Asherah? A number of scholars have believed so. The term *asherah*, it should be noted, not only refers to the Semitic mother-goddess Asherah, but also to a sacred tree or pole that stood near shrines to honor her. In this context, perhaps

273. Ibid.; Andersen and Freedman, *Hosea*, 256–58.
274. See Andersen and Freedman, *Hosea*, 257.
275. See Lang, *Monotheism*, 31.
276. It is to be read לוֹ instead of לִי in the MT, since it is Ephraim, not YHWH, who "has to do with idols" (see Hos 4:17). The LXX also reads as αὐτῷ (לוֹ in Hebrew).

we need to mention the suggestion raised by Wellhausen. Instead of the obviously bothersome phrase אֲנִי עִנִּיתִי וַאֲשׁוּרֶנּוּ ("I have humbled him, but I will prosper him"), Wellhausen suggests the phrase אֲנִי עֲנָתוֹ וַאֲשֵׁרָתוֹ ("I am his Anath and Asherah").[277] If he is right, then the God of Israel (through the mouth of his prophet) describes himself to his people as Anath (עֲנָת) and Asherah (אֲשֵׁרָה), as if God has become one with the goddesses in name, character, function, and even reality. His suggestion had been followed by G. Fohrer and E. Jacob.[278] The problem with his bold revision is that we do not expect to find allusions to the goddess Anath in Hebrew (or Phoenician) texts from the eighth century B.C.E. In this period, the goddess had already faded from the prominence she apparently enjoyed (based on the Canaanite literature of the Late Bronze Age), and was essentially forgotten, as indicated by the lack of theophoric names with the component Anath and her disappearance from votive inscriptions in the Iron Age.[279] Her successor Ashtoreth (Astarte; or Ashtoroth)[280] is less violent, and turns out to be a minor figure. On the basis of these observations, Day rejects Wellhausen's emendation, and suggests that there is only a mere allusion to the words Anath and Asherah in a play on the pronunciation of the wording אֲנִי עִנִּיתִי וַאֲשׁוּרֶנּוּ.[281] Although Day's suggestion is also problematic, a very persuasive understanding of this verse is seen in that at least YHWH's likening of himself to a "cypress" and his self-declaration as lord of fertility (מִמֶּנִּי פֶּרְיְךָ, "From me comes your fruit!") resulted from a part of Hosea's imperative to worship YHWH alone, which required a rejection of the fertility goddess(es) associated with the tree symbolism. Of course, the

---

277. J. Wellhausen, *Die Kleinen Propheten* (Berlin: de Gruyter, 1963), 134 (repr.).

278. G. Fohrer, *Studien zur Alttestamentlichen Prophetie* (BZAW 99; Berlin: Töpelmann, 1967), 230 n. 18; E. Jacob, *Osée, Joël, Amos* (Neuchâtel: Delachaux & Niestlé, 1965), 95, 97.

279. In the Bible, there are few names related to Anath, for example, Anathoth the birthplace of the prophet Jeremiah, as well as the judge Shamgar, who is described as the son of Anath (Judg 3:31). However, there does exist a reference to the deity Anathyahu from Elephantine, the Egyptian post-exilic military colony. For a detailed discussion relating to Anatyahu, see K. van der Toorn, "Anat–Yahu, some other deities, and the Jews of Elephantine," *Numen* 39, no. 1 (1992): 80–101.

280. In the Bible, Ashtoreth is listed as the goddess of the Sidonians (1 Kgs 11:5, 33; cf. 2 Kgs 22:13), and her plural form, Ashtoroth, appears in pairs with בְּעָלִים (Baalim) in Judg 10:6; 1 Sam 7:4; 12:10; cf. Judg 2:13; 1 Sam 7:3.

281. See J. Day, "A Case of Inner Scriptural Interpretation: The Dependence of Isaiah xxvi. 13–xxvii. 11 on Hosea xiii. 4–xiv. 10 (Eng. 9) and Its Relevance to Some Theories of the Redaction of the 'Isaiah Apocalypse,'" *JTS* 31 NS (1980): 309–19.

main goddess of this sort was Asherah. Nevertheless, one view holds that Asherah in the Bible is not the goddess, but rather, as alluded to above, a carved wooden object. In fact, until the discovery of the Ugaritic texts in 1929, it was common among scholars to deny the very existence of the goddess Asherah.[282] It seems that an examination of the verbs used together with the word *asherah* supports this view. These verbs are כרת ("cut," Exod 34:13; Judg 6:25, 26, 28; 2 Kgs 18:4; 23:14); גדע ("to cut down," Deut 7:5; 2 Chr 14:2; 31:1); שרף ("to burn," Deut 12:3; 2 Kgs 23:6, 15); עשה ("to make," 1 Kgs 14:15; 16:33; 2 Kgs 17:16); הציב ("to place," 2 Kgs 17:10); הסיר ("to remove," 2 Chr 17:6); ביער ("to burn," "to clear," "root out," 2 Chr 19:3); טיהר ("to purify," 2 Chr 34:3); נתץ ("to break down," 2 Chr 34:4).

However, there are some verses in which *asherah* does not seem to be an object, especially 1 Kgs 15:13; 18:19; 2 Kgs 21:7; 23:4; 2 Chr 15:16; and Judg 3:7. And the discovery of the Ugaritic texts ostensibly verifies the fact that there was a Canaanite goddess, Asherah, unrelated to Ashtoreth.[283] Moreover, in the ancient Near East, almost all the deities had their symbols, and the deity and the symbol were completely identified. Therefore, most scholars believe today, even though there remains disagreement, that the Hebrew term אשרה may refer both to the goddess and to her representation, including carved wooden statues, poles, and sacred trees.[284]

282.   W. L. Reed, *The Asherah in the Old Testament* (Fort Worth: Texas Christian University Press, 1949); E. Lipiński, "The Goddess Atirat in Ancient Arabia, in Babylon, and in Ugarit," *OLP* 3 (1972): 101–19; Lemaire, *Inscriptions hébraiques*, 595–608; A. Lemaire, "Who or What Was Yahweh's Asherah?," *BAR* 10, no. 6 (1984): 42–51.

283.   In Ugaritic texts, her name appears as *ʾaṯrt* (*athirat*). This term is the etymological equivalent to אשרה (Asherah) in Hebrew. The transformation of the early "th" (*ṯ*) to the later "sh" (*š*) is a well-attested change (see Cross, *Canaanite Myth*, 52f. n. 36). Similarly, the final *he* (ה) is a typical feminine singular suffix in Hebrew, and is to be seen as a normal adaptation of the Ugaritic feminine name (see J. M. Hadley, "Yahweh and 'His Asherah': Archaeological and Textual Evidence for the Cult of the Goddess," in Dietrich and Klopfenstein, eds., *Ein Gott allein?*, 237 n. 11).

284.   Cross, *Canaanite Myth*; J. Day, "Asherah in the Hebrew Bible and Northwest Semitic Literature," *JBL* 105 (1986): 385–408; Dever, "Material Remains"; J. Emerton, "New Light on Israelite Religion: The Implications of the Inscriptions from Kuntillet ʿAjrud," *ZAW* 94 (1982): 2–20; D. N. Freedman, "Yahweh of Samaria and His Asherah," *BA* 50 (1987): 241–49; J. M. Hadley, "Some Drawings and Inscriptions on Two Pithoi from Kuntillet ʿAjrud," *VT* 37 (1987): 180–213; R. Meshel, "Did Yahweh Have a Consort?," *BAR* 5, no. 2 (1979): 24–35; Olyan, *Asherah*; R. Patai, *The Hebrew Goddess* (New York: Ktav, 1967); Smith, *Early History of God*.

I will turn now to an examination of archaeological artifacts to show that trees were objects of worship as manifestations of goddesses in the ancient Near East. O. Keel shows the extent of the association between the goddess and the tree, and how ancient and widespread it was in the ancient Near East, at least since the third millennium B.C.E.[285] In Syria at the end of the third millennium B.C.E. and throughout the first quarter of the second millennium (Middle Bronze Age I and II A), tree images, some highly stylized, appear in portrayals of goddesses as their manifestations.[286] Goddesses are represented as tree trunks[287] or roots.[288] The goddess can appear as a palm tree flanked by fishes[289] or standing in anthropomorphic form next to her tree.[290] In these examples, the tree is closely related to water (fish). The goddess with the flowing vase[291] represents the possible connection between her and water and plant life. Similarly, but not in precisely the same way, painted images of this kind appear again and again throughout the Middle Bronze Age IIB, Late Bronze Age, and in the Egyptian New Empire.[292]

Precious objects, such as metal sheets, scarabs, and cylinder seals of the Middle Bronze Age IIB depict an anthropomorphic goddess,[293] in a stylized tree (or trees) sprouting out of her external sexual organs or navel,[294] and forming her head[295] or flanking her.[296] A tree worshipped by one or two people[297] is almost undoubtedly related to this goddess.[298] This is particularly clear on a scarab from Shechem (Nablus), in which the head of the goddess appears above the tree.[299] In the Late Bronze Age, the anthropomorphic goddess is to a large extent replaced by a tree flanked by caprids.[300] The tree is the same palm tree associated with the goddess from the third millennium B.C.E.

285.   O. Keel, *Goddesses and Trees, New Moon and Yahweh: Ancient Near Eastern Art and the Hebrew Bible* (Sheffield: Sheffield Academic, 1998).
286.   Ibid., 20ff., and esp. 23ff.
287.   Ibid., Fig. 7.
288.   Ibid., Fig. 16.
289.   Ibid., Fig. 11.
290.   Ibid., Fig. 14.
291.   Ibid., Figs. 8–10.
292.   Ibid., 24.
293.   Ibid., 29.
294.   Ibid., Figs. 17–20.
295.   Ibid., Fig. 12.
296.   Ibid., Figs. 22–27.
297.   Ibid., Figs. 28–32.
298.   Ibid., Figs. 28–32.
299.   Ibid., 30.
300.   Ibid., 35, Figs. 37–41.

There can be no doubt that the biblical Asherah in the time of the Iron Age is a continuation of the Late Bronze Age goddess. It is interesting to observe that throughout the Iron Age I, as well as the Iron Age IIA, the connection between the tree and the anthropomorphic goddess became less explicit.[301] It seems that this tendency reflects the aniconic attitude mentioned above. In the time of the Iron Age, two glyptic sources are noteworthy, which corroborate the link between the tree and the goddess.

First, there is an inscribed cult stand discovered in Taᶜanach, dating from the late tenth century B.C.E.[302] On the stand appear four registers: on the bottom register is depicted a nude female standing between two lions. Her outstretched arms grasp the lions' heads. The female is certainly to be viewed as the goddess Asherah, who is known as "the Lion Lady," *labiʾ(u)*, in West Semitic mythology.[303] Egyptian representations of Qudšu, thought to be the equivalent of Asherah (the word *qdš* is an epithet of Asherah in Ugarit), often show the goddess standing with her legs stretched apart on the back of a lion.[304] At Ugarit, the children of Asherah are called her "pride of lions" (*ṣbrt ary*).[305] The depictions of the lions and naked goddess on the bottom register of the Taᶜanach cult stand show a cult object permeated with the imagery of Asherah. So, it is significant to note that on the third register of the stand appears a sacred tree flanked by two lions identical to those on the bottom register. Thus, the third register has two major symbols associated with Asherah: the lion and the tree. This parallel surely reinforces the argument that the goddess (identified as Asherah) is represented by the tree.

Secondly, figurines dated to the eighth century B.C.E. have been found that have "pillar" bases, breasts, and a molded head, sometimes with no

---

301.   Ibid., 42.

302.   For photographs and discussion of the stand, see P. W. Lapp, "The 1968 Excavations at Tell Taᶜannek," *BASOR* 195 (1969): 42–44; A. E. Glock, "Taanach," *EAEHL* 4:1142, 1147; L. F. De Vries, "Cult Stands—A Bewildering Variety of Shapes and Sizes," *BAR* 13, no. 4 (1987): 32–33; R. Hestrin, "The Cult Stand from Taᶜanach and Its Religious Background," in *Phoenicia and the East Mediterranean in the First Millennium B.C.* (ed. E. Lipiński; Leuven: Peeters, 1987), 61–77; Keel, *Goddesses and Trees*, 42, Fig. 71.

303.   Cross, *Canaanite Myth*, 33–35; W. A. Maier, *ʾAšerah: Extrabiblical Evidence* (Atlanta: Scholars Press, 1986), 167.

304.   See, for example, I. E. S. Edwards, "A Relief of Qudshu–Astarte–Anath in the Winchester College Collection," *JNES* 14 (1955): 49–51; *ANEP* 470–74.

305.   *KTU* 1.3 V 45; 1.4 I 9; 1.4 II 25–26; for this translation, see Maier, *ʾAšerah*, 9. The use of animal names as titles for gods, royalty, and nobility is well described by P. D. Miller, "Animal Names as Designations in Ugaritic and Hebrew," *UF* 2 (1970): 177–86.

arms, sometimes arms holding breasts, and sometimes raised arms. These figurines were discovered in Jerusalem Cave 1 and Samaria locus E 207, both of which appear to be cultic sites. Such figurines were also found in domestic settings dated to the last years of settlement.[306] The design of these figures is instructive; the pillars have a distinctive form: the bottom part flares out, creating the effect of a skirt that slightly resembles a bell, but even more so a tree trunk. It is suggested that the pillar represents a tree trunk,[307] and that together with the large breasts it symbolizes the life-giving and nurturing mother-goddess.[308] Such a tree of nourishment is also known from an Egyptian painting in the tomb of Thutmosis III, in which the young king is depicted suckling from the breast of a large tree.[309] Here the tree is identified with the goddess Isis; elsewhere, such a tree is normally equated with Hathor.

In light of the above, it appears that archaeological evidence corroborates the argument that the word אֲשֵׁרָה in the Bible refers both to the goddess and to a stylized tree, pole, and/or living tree near the Israelite shrines and altars. Yet the living tree, as a symbol of the goddess, actually represents the power of growth or fertility. If so, since the goddess Asherah was the only major goddess surviving in Palestine from the end of the eighth century B.C.E., it is reasonable to assume that the tree, in its natural or stylized form, was named after her or associated with her.[310]

From the eighth century onward, real trees were increasingly considered a threat to pure Yahwism in general.[311] In Hos 4:13, the goddess Asherah might be represented as a tree, and specifically the oak (אַלּוֹן),

---

306.   Based on the dating of the Lachish layers, these figurines in Judah are dated to 720–587 B.C.E. or 610–587 B.C.E.; see J. S. Holladay, "Religion in Israel and Judah Under the Monarchy: An Explicitly Archaeological Approach," in Miller, Hanson, and McBride, eds., *Ancient Israelite Religion*, 249–99. T. A. Holland ("A Study of Palestinian Iron Age Baked Clay Figurines, with Special Reference to Jerusalem: Cave 1," *Levant* 9 [1977]: 134) states: "The Jerusalem material under discussion belongs to Iron Age II and is the outward expression of popular 'Israelite' religion derived from Canaanite prototypes, many of which were borrowed from Mesopotamia."

307.   Patai (*Hebrew Goddess*, 29–52) identifies this statuette as the goddess Asherah.

308.   Frymer-Kensky, *In the Wake of the Goddesses*, 160.

309.   Drawing in A. Mekhitarian, *Egyptian Painting* (Geneva: Skira, 1954), 34, reprinted in Hestrin, "The Cult Stand from Taʿanach," 61–77. See also R. Hestrin, "The Lachish Ewer and the ʾAsherah," *IEJ* 37 (1987): 212–23.

310.   R. Kletter, *The Judean Pillar-Figurines and the Archaeology of Asherah* (Oxford: Tempus Reparatum, 1996), 76–77 and passim.

311.   Keel, *Goddesses and Trees*, 56.

poplar (לִבְנֶה), and terebinth (אֵלָה).[312] In the hill country, these trees were probably the most common, and were also worshipped "upon the tops of the mountains, and…upon the hills."[313] The fact that Hosea describes YHWH as a luxuriant cypress tree (בְּרוֹשׁ רַעֲנָן) is a reminder that in his time the goddess Asherah was symbolized by the real tree, and presupposes that the goddess Asherah existed. Here a question arises: Does Hosea's displacement of a tree with YHWH aim to negate the people's coupling (in the marital sense) of him with Asherah, a coupling that is alluded to in the phrase "YHWH and his *A(a)shera*" (יהוה ואשרתה) in the inscriptions of Kuntillet ʿAjrud and Khirbet el-Qum?

Kuntillet ʿAjrud is a site not far from the main route between Gaza and Eilat on the border of the Sinai.[314] One of the inscriptions on a large storage jar discovered there contains the following words: ברכת אתכם ליהוה שמרן ולאשרתה ("I have blessed you by YHWH of Samaria and his Asherah/*asherah*"). The inscription appears to be dated between the mid-ninth and mid-eighth century B.C.E.[315] What is significant for our concern in this inscription is the phrase יהוה ואשרתה, that is, "YHWH and his Asherah/*asherah*." Such a phrase also appears in the inscription from Khirbet el-Qom, located some 13 kilometers west of Hebron.[316] What is meant by the word "his Asherah/*asherah*" (אשרתה)? Does it refer to the goddess Asherah or her wooden symbol, a tree?[317] The view that the term refers to the goddess Asherah has been rejected on the grounds that in biblical Hebrew proper nouns do not appear with a pronominal suffix.[318]

312. The name of this tree is a homonym with the feminine form of El, that is, the goddess *ʾēla* (אֵל). As an epithet of Asherah, *ʾēla* or *ʾēlat* is known both from Ugaritic and Phoenician texts.

313. Cf. Hestrin, "The Lachish Ewer," 212–23 (esp. 222–23).

314. Meshel (*Religious Centre*) was the first to publish the Kuntillet ʿAjrud findings. Since then, the number of studies examining them has multiplied considerably; see the various essays in Miller, Hanson, and McBride, eds., *Ancient Israelite Religion*; see also Olyan, *Asherah*; Smith, *Early History of God*.

315. Meshel, "Did Yahweh Have a Consort?," 34.

316. The inscription was found in a burial cave near the site, and has been dated to around 750 B.C.E. (see Lemaire, *Inscriptions hébraiques*, 603). Due to the poor quality of the rock on which it was engraved, the inscription is difficult to read. The inscription appears to read as follows: אריהו העשר. כתבה\ברך. |אריהו. ליהוה\ ומצריה לאשרתה הושעלה\...לאניהו\...לאשרתה...

317. Another suggestion of its meaning is "cella" or "chapel" (Lipiński, "The Goddess Atirat," 101–19). Although this meaning is attested in other Semitic languages, it is not found elsewhere in Hebrew and has little value for consideration here.

318. In any event, see M. Dietrich and O. Loretz, *Jahwe und seine Aschra. Anthropomorphes Kultbild in Mesopotamia,Ugarit and Israel. Das biblische*

Therefore, it seems that what is intended here is the tree or the symbolic representation of the goddess. When we take into account the complete fusion of the gods and their symbols in the ancient Near East, we can more safely say that the expression "YHWH and his Asherah/*asherah*" in these inscriptions provides sufficient reason to suppose that in certain circles YHWH was paired with the goddess Asherah (as husband and wife), something which could have naturally resulted from his equation with El.[319] There is no difficulty in supposing that Asherah could have been conceived as YHWH's wife in this syncretistic religious system, just as Athirat (= Asherah) was the wife of El in the Ugaritic pantheon. This supposition is quite well supported by Deut 16:21: "You shall not plant for yourself an Asherah of any kind of tree beside the altar of YHWH, your God, which you shall make for yourself"). This verse actually reveals two things: (1) the presence of the Asherah symbol next to YHWH's altar indicates that she was considered in syncretistic circles as YHWH's consort; and (2) the term כָּל עֵץ ("any kind of tree") in apposition of "Asherah" suggests that any kind of tree, whether stylized or a living "leafy tree" could have served to represent the goddess Asherah. Accordingly, this verse apparently reminds us of the expression בְּרוֹשׁ רַעֲנָן ("a leafy cypress tree") in Hos 14:9. This verse seems to indicate that the prophet Hosea was a pioneer of the Deuteronomic and Deuteronomistic circles, which were against the goddess Asherah and her symbols. So, Day rightly argues that Hos 14:9[320] should be seen as a kind of polemic against Asherah.[321]

3.3. *Know YHWH*
Israel's syncretistic association of YHWH with other religions, especially Baalism, resulted in the worship of other gods. Accordingly, at the height of this situation, Hosea endeavors to enlighten the spiritual blindness of the Israelites who have fallen deeply into syncretism with Baalism. Here we find why Hosea emphasizes the knowledge of God. Not only does he point out sharply the fundamental reason why the Israelites sunk into religious corruption—"they do not know YHWH"[322]—but he also resolutely

---

Bilderverbot (Münster: Ugarit-Verlag, 1992), 98–101, who note that in *KTU* 1.43.13 and *KTU* 2.31.41 a pronominal suffix appears attached to proper nouns. For a different view, see Emerton, "New Light," 14f.

319. Day, "Yahweh and the Gods," 181–96 (esp. 184).

320. Also Hos 4:12.

321. Day, "Inner Scriptural Interpretation," 314.

322. See Hos 5:4; cf. 2:10 (EV 8); 4:1, 6; 11:3. Terminologically, "know not" (לֹא יָדַע) is related to "forget" (שָׁכַח, Hos 2:15 [EV 13]; 5:14). In Deuteronomy, the direct object of the verb "forget" (שָׁכַח) is the "covenant" (4:23, 31), the

argues that the way to redemption from the sin of corruption is found in
reviving Israel's "knowledge of God."[323] The content of the "knowledge
of God" in the book of Hosea has in fact two dimensions: YHWH, the
God of Israel is not only the God of history but also the God of fertility;
that is, he has unique sovereignty over history and nature (fertility).

Hosea recounts YHWH's basic acts of redemption in the history of
Israel: the Exodus from Egypt (11:1); the feeding of Israel in the wilderness (9:10; 13:5–6); and the giving of the Land.[324] Each one of these acts
is related to YHWH's covenant with his people (6:7; 8:1) and the purpose
of the covenant is the "knowledge of God."[325] This "knowledge" is
directed to the commandment "You shall have no other gods but me,"
namely, the exclusive worship of YHWH (13:4).[326] Israel is to have no
other gods than YHWH, since no other deity has participated in its
history. Thus, Hosea enlightens his contemporaries who follow after
Baals in order to attain fertility that YHWH is the true giver of fertility:
YHWH is the only God in the sphere of fertility as well as in the world of
history; he is the One who gives them crops and wealth (2:10 [EV 8]),
who provides their pasture (4:16), who brings the rain (6:3), who will
restore their verdure in the end (14:5–8), and who definitely proclaims
himself as the Lord of fertility (14:9 [EV 8]). Therefore, Hosea's enlight-
enment movement is actually a demand to worship YHWH alone: he
emphasizes that YHWH alone has the unique lordship over history and
fertility; the authentic source of all fertility was YHWH, who liberated
Israel from its enslavement in Egypt.[327] Indeed, from the preface to ch. 1

"commandments" (26:13), and "YHWH" himself as Savior of Israel (6:12–14; 8:11,
14, 18). The last passages demonstrate again the close connection between Hosea
and the Deuteronomic circle in terms of their thought, since here, as well, those who
"forget YHWH" are described as those who "follow after other gods" (Deut 6:14;
8:19) (see Wolff, *Hosea*, 40).

323.   Hos 2:20 (EV 18); 6:3, 6; 8:2; 13:4; 14:10.

324.   Hosea refers to the Land as God's property (2:10 [EV 8]; 9:3), and thus he
terms it "the house of YHWH" (בֵּית יְהוָה, 8:1; 9:4). This term was already in use
among the groups who were concerned with the traditions of the tribal confederacy
(cf. Wolff, *Hosea*, 137; Mays, *Hosea*, 115–16). Emerton ("New Light," 2–13), however, contends unconvincingly that "the House of YHWH" be viewed as a reference
to a temple or a holy place at Bethel or a YHWH sanctuary in Samaria.

325.   Davies, *Hosea*, 79.

326.   Indeed, the basic covenant demand of YHWH toward Israel was to worship
him exclusively.

327.   P. D. Hanson, *The People Called: The Growth of Community in the Bible*
(San Francisco: Harper & Row, 1986), 167: "Hosea could remain true to the triadic
confession of his heritage [worship, righteousness, compassion], even as he

to the prophet's concluding words in ch. 14, Hosea's daring employment of key words from Canaanite mythology is nothing other than a ploy to display the advantage of the exclusive worship of YHWH. One can see that even though Israel's dependence upon Canaanite mythology and thought resulted in their unfaithfulness to YHWH and their "whoredom" (1:2; 2:4–7 [EV 2–5]; 3:3; 4:10–18; 5:3–7; 6:10; 9:1), Hosea's daring adaptation of the divine "husband" concept to YHWH (2:18 [EV 16]) serves to elucidate that YHWH is the only God of Israel, and thus stresses YHWH's claim of exclusiveness.[328] Israel was always in a covenantal bond with YHWH (6:7; 8:1), just as a wife is bonded to her husband (2:7)! Hosea delivers a wake-up call to the Israelites who have fallen into a mythical understanding of God due to syncretism with Baalism, and reminds them who the source of their existence is: remember the covenant with YHWH; know that he is the exclusive lord over nature, that he is the God of fertility; know YHWH!

In sum, Hosea's argument focuses on the fact that the Israelites must differentiate between YHWH who acts in the history of Israel and the Canaanite deities represented by Baal: know YHWH who holds the sovereignty over Israel's history and well-being (i.e. fertility). Therefore, Hosea prefers to call the deity "YHWH"[329] instead using the generic term "Elohim."[330] According to Hosea, Israel must know only the God who, since the time of Moses (12:14), has revealed himself in the proclamation of his law and through his liberating acts: "I am YHWH, your God from the land of Egypt" (12:10; 13:4). Israel is forbidden from knowing any other God: "You know no God besides me, and there is no savior but me" (13:4b). Hosea is familiar with the interpretation of YHWH's name in Exod 3:14, as he indicates in his negation of the old covenant formula. YHWH, the ancient God of Israel, is the God whom Hosea proclaims anew.[331] Other than the divine personal name "YHWH," there is almost no general reference to "Elohim" (אֱלֹהִים). Usually, possessive suffixes are appended to אֱלֹהִים in order to emphasize that he is the God of Israel: "YHWH, your God" in 12:10 (EV 9); 13:4; "YHWH, their God" in 3:5;

---

combined it with the freshness of a natural order revivified by the one true God, who was the Sovereign One not only of history but of nature as well."

328. Wolff, *Hosea*, xxvi. In Hosea's marriage metaphor (see 2:9, 18), YHWH's partner is not a goddess (Asherah), but rather historical Israel. Therefore, his metaphor rejects any suggestion of a plurality of divinities or even a sexually differentiated pantheon.

329. The word YHWH appears about 45 times in Hosea.

330. Elohim appears 26 times.

331. Wolff, *Hosea*, xxv.

7:10; "their God" in 4:12; 5:4; "your God" in 4:6; 9:1; 12:7a, 7b; "my God" is said by the people in 2:25 (EV 23); 8:2; and by Hosea in 9:17; "our God" in 14:4; and "her God," that is, "God of Samaria" in 14:1. In those few cases where the name "God" appears without possessive suffixes (3:1; 8:6; 13:4b), the word also serves to clarify Israel's proper exclusive relationship with YHWH; otherwise, the use of the word "God" on its own appropriately stands only in the pre-Mosaic Jacob tradition (12:4; cf. v. 7) and in formulaic expressions (4:1; 6:6).[332] Hosea's language clearly indicates that he is incapable of speaking of the God of Israel in a general sense; instead, he speaks precisely of YHWH, who has attested and proved himself in history as the God of Israel.

---

332.   Ibid., 63.

Chapter 5

THE MOTIVES BEHIND THE DEUTERONOMISTIC POLEMIC AGAINST THE CALF IMAGE AND THE PROHIBITION OF THE IMAGE

As we have seen above, the sin of the golden calf narrative in Deuteronomy (L–2[1]) was written with the criterion of the prohibition of the image in view. It seems that one can identify the motive behind the writing of L–2 through a consideration of the background to the crystallization of this prohibition. In order to inquire into the motives behind the Deuteronomistic polemic against the golden calf in L–2, we must examine the background to this crystallization in Deut 4:1–40, where the prohibition of the image is spoken of.[2] An observation of the prohibition of the image is essential if we wish to answer the question raised in Chapter 1 of the present study regarding the nature of Jeroboam's calves: Why are Jeroboam's calves associated with YHWH in 1 Kgs 12:28 and described in 2 Kgs 17:16 and 1 Kgs 14:9 as being other gods?

1. *Deuteronomy 4 and the Prohibition of the Image*

1.1. *The Central Issue of Deuteronomy 4:1–40*
In the same way that, generally speaking, a tension exists between the diachronic and synchronic approaches to the study of Deuteronomy,[3] one

---

1. Deut 9:9–19, 21, 25–29; 10:1–5, 10.
2. L–2 in Deut 9–10 has a number of similarities with Deut 4: (1) both texts include the expression מִתּוֹךְ הָאֵשׁ ("out of the midst of the fire," Deut 4:12, 15, 33; 9:10; 10:4) and the Ten Commandments (Deut 4:13; 9:9–11, 15, 17; 10:1–5), as well as Mount Horeb; (2) in Deut 4 and L–2, Israel's being chosen plays a dominant role (4:24–39; 9:25–29); (3) both texts speak of Israel as having become corrupt due to its violation of the prohibition of the image (4:16, 25, 31; 9:12, 26; 10:10); and (4) in both texts, forgiveness for the people's sin is based on YHWH's covenant with the Patriarchs (4:31; 9:27). Hence, it can reasonably be assumed that Deut 4:1–40 was composed by the second Deuteronomist (Dtr2), as was L–2. The attribution of Deut 4:1–40 will be discussed in detail in the following section.
3. For a historical survey of the research on Deuteronomy, see M. A. O'Brian, "The Book of Deuteronomy," *CurBS* 3 (1995): 95–128.

can notice the reflection of this tension specifically in the history of research on Deut 4.[4] It seems that the two approaches to the question of the formation of Deut 4 and of its literary structure are irreconcilable.[5] The diverse arguments regarding the existence of different "hands" or "layers" in Deut 4:1–40 appear to be unconvincing. The claim regarding the style, namely, the shift of the address from the plural to the singular form as a criterion for distinguishing different sources is unconvincing, since such shifting characterizes the work of D as a whole, as argued long ago by Lohfink.[6] Some contend that in Deut 4:1–40 one can discern different layers from a thematic[7] and terminological[8] perspective. However, it seems that these arguments ignore the literary structure of the chapter, edited in accordance with the central theme of all of Deut 4:1–40. This assumption supports the literary unity of the passage, that is, its terminological unity, in recurrent phrases and motifs.[9]

If this is the case, is there a central theme interwoven throughout this text? Before addressing this question, it is worthwhile examining the

4. On the different approaches to the study of Deut 4, see K. Holter, "Literary Critical Studies of Deut 4: Some Criteriological Remarks," *BN* 81 (1996): 91–103.

5. On diachronic interpretations of Deut 4, see Begg, "Literary Criticism of Deut 4,1–40," 10–55; on synchronic literary analyses of Deut 4, see J. G. Millar, "Living at the Place of Decision," in *Time and Place in Deuteronomy* (ed. J. G. McConville and J. G. Millar; JSOTSup 179; Sheffield: Sheffield Academic, 1994), 32–49.

6. N. Lohfink, "Auslegung deuteronomischer Texte IV. Verkündigung des Hauptgebots in der jüngsten Schicht des Deuteronomiums (Dt 4,1–40)," in *Höre Israel! Auslegung von Texten aus dem Buch Deuteronomium* (Düsseldorf: Patmos, 1965), 90ff. The interchanging of second person singular and second person plural occurs frequently in ancient Near Eastern literature (see Weinfeld, *Deuteronomy 1– 11*, 15–16, 223). According to A. D. H. Mayes ("Deuteronomy 4 and the Literary Criticism of Deuteronomy," *JBL* 100 [1981]: 30), the Deuteronomist uses the plural form, but intentionally left the singular form of Deuteronomic law, in order to show that the latter was a citation.

7. For example, D. Knapp (*Deuteronomium 4: Literarische Analyse und theologische Interpretation* [Göttingen: Vandenhoeck & Ruprecht, 1987], 31–32) argues that vv. 5–8 are an insertion between vv. 1–4 and vv. 9–14, based on the fact that v. 9 is iterant of v. 4 from the viewpoint of theme and terminology.

8. For instance, G. von Rad claims (*Das fünfte Buch Mose: Deuteronomium* [ATD 8; Göttingen: Vandenhoeck & Ruprecht, 1964], 49) that the law in vv. 9–14 implied a general term, but in vv. 15–20, 23–24 it refers to a specific term, namely, the law prohibiting the image, and that therefore the latter verses cannot be original.

9. Regarding these factors, see A. D. H. Mayes, "Deuteronomy 4 and the Literary Criticism of Deuteronomy," *JBL* 100 (1981): 25; Weinfeld, *Deuteronomy 1–11*, 221–22. Several scholars note the literary unity of Deut 4:1–40: Levenson, "Book of the Torah?," 203ff.; Mayes, *Story of Israel*, 27–28; Millar, "Place of Decision," 32–49.

structure of the text, which is composed of five passages: vv. 1–8,[10] 9–14, 15–22, 23–31, and 32–40. Each passage, with the exception of the last one, begins with a warning[11] to Israel to abide by the Law or to avoid violating YHWH's prohibitions. In particular, the three passages vv. 9–14, 15–22, and 23–31 fall under the same theme—the prohibition of making images—and hence, they are considered a single unit. This central passage, vv. 9–31, is then framed by vv. 1–8 and 32–40, which serve respectively as prologue and epilogue. Thus, the structure of the text and themes may be understood as follows:

A. Prologue (vv. 1–8): Statutes, ordinances, and Israel's uniqueness.
B. Central Passage (vv. 9–31): Prohibition of the image and repercussions of violating the prohibition.
C. Epilogue (vv. 32–40): Israel's uniqueness, statutes, and ordinances.

It could be said that the themes of the prologue and epilogue are not oriented to two different concerns (namely, Israel's uniqueness and YHWH's uniqueness) but rather one inseparable concern. On the other hand, it could be argued that there is a difference between the themes of the two passages: Israel's uniqueness gains recognition through its adherence to YHWH's laws in contrast to the other nations (vv. 1–8), and the uniqueness of God is recognized through his mighty deeds on behalf of Israel in Egypt and Horeb (vv. 32–40).[12] In vv. 1–8, Israel is represented as unique in comparison to the nations, and in vv. 32–40, YHWH is unique in comparison to other gods. This difference is especially clear in the parallel between the questions in v. 7 and v. 34: "For what great nation is there, that has gods so close to it?" (v. 7) and "Or did any god venture to go and take a nation from the midst of another nation...?" (v. 34). However, the two themes cannot be separated from one another completely. Israel's uniqueness presupposes YHWH's uniqueness, and YHWH's uniqueness relates to that of Israel. Israel is unique only because it received YHWH's Torah (Law) and upholds it, while YHWH is unique because he saved Israel from enslavement in Egypt, and gave them the Torah at Horeb. In spite of the close relationship between the two themes, priority is given to YHWH's uniqueness in terms of the Law,

---

10. According to Mayes ("Deuteronomy 4," 25), vv. 1–8 are divided into two passages: vv. 1–4 and 5–8.

11. Note the words specifically conveying warning, such as שְׁמַע ("hear,!" v. 1), הִשָּׁמֶר ("take heed to yourself!," v. 9), וְנִשְׁמַרְתֶּם ("you will watch yourselves carefully," v. 15), and הִשָּׁמְרוּ ("take heed to yourselves!," v. 23). See Weinfeld, *Deuteronomy 1–11*, 221.

12. J. H. Le Roux, "A Holy Nation was Elected," *OTWSA* 25–26 (1982–83): 64–65.

since the laws, which are intimately linked to Israel's uniqueness (v. 8), were given by YHWH at Horeb (v. 33[13]). Hence, we may conclude that there is interdependence between the uniqueness of Israel and that of YHWH, and that the former is dependent upon the latter through the Torah. In other words, the Torah is not only something within which the two themes (Israel's uniqueness and YHWH's uniqueness) merge into one, but it is also essential to the institutionalization of YHWH's uniqueness. Therefore, Deut 4:1–40 begins and ends with an exhortation against not keeping the Torah: "And now, O Israel, listen to the statutes and the ordinances..." (v. 1); "So you shall keep his statutes and commandments..." (v. 40).[14]

In turn, observance of the laws, which is related to YHWH's uniqueness, is demanded of Israel emphatically in the central passage (vv. 9–31). As observed above, the central passage is divided into three parts: vv. 9–14, 15–22, and 23–31. Each part begins with a form of the verb שָׁמַר ("to keep, watch"), accompanied by expressions such as לְךָ/לָכֶם ("yourself"/"yourselves") or לְנַפְשְׁךָ/לְנַפְשֹׁתֵיכֶם ("for your soul"/"for your souls") and פֶּן ("lest").[15] The three parts are joined in a continuous sequence in terms of principal content: in the first part (vv. 9–14), it is said of the Israelites that they did not see YHWH, but only heard his voice; in the second part (vv. 15–22), the people of Israel are warned not to make graven images; the third part (vv. 23–31) speaks of Israel's exile from the Land as punishment for violating the prohibition of the image. Hence, it seems that the content of the central passage is related to the commandment "You shall not make for yourself a graven image" appearing in the Decalogue.[16] Although the Decalogue ("Ten Words")

---

13. According to D, in his oration at the Moab plain, Moses gives the laws to the people of Israel almost 40 years after he received them from YHWH at Horeb.

14. On the similarity between the two verses, see Weinfeld, *Deuteronomy 1–11*, 199.

15. See G. Braulik, *Die Mittel deuteronomischer Rhetorik: Erhoben aus Deuteronomium 4, 1–40* (Rome: Biblical Institute, 1978), 82–83; also Weinfeld, *Deuteronomy 1–11*, 221.

16. According to K. Holter (*Deuteronomy 4 and the Second Commandment* [New York: Lang, 2003], 13), the content of the central passage in Deut 4:1–40 parallels the commandment "You shall not make for yourself a graven image..." in Deut 5:8–9 as follows: Deut 4:9–14 / 5:8aα (וּתְמוּנָה אֵינְכֶם רֹאִים, "but you saw no form"); 4:15–16a / 5:8aα (לֹא רְאִיתֶם כָּל תְּמוּנָה, "you did not see any form"); 4:16b–18 / 5:8aβ–b (כָּל סָמֶל תַּבְנִית זָכָר אוֹ נְקֵבָה, "even the form of any figure, the likeness of male or female"); 4:19–20 / 5:9a (וְנִדַּחְתָּ וְהִשְׁתַּחֲוִיתָ לָהֶם וַעֲבַדְתָּם, "you be drawn away and worship them, and serve them"); 4:21–24 / 5:8aα + 9a (הוּא אֵל קַנָּא, "a jealous God"); 4:25–31 / 5:8aα + 9b (בָּנִים וּבְנֵי בָנִים, "children, and children's children").

itself is merely a manner of YHWH's revelation to the people of Israel at Horeb, and does not comprise laws and ordinances,[17] it seems to consist of laws in terms of the content, since YHWH commands the people of Israel "to perform even the Decalogue" (v. 13). Hence, the prohibition of the image, which is addressed in the central passage (vv. 9–31), is a "commandment" of YHWH that Israel is ordered to keep, and serves as the basis for YHWH's uniqueness, as expressed in the prologue (vv. 1–8) and epilogue (vv. 32–40).

We may sum up as follows: Deut 4:1–40 is uniform in terms of its main theme, which is interwoven throughout the text, in addition to a number of other factors that support the unity and cohesion of the text; there is an interrelatedness between Israel's uniqueness and YHWH's uniqueness, which comprise the major themes of the prologue (vv. 1–8) and epilogue (vv. 32–40). Yet the former is dependent upon the latter, since the former is based on the laws given by YHWH; Israel's uniqueness derives from the laws, and YHWH's uniqueness is institutionalized by the laws held and upheld by the people of Israel. The central passage (vv. 9–31) deals with Israel's observance of the prohibition of the image, which is related to the institutionalization of YHWH's uniqueness.

1.2. *The Objective of the Prohibition of the Image*
As aforesaid, the prohibition of the image serves as a means of developing the central theme of Deut 4, namely, the institutionalization of the uniqueness of YHWH. If so, to which deity does the image refer in this prohibition? In Moses' exhortation to the people of Israel in Deut 4:16 refers directly to the prohibition of the image. Here, the making of a "graven image" is forbidden through the use of the words "lest you corrupt yourselves and make…" (…פֶּן תַּשְׁחִתוּן וַעֲשִׂיתֶם). The conjunction פֶּן ("lest") appears five times in Deut 4: vv. 9 (twice), 16, 19, and 23. In vv. 9 and 23, פֶּן is linked to the Niphal imperative form of שׁמר (i.e. הִישָׁמֶר), which expresses an admonition of the "Do not…" type.[18] In vv. 16 and 19, the word follows the Niphal form of שׁמר. The expression וְנִשְׁמַרְתֶּם ("[You shall] take good heed to yourselves") in v. 15 is directly linked to a "lest (פֶּן)… lest (פֶּן)…" sequence in vv. 16–19, in which פֶּן in v. 16 and פֶּן in v. 19 create a parallel between vv. 16–18 and v. 19.[19]

---

17. According to D, the Decalogue ("Ten Words") alone was transmitted to the people of Israel at Horeb. It was not laws and ordinances. The "laws and ordinances" (וּמִשְׁפָּטִים חֻקִּים) were told there to Moses alone, and he was commanded to transmit them to Israel, but not immediately, only some time later.

18. Holter, *Deuteronomy 4*, 38.

19. Ibid., 38–39.

Therefore, the head of the "lest (פֶּן)…lest (פֶּן)…" sequence in vv. 16–19 is v. 15, which contains a strong exhortation to Israel (v. 15a: וְנִשְׁמַרְתֶּם מְאֹד לְנַפְשֹׁתֵיכֶם, "take heed to yourselves very carefully"), based on Israel's experience of seeing no likeness on the day that YHWH spoke out of the fire (v. 15b: "since you did not see any form on the day that YHWH spoke to you at Horeb out of the midst of the fire"). The reference here to this experience seems to echo v. 12. In v. 12, the objective of the reference is to indicate the manner of YHWH's revelation at Horeb: he reveals himself not through a "likeness" (תְּמוּנָה), but rather through "the sound (or voice) of words" (קוֹל דְּבָרִים). "The sound of words" is a way that YHWH chooses to reveal Himself, and what is actually heard by the people of Israel is the "Ten Words" (עֲשֶׂרֶת הַדְּבָרִים, v. 13), that is, the Decalogue. On the other hand, when this reference to Israel's experience of YHWH's revelation (v. 15b) is linked to the exhortation in v. 16 ("lest you corrupt yourselves and make you a graven image…"), this exhortation sounds like the commandment "You shall not make for yourself a graven image." In order to clarify whether the "graven image" (פֶּסֶל) in this commandment refers to an image made for idolatrous purposes or for the worship of YHWH, it is worth examining Deut 4:16 in isolation from Deut 5:8. Did the prohibition of the image seek to forbid graven images of any deity or only of YHWH specifically?

Before proceeding to the verses relevant to the prohibition of the image (Deut 4:16; 5:8), we should recall the absence of any anthropomorphic or theriomorphic image of YHWH in Israelite religion (both in the southern kingdom of Judah and in the northern kingdom of Israel during the First Temple period), due to its aniconic custom, as discussed in Chapter 1. Here let us take a look at the following questions: If indeed there was no graven image of YHWH in Israelite religion, could it be that there was actually a need for a prohibition of YHWH's image? And if so, does it not make sense to assume that the prohibition of the image was not meant to forbid the making of graven images of other gods, but rather graven images of YHWH?

However, considering that the prohibition of making images in Israel (Deut 4:16) is based on the fact that the people of Israel did not see "any likeness" (תְּמוּנָה כָל) when YHWH spoke to them "out of the midst of the fire" at Horeb (Deut 4:15), it becomes evident that the prohibition of the image in Deut 4:16 became crystallized in order to prevent the making of images of YHWH.[20] It appears, then, that the prohibition of the image became crystallized, at the very least, in order to forbid the manufacture of images of YHWH.

---

20. Miller, *Religion of Ancient Israel*, 16.

2. *The Time of Crystallization of the Prohibition of the Image and Its Motive*

2.1. *The Time of Crystallization of the Prohibition of the Image*

When did the law prohibiting the image, which was intended specifically to forbid the making of images of YHWH, become crystallized? Regarding this question, we should recall what was said in §2.3 of Chapter 3: the aniconic measures carried out in the framework of Josiah's reforms were not based on the prohibition of the image, but rather the requirement to worship YHWH alone, namely, the commandment forbidding other gods. Practically, there is little difference between the prohibition of other gods and the prohibition of images of other gods, since, as previously mentioned, all of the gods in the ancient Near East were represented by symbols or graven images.[21] The prohibition of the image is not included in the "Book of the Law" (סֵפֶר הַתּוֹרָה) mentioned in 2 Kgs 22:8, which was based on the code of the laws in Deut 12–26 and believed to be the guide for Josiah's reforms. Hence, it is improbable that Josiah's version of the Deuteronomistic History (Dtr1)[22] presupposed the existence of the law prohibiting the image.[23] It is likely that there was no law designed to prohibit images of YHWH prior to the Exile. This assumption is reinforced by the text of Deut 4:1–40, which includes the prohibition of the image, and is the work of the Deuteronomist during the Exile. The ascription of Deut 4:1–40 to this later period is based on the following arguments. First, the elaboration of the prohibition of the image with the emphasis on the uniqueness of YHWH, and Israel as the object of the divine revelation, is reminiscent of the description in the Second Isaiah.[24] Second, vv. 23–31 ostensibly reflect the situation in which Israel is no longer in Israel, namely, the state of exile. This

---

21. See Weinfeld, *Deuteronomy 1–11*, 288; Morenz, *Egyptian Religion*, 150–56. According to Faur ("Idolatry," 6–7), the fundamental essence of pagan religion is the identification of the god with his image.

22. The term "Josiah's version" is based on the double-redaction theory proposed by American scholars (Levenson, "Book of the Torah?," 203–33; Halpern, *The First Historians*, 107–21, 207–40; Nelson, *Double Redaction*; Tadmor and Cogan, *2 Kings*; Provan, *Hezekiah*; McKenzie, *The Trouble with Kings*), following Cross's work (*Canaanite Myth*, 274–89) on the Deuteronomistic History.

23. As we saw in §2.3 in Chapter 3, the Josiah phase of Deuteronomy reflects a monolatric perspective rather than a monotheistic one. In the Exilic phase of the Deuteronomistic editing (especially Deut 4), a clearly monotheistic character is apparent, which is reminiscent of Second Isaiah; see Rose, *Ausschliesslichkeitsanspruch Jahwes*, 185ff., and also Rofé, "Monotheistic Argumentation," 434–45.

24. Compare vv. 15–18, 32, 35, and 39 with Isa 40:19–20; 44:19–20; 45:18, 21–22; and 46:9–9.

condition is expressed in such phrases as ...כִּי אָבוֹד תֹּאבֵדוּן ("that you will surely perish...," v. 26) and וְהֵפִיץ יְהוָה אֶתְכֶם ("and YHWH will scatter you," v. 27) regarding the banishment of Israel from the Land. Had these words been expressed to the people of Israel while they were still in the Land, sometime before the Exile, as a threat suggesting what would happen should they violate the prohibition of the image, expressions concerning restoration (vv. 29–31) would not have been included, since providing them in advance would have weakened the effectiveness of the threat. This assumption leads to the conclusion that the author was already in exile, and wanted to arouse hope of Israel's restoration through the phrase כִּי אֵל רַחוּם יְהוָה אֱלֹהֶיךָ ("For YHWH your God is a merciful God," v. 31). Third, the declaration of YHWH's uniqueness and the demand to keep the laws and ordinances (vv. 39–40) are important characteristics of the exhortation to the people of Israel in the Exile period.[25] In the Torah, the people of Israel were commanded in Moses' oration to avoid the iconic representation of YHWH, but the prohibition of the image actually became crystallized only during the Exile. Although an aniconic custom existed, one which rejected the iconic representation of YHWH already in the First Temple period, its literary expressions, as articulated in Deut 4:16, appear only during the Exile.

If the prohibition of the image did not exist prior to the Exile, one may conclude that it became crystallized during the Exile. Here we must ask the following question: If the prohibition of the image became crystallized during the Exile period, how can we explain the existence of the commandment "You shall not make for yourself a graven image" in the Decalogue of E, namely, in Exod 20?[26]

In order to answer this question, it is advisable to clarify which version of the commandment "You shall not make for yourself a graven image"—that of E or that in Deuteronomy—is the earlier one. The version in E reads לֹא תַעֲשֶׂה...פֶּסֶל וְכָל-תְּמוּנָה ("You shall not make...a

---

25. See Weinfeld, *Deuteronomy 1–11*, 224; Mayes, *Deuteronomy*, 149.

26. Regarding this question, we must deal with Exod 20:23 ("You shall not make with me gods of silver, or gods of gold, you shall not make for yourselves") and 34:17 ("You shall not make for yourself molten gods"), since these verses are attributed to E and J respectively, and may be considered laws prohibiting the image. However, the expression אִתִּי ("with me") in 20:23 suggests that what is actually intended is the prohibition of other gods (see Hyatt, *Exodus*, 225). Exod 34:17 also does not seem to be concerned with the making of images of YHWH, but rather idolatrous worship, since the verse appears in a context dealing with the prohibition of other gods (vv. 14–16). Hence, in both texts, the focus is actually on the forbiddance of other gods, which are YHWH's competitors (see Durham, *Exodus*, 319, 460–61; Childs, *Exodus*, 466; Houtman, *Exodus*, 104).

graven image *and* any likeness," Exod 20:4), while the version in Deuteronomy reads לֹא תַעֲשֶׂה...פֶּסֶל כָּל תְּמוּנָה ("You shall not make...a graven
image, any likeness," Deut 5:8). In other words, the Elohistic version
includes the conjunction -וְ ("and") between פֶּסֶל and כָּל תְּמוּנָה, while in
Deuteronomy it is absent. If the commandment "You shall not make for
yourself a graven image" is included in the Decalogue of a version
preceding the formulation of Deut 5, one can infer from such that the
author of Deut 5 accidentally omitted the conjunction -וְ from the phrase
פֶּסֶל וְכָל תְּמוּנָה in the Elohistic version. However, it is difficult to accept
the suggestion that the conjunction -וְ ("and") was mistakenly left out
by the author of Deut 5 when he copied the Elohistic version of the
Decalogue. Grammatically speaking, the form of the commandment in
Deut 5 is more ancient than that in E. The phrase פֶּסֶל כָּל תְּמוּנָה, without
the conjunction -וְ, does not indicate the plural but rather the singular, and
therefore does not refer to the objects that follow, namely, the "them" of
the phrases "bow down to them" and "worship them." If we assume that
the form of the text in E is more ancient than that in Deut 5, then the
earlier and more grammatically correct version, namely, פֶּסֶל וְכָל תְּמוּנָה,
was revised by the later author in a grammatically and syntactically
incorrect form, namely, פֶּסֶל כָּל תְּמוּנָה. However, this assumption does
not hold up under the rules of textual criticism, according to which the
text that is more difficult to read is more ancient. Therefore, it makes
sense to argue that the text was altered from the original form without -וְ
(פֶּסֶל כָּל תְּמוּנָה) to the form with -וְ (פֶּסֶל וְכָל תְּמוּנָה). In other words, the
phrase פֶּסֶל כָּל תְּמוּנָה, without the conjunction -וְ is actually anterior to
the version with -וְ, that is, the version without -וְ is the original one. This
implies that the commandment "You shall not make for yourself a graven
image" did not exist in the Elohistic version of the Decalogue when it
was copied by the author of Deut 5, and that it was the author of Deut 5
who inserted that commandment into his own text. This conclusion is
verified through a grammatical and syntactical analysis of Deut 5:7–9.

At this point, there is a need to examine in detail the relation between
the verbs in vv. 8 and 9 (תַּעֲשֶׂה, "make"; תִשְׁתַּחֲוֶה, "bow down") and the
objects (פֶּסֶל כָּל תְּמוּנָה, "a graven image, any likeness"; לָהֶם, "to *them*";
תָּעָבְדֵם, "worship *them*"). Although the words פֶּסֶל and תְּמוּנָה are
singular, their pronouns ("*them*") as the objects of the verbs תִשְׁתַּחֲוֶה and
תָּעֲבֹד appear in the plural.[27] From a grammatical perspective, the phrase
פֶּסֶל כָּל תְּמוּנָה in v. 8 does not signify the plural objects, but rather stands
in an appositional relation without the conjunction -וְ, and therefore is
given not in the plural, but rather in the singular. פֶּסֶל כָּל תְּמוּנָה, as direct

27. See v. 8: לֹא תִשְׁתַּחֲוֶה לָהֶם וְלֹא תָעָבְדֵם.

object of the verb תַּעֲשֶׂה ("make"), does not refer to the pronoun לָהֶם ("to *them*") as indirect object of the verb תִשְׁתַּחְוֶה ("bow down") and to the pronoun ־ם ("them") as direct object of the verb תָעֲבֹד ("worship"). Therefore, the plural pronoun in the sentence לֹא תִשְׁתַּחְוֶה לָהֶם וְלֹא תָעָבְדֵם ("You shall not bow down to them, nor worship them," v. 9a) refers appropriately to אֱלֹהִים אֲחֵרִים ("other gods") in the preceding verse, לֹא יִהְיֶה לְךָ אֱלֹהִים אֲחֵרִים עַל פָּנָי ("You shall have no other gods before me," v. 7). This interpretation gains further reinforcement by a number of linguistic arguments. The pair of verbs הִשְׁתַּחְוֶה/עָבַד ("to worship/to bow down"), which is an outstanding Deuteronomic expression, refers without exception to the worship of other gods, and פֶּסֶל ("graven image") or פְּסָלִים never serves as object to these verbs.[28] This analysis indicates that v. 9 was originally placed after v. 7, and only afterwards was v. 8 inserted between vv. 7 and 9. This assertion is confirmed by the fact that the prohibition of the images is non-existent in proto-Deuteronomy, to which Deut 5 is attributed.[29] Therefore, we may conclude that originally the commandment "You shall not make for yourself a graven image," which forbids images of YHWH, became crystallized on the background of Deut 4:16, as previously noted. When the commandment "You shall not make for yourself a graven image" was inserted within the scheme of the commandment "You shall have no other gods before me…," the latter commandment was meant to prohibit graven images of other gods.

If this is the case, did the author of Deut 5 add the commandment "You shall not make for yourself a graven image" when he copied the Decalogue of the Elohist? As observed above, in the proto-Deuteronomy there is no sign of the law prohibiting the image, and based on an examination of Deut 4:1–40, this prohibition was crystallized during the Exile period. If so, it is likely that the commandment "You shall not make for yourself a graven image" was inserted into the Decalogue in D during the Exile by the second Deuteronomist (Dtr2).[30] Here a question

---

28. Each of the two verbs (הִשְׁתַּחְוֶה/עָבַד) could technically be linked to פְּסָלִים as grammatical objects. Yet what is meant here is not each verb on its own, but rather the two verbs together as a pair (the verb עָבַד appears three times with פֶּסֶל or פְּסָלִים [2 Kgs 17:41; 2 Chr 33:22; Ps 95:7], while the verb הִשְׁתַּחְוֶה appears ten times with פֶּסֶל or פְּסָלִים [Exod 34:14; Lev 26:1; Isa 2:8, 20; 44:15, 17; 46:6; Jer 1:16; Mic 5:12; Ps 106:19]). Regarding the pair of verbs חוה/עבד, see Deut 8:19; 11:16; 17:3; 29:25; 30:17; Josh 23:16; Judg 2:19; 1 Kgs 9:6, 9; 2 Kgs 17:35; Jer 13:10; 16:11; 22:9; 25:6. See Zimmerli, "Das zweite Gebot," 237ff.

29. As previously seen in §2.3 in Chapter 3, the scope of the proto-Deuteronomic book is Deut 4:44–28:68 and does not include the law prohibiting the image.

30. As aforementioned in §2.3 in Chapter 3, the first Deuteronomist (Dtr1) is dated to the time of Josiah, prior to his death in 609 B.C.E.

arises: Was the commandment "You shall not make for yourself a graven image" inserted into E's Decalogue by the second Deuteronomist as well? This seems improbable. If we accept that the second Deuteronomist inserted it, we cannot explain why he added the conjunction -וְ between פֶּסֶל and כָּל תְּמוּנָה in the Elohistic text, while in Deuteronomy he left the text without the addition of -וְ. It appears, then, that the addition of the commandment "You shall not make for yourself a graven image" into the Decalogue in E was made by an author later than the second Deuteronomist, and he likely added the conjunction -וְ between פֶּסֶל and כָּל תְּמוּנָה in order to create grammatical congruity.

2.2. *The Motive Behind the Crystallization of the Prohibition of the Image*

What was the motive behind the crystallization of the prohibition of the image, which was designed to forbid the images of YHWH in the period of the Exile? In order to answer this question, we first need to answer a question regarding the background to Deut 4, which contains the prohibition of the image. It is likely that Deut 4 was composed as an answer to some of the questions raised by the Babylonian Exile. For example, how could something like this (the destruction of Israel and its exile to Babylon) happen if YHWH is the God of Israel? Who is YHWH to Israel? And what is Israel supposed to do in such a situation?[31]

Deuteronomy 4:23–31 provides the Deuteronomist's answer to the first question: Israel violated the Horeb covenant and aroused YHWH's wrath (vv. 23 and 25). Hence, Deut 4:23–31 comprises the author's most scathing utterances regarding the making of "a graven image of anything" (v. 25). Here, it is not the worship of other gods that provoked YHWH's fury and brought about Israel's exile. In other words, the Deuteronomist attributes the destruction (and exile) of Israel to "making graven images" (vv. 26–27), and does not refer at all to "worship of other gods." According to Deut 4, Israel's ruin (v. 26) was caused by the breach of the Horeb covenant (v. 23). In his view, the ordinances of the Horeb covenant center mainly on the prohibition of the image (the commandment "You shall not make for yourself a graven image," vv. 12–16, 23). Therefore, according to the Deuteronomist, the infringement of the law forbidding the image comprises an infringement of the Horeb covenant, and constitutes the reason for the Exile.

---

31. Regarding these questions, see L. Perlitt, "Anklage und Freispruch Gottes: Theologische Motive in der Zeit des Exils," *ZTK* 69 (1972): 298, cited in Braulik, *Theology of Deuteronomy*, 110.

This matter raises a certain problem: If the prohibition of the image did not exist before the Exile, could the author of Deut 4 have in fact attributed Israel's ruin and exile to its violation of the prohibition of the image? That is, if the prohibition of the image did not predate the Exile, the suggestion that the author of Deut 4 attributes the destruction and exile of Israel to the violation of the prohibition of the image does not make sense. Here we should recall the people of Israel's aniconism, as previously examined in Chapter 1. It is probable that for the readers of the verses related to the prohibition of the image (v. 16) and to the accusation that Israel's ruin and exile were a punishment for its violation (vv. 25–28), there was no problem identifying this custom with the prohibition of the image.

Now, it should be noted that the Deuteronomist emphasized the importance of the prohibition of the image in relation to YHWH's words at the time of his revelation at Horeb, not only as the reason for Israel's destruction and exile (see Deut 4:25–28), but also with the aim of institutionalizing YHWH's uniqueness (vv. 32–40, especially vv. 35 and 39). What the Deuteronomist preaches to Israel in exile is the adoption of belief in YHWH's uniqueness. The Deuteronomist—who composed Deut 4:1–40 as a reply to the question "Who is YHWH to Israel, and what should Israel do in such a state of exile?"—proposes the seeking of YHWH, the finding of him, and the return to him (vv. 29–30). The God of Israel, whom his people found again in the land of their exile, is YHWH, who is unlike the gods of other people, the impotent gods of "wood and stone"; he is the unique God, and there is no other like him (vv. 32–40). It seems that behind the Deuteronomist's declaration of YHWH as the unique God is found the following conception: in the ancient Near East, there was a perception that a war between nations comprises a war between gods.[32] Consequently, a view pervaded among the Israelites in the Babylonian Exile that YHWH was not as strong as the gods of Babylon, and that was the cause of the Israelites' defeat to the Babylonians. In reply to this assertion, the Deuteronomist informs the people that the destruction and exile of Israel was not the result of YHWH's defeat by Babylonian gods, but rather YHWH's judgment of his people for their violation of the Horeb covenant (vv. 23, 26–27); for the Deuteronomist, what Israel must know above all is that only YHWH is God, and that there is no other God but him—in other words, YHWH is a monotheistic God (vv. 35 and 39).

For the Deuteronomist, the realistic way to actualize YHWH as a monotheistic God is by asserting the prohibition of making images of

32. See Weippert, "Heiliger Krieg," 484.

him. This prohibition is based on the fact that YHWH is an imageless god, and that any attempt to create an iconic representation of him reduces him to the status of one of the pagan gods and their graven images.[33] In the Deuteronomist's conception, the description of pagan gods as idols of "wood and stone," that is, as gods who are "the work of men's hands" (v. 28), entails a declaration that in fact the foreign gods are not true gods.[34] Therefore, the Deuteronomist's declaration of the prohibition of images of YHWH comprises a declaration of monotheism (vv. 35 and 39).

Here we must clarify another issue: If we accept the claim that the objective of the crystallization of the prohibition of the image was the establishment of monotheistic belief in YHWH, then is it possible to date monotheism's foundation[35] to the period of the Exile? There is controversy regarding the time of the appearance of monotheistic belief in YHWH in Israelite religion, and whether monotheism evolved gradually or appeared suddenly, or even in both ways simultaneously.

Since the nineteenth century, scholars have been divided into two schools on the issue of the origin and genesis of monotheism in Israelite religion. One view espouses the notion of evolution, while the other supports the idea of revolution. The first is based on Darwin's evolution theory, which had a far-reaching impact on the sciences in the nineteenth century. The pioneers of the evolutionary method in the field of historical research on Israelite religion were Wellhausen and Kuenan. According to them, "moral monotheism"[36] emerged among the classical prophets of the eighth and seventh centuries B.C.E.[37] Monotheism developed gradually, rather than suddenly.[38] Eventually monotheism appeared in the shadow of the Exile in the sense of the total negation of other gods.[39]

---

33. Mayes, "Deuteronomy 4," 27.

34. See the phrase "which neither see, nor hear, nor eat, nor smell" (v. 28b).

35. A definition of monotheism entails the belief in one god, who is supernatural and universal, and denies the existence of other gods (see A. Bertholet, *Wörterbuch der Religionen* [Stuttgart: Cröner, 1952], 320; Meek, *Hebrew Origins*, 214–15; Rowley, *Unity of the Bible*, 42; Kaufmann, *Religion of Israel*, 127). In contrast to monotheism, henotheism indicates the temporal worship of a particular god, while monolatry refers to the consistent worship of a unique deity without denial of the existence of other gods.

36. In their view, "moral monotheism" was monotheism at the beginning of its evolution, before it became absolute monotheism, that is, in the transition between monolatrism and monotheism.

37. Wellhausen, *Prolegomena*, 411–25; A. Kuenen, *National Religions and Universal Religions* (London: Williams & Norgate, 1882), 119, 319.

38. Kuenen, *National Religions*, 319.

39. A. Kuenen, "Yahweh and the 'Other Gods,'" *TRev* 13 (1876): 346.

Evolutionary theory retained its hegemonic status in the field of historical research on Israelite religion until around World War II. At this time, two scholars, one in the United States and the other in Israel, Albright and Kaufmann, presented theories that countered "the Wellhausen hypothesis." In Albright's view, there were two major problems with Wellhausen's research: data and methodology. Followers of Wellhausen did not take into account the most recent archaeological findings, and interpreted the biblical texts based on Hegelian theory, which posited progressive evolution.[40] Above all, what bothered Albright was Wellhausen's claim that monotheism is a late development in Israelite history.[41] In many of his studies, and particularly in *From the Stone Age to Christianity*, Albright argues that Moses was a monotheist,[42] and that monotheism was his creation.[43] Like Albright, Kaufmann[44] too saw Israelite monotheism as Moses' creation. In his conception, all of the Bible and Israelite religion are essentially monotheistic.[45]

The fundamental reason why Albright and his students[46] saw Moses as the founder of monotheism in Israel was that in their opinion "the Bible was true, not only in terms of precepts and concepts probably articulated and formulated, but in a historical sense as well."[47] On the other hand, today some scholars hold the view that the Bible provides only secondary (or even tertiary) sources (or accounts) regarding what happened prior to the Babylonian Exile in the religious history of Israel. This is

40. Albright, *Stone Age to Christianity*, 82–126.

41. B. O. Long, *Planting and Reaping Albright: Politics, Ideology, and Interpreting the Bible* (University Park: Pennsylvania State University Press, 1997), 38; W. F. Albright, *Archaeology of Palestine and the Bible* (New York: Fleming H. Revell, 1932), 163.

42. Albright (*Stone Age to Christianity*, 271–72) contends that "If…the term 'monotheist' means one who teaches the existence of only one God, the creator of everything, the source of justice, who is equally powerful in Egypt, in the desert, and in Palestine…then the founder of Yahwism was certainly a monotheist."

43. Albright, *Archaeology of Palestine*, 163–67, and *Stone Age to Christianity*, 82–126.

44. His book *History of Israelite Religion* (in Hebrew; 8 vols.) was published in 1937 and 1956, and was abridged and translated into English with the title *The Religion of Israel* in 1960 by M. Greenberg.

45. Kaufmann, *Religion of Israel*, 60–131.

46. J. Bright, *The Kingdom of God: The Biblical Concept and Its Meaning for the Church* (Nashville: Abingdon, 1953); E. Jacob, *Theology of the Old Testament* (trans. A. Heathcote and P. Allcock; New York: Harper, 1958) (Jacob was a German scholar, but supported Albright's view).

47. D. N. Freedman, "Albright as a Historian," in *The Scholarship of William Foxwell Albright* (ed. G. W. Van Beek; Atlanta: Scholars Press, 1989), 37.

argued on the basis that it does not describe historical facts as they occurred.[48] The primary sources of ancient Israelite history are archaeological remnants (buildings, artifacts, clay tablets, pottery sherds, papyri, etc.). In the opinion of some scholars, the Bible's function in the reconstruction of the history of the people of Israel is to aid in compiling and interpreting the information dispersed in other documents.[49] Now, although we assume the veracity of the biblical descriptions of Mosaic religion even in the absence of archaeological findings proving the existence of a historical Moses, and the reality of Mosaic religion apart from the "Torah," Albright's hypothesis, according to which Moses integrated aspects of the monotheistic religion of Pharaoh Amenophis IV or Akhenaten (1364–1347 B.C.E.) of Egypt into Israelite religion, remains unconvincing. The monotheistic influence of Amenophis IV was short-lived in Egypt of the fourteenth century B.C.E. It was followed by a counter-reaction to his monotheistic policies. After his death, his monotheistic revolution was overturned.[50] Moreover, the critical factor in monotheism is the belief in one god, without other gods, yet in the literary sources ascribed to the pre-exilic period, this worldview is far from clearly formulated.[51]

However, the negative appraisal of Albright's and Kaufmann's conception of a revolutionary notion of monotheism does not mean we should return to the evolutionary conception, according to which Israel

48. See E. A. Knauf, "From History to Interpretation," in *The Fabric of History: Text, Artifact and Israel's Past* (ed. D. V. Edelman; JSOTSup 127; Sheffield: JSOT, 1991), 46 n. 1.

49. J. M. Miller, "Is it Possible to Write a History of Israel without Relying on the Hebrew Bible?," in Edelman, ed., *The Fabric of History*, 93–102; G. W. Ahlström, "The Role of Archaeological and Literary Remains in Reconstructing Israel's History," in Edelman, ed., *The Fabric of History*, 116–41 (esp. 119–41); T. L. Thompson, *Early History of the Israelite People: From the Written and Archaeological Sources* (Leiden: Brill, 1992), 110–11, 404–5. For a methodology for determining the historicity of texts in the Bible, see K. A. D. Smelik, "The Use of the Hebrew Bible as a Historical Source," in *Converting the Past: Studies in Ancient Israelite and Moabite Historiography* (Leiden: Brill, 1992), 1–34 (esp. 22–25); D. V. Edelman, "Doing History in Biblical Studies," in Edelman, ed., *The Fabric of History*, 13–25.

50. F. Stolz, *Einführung in den biblischen Monotheismus* (Darmstadt: Wissenschaftliche Buchgesellschaft, 1996), 77. Also unconvincing is Propp's view that Akhenaten's regime had its influence on the Israelites, not in its earliest days, but rather at the time of the monarchy, and this influenced Deuteronomic theology (see W. H. C. Propp, "Monotheism and 'Moses,'" *UF* 31 [1999]: 573).

51. H. H. Rowley, "Moses and Monotheism," in *From Moses to Qumran: Studies in the Old Testament* (London: Lutterworth, 1963), 42.

underwent a number of stages of development (namely, animism, poly-
theism, henotheism, and monolatry) before it came to its final form, as
Wellhausen et al. argued. The concept of a linear evolution of Israelite
religion culminating in monotheism is based on the view[52] that originally
Israelite religion and Canaanite religions were indistinguishable. However, as observed in Chapter 1, from an archaeological perspective, the
existence of aniconism among the Israelites is a proven fact, that is, they
did not produce graven images of YHWH, and thus the Israelite religion
was different[53] from other religions in the ancient East. In my opinion, if
we wish to assert that the Torah's account of ancient Israelite religion is
reliable, we had better use the term "monolatry"[54] to indicate the perspective on divinity in ancient Israelite religion.[55]

In light of the critical analysis of the Israelite religion as described in
the Bible, we cannot ignore its polytheistic reality in the period before
the Exile. At an early stage, it seems that in Israelite religion there was
an almost total identification between YHWH and El.[56] It is also clear that
there was a widespread co-existence or identification of YHWH with

52. See N. P. Lemche, "The Development of the Israelite Religion in the Light of
Recent Studies on the Early History of Israel," in *Congress Volume: Leiden 1989*
(ed. J. A. Emerton; VTSup 43; Leiden: Brill, 1991), 107–15.

53. For example, in contrast to the view of the divinities in other religions, the
Israelite religion had the perspective of a non-mythological, transcendent divinity,
anti-magicism, and of an aniconic deity, and so on. See Albright, *Stone Age to
Christianity*, 249–72; Kaufmann, *Religion of Israel*, 60–149.

54. The Commandment ("You shall have no other gods before me") does not
deny the existence of other gods.

55. A number of scholars are convinced that true monotheism is the product of a
series of revolutions, which took place over several hundreds of years (Lang,
Monotheism, 55–56; Keel and Uehlinger, *Gods, Goddesses, and Images of God*, 248;
de Moor, *Rise of Yahwism*). In other words, these scholars are positioned between
Wellhausen and Albright, and attempt to explain the phenomenon of monotheism as
an evolutionary process occurring in a revolutionary way (see R. K. Gnuse, *No
Other Gods: Emergent Monotheism in Israel* [JSOTSup 241; Sheffield: Sheffield
Academic, 1997], 69).

56. Although undoubtedly from an early stage, El was worshipped under the
name YHWH as the god who brought Israel out of Egypt (Exod 15:1–18), it can
reasonably be assumed that many Israelites worshipped this god under the name El
(Num 23:22; 24:8). Apparently, the tension between these two traditions was
resolved through the notion that YHWH originated in the image of El (see Cross,
Canaanite Myth, 44–75; de Moor, *Rise of Yahwism*, 233–66; J. Milbank, "The
History of One God," *HeyJ* 38 [1997]: 373) or the concept that identified YHWH with
El after worshippers of YHWH entered the Land of Canaan, where El was
worshipped (see Eissfeldt, "El and Yahweh," 35–37). On the detailed discussion of
the assimilation of YHWH with El, see §2.3.1 in Chapter 4.

Baal. However, it seems that the number of deities recognized by Israel, in comparison to the Ugaritic, Mesopotamian, and Egyptian pantheons of gods, was rather limited.[57] In the Judges period, Israel worshipped YHWH, El, Baal, Asherah (perhaps), and also celestial deities (sun, moon, and stars). During the monarchical period, both in northern Israel and southern Judah, YHWH, El, Baal, Ashtoreth, and the celestial deities were worshipped.[58] Of these deities, it was Baal who most profoundly influenced the Yahwistic religion. In Hosea, the term בְּעָלִים ("Baalim") refers to other gods (as observed in §3.2.1 in Chapter 4). In such a polytheistic situation, monolatry re-emerged in Israelite religion, which was represented by the "YHWH-alone movement,"[59] which was led by the prophets of the eighth and seventh centuries B.C.E.[60] However, Israel did not achieve true monotheism through this movement. Monotheistic expressions are not found from the biblical texts written before the Exile.

Even the statement שְׁמַע יִשְׂרָאֵל יְהוָה אֱלֹהֵינוּ יְהוָה אֶחָד ("Hear, O Israel, YHWH is our God, YHWH is one") in Deut 6:4, which is accepted in both Judaism and Christianity as an avowal of YHWH's monotheism, and which is attributed to the "proto-Deuteronomy" of King Josiah,[61] implies "poly-Yahwism." The proper name associated with the divine entity cannot be counted as "one, two, three…" The word YHWH as proper name is incompatible with אֶחָד ("one"), which is a cardinal number, without assuming YHWH's multi-manifestations at various places. Suggestions have been made for interpreting the word אֶחָד ("one") in a sense other than as a cardinal number. According to Gordon, אֶחָד should be understood as a proper name, and that one should read Deut 6:4 in the sense of "YHWH is our God, YHWH is 'One.'"[62] Gordon's suggestion is based on Zech 14:9, and on a comparison with names of deities in the ancient Near East. Yet, one should not necessarily understand the two clauses in Zech 14:9, יְהְיֶה יְהוָה אֶחָד וּשְׁמוֹ אֶחָד ("YHWH will be one, and his name is one") as synonymous. Even if אֶחָד is indeed used as a proper noun, the question remains as to what is meant by calling YHWH by the

---

57. Smith, *Early History of God*, 182.

58. Ibid. Deities who appeared in the later period of the Kingdom of Judah are "Queen of Heaven" (Jer 7:18; 44:18–19), Tammuz (Ezek 8:14), Haddad-Rimmon (Zech 12:11), and Bethel (Jer 48:13).

59. On the "YHWH-alone movement," see Lang, *Monotheism*, 30ff.

60. It can be said that the pioneers of the movement were Elijah and Elisha in the ninth century B.C.E., who clashed with the prophets of Baal.

61. H. D. Preuss, *Deuteronomium* (Darmstadt: Wissenschaftliche Buchgesell-schaft, 1982), 100–101.

62. C. H. Gordon, "His Name is 'One'," *JNES* 29 (1970): 198–99.

name אֶחָד.[63] Another suggestion is to interpret אֶחָד ("one") as an adjective, in the sense of "single," "sole," "unique." Mayes cites Isa 51:2; Ezek 33:24; 37:22; Zech 14:9, and 1 Chr 29:1 in support of this proposal.[64] However, none of these references provides a convincing example of the meaning of the word אֶחָד as "singular." In Isa 51:2 and Ezek 33:24, there is a contrast between Abraham as one man and the masses of his offspring. There is also a numerical contrast in Ezek 37:22 between Israel as two nations in the past and its future as one nation. The number אֶחָד ("one") indicates this contrast well.[65] It seems that Zech 14:9 is nothing other than a citation of Deut 6:4.[66] First Chronicles 29:1 states: שְׁלֹמֹה בְנִי אֶחָד בָּחַר בּוֹ אֱלֹהִים נַעַר וָרָךְ ("My son Solomon, whom *alone* God has chosen, is yet young and tender"). Moberly contends that in this version, the author omitted the word אֲשֶׁר ("which"),[67] and that the proper context of אֶחָד is Solomon's election among David's sons in 1 Chr 28:4–5. However, the immediate context is David's speech to the assembly of officials, whose aid Solomon requires (1 Chr 28:8, 21).[68] This context also implies that the contrast is numerical. Thus, in none of the examples does אֶחָד demand the translation "singular" or "unique."[69] Sperling thinks that the text was corrupted, and that אֶחָד should be read instead as אָהוּב ("loved").[70] Yet there is no textual basis for this arbitrary reading. Hence, it seems that the difficulty involved in the interpretation of אֶחָד finds its resolution in the references to "YHWH of Samaria" and "YHWH of Teman (Yemen)"[71] in the Kuntillet ʿAjrud inscriptions,[72] dated

63. N. MacDonald, *Deuteronomy and the Meaning of Monotheism* (Tübingen: Mohr Siebeck, 2003), 70.

64. Mayes, *Deuteronomy*, 176.

65. MacDonald, *Deuteronomy*, 70.

66. R. W. L. Moberly, "'Yahweh is One': The Translation of the Shema," in Emerton, ed., *Studies in the Pentateuch*, 214–15.

67. Ibid., 212.

68. MacDonald, *Deuteronomy*, 70.

69. Ibid.

70. S. D. Sperling, "The One We Ought to Love," in *Ehad: The Many Meanings of God is One* (ed. E. B. Borowitz; Port Washington, N.Y.: Sh'ma, 1988), 83–85.

71. Apparently, "Teman" (Yemen) refers to the shrine in the desert where YHWH was worshipped, or the place where the ancient cult of YHWH originated (see Gnuse, *No Other Gods*, 70).

72. On the Kuntillet ʿAjrud inscriptions, see Meshel, "Did Yahweh Have a Consort?," 24–35, and "Two Aspects," 99–104; W. G. Dever, "Recent Archaeological Confirmation of the Cult of Asherah in Ancient Israel," *HS* 23 (1982): 37–44; Weinfeld, "Kuntillet ʿAjrud Inscriptions," 121–30; Emerton, "New Light," 385–408; Day, "Yahweh and the Gods," 181–96.

to the ninth and eighth centuries B.C.E.[73] The "Samaria" and "Teman" ("Yemen") references in connection with the God YHWH seem to suggest that many worshippers of YHWH believed in YHWH's regional manifestations.[74] Israelites influenced by Baalism, according to which Baal manifested himself at a range of cultic sites,[75] could have accepted YHWH's multi-manifestations in different places of worship. Accordingly, the majority of scholars agree that the declaration יְהוָה אֶחָד ("YHWH is one") in Deut 6:4 appears in the framework of a polemic against poly-Yahwism.[76] This proclamation expresses the view that YHWH is indivisible, and does not exist in different forms at different shrines. The application of this declaration is found in Deut 12. The formula, "the place where YHWH will choose," always refers to Jerusalem, and the first version of this chapter (Deut 12:13–14a, 15–18) was written during the reign of Josiah.[77]

This being the case, I will turn now to an examination of whether monotheism is indeed described in Deut 4:1–40, which is attributed to the period of the Babylonian Exile, as previously observed. The verses deserving of attention regarding monotheism are vv. 35 and 39, which read respectively as follows: "...YHWH, he is God; there is none else beside him" and "YHWH, he is God in heaven above and on the earth below; there is none else." Such an expression is reminiscent of Second Isaiah, as most scholars acknowledge,[78] in which absolute monotheism is

---

73. Scholars date them to 850–837 B.C.E., that is, to the time that Israel ruled Judah under the extended family of Omri (Jehoram, Ahaziah, Athaliah; 2 Kgs 8:25–29), or to the time of Joash, King of Israel (801–786 B.C.E.; 2 Kgs 13:8–9) (see Gnuse, *No Other Gods*, 70).

74. Ibid.

75. Smith, *Early History of God*, 47.

76. Regarding poly-Yahwism, see Römer, "History of Israel's Traditions," 200–201.

77. See Albertz, *Israelite Religion*, 206ff.

78. F. Stolz, "Der Monotheism Israels im Kontext der altorientalischen Religionsgeschichte-Tendenzen neuerer Forschung," in Dietrich and Klopfenstein, eds., *Ein Gott allein?*, 179–80; Lang, *Monotheism*, 41–50; M. Lind, "Monotheism, Power, and Justice: A Study in Isaiah 40–55," *CBQ* 46 (1984): 432–46; H. Klein, "Der Beweis der Einzigkeit Jahwes bei Deutero-Jesaja," *VT* 35 (1985): 267–73; S. D. Sperling, "Israel's Religion in the Ancient Near East," in *Jewish Spirituality: From the Bible through the Middle Ages* (ed. A. Green; New York: Crossroad, 1986), 6, 28; T. N. D. Mettinger, *In Search of God: The Meaning and Message of the Everlasting Names* (Philadelphia: Fortress, 1988), 204–5; Albertz, *Israelite Religion*, 417–18; O. Loretz, "Das 'Ahnen- und Götterstatuen- Verbot' im Dekalog und die Einzigkeit Jahwes: Zum Begriff des Göttlichen in altorientalischen und alttestamentalichen Quellen," in Dietrich and Klopfenstein, eds., *Ein Gott allein?*, 512–14.

declared: "…I am he; before me there was no God formed, neither shall any be after me; I, even I, am YHWH; and beside me there is no savior" (Isa 43:10–11); "…I am the first, and I am the last; and beside me there is no God" (Isa 44:6); "…I am YHWH, and there is none else, beside me there is no God…" (Isa 45:5); "I am YHWH, and there is none else" (Isa 45:18); "…is it not I, YHWH? And there is no other God besides me…for I am God, and there is none else" (Isa 45:21–22); and "…I am God, and there is none else; I am God, and there is none like Me" (Isa 46:9). Here, the expression "there is none else" (עוֹד אֵין) reflects the monotheistic character of the text, which denies the existence of other gods. Consequently, most scholars appraise Deut 4:35 and 39 as an explicit account of monotheism.[79]

However, it seems that the reference to the celestial bodies (sun, moon, stars) described in v. 19 contradict the denial of the existence of other gods implied in the expression "there is none else." Verse 19 says that the celestial entities that the peoples are drawn to worship were allotted by YHWH himself. The stars themselves are considered divine beings (sons of god/gods).[80] Yet another understanding of the celestial bodies in v. 19 might be deduced from the literary structure of …פֶּן…פֶּן ("lest…lest…"), which appears in vv. 16–18 and 19. The conjunction פֶּן ("lest, for fear that") serves normally to indicate a warning,[81] and functions

79. I. Cairns, *Deuteronomy: Word and Presence* (Edinburgh: Handsel, 1992), 61; P. C. Craigie, *The Book of Deuteronomy* (London: Hodder & Stoughton, 1976), 143; D. G. Dawe, "Deuteronomy 4:32–40," *Int* 47 (1993): 45; Lang, *Monotheism*, 45; J. Pakkala, *Intolerant Monolatry in the Deuteronomistic History* (Göttingen: Vandenhoeck & Ruprecht, 1999), 223; Rofé, "Monotheistic Argumentation," 434–45; J. H. Tigay, *Deuteronomy: The Traditional Hebrew Text with the New JPS Translation* (Philadelphia: The Jewish Publication Society of America, 1996), 57; Weinfeld, *Deuteronomy 1–11*, 212; Mayes, *Deuteronomy*, 157–58; Stolz, "Der Monotheism Israels," 181–82; Sperling, "Israel's Religion," 23; Loretz, "Das 'Ahnen- und Götterstatuen- Verbot'," 509–11; Braulik, *Theology of Deuteronomy*, 115–26. However, MacDonald claims that the phrase "YHWH, he is God; there is none else" in Deut 4:35, 39 means the unity of YHWH with the one God of Israel, and does not deny the existence of other gods (see MacDonald, *Deuteronomy*, 79–85). Gnuse, as well, contends that Deut 4:39 does not comprise a total denial of the existence of gods other than YHWH. In his view, the phrase "He is God in heaven above and on the earth below" is an exaggeration found in hymns and prayers to particular gods in the ancient Near East (see Gnuse, *No Other Gods*, 206).

80. Weinfeld, *Deuteronomy 1–11*, 206.

81. According to Muraoka, פֶּן indicates "a negative wish of a speaker or speakers" (P. Joüon and T. Muraoka, *A Grammar of Biblical Hebrew* [Rome: Pontifical Biblical Institute, 1991], 635).

as a substitute for לֹא ("no," "not").[82] Consequently, the phrase פֶּן +
incomplete verb, in the second person is understood as a negative
imperative. Hence, vv. 16–18 are a reminder of the commandment "You
shall not make for yourself a graven image" in the Decalogue, while
v. 19 echoes the commandment "You shalt have no other gods before
me." These two negative imperatives, within the ...פֶּן...וּפֶן form, are
intimately linked with v. 15 in terms of literary structure. The conjunction פֶּן appears five times in Deut 4 (vv. 9 [twice], 16, 19, and 23),
while in three instances it is immediately followed by the imperative of
the Niphal form of the verb שָׁמַר (vv. 9, 15, 23), which indicates a warn-
ing/rebuke.[83] Therefore, the meaning of both negative imperatives in
vv. 16–18 and 19 is found in v. 15: "Watch yourselves carefully, since
you did not see any form on the day YHWH spoke to you at Horeb from
the midst of the fire." In other words, both imperatives refer to the fact
that because YHWH, as a monotheistic god, is formless, explicit representation of him is forbidden. Consequently, entities that assume any
explicit form are not gods at all. This intent is clearly revealed in the
description of the impotence of entities recognized and worshipped as
deities by other nations (vv. 28 and 34). Therefore, when Deut 4 refers to
the gods of other nations, the term אֱלֹהִים ("god") does not serve to
indicate the existence of other gods, but rather to reinforce the polemic
denying their divinity (vv. 28, 34). Hence, the declaration of YHWH as a
monotheistic god in vv. 35 and 39 is a logical extension of the claim that
there are no gods other than him (vv. 28, 34).

The prohibition of the image, based on the theology according to
which it is forbidden to represent YHWH in an explicit form because he is
formless (v. 15), determines that deific entities that are represented in
explicit form are in fact not gods at all. This theology, embedded within
the prohibition of the image, strongly resembles the conception of Second
Isaiah, who declares YHWH to be a monotheistic deity: only YHWH is
God, because only he has the power to redeem and to control every entity
on earth and in heaven, in contrast to the lifeless idols that represent
other gods.[84]

Therefore, it can be concluded that YHWH is an imageless God;
accordingly, worshipping him by way of an image or icon is tantamount

---

82. Holter, *Deuteronomy 4*, 40.

83. Ibid., 38.

84. On the relationship between the monotheistic declaration and the mockery of
idols in Second Isaiah, see Isa 44:6–22; 46:1–13. Regarding the function and use of
the idolatry verses in Second Isaiah, see R. J. Clifford, "The Function of Idol
Passages in Second Isaiah," *CBQ* 42 (1980): 450–64.

to worshipping a pagan god; the law prohibiting images of YHWH, then, comprises a proclamation that YHWH alone is God, and there is no other beside him.[85]

3. *The Deuteronomist's Polemic Against the Golden Calf*

At this juncture, we can sum up the Deuteronomistic polemic against the golden calf in light of his understanding of the law forbidding the image. The texts deserving attention in this context are 1 Kgs 12; 14:9; 2 Kgs 17:16; and L–2 (Deut 9:9–19, 21; 10:1–5, 10). According to the double-redaction theory, as we saw in §2.3 in Chapter 3, the Deuteronomistic school created two Deuteronomistic layers. The first Deuteronomistic layer (Dtr1) is dated to the time of Josiah, prior to his death in 609 B.C.E., while the second (Dtr2) is dated to the period of the Babylonian Exile. Attributed to the exilic Deuteronomist (Dtr2) are the final two-and-a-half chapters of the books of Kings, after Josiah (namely, 2 Kgs 23:26–37; 24; 25), as well as some passages ascribed to the exilic period.[86] Notwithstanding the question of the existence of a Deuteronomistic school,[87] I accept the argument that the Deuteronomistic History was created through double redaction, since only thus is it possible to explain both the continuity and the inconsistency in the Deuteronomistic History. In any case, through this reasoning, 1 Kgs 14:9 and 2 Kgs 17:16 are attributed to the first Deuteronomist (Dtr1). In other words, in these verses, which belong to the version written before the Exile, Jeroboam's golden calves are not measured up in light of the prohibition of the image, but rather the prohibition of worshipping other gods. Jeroboam's calves, which were originally associated in the cultic formula of 1 Kgs 12:28 with YHWH,[88] are identified with other gods in 1 Kgs 14:9, and 2 Kgs 17:16, in which Jeroboam's calves are decried as other gods. On this point, there is no difference between the position of the first Deuteronomist and that of the Elohist. It can be said that the first Deuteronomist adopted the theological stance of the Elohist in relation to the calf image in order to describe the history of the northern kingdom of Israel. In this way, the first Deuteronomist inherited the traditions of the northern kingdom.

85. See Mayes, *Story of Israel*, 29.
86. According to Cross (*Canaanite Myth*, 287), the following passages are attributed to Dtr2: Deut 4:27–31; 28:36–46, 63–68; 29:27; 10:1–10; Josh 23:11–13, 15–16; 1 Sam 12:25; 1 Kgs 2:4; 6:11–13; 8:25b, 46–53; 9:4–9; 2 Kgs 17:19; 20:17–18; 21:2–15.
87. On this issue, see Porter, "Supposed Deuteronomistic Redaction," 69–78.
88. See §4 in Chapter 1.

On the other hand, the second Deuteronomist, being in exile, dealt with the matter of the prohibition of images of YHWH in light of his theological ruminations on the question of how such a disaster occurred and who YHWH is in relation to Israel. According to the Deuteronomist's ideas, which emerge from an observation of Deut 4:1–40, Israel's ruin and exile are YHWH's judgment upon Israel for violating the law forbidding the image, while the justification for Israel's exilic existence is discovering YHWH as the unique God, that is, establishing of monotheistic belief in YHWH, as expressed through observance of the law prohibiting the image. Consequently, the second Deuteronomist's emphasis on the prohibition of the image, which is seen as a necessary condition for Israel's future existence, forces him to reconstruct the Elohistic polemic against the golden calf in light of his understanding of it as a violation of the prohibition of the image.

In Deut 4:1–40, the second Deuteronomist has Moses orate on the importance of the prohibition of the image and on YHWH's uniqueness: the destruction and exile of Israel result from YHWH's judgment of Israel's violation of the Horeb covenant, and according to v. 23 the major infraction in this respect was Israel's disregard of the law forbidding the image. YHWH is the unique sovereign of all the creatures and beings on earth and in heaven, even the celestial bodies, which are worshipped by other peoples (v. 19). These entities, which are termed אֱלֹהִים ("gods"), are visible or explicitly represented, yet they lack power, knowledge, emotion, desire (v. 28), and are fundamentally impotent (v. 34). Consequently, they are not true gods; only YHWH is God and there is no other (vv. 35, 39); YHWH, as the unique God, revealed himself in no form other than his "words" (vv. 12–15) and, therefore, any attempt to represent him explicitly (including graven images, etc.) will reduce belief in him to the level of belief in other gods, which are in fact not gods at all. Hence, behind the replacement, during the exilic period, of the aniconic custom in Israelite religion with the law prohibiting images, lies the monotheistic theology of YHWH, who cannot be represented explicitly (in iconic form). Only the prohibition of the image functions as a means of ensuring monotheistic belief in YHWH.

In order to teach the people in exile a lesson regarding the importance of the law forbidding the image, the second Deuteronomist used the sin of the golden calf as an example of what happens when this law is infracted and YHWH is represented as an image. He reinterpreted the Elohist's version of the sin of the golden calf from the perspective of the prohibition of the image, and created L–2 (Deut 9:9–19, 21; 10:1–5, 10).

Chapter 6

SUMMARY AND CONCLUSION

(1) In the earliest stage, the image of the calf was not considered negative or contradictory to the aniconic Israelite religious tradition. Far from representing a heathen god (or gods), it was in fact regarded within Israelite religion as a footstool of their invisible God, YHWH. At the time of Jeroboam I's establishment of an official form of calf worship in the northern kingdom of Israel in the tenth century B.C.E., there are no indications whatsoever of a negative approach to the calf figure. The first negative critique was voiced by the prophet Hosea in the eighth century B.C.E., who was followed by the Elohistic historian (E). One can infer from this fact that prior to the time of Hosea and the Elohist, a positive approach to the calf image prevailed in Israel. Opposition originated in the northern kingdom. Even within the Elohistic narrative (Exod 32), which condemns the calf image, there are hints suggesting that originally there was a positive attitude to it. The god referred to upon presentation of the golden calf is in fact YHWH himself (Exod 32:4b). The phrase "who brought you up out of Egypt" in the Torah and in Deuteronomistic History always refers to YHWH. This understanding is reinforced by Aaron's expression "a festival for YHWH (חַג לַיהוָה) tomorrow" (Exod 32:5b), that is refers to the calf. These positive allusions to the calf image, namely, expressions indicating that the calf image was originally linked with YHWH, were certainly not an innovation of the Elohist, who denounced the calf as an idol, but rather were already present before his time.

(2) The origin of the positive approach to the calf image in Israelite religion can be traced to worship in the sanctuary at Bethel. Indications of such can be found, first of all, in the cultic formula in Exod 32:4a, and the expression "a festival for YHWH" in v. 5b. They not only attest to a positive public notion with respect to calf worship but also to the fact that Aaron established it, given his own fabrication of the calf (v. 4a) and

construction of the altar (v. 5a). In Judg 20:27b–28a, as well, it is reported that the Aaronic priests served at Bethel. So, from Exod 32:4a and 5a, and Judg 20:27b–28a, it can be deduced that calf worship originated at Bethel. Although there is some doubt surrounding the authenticity of Judg 20:27b–28a, which may be a late insertion, it is evident that "before YHWH" (לִפְנֵי לַיהוָה) in Judg 20:23, 26 is another way of saying "before the Ark of the Covenant," and the expression "and went up to Bethel" in vv. 23, 26 means that the Israelites went up to the sanctuary at Bethel, which housed the Ark of the Covenant. It seems that the Deuteronomist deliberately omitted the reference to the Bethel sanctuary and Aaron's priesthood in light of the theology underlying his program of centralization of worship. In accordance with this theology, which delegitimizes all temples other than the Jerusalem Temple, the Deuteronomist did not wish to make reference to the sanctuary at Bethel and the Ark it housed, much less the priesthood that served there.

It seems that calf worship at Bethel emerged in the wake of the fall of the Tribe of Benjamin in the civil war between the tribes of Israel. This proposition is based on the fact that the Ark, which was housed at Bethel as a central place of worship during the period of the Judges, was moved to Shiloh (1 Sam 3:3). As recounted in Judg 20, the tribe of Benjamin was segregated from the other tribes of Israel, and hence the tribes considered it inappropriate to leave the Ark at Bethel, situated as it was on the border of Benjamin's territorial boundaries. For the priests of Bethel, the loss of the Ark symbolized the loss of God's presence, as well as the loss of their own authority and honor. Hence, these priests were forced to seek out an alternative to the Ark, which was considered the seat of God. The calf image suited this purpose. It is likely that at least before the establishment of the kingdom, the calf image was known as a symbol that, like the Ark, served as a pedestal of YHWH who liberated Israel from Egypt, in the light of the glosses of Num 23:22 (= 24:8) and Ps 22:22, in which God is perceived as being crowned upon the horns of a bull. A bronze calf image unearthed from the area of the tribe of Manasseh, dated to the Judges period (early Iron Age), bears witness to the antiquity of calf worship in Israel. The Bethel priests used the calf image to compensate for the absence of the Ark, in an attempt to preserve their religious authority. It is possible that the ritual formula, "This is your god, O Israel, who brought you up out of the land of Egypt," was a product of the Bethel priesthood during the period of the Judges. "God" here does not refer to the image of the calf itself but rather to an invisible deity imagined as seated upon the back of the calf. Jeroboam inherited the Bethel cult, which had been existent before his enthronement, and turned it into the official national cult of Israel. The cultic formula involving Jeroboam's calves, as it appears in 1 Kgs 12:28, seems to have already been in practice at Bethel prior to Jeroboam's reign. It follows from this that the cultic formula preserved in Exod 32:4b and 1 Kgs 12:28 was invented neither by the Elohist, with the aim of denouncing calf worship, nor by Jeroboam. It did not stem from the interdependence of the two texts, or from the preference of one over the other, as some scholars claim, but rather from the same cultic background.

(3) The first polemical narrative against calf worship was that of the Elohist in the eighth century B.C.E., as found in the E narrative preserved in Exod 32–34 (31:18; 32:1–25, 30–35; 33:6–11; 34:1, 4, 28). Here, the Elohist invented the expression "make for us gods" (עֲשֵׂה לָנוּ אֱלֹהִים) in order that "God" (אֱלֹהִים) in the cultic formula (32:4b), which has referred to YHWH until his time, would be identified with foreign gods. Furthermore, through the use of negative expressions aimed at the calf cult—such as, "Let my anger flare up against them and I shall annihilate them" (32:10); "He threw down the tablets from his hands and shattered them at the foot of the mountain" (32:19); and "He took the calf that they had made and burned it in the fire" (32:20)—the Elohist expressed this wholly negative attitude toward the calf image. Above all, the expression "god of gold" (32:31) makes it clear that in the view of the Elohist the calf image was totally extrinsic to YHWH. The Elohist, in his condemnation of the calf image as a foreign deity, uses terms such as צִיחֵק and פָּרוּעַ to describe the calf cult as the perverted version of the normative Yahwistic one, resulting from the influence of cults that worship other deities.

The basic factor that led the Elohist to condemn the calf image as symbolizing other deity is found in the identification of YHWH with Baal. As we know from the oracles of the prophet Hosea, a contemporary of the Elohist, from the northern kingdom, Israelite religion in the eighth century B.C.E. was profoundly influenced by Baalism. It is within this religious context that one must understand the backgrounds of the Elohist's and Hosea's condemnations of the calf image. The profound interfusion of Yahwism and Baalism made for a reality in which the calf was no longer perceived as YHWH's pedestal but rather as a deity in its own right. It is most likely against this background that Hosea made his declaration that the calf was "not God" (8:6).

The Yahwistic cult under the influence of Baalism was accompanied by cultic activities that were unacceptable within normative worship of YHWH, including illicit sexual activity resulting from intoxication

(Hos 4:10–14). The Elohist used the word צִיחֵק to describe such cultic behavior that deviated from the normative cult of YHWH. There is no clear evidence in the book of Hosea that the calf cult necessarily entailed sexual activity. However, one may agree that the calf cult, as described by the Elohist, was accompanied by sexual activity, given the inclusion of the word צִיחֵק (Exod 32:6b), which has a sexual connotation, and in light of the fact that Hosea, a contemporary of the Elohist, spoke out against a ritual involving sexual activity. Notwithstanding this fact, the reason that the Elohist did not use the term זָנָה, which more clearly denotes sexual behavior, but rather the word צִיחֵק, which has multiple meanings including ritual dancing (or sport), song (or a joyous cry), may be that he intended to encapsulate in one word the deviant cultic feature in its various manifestations.

(4) When examining the factors involved in the Deuteronomist's negative attitude toward the calf image, it is appropriate to take note of the two criteria on the basis of which he condemned it. The first is the prohibition of other gods, which is an issue of exclusive loyalty to YHWH, and the second is the prohibition of images, which is intended to prohibit all visible representation of YHWH. In the books of Kings, the calf image is denounced as the image of other gods (1 Kgs 14:9; 2 Kgs 17:16). Based on the double-redaction theory of Deuteronomistic History, and the absence of a law prohibiting images of YHWH prior to the Exile, it can be deduced that the author dealing with the sin of the golden calf in the books of Kings, in terms of the prohibition of other gods, is the first Deuteronomist (Dtr1), whose work is dated to the period of Josiah. He had the same critical viewpoint toward the calf image as that of the Elohist, who also denounced the calf image as a transgression of the prohibition against other gods. Dtr1 included in his work the cultic formula "This is your god, O Israel, who brought you up out of the land of Egypt" in order to belittle Jeroboam as an idolater. The rationale for including the ancient formula was that he could not efficiently achieve the objective of his polemic against calf worship without dealing with the cultic formula aimed at YHWH, on the basis of which the calf image was perceived as legitimate. The Elohist's reason for condemning the calf figure was in order to counter the influence of Baal worship, which was responsible for the calf figure no longer being considered the pedestal of YHWH but rather a representation or image of him, while the main factor behind Dtr1's denunciations was his point of view regarding "the sins of Jeroboam." The reason that Dtr1 does not attribute the fall of Israel to the sin of Baal worship but rather to the sin of the calf (see 2 Kgs

17:20–23 and 1 Kgs 14:14–16) stems from his polemic against Jeroboam, whose actions ran counter to the Deuteronomistic point of view. From an analysis of 1 Kgs 12:26–33; 13:1–10, and 2 Kgs 23:15–20 it emerges that the motivation behind Dtr1's polemic against the calf image is condemnation of the Bethel sanctuary, which contradicted his centralization theology. A second motivation was Dtr1's desire to blame Jeroboam for bringing about the division of the united kingdom of Israel.

In contrast to Dtr1, the second, exilic, Deuteronomist (Dtr2) judged the calf image according to the criteria of the law prohibiting images. He rewrote the Elohist's narrative of the golden calf from the point of view of a prohibition of images. For, despite the long-standing prevalence of aniconic practice in Israelite religion, an actual law prohibiting images, specifically intended to outlaw the making of images of YHWH, was a product of the exilic period. During the Exile, when Israel's ruin could have been interpreted, particularly in Babylon, as the result of YHWH's defeat by heathen gods, Dtr2, the author of Deut 4:1–40, crystallized the idea of monotheism in order to overcome such ideas, and placed emphasis on the prohibition of images in order to institutionalize the monotheistic concept of YHWH. He needed to present the historical lesson of the violation of this law so as to emphasize the significance of the prohibition of images, and thus he adapted and revised the Elohist's sin of the golden calf to suit the prohibition of images, as is evident in Deut 9:9–19, 21, 25–29, and 10:1–5, 10.

BIBLIOGRAPHY

Aberbach, M., and L. Smolar. "Aaron, Jeroboam, and the Golden Calves." *JBL* 86 (1967): 129–40.

Aḥituv, S. *Handbook of Ancient Hebrew Inscriptions from the Period of the First Commonwealth and the Beginning of the Second Commonwealth (Hebrew, Philistine, Edomite, Moabite, Ammonite and the Bileam Inscription)*. Jerusalem: Mosad Bialik, 1992.

Ahlström, G. W. "The Battle of Ramoth-Gilead in 841 B.C." Pages 157–66 in *"Wünschet Jerusalem Frieden": Collected Communications to the 12th Congress of the International Organization for the Study of the Old Testament, Jerusalem 1986*. Edited by M. Augustin and K. D. Schunk. New York: Lang, 1988.

———. "An Israelite God Figurine from Hazor." *Orientalia Suecana* 19–20 (1970–71): 54–62.

———. "An Israelite God Figurine, Once More." *VT* 25 (1975): 106–9.

———. "The Role of Archaeological and Literary Remains in Reconstructing Israel's History." Pages 116–41 in Edelman, ed., *The Fabric of History*.

Albertz, R. *A History of Israelite Religion in the Old Testament Period*, vol. 1. Translated by J. Bowden. London: SCM, 1994.

———. "In Search of the Deuteronomists: A First Solution to a Historical Riddle." Pages 1–17 in *The Future of the Deuteronomistic History*. Edited by T. Römer. Leuven: Leuven University Press, 2000.

Albright, W. F. "Anath and Dragon." *BASOR* 84 (1941): 14–17.

———. *Archaeology of Palestine and the Bible*. New York: Revell, 1932.

———. *Archaeology and the Religion of Israel*. Baltimore: Johns Hopkins University Press, 1946.

———. *From the Stone Age to Christianity: Monotheism and the Historical Process*. Baltimore: Johns Hopkins University Press, 1957.

———. "The Oracles of Balaam." *JBL* 63 (1944): 207–33.

———. *Yahweh and the Gods of Canaan*. London: Athlone, 1968.

Allen, L. C. *Greek Chronicles*. Part II, *Textual Criticism*. VTSup 27. Leiden: Brill, 1974.

Andersen, F. I. "A Lexicographical Note on Exodus xxxii 18." *VT* 16 (1966): 108–12.

Andersen, F. I., and D. N. Freedman. *Hosea*. AB 24. Garden City, N.Y.: Doubleday, 1980.

Armayor, O. K. "Did Herodotus Ever Go to Egypt?" *JARCE* 15 (1978): 59–73.

Astour, M. C. "Tamar the Hierodule." *JBL* 85 (1966): 185–96.

Aurelius, E. *Der Fürbitte Israels: Eine Studie zum Mosebild im Alten Testament*. Stockholm: Almqvist & Wiksell, 1988.

Ausloos, H. "The Risks of Rash Textual Criticism Illustrated on the Basis of the '*Numeruswechel*' in Exod 23, 20–33." *BN* 97 (1999): 5–12.

Axelsson, L. E. *The Lord Rose up from Seir: Studies in the History and Traditions of the Negev and Southern Judah*. Translated by F. H. Cryer. Lund: Almqvist & Wiksell, 1987.

Bailey, L. "The Golden Calf." *HUCA* 42 (1971): 97–115.

Barrick, W. B. "Burning Bones at Bethel: A Closer Look at 2 Kgs 23:16a." *SJOT* 14 (2000): 3–16.

———. "What Do We Really Know about 'High-places'?" *SEÅ* 45 (1980): 50–57.

Baumgartner, W. "Herodots babylonische und assyrische Nachrichten." Pages 282–331 in *Zum Alten Testament und seiner Umwelt*. Leiden: Brill, 1959.

Baumgartner, W., et al., eds. *Festschrift Alfred Bertholet*. Tübingen: Mohr, 1950.

Beck, A. B., et al. *Fortunate the Eyes That See: Essays in Honor of David Noel Freedman in Celebration of His Seventieth Birthday*. Grand Rapids: Eerdmans, 1995.

Beer, G. *Exodus*. Tübingen: Mohr Siebeck, 1939.

Begg, C. T. "The Destruction of the Calf (Exod 32,20/Deut 9,21)." Pages 208–51 in Lohfink, ed., *Das Deuteronomium*.

———. "The Literary Criticism of Deut 4,1–40." *ETL* 56 (1980): 10–55.

———. "The Significance of the *Numeruswechsel* in Deuteronomy—The Pre-history of the Question." *ETL* 55 (1979): 116–24.

Bentzen, A. *Introduction to the Old Testament*, vol. 2. Copenhagen: Gad, 1952.

Berger, P. L. *The Social Reality of Religion*. Harmondsworth: Penguin, 1987.

Bertholet, A. *Wörterbuch der Religionen*. Stuttgart: Cröner, 1952.

Beyerlin, W. *Origins and History of the Oldest Sinaitic Traditions*. Oxford: Blackwell, 1965.

Biran, A. "Tel Dan: Biblical Texts and Archaeological Data." Pages 1–17 in Coogan et al., eds., *Scripture and Other Artifacts*.

Bird, P. A. "The End of the Male Cult Prostitute: A Literary-historical and Sociological Analysis of Hebrew *QĀDĒŠ-QĔDĒŠÎM*." Pages 37–80 in *Congress Volume, Cambridge 1995*. VTSup 66. Leiden: Brill, 1997.

———. "The Harlot as Heroine in Biblical Texts: Narrative Art and Social Presupposition." *Semeia* 46 (1989): 119–39.

———. "The Place of Women in the Israelite Cultus." Pages 397–419 in *Ancient Israelite Religion*. Edited by P. D. Hanson et al. Philadelphia: Fortress, 1987.

———. "'To Play the Harlot': An Inquiry Into An Old Testament Metaphor." Pages 75–94 in Day, ed., *Gender and Difference*.

Bole, M. *The Book of Jeremiah*. Jerusalem: Mosad Harav Kook. 1984 (Hebrew).

Bracke, J. M. *Jeremiah 1–29*. Louisville, Ky.: Westminster John Knox, 2000.

Braulik, G. *Die Mittel deuteronomischerRhetorik: Erhoben aus Deuteronomium 4, 1–40*. Rome: Biblical Institute, 1978.

———. *The Theology of Deuteronomy*. Translated by U. Lindblad. N. Richland Hills, Tex.: BIBAL, 1994.

Brenner, A. *A Feminist Companion to the Latter Prophets*. Sheffield: Sheffield Academic, 1995.

Bright, J. "The Date of the Prose Sermons of Jeremiah." *JBL* 70 (1951): 15–35.

———. *A History of Israel*. Philadelphia: Westminster, 1981.

————. *The Kingdom of God: The Biblical Concept and Its Meaning for the Church.* Nashville: Abingdon, 1953.

Broshi, M. "The Expansion of Jerusalem in the Reigns of Hezekiah and Manasseh." *IEJ* 24 (1974): 21–26.

Buber, M. *Moses.* New York: Harper, 1958.

Cairns, I. *Deuteronomy: Word and Presence.* Edinburgh: Handsel, 1992.

Cancik, H. "Ikonoklasmus." Pages 217–21 in *Handbuch religionswissenschaftlicher Grundbegriffe*, vol. 3. Stuttgart: Kohlhammer, 1993.

Carpenter, J. E., and G. Barford-Battersby. *The Hexateuch.* London: Longmans, Green & Co., 1900.

Cassuto, U. *A Commentary on the Book of Exodus.* Translated by I. Abrahams. Jerusalem: Magnes, 1967.

Catron, J. E. "Temple and *bāmāh*: Some Considerations." Pages 150–65 in Holloway and Handy, eds., *The Pitcher is Broken.*

Cazelles, H. "The Problem of the Kings in Osee, 8:4." *CBQ* 11 (1949): 14–25.

Childs, B. S. *The Book of Exodus.* OTL. Louisville, Ky.: Westminster John Knox, 1976.

————. "The Etiological Tale Re-Examined." *VT* 24: 387–97.

Christensen, L. "The *Numeruswechsel* in Deuteronomy 12." Pages 61–68 in *A Song of Power and the Power of Song: Essays on the Book of Deuteronomy.* Edited by D. L. Christensen. Winona Lake: Eisenbrauns, 1993.

Clements, R. E. *Deuteronomy.* Sheffield: JSOT, 1989.

————. *Exodus.* CBC. Cambridge: Cambridge University Press, 1972.

————. "Understanding the Book of Hosea." *RevExp* 72 (1975): 417–19.

Clifford, R. J. "The Function of Idol Passages in Second Isaiah." *CBQ* 42 (1980): 450–64.

Clines, D. J. "Hosea 2; Structure and Interpretation." *StudBib* 1 (1978): 83–103.

Coats, G. W. *Rebellion in the Wilderness: The Murmuring Motif in the Wilderness Tradition of the Old Testament.* Nashville: Abingdon, 1968.

————. *The Moses Tradition.* Sheffield: JSOT, 1993.

Coogan, M. D. *Scripture and Other Artifacts.* Edited by M. D. Coogan et al. Louisville, Ky.: Westminster John Knox, 1994.

Craigie, P. C. *The Book of Deuteronomy.* London: Hodder & Stoughton, 1976.

Cross, F. M. *Canaanite Myth and Hebrew Epic: Essays in the History of the Religion of Israel.* Cambridge, Mass.: Harvard University Press, 1973.

Culican, W. "Melqart Representations on Phoenician Seals." *AbrN* 2 (1960–61): 41–54.

Dahood, M. "Hebrew–Ugaritic Lexicography X." *Bib* 53 (1972): 386–403.

Danelius, E. "The Sins of Jeroboam ben-Nabat." *JQR* 58 (1967): 95–114.

Davenport, J. W. "A Study of the Golden Calf Tradition in Exodus 32." Ph.D. diss., Princeton Theological Seminary, 1973.

Davies, G. I. *Hosea.* NCBC. London: Marshall Pickering, 1992.

Davies, G. I., et al. *Ancient Hebrew Inscriptions: Corpus and Concordance.* Cambridge: Cambridge University Press, 1991.

Dawe, D. G. "Deuteronomy 4:32–40." *Int* 47 (1993): 159–62.

Day, J. "Asherah in the Hebrew Bible and Northwest Semitic Literature." *JBL* 105 (1986): 385–408.

———. "A Case of Inner Scriptural Interpretation: The Dependence of Isaiah xxvi. 13-xxvii. 11 on Hosea xiii. 4–xiv. 10 (Eng. 9) and Its Relevance to Some Theories of the Redaction of the 'Isaiah Apocalypse.'" *JTS* 31, no. 2 (1980): 309–19.

———. "Yahweh and the Gods and Goddesses of Canaan." Pages 181–96 in Dietrich and Klopfenstein, eds., *Ein Gott allein?*

Day, P., ed. *Gender and Difference in Ancient Israel*. Minneapolis: Fortress, 1989.

Deen, A. "The Goddess Anath and some Biblical Hebrew Cruces." *JTS* 23 (1978): 25–30.

Dever, W. G. "Material Remains and the Cult in Ancient Israel: An Essay in Archeological Systematics." Pages 571–87 in *The Word of the Lord Shall Go Forth*. Edited by C. L. Meyers and M. C. O'Connor. Winona Lake: Eisenbrauns, 1983.

———. "Recent Archaeological Confirmation of the Cult of Asherah in Ancient Israel." *HS* 23 (1982): 37–44.

———. *Recent Archaeological Discoveries and Biblical Research*. Seattle: University of Washington Press, 1990.

———. "The Silence of the Text: An Archaeological Commentary on 2 Kings 23." Pages 143–68 in Coogan et al., eds., *Scripture and Other Artifacts*.

De Vries, L. F. "Cult Stands—A Bewildering Variety of Shapes and Sizes." *BAR* 13, no. 4 (1987): 32–42.

Diebner, B. J., and C. Nauerth. "Die Inventio des ספר התורה in 2 Kön 22: Struktur, Intention und Funktion von Auffindungslegenden." *DBAT* 18 (1984): 95–118.

Dietrich, M., and M. A. Klopfenstein, eds. *Ein Gott allein?* Göttingen: Vandenhoeck & Ruprecht, 1994.

Dietrich, M., and O. Loretz. *Jahwe und seine Aschra. Anthropomorphes Kultbild in Mesopotamia,Ugarit and Israel. Das biblische Bilderverbot*. Münster: Ugarit-Verlag, 1992.

Donner, H. "Hier sind deine Götter, Israel!" Pages 45–50 in *Wort und Geschichte: Festschrift K. Elliger*. AOAT 18. Neukirchen–Vluyn: Neukirchener, 1973.

———. "The Separate States of Israel and Judah." Pages 407–13 in *Israelite and Judaean History*. Edited by J. H. Mays and M. M. Miller. Philadelphia: Westminster, 1977.

Driver, S. R. *The Book of Exodus*. Cambridge: Cambridge University Press, 1953.

———. *Canaanite Myths and Legends*. Edinburgh: T. & T. Clark, 1977.

———. *Notes on the Hebrew Text and the Topography of the Books of Samuel*. Oxford: Clarendon, 1960.

Durham, J. *Exodus*. WBC 3. Waco, Tex.: Word.

Eakin, F. E. "Yahwism and Baalism before the Exile." *JBL* 84 (1965): 407–14.

Edelman, D. V. "Doing History in Biblical Studies." Pages 13–25 in Edelman, ed., *The Fabric of History*.

———, ed. *The Fabric of History: Text, Artifact and Israel's Past*. JSOTSup 127. Sheffield: JSOT, 1991.

———. "The Meaning of QIṬṬĒR." *VT* 35 (1985): 395–404.

———, ed. *The Triumph of Elohim: From Yahwisms to Judaisms*. Grand Rapids: Eerdmans, 1996.

Edelmann, R. "To *'annôt* Exodus xxxii 18." *VT* 16 (1966): 355.

Edwards, I. E. S. "A Relief of Qudshu-Astarte-Anath in the Winchester College Collection." *JNES* 14 (1955): 49–51.

Ehrlich, E. L. *Geschichte Israels von den Anfängen bis zur Zerstörung des Tempels (70 n. Chr)*. Berlin: de Gruyter, 1958.

Eissfeldt, O. "El and Yahweh." *JSS* 1 (1956): 25–37.

———. *The Hebrew Kingdom*. Cambridge: Cambridge University Press, 1965.

———. *Hexateuch-Synopse*. Leipzig: J. C. Hinrichs, 1929.

———."Lade und Stierbild." *ZAW* 58 (1940–41): 190–215.

Emerton, J. "New Light on Israelite Religion: The Implications of the Inscriptions from Kuntillet ʿAjrud." *ZAW* 94 (1982): 2–20.

Emmerson, G. I. *Hosea: An Israelite Prophet in Judean Perspective*. Sheffield: JSOT, 1984.

Ewald, H. *Geschichte des Volkes Israel*. Bd. 2, *Geschichte Moses und der Gotterrschaft in Israel*. Göttingen: Dieterichschen Buchhandlung, 1865.

Faur, J. "Biblical Idea of Idolatry." *JQR* 69 (1978–79): 1–15.

Fensham, F. C. "A Few Observations on the Polarisation between Yahweh and Baal in 1 Kings 17–19." *ZAW* 92 (1980): 227–36.

Fisher, L. R. *Ras Shamra Parallels: The Texts from Ugarit and the Hebrew Bible*, vol. 2. Rome: Pontifical Biblical Institute, 1972.

Fitzmyer, J. A. *The Aramaic Inscriptions of Sefire*. Rome: Pontifical Biblical Institute, 1967.

Fohrer, G. *History of Israelite Religion*. Translated by D. E. Green. London: SPCK, 1973.

———. *Introduction to the Old Testament*. London: SPCK, 1976.

Fontaine, C. R. "Hosea." Pages 40–69 in Brenner, ed., *A Feminist Companion to the Latter Prophets*.

Fowler, J. D. *Theophoric Personal Names in Ancient Hebrew*. JSOTSup 49. Sheffield: JSOT, 1988.

Frankel, D. "The Destruction of the Golden Calf: A New Solution." *VT* 44 (1994): 330–39.

Frazer, J. *The Golden Bough: A Study in Magic and Region*. New York: Macmillan, 1935.

Freedman, D. N. "Albright as a Historian." Pages 33–43 in *The Scholarship of William Foxwell Albright*. Edited by G. W. Van Beek. Atlanta: Scholars Press, 1989.

———. "Divine Names and Titles in Early Hebrew Poetry." Pages 55–107 in *Magnalia Dei. Festschrift G. E. Wright*. Edited by F. M. Cross et al. Garden City, N.Y.: Doubleday, 1976.

———. "Yahweh of Samaria and His Asherah." *BA* 50 (1987): 241–49.

Friedman, R. E. "The Deuteronomic School." Pages 70–80 in Beck et al., eds., *Fortunate the Eyes That See*.

———. "From Egypt to Egypt: Dtr¹ and Dtr²." Pages 167–92 in *Traditions in Transformation*. Edited by B. Halpern and J. D. Levenson. Winona Lake: Eisenbrauns, 1981.

Frymer-Kensky, T. *In the Wake of the Goddesses: Women, Culture, and the Biblical Transformation of Pagan Myth*. New York: Maxwell Macmillan, 1992.

Gagnon, J. H. "Prostitution." Pages 592–98 in *The International Encyclopedia of the Social Sciences*. Edited by D. L. Sills. New York: Macmillan, 1969.

Gese, H. *Die Religionen Altsyriens. Die Religionen Altsyriens, Altarabiens und der Mandäer.* Die Religionen der Menschheit 10/2. Stuttgart: Kohlhammer, 1970.

Geus, C. de. *The Tribes of Israel.* Assen: Van Gorcum, 1976.

Ginsberg, H. L."Hosea, book of." *EncJud* 8: 1010–24.

———. "Lexicographical Notes." Pages 71–82 in *Hebräische Wortforschung.* VTSup 16. Leiden: Brill, 1967.

Gladigow, B. *Handbuch religionswissenschaflicher Grundbegriffe,* vol. 1. Stuttgart: Kohlhammer, 1988.

Glock, A. E. "Taanach." *EAEHL* 4:1138–47.

Gnuse, R. K. *No Other Gods: Emergent Monotheism in Israel.* JSOTSup 241. Sheffield: Sheffield Academic, 1997.

Good, R. M. "Exodus 32:18." Pages 137–42 in *Love and Death in the Ancient Near East: Festschrift M. H. Pope.* Edited by J. H. Marks and R. M. Good. Guilford, Conn.: Four Quarters, 1987.

Gordon, C. H. "His Name is 'One'." *JNES* 29 (1970): 198–99.

———. *Ugaritic Textbook.* Rome: Pontifical Biblical Institute, 1965.

Goulder, M. D. "Asaph's History of Israel (Elohist press, Bethel, 725 BCE)." *JSOT* 65 (1995): 71–81.

———. *The Psalms of the Sons of the Korah.* JSOTSup 20. Sheffield: JSOT, 1982.

Graetz, H. *Geschichte der Israeliten.* Bd. 1, *von ihren Uranfängen (um 1500) bis zum Tode des Königs Salomo (um 977).* Leipzig: Leiner, 1874.

Gray, G. B. *Studies in Hebrew Proper Names.* London: Black, 1896.

Gray, J. *I and II Kings.* Philadelphia: Westminster, 1970.

Green, A., ed. *Jewish Spirituality: From the Bible through the Middle Ages.* New York: Crossroad, 1986.

Greenberg, M. "Moses' Intercessory Prayer." *Tantur Yearbook 1977–78* (1978): 21–36.

———. "On the Refinement of the Conception of Prayer in the Hebrew Scriptures." *AJSR* 1 (1976): 57–92.

Gressmann, H. *Die Anfange Israels.* Göttingen: Vandenhoeck & Ruprecht, 1929.

Gruber, M. "Hebrew *qedešah* and Her Canaanite and Akkadian Cognates." *UF* 18 (1983): 133–48.

———. "Marital Fidelity and Intimacy: A View from Hosea." Pages 169–79 in Brenner, ed., *A Feminist Companion to the Latter Prophets.*

Gubel, E. "The Iconography of the Ibiza MAI 3650 Reconsidered." *AuOr* 4 (1986): 111–18.

Hacham, N. "ʿanna." *Tarbiz* 69 (2000): 144–45 (Hebrew).

Hadad, E. "The Sin of the Calf." *Maggadim* 21 (1994): 29–36 (Hebrew).

Hadley, J. M. "Some Drawings and Inscriptions on Two Pithoi from Kuntillet ʿAjrud." *VT* 37 (1987): 180–213.

———. "Yahweh and 'His Asherah': Archaeological and Textual Evidence for the Cult of the Goddess." Pages 235–68 in Dietrich and Klopfenstein, eds., *Ein Gott allein?*

Hallo, W. W. "Cult Statue and Divine Image: A Preliminary Study." Pages 1–16 in *Scripture in Context II: More Essays on the Comparative Method.* Edited by L. G. Perdue. Winona Lake: Eisenbrauns, 1983.

Halpern, B. "'Brisker Pipes than Poetry': The Development of Israelite Monotheism." Pages 77–115 in *Judaic Perspectives on Ancient Israel*. Edited by J. A. Neusner et al. Philadelphia: Fortress, 1987.

———. "The Centralization Formula in Deuteronomy." *VT* 31 (1981): 20–38.

———. *The First Historians: The Hebrew Bible and History*. San Francisco: Harper & Row, 1988.

———. "Levitic Participation in the Reform Cult of Jeroboam I." *JBL* 95 (1976): 31–42.

Hamilton, V. P. *The Book of Genesis: Chapters 18–50*. Grand Rapids: Eerdmans, 1995.

Handy, L. K. "Hezekiah's Unlikely Reform." *ZAW* 100 (1988): 111–15.

Hanson, P. D. *The People Called: The Growth of Community in the Bible*. San Francisco: Harper & Row, 1986.

Haran, M. "The Ark and the Cherubim: Their Symbolic Significance in Biblical Ritual." *IEJ* 9 (1959): 30–38.

———. "The Divine Presence in the Israelite Cult and the Cultic Institution." *Bib* 50 (1969): 251–67.

———. "Removal of the Ark of Covenant." *Yediot Hahevra Lehaqirat Eretz Israel Ve 'Atiqoteha* 25 (1961): 211–23 (Hebrew).

———. *Temple and Temple-Service in Ancient Israel*. Oxford: Clarendon, 1978.

———. "Temples and Cultic Open Areas as Reflected in the Bible." Pages 31–37 in *Temples and High Places*. Edited by A. Biran. Jerusalem: Hebrew Union College Press, 1981.

Hauer, C. "Who was Zadok?" *JBL* 82 (1963): 89–94.

Hehn, J. *Die biblische und die babylonische Gottesidee*. Leipzig: Hinrichs, 1913.

Hendel, R. "Nehushtan." *DDD* 1159.

———. "The Social Origins of the Aniconic Tradition in Early Israel." *CBQ* 50 (1988): 365–82.

Herrmann, S. *A History of Israel in Old Testament Times*. Philadelphia: Fortress, 1975.

Hestrin, R. "The Cult Stand from Taʿanach and Its Religious Background." Pages 61–77 in *Phoenicia and the East Mediterranean in the First Millennium B.C.* Edited by E. Lipiński. Leuven: Peeters, 1987.

———. "The Lachish Ewer and the ʾAsherah." *IEJ* 37 (1987): 212–23.

Hoffmann, H. D. *Reform und Reformen*. Zurich: Theologischer Verlag, 1980.

Hoffner, H. A, ed. *Orient and Occident: Essays Presented to C. H. Gordon*. AOAT 22. Neukirchen–Vluyn: Neukirchener Verlag, 1973.

Holladay, J. S. "Religion in Israel and Judah Under the Monarchy: An Explicitly Archaeological Approach." Pages 249–99 in Miller, Hanson, and McBride, eds., *Ancient Israelite Religion*.

Holladay, W. L. "On Every High Hill and Under Every Green Tree." *VT* 11 (1961): 170–76.

Holland, T. A. "A Study of Palestinian Iron Age Baked Clay Figurines, with Special Reference to Jerusalem: Cave 1." *Levant* 9 (1977): 122–55.

Holloway, S. W., and L. K. Handy, eds. *The Pitcher is Broken: Memorial Essays for Gösta W. Ahlström*. JSOTSup 190. Sheffield: Sheffield Academic, 1995.

Holter, K. *Deuteronomy 4 and the Second Commandment*. New York: Lang, 2003.

———. "Literary Critical Studies of Deut 4: Some Criteriological Remarks." *BN* 81 (1996): 91–103.

Holzinger, H. *Exodus*. Tübingen: Mohr Siebeck, 1900.

Hoppe, L. J. "Jerusalem in the Deuteronomistic History." Pages 107–10 in Lohfink, ed., *Das Deuteronomium.*

Houtman, C. *Exodus*, vol. 3. Leuven: Peeters, 2000.

Hubbard, D. A. *Hosea.* Leicester: Inter-Varsity, 1989.

Hyatt, J. P. *Exodus.* NCBC. Grand Rapids: Eerdmans, 1983.

Jacob, E. *Osée, Joël, Amos.* Neuchâtel: Delachaux & Niestlé, 1965.

———. *Theology of the Old Testament.* Translated by A. Heathcote and P. Allcock. New York: Harper, 1958.

Jenks, A. W. *The Elohistic and North Israelite Traditions.* Missoula, Mont.: Scholars Press, 1976.

Joines, K. R. "Feasts and Festivals." *MDB* 297–98.

Jones, G. H. *1 and 2 Kings.* NCBC 1. Grand Rapids: Eerdmans, 1984.

Joüon, P., and T. Muraoka. *A Grammar of Biblical Hebrew.* Rome: Pontifical Biblical Institute, 1991.

Kallai, Z. "Beth-el-Luz and Beth-aven." Pages 171–88 in *Prophetie und geschicht-liche Wirklichkeit im alten Israel. Festschrift für S. Hermann.* Edited by R. Liwak and S. Wagner. Stuttgart: Kohlhammer, 1991.

Katz, P. "*Katapaúsai* as a Corruption of *katalýsai* in the Septuagint." *JBL* 65 (1946): 319–24.

Kaufman, I. T. "The Samaria Ostraca: An Early Witness to Hebrew Writing." *BA* (1982): 229–39.

Kaufmann, Y. *The Religion of Israel.* Translated by M. Greenberg. Chicago: University of Chicago Press, 1960.

Keel, O. "Das Vergraben der 'fremden Götter' in Genesis XXXV 4b." *VT* 23 (1973): 305–36.

———. *Die Welt der altorientalischen Bildsymbolik und das Alte Testament: Am Beispiel der Psalmem.* Zurich: Benziger, 1977.

———. *Goddesses and Trees, New Moon and Yahweh: Ancient Near Eastern Art and the Hebrew Bible.* JSOTSup 261. Sheffield: Sheffield Academic, 1998.

Keel, O., and C. Uehlinger. *Gods, Goddesses, and Images of God in Ancient Israel.* Minneapolis: Fortress, 1998.

Kennett, R. H. "The Origin of the Aaronite Priesthood." *JTS* 6 (1905): 161–85.

Key, A. F. "Traces of the Worship of the Moon God Sîn among the Early Israelites." *JBL* 84 (1965): 20–26.

Klein, H. "Der Beweis der Einzigkeit Jahwes bei Deutero-Jesaja." *VT* 35 (1985): 267–73.

Kletter, R. *The Judean Pillar-Figurines and the Archaeology of Asherah.* Oxford: Tempus Reparatum, 1996.

Knapp, D. *Deuteronomium 4: Literarische Analyse und theologische Interpretation.* Göttingen: Vandenhoeck & Ruprecht, 1987.

Knauf, E. A. "From History to Interpretation." Pages 26–64 in Edelman, ed., *The Fabric of History.*

Knoppers, G. N. *Two Nations Under God: The Deuteronomistic History of Solomon and the Dual Monarchies 2.* Atlanta: Scholars Press, 1994.

Koch, K. *The Prophets*, vol 1. Philadelphia: Fortress, 1982.

Kraus, H.-J. *Worship in Israel.* Translated by G. Buswell. Oxford: Blackwell, 1966.

Kuenen, A. *National Religions and Universal Religions.* London: Williams & Norgate, 1882.

————. "Yahweh and the 'Other Gods.'" *TRev* 13 (1876): 329–66.

Kugel, J. "Topics in the History of the Spirituality of the Psalms." Pages 113–44 in Green, ed., *Jewish Spirituality*.

Lambert, W. G. *Babylonian Wisdom Literature*. Oxford: Clarendon, 1960.

Lang, B. *Monotheism and the Prophetic Minority*. Social World of Biblical Antiquity 1. Sheffield: Sheffield Academic, 1983.

Lapp, P. W. "The 1968 Excavations at Tell Taᶜannek." *BASOR* 195 (1969): 42–49.

Lehming, S. "Versuch zu Ex. xxxii." *VT* 19 (1960): 16–50.

Lemaire, A. *Inscriptions hébraïques*. Paris: Cerf, 1977.

————. "Who or What Was Yahweh's Asherah?" *BAR* 10, no. 6 (1984): 42–51.

Lemche, N. P. "The Development of the Israelite Religion in the Light of Recent Studies on the Early History of Israel." Pages 97–111 in *Congress Volume, Leuven 1989*. Edited by J. A. Emerton. VTSup 43. Leiden: Brill, 1991.

Le Roux, J. H. "A Holy Nation was Elected." *OTWSA* 25–26 (1982–83): 59–78.

Levenson, J. "Who Inserted the Book of the Torah?" *HTR* 68 (1975): 203–33.

Levy, T. E., et al. "Archaeology and the Shasu Nomads: Recent Excavations in the Jabal Hamrat Fidan, Jordan." Pages 63–89 in *"Le-David Maskil": A Birthday Tribute for Noel Friedman*. Edited by R. E. Friedman and W. H. C. Propp. Winona Lake: Eisenbrauns, 2004.

Lewis, T. J. "Divine Images and Aniconism in Ancient Israel." *JAOS* 118 (1998): 36–53.

————. "The Identity and Function of El/Baal Berith." *JBL* 115 (1996): 418–22.

Lewy, J. "The Late Assyro-Babylonian Cult of the Moon and Its Culmination at the Time of Nabonidus." *HUCA* 19 (1945): 405–89.

Lind, M. "Monotheism, Power, and Justice: A Study in Isaiah 40–55." *CBQ* 46 (1984): 432–46.

Lipiński, E. "The Goddess Atirat in Ancient Arabia, in Babylon, and in Ugarit." *OLP* 3 (1972): 101–19.

Lipschits, O. "The History of the Benjamin Region under Babylonian Rule." *Tel Aviv* 26, no. 2 (1999): 155–90.

Lohfink, N. "Auslegung deuteronomischer Texte IV. Verkündigung des Hauptgebots in der jüngsten Schicht des Deuteronomiums (Dt 4,1–40)." Pages 87–120 in *Höre Israel! Auslegung von Texten aus dem Buch Deuteronomium*. Düsseldorf: Patmos, 1965.

————. "Culture Shock and Theology: A Discussion of Theology as a Cultural and Sociological Phenomenon Based on the Example of Deuteronomic Law." *BTB* 7 (1977): 12–22.

————, ed. *Das Deuteronomium. Entstehung, Gestalt und Botschaft*. Leuven: Leuven University Press, 1985.

————. *Das Hauptgebot: Eine Untersuchung literarischen Einleitungsfragen zu Deut 5–11*. Rome: Pontifical Biblical Institute, 1963.

————. "Was There A Deuteronomistic Movement?" Pages 36–66 in *Those Elusive Deuteronomists*. Edited by L. S. Schearing and S. L. McKenzie. JSOTSup 268. Sheffield: Sheffield Academic, 1999.

————. "Zum '*Numeruswechsel*' in Deut 3,21f." *BN* 49 (1989): 39–52.

Long, B. O. *Planting and Reaping Albright: Politics, Ideology, and Interpreting the Bible*. University Park: Pennsylvania State University Press, 1997.

Loretz, O. "Das 'Ahnen- und Götterstatuen- Verbot' im Dekalog und die Einzigkeit Jahwes: Zum Begriff des Göttlichen in altorientalischen und alttestamentalichen Quellen." Pages 491–527 in Dietrich and Klopfenstein, eds., *Ein Gott allein?*

Losa, J. "Exode xxxii et la Redaction JE." *VT* 23 (1973): 31–55.

Loewenstamm, S. E. *The Evolution of the Exodus Tradition.* Translated by B. J. Schwartz. Jerusalem: Magnes, 1992.

———. "The Making and Destruction of the Golden Calf." *Bib* 48 (1967): 481–90.

MacDonald, N. *Deuteronomy and the Meaning of Monotheism.* Tübingen: Mohr Siebeck, 2003.

Macintosh, A. A. *Hosea.* ICC. Edinburgh: T. & T. Clark, 1997.

Maier, W. A. *ʾAšerah: Extrabiblical Evidence.* Atlanta: Scholars Press, 1986.

Margalit, B. "KTU 1.92 (Obv): A Ugaritic Theophagy." *AuOr* 7 (1989): 67–80.

Mastin, B. A. "Yahweh's Asherah, Inclusive Monotheism and the Question of Dating." Pages 326–51 in *In Search of Pre-Exilic Israel: Proceedings of the Oxford Old Testament Seminar.* Edited by J. Day. JSOTSup 406. London: T&T Clark International.

Mayes, A. D. H. *Deuteronomy.* NCBC. London: Marshall, Morgan & Scott, 1991.

———. "Deuteronomy 4 and the Literary Criticism of Deuteronomy." *JBL* 100 (1981): 23–51.

———. *The Story of Israel between Settlement and Exile.* London: SCM, 1983.

Mays, J. L. *Hosea: A Commentary.* London: SCM, 1969.

Mazar, A. "The 'Bull Site'—An Iron Age I Open Cult Place." *BASOR* 247 (1982): 27–42.

———. "Iron Age I." Pages 258–99 in *The Archaeology of Ancient Israel.* Edited by A. Ben-Tor. New Haven: Yale University Press, 1992.

McCarthy, D. J. *Treaty and Covenant.* Rome: Pontifical Biblical Institute, 1978.

McKenzie, S. L. *The Trouble with Kings: The Composition of the Book of Kings in the Deuteronomistic History.* VTSup 42. Leiden: Brill, 1991.

Meek, T. J. "Aaronites and Zadokites." *AJSL* 45 (1929): 149–66.

———. *Hebrew Origins.* New York: Harper, 1960.

Mekhitarian, A. *Egyptian Painting.* Geneva: Skira, 1954.

Mendenhall, G. "Covenant Forms in Israelite Tradition." *BA* 17 (1954): 50–76.

Meshel, Z. "Did Yahweh Have a Consort?" *BAR* 5, no. 2 (1979): 24–35.

———. *A Religious Centre from the Time of the Judaean Monarchy on the Border of Sinai.* Israel Museum Catalogue 175. Jerusalem: Israel Museum, 1978.

———. "Two Aspects in the Excavation of Kuntillet ʿAjrud." Pages 99–104 in Dietrich and Klopfenstein, eds., *Ein Gott allein?*

Mettinger, T. N. D. "The Elusive Essence: YHWH, El and Baal and the Distinctiveness of Israelite Faith." Pages 393–417 in *Die hebräische Bibel und ihre zweifache Nachgeschichte.* Edited by E. Blum et al. Neukirchen–Vluyn: Neukirchener Verlag, 1990.

———. *No Graven Image? Israelite Aniconism in Its Ancient Near Eastern Context.* Stockholm: Almqvist & Wiksell, 1995.

———. *In Search of God: The Meaning and Message of the Everlasting Names.* Philadelphia: Fortress, 1988.

———. "The Veto on Images and the Aniconic God in Ancient Israel." Pages 15–29 in *Religious Symbols and Their Functions.* Edited by H. Biezais. Stockholm: Almqvist & Wiksell, 1979.

Milbank, J. "The History of One God." *HeyJ* 38 (1997): 371–400.

Milgrom, J. "Does H Advocate the Centralization of Worship?" *JSOT* 88 (2000): 59–76.

Millar, J. G. "Living at the Place of Decision." Pages 15–88 in *Time and Place in Deuteronomy.* Edited by J. G. McConville and J. G. Millar. JSOTSup 179. Sheffield: Sheffield Academic, 1994.

Miller, J. M. *The Old Testament and the Historian.* Philadelphia: Fortress, 1976.

———. "Is it Possible to Write a History of Israel without Relying on the Hebrew Bible?" Pages 93–102 in Edelman, ed., *The Fabric of History.*

Miller, P. D. "Animal Names as Designations in Ugaritic and Hebrew." *UF* 2 (1970): 177–86.

———. "El, The Creator of Earth." *BASOR* 239 (1980): 43–46.

———. *The Religion of Ancient Israel.* London: SPCK, 2000.

Miller, P. D., P. D. Hanson, and S. D. McBride, eds. *Ancient Israelite Religion.* Philadelphia: Fortress, 1987.

Moberly, R. W. L. *At the Mountain of God.* JSOTSup 22. Sheffield: JSOT, 1983.

———. "'Yahweh is One': The Translation of the Shema." Pages 209–15 in *Studies in the Pentateuch.* VTSup 41. Edited by J. A. Emerton. Leiden: Brill, 1990.

Moor, J. C. de. *The Rise of Yahwism: The Roots of Israelite Monotheism.* Leuven: Peeters, 1997.

Morag, S. "Question of the Uniqueness of Hosea's Language: Semantic and Lexical Traits." *Tarbiz* 53 (1984): 489–510 (Hebrew).

Morenz, S. *Egyptian Religion.* Translated by A. E. Keep. Ithaca, N.Y.: Cornell University Press, 1973.

Morgenstern, J. "The Festival of Jeroboam I." *JBL* 83 (1964): 109–18.

Motzki, H. "Ein Beitrag zum Problem des Stierkultes in der Religionsgeschichte Israels." *VT* 25 (1975): 470–85.

Mowinckel, S. *The Psalms in Israel's Worship.* 2 vols. New York: Abingdon, 1962.

Mullen, E. T. "The Sins of Jeroboam: A Redactional Assessment." *CBQ* 49 (1987): 212–32.

Murray, M. *The Splendour that was Egypt.* London: Sidgwick & Jackson, 1964.

Na'aman, N. "The Debated Historicity of Hezekiah's Reform in the Light of Historical and Archaeological Research." *ZAW* 107 (1995): 179–95.

———. "No Anthropomorphic Graven Image: Notes on the Assumed Anthropomorphic Cult Statues in the Temples of YHWH in the Pre-Exilic Period." *UF* 31 (1999): 391–415.

Nagy, G. *The Best of the Achaeans: Concepts of the Hero in Archaic Greek Poetry.* Baltimore: Johns Hopkins University Press, 1979.

Negbi, O. *Canaanite Gods in Metal.* Tel Aviv: Tel Aviv University, 1976.

Nelson, R. *The Double Redaction of the Deuteronomistic History.* JSOTSup 18. Sheffield: JSOT, 1981.

Nicholson, E. W. *Exodus and Sinai in History and Tradition.* Atlanta: John Knox, 1973.

Niehr, H. "In Search of YHWH's Cult Statue in the First Temple." Pages 73–95 in van der Toorn, ed., *The Image and the Book.*

Nielsen, K. *Incense in Ancient Israel.* VTSup 38. Leiden: Brill, 1986.

North, C. R. "The Essence of Idolatry." Pages 151–60 in *Von Ugarit nach Qumran.* Edited by J. Hempel. BZAW 77. Berlin: Töpelmann, 1958.

North, F. S. "Aaron's Rise in Prestige." *ZAW* 66 (1954): 192–99.

Noth, M. *The Deuteronomistic History.* JSOTSup 15. Sheffield: JSOT, 1981.

———. *Exodus.* OTL. Translated by J. S. Bowden. Philadelphia: Westminster, 1962.

———. *A History of Pentateuchal Traditions.* Translated by B. W. Anderson. Englewood Cliffs, N.J.: Prentice-Hall, 1972.

———. *Das System der Zwölf Stämme Israels.* Darmstadt: Wissenschaftliche Buchgesellschaft, 1930.

———. *Überlieferungsgeschichte des Pentateuch.* Stuttgart: Kohlhammer, 1948.

Nyberg, H. *Studien zum Hoseabuche.* Uppsala: Almqvist & Wiksell, 1935.

Obbink, H. T. "Jahwebilder." *ZAW* 47 (1929): 264–74.

O'Brian, M. A. "The Book of Deuteronomy." *CurBS* 3 (1995): 95–128.

Oden, R. A. *The Bible Without Theology: The Theological Tradition and Alternatives to It.* San Francisco: Harper & Row, 1987.

Olyan, S. M. *Asherah and the Cult of Yahweh in Israel.* Atlanta: Scholars Press, 1988.

———. "Zadok's Origins and the Tribal Politics of David." *JBL* 10 (1982): 177–93.

Orlinsky, H. M. "Critical Notes on Gen 39:14, 17; Jud 11:37." *JBL* 61 (1942): 87–90.

Östborn, G. *Yahweh and Baal: Studies in the Book of Hosea and Related Documents.* Lund: Gleerup, 1955.

Oswalt, J. N. *The Book of Isaiah: Chapters 1–39.* Grand Rapids: Eerdmans, 1986.

———. "The Golden Calves and the Egyptian Concept of Deity." *EvQ* 5: 13–20.

Pakkala, J. *Intolerant Monolatry in the Deuteronomistic History.* Göttingen: Vandenhoeck & Ruprecht, 1999.

———. "Jeroboam's Sin and Bethel in 1 Kgs 12:25–33." *BN* 112 (2002): 82–94.

Patai, R. *The Hebrew Goddess.* New York: Ktav, 1967.

Peckham, B. "The Composition of Deut 9:1–10:11." Pages 3–59 in *Word and Spirit.* Edited by J. Plernik. Willowdale: Ontario, 1975.

Perlitt, L. "Anklage und Freispruch Gottes: Theologische Motive in der Zeit des Exils." *ZTK* 69 (1972): 290–333.

Pfeiffer, R. "Images of Yahweh." *JBL* 45 (1926): 211–22.

Plastaras, J. *The God of Exodus: The Theology of the Exodus Narratives.* Milwaukee: Bruce, 1966.

Podella, T. *Das Lichtkleid JHWHs.* Tübingen: Mohr Siebeck, 1996.

Polak, F. H. "The Covenant at Mount Sinai in the Light of Texts from Mari." Pages 119–34 in *Sefer Moshe: The Moshe Weinfeld Jubilee Volume.* Edited by C. Cohen, A. Hurvitz, and S. M. Paul. Winona Lake: Eisenbrauns, 2004.

Porter, J. R. "The Supposed Deuteronomistic Redaction of the Prophets." Pages 69–78 in *Schöpfung und Befreiung.* Edited by R. Albertz et al. Stuttgart: Calwer, 1989.

Preuss, H. D. *Deuteronomium.* Darmstadt: Wissenschaftliche Buchgesellschat, 1982.

———. *Old Testament Theology,* vol. 1. Translated by L. G. Perdue. Edinburgh: T. & T. Clark, 1996.

Propp, W. H. C. "Monotheism and 'Moses.'" *UF* 31 (1999): 537–75.

Provan, I. *Hezekiah and the Books of Kings: A Contribution to the Debate about the Composition of the Deuteronomistic History.* BZAW 172. Berlin: de Gruyter, 1988.

Rabban, N. "Before the Lord." *Tarbiz* 23 (1952): 1–8 (Hebrew).

Rad, G. von. *Das fünfte Buch Mose: Deuteronomium.* ATD 8. Göttingen: Vandenhoeck & Ruprecht, 1964.

————. *Old Testament Theology*, vol. 1. Translated by D. M. Stalker. Edinburgh: Oliver & Boyd, 1967.

————. *Old Testament Theology*. vol. 2. New York: Harper, 1965.

————. *Studies in Deuteronomy*. Translated by D. M. Stalker. London: SCM, 1963.

Rainey, A. F. "Israel in Merneptah's Inscription and Reliefs." *IEJ* 51 (2001): 57–85.

Reed, W. L. *The Asherah in the Old Testament.* Fort Worth: Texas Christian University Press, 1949.

Rendtorff, R. *The Old Testament: An Introduction*. Philadelphia: Fortress, 1983.

Reuter, E. *Kultzentralisation: Entstehung und Theolgogie von Deut 12.* Frankfurt: Anton Hain, 1993.

Ringgren, H. *Israelite Religion.* Translated by D. Green. Philadelphia: Fortress, 1966.

Robertson, J. *The Early Religion of Israel.* Edinburgh: Blackwood, 1892.

Rofé, A. *Introduction to Deuteronomy*. Jerusalem: Magnes, 1988. (Hebrew)

————. "The Monotheistic Argumentation in Deuteronomy IV 32–40: Contents, Composition and Text." *VT* 35 (1985): 434–45.

————. "The Strata of the Law about the Centralization of the Worship in Deuteronomy and the History of the Deuteronomic Movement." Pages 221–26 in *Congress Volume, Uppsala 1971.* VTSup 22. Leiden: Brill, 1972.

Römer, T. "The History of Israel's Traditions." Pages 178–212 in *The History of Israel's Traditions.* Edited by S. L. McKenzie and M. P. Graham. JSOTSup 182. Sheffield: JSOT, 1994.

Rose, M. *Der Ausschliesslichkeitsanspruch Jahwes: Deuteronomische Schultheologie und die Volksfrömmigkeit in der späten Königszeit.* Stuttgart: Kohlhammer, 1975.

Rösel, H. N. *Israel in Kanaan: Zum Problem der Entstehung Israels.* New York: Lang, 1992.

Rosenberg, R. "The God *Sedeq.*" *HUCA* 36 (196): 161–77.

Rössler, E. "Jahwe und die Götter im Pentateuch und im Deuteronomistischen Geschichtswerk." Ph.D. diss., Phil. Bonn, 1966.

Rost, L. "Erwägungen zu Hos 4:13f." Pages 451–60 in Baumgartner et al., eds., *Festschrift Alfred Bertholet.*

Rothenberg, B. "Timna." *NEAEHL* 4: 1475–86.

Rowley, H. H. "Melchizedek and Zadok." Pages 491–72 in Baumgartner et al., eds., *Festschrift Alfred Bertholet.*

————. "Moses and Monotheism." Pages 35–63 in *From Moses to Qumran: Studies in the Old Testament.* London: Lutterworth, 1963.

————. *Unity of the Bible*. New York: Meridien, 1957.

————. *Worship in Ancient Israel*. London: SPCK, 1967.

————. "Zadok and Nehushtan." *JBL* 58 (1939): 113–41.

Rudolph, W. *Hosea*. Gütersloh: Mohn, 1966.

Sarna, N. M. *Exploring Exodus*. New York: Schocken, 1986.

Sasson, J. M. "The Worship of the Golden Calf." Pages 151–59 in Hoffner, ed., *Orient and Occident.*

Schmidt, B. B. "The Aniconic Tradition: On Reading Images and Viewing Texts." Pages 75–105 in *The Triumph of Elohim: From Yahwisms to Judaism.* Edited by D. V. Edelman.Grand Rapids: Eerdmans, 1996.

Schwartz, B. J. *The Holiness Legislation: Studies in the Priestly Code.* Jerusalem: Magnes, 1999 (Hebrew).

———. "The Priestly Account of the Theophany and Lawgiving at Sinai." Pages 103–34 in *Texts, Temples, and Traditions: A Tribute to Menahem Haran.* Edited by V. F. Michael et al. Winona Lake: Eisenbrauns, 1996.

———. "Torah from Zion: Isaiah's Temple Vision (Isaiah 2:1–4)." Pages 11–26 in *Sanctity of Time and Space in Tradition and Modernity.* Edited by A. Houtman, M. Roorthuis, and J. Schwartz. Leiden: Brill, 1998.

———. "What Really Happened at Mount Sinai?" *BR* 8, no. 5 (1997): 20–30, 46.

Seitz, G. *Redaktioinsgeschichtliche Studien zum Deuteronomium.* Stuttgart: Kohlhammer, 1971.

Shalom-Guy, H. "Between the Description of Jeroboam's Reforms and the Golden Calf Episode." *Shunaton Leheqer Hamiqr'a Vehamizrach Haqadum* 17 (2006): 15–27 (Hebrew).

Simpson, C. A. *The Early Traditions of Israel.* Oxford: Blackwell, 1948.

Skinner, J. *Genesis.* ICC. Edinburgh: T. & T. Clark, 1951.

Smelik, K. A. D. *The Early History of God.* San Francisco: Harper & Row, 1990.

———. *The Ugaritic Baal Cycle.* Vol. 1, *Introduction with Text, Translation and Commentary of KTU 1.1–1.2* VTSup 55. Leiden: Brill, 1994.

———. "The Use of the Hebrew Bible as a Historical Source." Pages 1–34 in *Converting the Past: Studies in Ancient Israelite and Moabite Historiography.* Edited by K. A. D. Smelik. Leiden: Brill, 1992.

Smith, M. S. *The Early History of God: Yahweh and the Other Deities in Ancient Israel.* Grand Rapids: Eerdmans, 2002.

Sperling, S. D. "Israel's Religion in the Ancient Near East." Pages 5–31 in Green, ed., *Jewish Spirituality.*

———. "The One We Ought to Love." Pages 83–85 in *Ehad: The Many Meanings of God is One.* Edited by E. B. Borowitz. Port Washington, N.Y.: Sh'ma, 1988.

Spieckermann, H. *Juda unter Assur in der Sargonidenzeit.* Göttingen: Vandenhoeck & Ruprecht, 1982. Grand Rapids: Eerdmans, 1989.

Stager, L. E., and S. R. Wolff. "Production and Commerce in Temple Courtyards: An Olive Press in the Sacred Precinct at Tel Dan." *BASOR* 243 (1981): 95–102.

Stolz, F. *Einführung in den biblischen Monotheismus.* Darmstadt: Wissenschaftliche Buchgesellschaft, 1996.

———. "Der Monotheism Israels im Kontext der altorientalischen Religionsgeschichte-Tendenzen neuerer Forschung." Pages 33–50 in Dietrich and Klopfenstein, eds., *Ein Gott allein?*

Suzuki, Y. "A New Aspect of the Occupation Policy by King Josiah." *AJBI* 18 (1992): 31–61.

Tadmor, H., and M. Cogan. *2 Kings.* AB 11. Garden City, N.Y.: Doubleday, 1988.

Tadmor, M. "Female Cult Figurines in Late Canaan and Early Israel: Archaeological Evidence." Pages 139–73 in *Studies in the Period of David and Solomon and Other Essays.* Edited by T. Ishida. Winona Lake: Eisenbrauns, 1982.

Talmon, S. "Divergences in Calendar-Reckoning in Ephraim and Judah." *VT* 8 (1958): 48–74.

Thompson, T. L. *Early History of the Israelite People: From the Written and Archaeological Sources.* Leiden: Brill, 1992.

Tigay, J. H. *Deuteronomy: The Traditional Hebrew Text with the New JPS Translation.* Philadelphia: Jewish Publication Society of America, 1996.

————. *You Shall Have No Other Gods: Israelite Religion in the Light of Hebrew Inscriptions*. Atlanta: Scholars Press, 1986.

Toews, W. I. *Monarchy and Religious Institution in Israel under Jeroboam I*. Atlanta: Scholars Press, 1993.

Tosato, A. "The Literary Structure of the First Two Poems of Balaam (Num xxiii 7–10, 18–24)." *VT* 29 (1979): 101–4.

Tur-Sinai, N. H. "Dunkele Bibelstellen." Pages 274–80 in *Vom Alten Testament. Festschrift K. Marti*. Edited by K. Budde. BZAW 41. Berlin: Töpelmann, 1925.

Uehlinger, C. "Anthropomorphic Cult Statuary in Iron Age Palestine and the Search for Yahweh's Cult Images." Pages 97–155 in van der Toorn, ed., *The Image and the Book*.

Van der Toorn, K. "Anat–Yahu, Some Other Deities, and the Jews of Elephantine." *Numen* 39, no. 1 (1992): 80–101.

————. "Cultic Prostitution." *ABD* 5:510–13.

————. "Female Prostitution in Payment of Vows in Ancient Israel." *JBL* 108 (1989): 193–205.

————, ed. *The Image and the Book. Iconic Cults, Aniconism, and the Rise of Book Religion in Israel and the Ancient Near East*. Leuven: Peeters, 1997.

Van Seters, J. *Abraham in History and Tradition*. New Haven: Yale University Press, 1975.

————. "The Golden Calf: Exodus 32." Pages 290–318 in *The Life of Moses: The Yahwist as Historian in Exodus–Numbers*. Kampen: Kok, 1994.

————. "Law and the Wilderness Rebellion Tradition: Exod 32." *SBLSP* 27 (1990): 583–91.

de Vaux, R. *Ancient Israel 2: Religious Institutions*. New York: McGraw-Hill, 1965.

Vermeylen, J. "L'affaire du veau d'or (Exod 32–34)." *ZAW* 97 (1985): 1–23.

Waterman, L. "Bull Worship in Israel." *AJSL* 31 (1915): 229–55.

Watts, J. D. *Isaiah 1–33*. WBC 24. Waco, Tex.: Word, 1985.

Weimar, P. "Das Goldene Kalb: Redaktionskritische Erwägungen zu Exod 32." *BN* 38–39 (1987): 117–60.

Weinfeld, M. *Deuteronomy and the Deuteronomic School*. Oxford: Clarendon, 1972.

————. *Deuteronomy 1–11*. AB 5. New York: Doubleday, 1991.

————. "The Emergence of the Deuteronomic Movement and Its Antecedents." Pages 76–98 in Lohfink, ed., *Das Deuteronomium*.

————. "Kuntillet ʿAjrud Inscriptions and Their Significance." *SEL* 1 (1984): 121–30.

————. "The Pattern of the Israelite Settlement in Canaan." Pages 270–83 in *Congress Volume: Jerusalem, 1986*. VTSup 40. Leiden: Brill, 1986.

Weippert, M. "Heiliger Krieg in Israel und Assyrian." *ZAW* 84 (1972): 460–93.

Wellhausen, J. *Die Composition des Hexateuchs und der historischen Bücher des Alten Testaments*. Berlin: Reimer, 1889.

————. *Die Kleinen Propheten*. Berlin: de Gruyter, 1963.

————. *Prolegomena to the History of Ancient Israel*. Translated by J. S. Black and A. Menzies. 3d printing. Cleveland: World, 1961.

Westenholz, J. G. "Tamar, Qedeša, Qadištu, and Sacred Prostitution in Mesopotamia." *HTR* 82 (1989): 245–65.

Westermann, C. *Die Geschichtsbücher des Alten Testament: gab es ein deuteronomistisches Geschichtswerk?* Gütersloh: Kaiser, 1994.

————. *Praise and Lament in the Psalms*. Atlanta: John Knox, 1981.

White, M. "The Elohistic Depiction of Aaron: A Study in the Levite–Zadokite Controversy." Pages 49–59 in *Studies in the Pentateuch*. VTSup 41. Edited by J. A. Emerton. Leiden: Brill, 1990.

Whybray, R. N. "ענות in Exodus xxxii 18." *VT* 17 (1967): 122.

Wiggins, S. "The Myth of Asherah: Lion Lady and Serpent Goddess." *UF* 23 (1991): 383–94.

Wildberger, H. *Isaiah 13–27*. Translated by T. H. Trapp. CC. Minneapolis: Fortress, 1997.

———. *Isaiah 28–39*. Translated by T. H. Trapp. Minneapolis: Fortress, 2002.

Willis, J. T. "Redaction Criticism and Historical Reconstruction." Pages 83–89 in *Encounter With the Text: Form and History in the Hebrew Bible*. Edited by M. Buss. Philadelphia: Fortress, 1979.

Wolff, H. W. *Hosea*. Translated by G. Standsell. Philadelphia: Fortress, 1974.

Woolley, C. L. *Carchemish*, vol. 3. Oxford: Oxford University Press, 1914.

Yamauchi, E. M. "Cultic Prostitution." Pages 213–22 in Hoffner, ed., *Orient and Occident*.

Yee, G. *Composition and Tradition in the Book of Hosea*. Atlanta: Scholars Press, 1987.

Zakovitch, Y. "Assimilation in Biblical Narrative." Pages 175–96 in *Empirical Models of Biblical Criticism*. Edited by J. H. Tigay. Philadelphia: University of Pennsylvania Press, 1985.

Zenger, E. *Die Sinaitheophanie, Untersuchung zum jahwistischen und elohistischen Geschichtswerk*. Wurzburg: Echter, 1971.

Zevit, Z. "Deuteronomistic Historiography in 1 Kings 12–2 Kings 17 and the Reinvestiture of the Israelian Cult." *JSOT* 32 (1985): 57–73.

Zimmerli, W. "Das Bilderverbot in der Geschichte des alten Israel: Goldenes Kalb, Eherne Schlange, Mazzeben und Lade." Pages 86–96 in *Studien zu Glaube und Geschichte Israels*. A. Jepsen zum 70 Geburtstag. Stuttgart: Calwer, 1971.

———. *Old Testament Theology in Outline*. Edinburgh: T. & T. Clark, 1978.

———. *Studien zur alttestamentlichen Theologie und Prophetie*. Munich: Kaiser, 1974.

———. "Das zweite Gebot." Pages 234–48 in *Gottes Offenbarung*. Munich: Kaiser, 1969.

INDEX OF AUTHORS

Emmerson, G. I. 115, 116
Ewald, H. 3

Fabry, H.-J. 119, 120
Faur, J. 90, 187
Fensham, F. C. 14
Fisher, L. R. 56
Fitzmyer, J. A. 65
Fohrer, G. 15–17, 49, 88, 90, 96, 119,
        120, 171
Fontaine, C. R. 111
Fowler, J. D. 122
Frankel, D. 42, 83
Frazer, J. 158
Freedman, D. N. 111, 112, 118, 122–24,
        131, 133, 134, 138, 147–49, 155,
        156, 161, 162, 168, 170, 172, 194
Friedman, R. E. 94, 95
Frymer-Kensky, T. 143, 159, 160, 175

Gagnon, J. H. 157
Gese, H. 135
Geus, C. de 137
Ginsberg, H. L. 111, 148, 162
Gladigow, B. 11
Glock, A. E. 174
Gnuse, R. K. 196, 198–200
Good, R. M. 103
Gordon, C. H. 83, 197
Goulder, M. D. 44
Graetz, H. 3
Gray, G. B. 122
Gray, J. 6
Greenberg, M. 40, 64, 100
Gressmann, H. 31
Gruber, M. 159, 162
Gubel, E. 135

Hacham, N. 104, 105
Hadad, E. 79, 81, 82, 84, 85
Hadley, J. M. 172
Hallo, W. W. 9
Halpern, B. 15, 24, 28, 93, 169, 187
Hamilton, V. P. 98
Handy, L. K. 27
Hanson, P. D. 176, 178

Haran, M. 12, 38, 47, 50–53, 86, 151,
        152
Hauer, C. 38
Hehn, J. 4
Hendel, R. 8, 9
Herrmann, S. 87
Hestrin, R. 174–76
Hoffmann, H. D. 6, 70
Holladay, W. L. 150, 175
Holland, T. A. 175
Holter, K. 182, 184, 185, 201
Holzinger, H. 31
Hoppe, L. J. 90
Houtman, C. 34, 188
Hubbard, D. A. 114
Hyatt, J. P. 6, 36, 37, 43, 71, 106, 164,
        188

Jacob, E. 171, 194
Jenks, A. W. 6, 7, 17–19, 119, 121
Joines, K. R. 121
Jones, G. H. 24
Joüon, P. 200

Kallai, Z. 132
Kapelrud, A. S. 139
Katz, P. 99
Kaufman, I. T. 122
Kaufmann, Y. 109–12, 122, 193, 194,
        196
Keel, O. 9, 13, 122, 173–75, 196
Kennett, R. H. 5
Key, A. F. 4
Klein, H. 199
Kletter, R. 175
Knapp, D. 182
Knauf, E. A. 195
Knoppers, G. N. 25, 93
Koch, K. 141
Kraus, H.-J. 51, 126
Kuenen, A. 193
Kugel, J. 100

Lambert, W. G. 159
Lang, B. 167, 170, 196, 197, 199, 200
Lapp, P. W. 174